CIVIL LITIGATION

CIVIL LITIGATION

Kevin Browne LLB, Solicitor

Margaret J Catlow BA (Law), Solicitor

CLP

Published by

College of Law Publishing
Braboeuf Manor, Portsmouth Road, St Catherines, Guildford GU3 1HA

© The College of Law 2004

All rights reserved. No part of this publication may be reproduced, stored in a retrieval system, or transmitted in any way or by any means, including photocopying or recording, without the written permission of the copyright holder, application for which should be addressed to the publisher.

British Library Cataloguing-in-Publication Data
A catalogue record for this book is available from the British Library.

ISBN 0 905835 68 9

Typeset by Style Photosetting Ltd, Mayfield, East Sussex
Printed in Great Britain by Antony Rowe Ltd, Chippenham

Preface

This book has been written as a tool for learning about civil procedure in England and Wales. In it we examine the practical issues which arise from the start of a case until its ultimate conclusion, whether that is by settlement, court judgment or otherwise.

We have divided up the civil process into five stages. But it is important to remember that each stage cannot be learnt in isolation from the others. We urge anyone using this book to make frequent reference to the overview of the five stages at **1.3** and the flow diagram at **Appendix C(1)**. These will serve as a reminder of the various steps and how one part fits into the whole process.

In the interest of brevity, the masculine pronoun has been used throughout to include the feminine.

KEVIN BROWNE AND MARGARET J CATLOW
The College of Law
London

Contents

PREFACE		v
TABLE OF CASES		xiii
TABLE OF STATUTES		xvii
TABLE OF STATUTORY INSTRUMENTS AND CODES OF PRACTICE		xix
TABLE OF ABBREVIATIONS		xxiii

Chapter 1	INTRODUCTION TO CIVIL LITIGATION	1
1.1	The Woolf reforms	1
1.2	The Rules	4
1.3	An overview of a civil claim	4
1.4	Case analysis	7
1.5	Useful websites	7

Chapter 2	CONSIDERATIONS AT THE FIRST INTERVIEW AND FUNDING THE CLAIM	9
2.1	Purpose of the first interview	9
2.2	Limitation	9
2.3	Viability and burden of proof	11
2.4	Remedy sought	12
2.5	Funding	15
2.6	Ethics and conflict of interest	23
2.7	Foreign element and choice of forum	24
2.8	Alternatives to a civil claim	26
2.9	Human rights	28
2.10	Pre-action checklist	29

Chapter 3	EARLY ACTION	31
3.1	Writing to the client	31
3.2	Interviewing witnesses	31
3.3	Preserving documents	32
3.4	Obtaining expert evidence	33
3.5	Site visits	34
3.6	Instructing counsel	35
3.7	Pre-action protocols	36
3.8	Sending the letter of claim	37
3.9	Pre-action disclosure	38
3.10	Settlement	39
3.11	Researching the law	40
3.12	Summary of pre-action steps	41

Chapter 4	COMMENCING PROCEEDINGS	43
4.1	Choice of court	43
4.2	Court personnel	45
4.3	Issuing proceedings	45
4.4	Parties to the proceedings	47
4.5	Service	50
4.6	Time for service of claim form	55
4.7	Service of particulars of claim	55

Chapter 5	RESPONDING TO PROCEEDINGS AND JUDGMENT IN DEFAULT		57
	5.1	Introduction	57
	5.2	Computation of time (r 2.8)	57
	5.3	Acknowledgement of service (Part 10)	58
	5.4	The defence (Part 15)	59
	5.5	Admissions (Part 14)	59
	5.6	Default judgments (Part 12)	62
	5.7	Human rights	64
Chapter 6	STATEMENTS OF CASE		65
	6.1	Introduction	65
	6.2	Contents of the particulars of claim	66
	6.3	The defence	74
	6.4	Reply to defence	76
	6.5	The role of statements of case	77
	6.6	Amendments to statements of case (Part 17)	79
	6.7	Requests for further information (Part 18)	80
Chapter 7	PART 20 PROCEEDINGS AND PART 8 CLAIMS		83
	7.1	Introduction	83
	7.2	Procedure	84
	7.3	Part 8 claims	87
Chapter 8	CASE MANAGEMENT AND ALLOCATION OF CASES		89
	8.1	Introduction	89
	8.2	The court's powers	89
	8.3	Striking out and other sanctions	90
	8.4	Relief from sanctions	92
	8.5	Allocation	93
	8.6	Allocation to a county court track	96
	8.7	Costs estimates	105
Chapter 9	APPLICATIONS TO THE COURT		107
	9.1	Introduction	107
	9.2	Applications generally	107
	9.3	Interim costs	110
	9.4	Appeals against an interim order	112
	9.5	Particular types of application	113
	9.6	Interim remedies	118
	9.7	Interim payments	119
	9.8	Security for costs	122
	9.8	Human rights	122
Chapter 10	DISCLOSURE AND INSPECTION OF DOCUMENTS – CPR 1998, PART 31		125
	10.1	Purpose of disclosure and inspection	125
	10.2	Definition of 'disclosure' (r 31.2)	126
	10.3	Definition of 'documents' (r 31.4)	126
	10.4	Standard disclosure (r 31.6)	126
	10.5	Disclosure of copies (r 31.9)	126
	10.6	The duty to search (r 31.7)	126
	10.7	The right of inspection (r 31.3)	127
	10.8	Procedure for standard disclosure	127
	10.9	The disclosure statement	128
	10.10	Continuing obligation (r 31.11)	128
	10.11	Withholding inspection	128
	10.12	Disclosing the existence of documents: the list	131
	10.13	Failure to disclose (r 31.21)	132

Contents ix

10.14	Subsequent use of disclosed documents (r 31.22)	132
10.15	Applying for specific disclosure (r 31.12)	132
10.16	Pre-action disclosure (r 31.16)	133
10.17	Non-party disclosure (r 31.17)	133
10.18	Human rights	134
10.19	Summary of key points	134
10.20	Disclosure obligations and solicitors' duties	135

Chapter 11 EVIDENCE 137

11.1	Introduction	137
11.2	Witness evidence	137
11.3	Form of witness statements	138
11.4	Use of witness statements at trial	139
11.5	Witness summaries (r 32.9)	140
11.6	Sanctions for non-service of witness statements (r 32.10)	140
11.7	Affidavits	141
11.8	Opinion evidence	141
11.9	Hearsay evidence	142
11.10	Use of plans, photographs and models as evidence (r 33.6)	145
11.11	Notice to admit facts (r 32.18)	146
11.12	Notice to admit or prove documents (r 32.19)	146
11.13	Expert evidence (Part 35)	146
11.14	Assessors (r 35.15)	151
11.15	Human rights	151

Chapter 12 SETTLEMENT 153

12.1	Negotiations	153
12.2	Pre-action settlements	153
12.3	Settlements reached after the issue of proceedings	154
12.4	Part 36	154
12.5	Claims involving children and patients	165
12.6	Discontinuance (Part 38)	165

Chapter 13 FINAL PREPARATIONS FOR TRIAL, TRIAL AND ASSESSMENT OF COSTS 167

13.1	Final preparations for trial	167
13.2	Trial	169
13.3	Costs	174
13.4	Human rights	183

Chapter 14 ENFORCEMENT OF MONEY JUDGMENTS 185

14.1	Introduction	185
14.2	Interest on judgment debts	185
14.3	Tracing the other party	186
14.4	Investigating the judgment debtor's means	186
14.5	Methods of enforcement	187

Chapter 15 ALTERNATIVE DISPUTE RESOLUTION 195

15.1	The nature of ADR	195
15.2	Advantages of ADR	196
15.3	Disadvantages of ADR	197
15.4	Types of ADR	198
15.5	Organisations providing ADR	200
15.6	Using ADR	200
15.7	Choosing ADR	201
15.8	Summary	201

x   Civil Litigation

Appendix A		COURT FORMS AND PROTOCOLS	203
	1	Forms N1 and N1A – Claim Form and Notes for Claimant	205
	2	Form N1C – Notes for Defendant on Replying to the Claim Form	209
	3	Form N9, Including Forms N9A–N9D – Response Pack	211
	4	Form N225 – Request for Judgment	220
	5	Form 227 – Request for Judgment by Default	221
	6	Form N211, Including Forms N211A and N211C – Part 20 Claim Form	222
	7	Form N251 – Notice of Funding	227
	8	Form N215 – Certificate of Service	228
	9	Form N218 – Notice of Service on Partner	230
	10	Form N266 – Notice to Admit Facts	231
	11	Form N265 – List of Documents	232
	12	Form N150 – Allocation Questionnaire	234
	13	Precedent H – Estimate of Costs	239
	14	Form N242A – Notice of Payment into Court	242
	15	Form N243A – Notice of Acceptance and Request for Payment	244
	16	Form N244 – Application Notice	245
	17	Form N260 – Statement of Costs for Summary Assessment	247
	18	Form N170 – Pre-trial Checklist, Listing Questionnaire	249
	19	Appendix to Part 28	252
	20	QBD PF52 – Order for Case Management Directions in the Multi-track (Part 28)	255
	21	Form N252 – Notice of Commencement of Assessment of Bill of Costs	261
	22	Precedent A – Bill of Costs	262
	23	Precedent G – Points of Dispute	267
	24	Practice Direction – Protocols	269
	25	Professional Negligence Pre-action Protocol	273
Appendix B		MISCELLANEOUS DOCUMENTS	279
	1	*Tomlin* Order	281
	2	Guideline figures for summary assessment of costs	283
Appendix C		FLOW DIAGRAMS	289
	1	Overview of the Five Stages of Litigation	291
	2	Determining Jurisdiction where the Defendant is Domiciled in an EU State	292
	3	Consequences of Part 36 Payment	293
	4	Consequences of Offer Made by Claimant under Part 36 – Defendant Accepts Offer	294
	5	Consequences of Offer Made by Claimant Under Part 36 – Claimant Beats Own Offer at Trial	295
	6	Consequences of Offer Made by Claimant under Part 36 – Claimant Fails to Beat Offer	296
	7	Consequences of Offer Made by Claimant Under Part 36 – Claimant Loses at Trial	297
	8	Possible Responses by Defendant to a Claim	298
	9	Table 1 – Admission of Claim in Whole but Request Time to Pay	299
	10	Table 2 – Admission of Part of Claim – Specified Amount	300
	11	Table 3 – File Acknowledgement of Service	301
	12	Table 4 – Default Judgment	302
Appendix D		CASE STUDY DOCUMENTS	303
	1	Letter of Claim	305

	2	Particulars of Claim	307
	3	Defence and Part 20 Counterclaim	309
	4	Reply and Defence to Part 20 Counterclaim	311
	5	Case Summary for Use at Case Management Conference	313
	6	Order for Directions	316
	7	Experts' Without Prejudice Meeting Statement	318
	8	(Defendant's) Brief to Counsel	320
	9	Consent Order	323

INDEX 325

Table of Cases

A

Airey v Ireland (1979–80) 2 EHRR 305	29
Alex Lawrie Factors Ltd v Morgan, Morgan and Turner (1999) The Times, 18 August	138
Amber v Stacy [2001] 2 All ER 88	165
Anderton v Clwyd County Council [2002] EWCA Civ 933, [2002] 3 All ER 813	52
Andronicou and Constantinou v Cyprus (1998) 25 EHRR 491	29
Arrow Nominees Inc v Blackledge [2000] 1 BCLC 709	91
AXA Insurance Co Ltd v Swire Fraser (2000) The Times, 19 January	92

B

Barclays Bank plc v O'Brien [1994] 1 AC 180	139
Baron v Lovell [1999] CPLR 630	103
Bates v Microstar Ltd [2000] LTL, 4 July	116
Beathem v Carlisle Hospitals NHS Trust (1999) The Times, 20 May	48
Biguzzi v Rank Leisure plc [1999] 1 WLR 1926	91
British and Commonwealth Holdings plc v Quadrex Holdings Inc [1989] 3 WLR 723	121
Burrells Wharf Freeholders Ltd v Galliard Homes Ltd [1999] 2 EGLR 81	39

C

Cable & Wireless v IBM UK Ltd [2002] BLR 89	197
Channel Tunnel Group Ltd and France Manche SA v Balfour Beatty Construction Ltd [1993] 2 WLR 262	197
Chapple v Williams [1999] CPLR 731	123
Craven Textile Engineers Ltd v Batley Football Club Ltd [2000] LTL, 7 July	176
Cutts v Head [1984] Ch 290	39, 40

D

Daniels v Walker [2000] 1 WLR 1382	150
Darbishire v Warran [1963] 1 WLR 1067	13
Daryanani v Kumar & Co and Another [2000] LTL, 15 March	93
Davies v Eli Lilly & Co [1987] 1 WLR 428	125
Dunnett v Railtrack plc (in Railway Administration) [2002] EWCA Civ 303, [2002] 2 All ER 850	177

E

Elmes v Hygrade Food Products plc [2001] EWCA Civ 121, [2001] LTL, 27 February	54

F

Field v Leeds City Council [2000] 1 EGLR 54	147
Ford v GKR Construction and Others [2000] 1 All ER 802	164
Frost v Knight (1872) LR 7 Ex 111	13

G

Garratt v Saxby [2004] LTL, 18 February	164
Gibbons v Wall (1988) The Times, 24 February	121

H

Habib Bank Ltd v Abbeypearl Ltd and Others [2001] EWCA Civ 62, [2001] 1 All ER 185	91

Hannigan v Hannigan [2000] 2 FCR 650 — 2
Huck v Robson [2002] EWCA Civ 398, [2002] 3 All ER 263 — 155
Hunt v RM Douglas (Roofing) Ltd [1990] 1 AC 398 — 174
Hussain v Woods and Another [2001] Lloyd's Rep PN 134 — 116
Hyams v Pender [2000] 1 WLR 32 — 183

I

IBM Corporation and Another v Phoenix International (Computers) Ltd [1995] 1 All ER 413 — 131

K

Kirschel & Others v Fladgate Fielder (a firm) [2000] LTL, 22 December — 115

L

Leigh v Michelin Tyres plc [2003] EWCA Civ 1766 — 106, 175
Little and Others v George Little Sebire & Co [2001] EWCA Civ 894, [2001] STC 1065 — 162
Lucas v Barking, Havering and Redbridge Hospitals NHS Trust [2003] EWCA Civ 1102 — 148

M

Maltez v Lewis (1999) The Times, 4 May — 1
Mann and Holt v Lexington Insurance Co [2001] 1 Lloyd's Rep 1 — 162
Mars UK Ltd v Teknowledge Ltd (No 2) [1999] Masons CLR 322 — 175, 182
Matthews v Tarmac Bricks and Tiles Ltd [1999] CPLR 463 — 95
McGinley and Egan v UK (1998) 27 EHRR 1 — 134
McPhilemy v Times Newspapers Limited and Others [1999] 3 All ER 775 — 77
Mealey Horgan plc v Horgan (1999) The Times, 6 July — 141
Molins plc v GD SpA (2000) The Times, 1 March — 51
Morris v Wentworth-Stanley [1999] QB 1004 — 5
Murphy v Staples UK Limited [2003] 3 All ER 129 — 52
Myers v Elman [1940] AC 282 — 135

N

Nanglegan v Royal Free Hampstead NHS Trust [2001] EWCA Civ 127, [2001] 3 All ER 793 — 54, 55
Necati v Commissioner of Police for the Metropolis [2001] LTL, 19 January — 91
Norman Roger Breeze v John Stacy & Sons Ltd (1999) The Times, 8 July — 131

O

Olatawura v Abiloye [2002] EWCA Civ 998, [2002] 4 All ER 903 — 122

P

Peet v Mid-Kent Healthcare Trust (Practice Note) [2001] EWCA Civ 1703, [2002] 3 All ER 688 — 150
Peskin v Anderson and Others [2001] 1 BCLC 372 — 116
Petrotrade Inc v Texaco Ltd [2001] 1 WLR 947 — 162
Practice Statement (Alternative Dispute Resolution) (No 2) [1996] 1 WLR 1024 — 196

R

R (Clingham) v Marylebone Magistrates' Court [2001] LTL, 22 January — 151
Royal Brompton Hospital NHS Trust v Hammond & Others [2000] LTL, 4 December — 65
Rush & Tomkins Ltd v Greater London Council [1989] AC 1280 — 131

S

Sarwar v Alam [2001] EWCA Civ 1401, [2002] 1 WLR 125 — 22

Satwinder Kaur v CTP Coil Ltd [2000] LTL, 10 July	55
Scammell and Others v Dicker [2001] 1 WLR 631	160
Scott Paper Co v Drayton Paper Works Ltd [1927] 44 RPC 151	39
Secretary of State for Health v Norton Healthcare Ltd and Others [2004] LTL, 25 February	115
Sinclair v Chief Constable of West Yorkshire and Another [2000] LTL, 12 December	116
Smith v Probyn (2000) The Times, 29 March	54
Spencer v Gordon Wood (t/a Gordon's Tyres) [2004] LTL, 15 March	19
Stevens v Gullis [1999] BLR 394	146
Stringman v McArdle [1994] 1 WLR 1653	120
Stroh v London Borough of Haringey [1999] LTL, 13 July	141
Stubbings and Others v The United Kingdom [1997] 1 FLR 105	28
Swain v Hillman [2001] 1 All ER 91	115
Sweetman v Shepherd (2000) The Times, 29 March	117

T

Tarajan Overseas Ltd v Kaye (2002) The Times, 22 January	103
Three Rivers District Council and Others v Governor and Company of the Bank of England (No 10) [2004] EWCA Civ 218	129
Three Rivers District Council and Others v Governor and Company of the Bank of England (No 3 bis) [2001] 2 All ER 513, HL	115
Tolstoy Miloslavsky v UK (1995) 20 EHRR 442	123
Totty v Snowden; Hewett v Wirrall and West Cheshire Community NHS Trust [2001] EWCA Civ 933, [2002] 1 WLR 1384	55

U

UCB Corporate Services Ltd v Halifax (SW) Ltd [1999] 1 Lloyd's Rep 154	92

V

Van de Hurk v Netherlands (1994) 18 EHRR 481	183
Vinos v Marks & Spencer plc [2001] 3 All ER 784	55

W

Winer v UK (1986) 48 DR 154	29
Woods v Martin's Bank [1959] 1 QB 55	135

Table of Statutes

Access to Justice Act 1999 22
  s30 18
Administration of Justice Act 1920 194
Arbitration Act 1996 26, 197, 199
  s66 26, 197

Children Act 1989
  s96(2) 172, 173
Civil Evidence Act 1972
  s3(1) 34
  s3(2) 142
Civil Evidence Act 1995 144, 145, 151, 169, 320, 322
  s1 143
  s1(2)(a) 142
  s2 143
  s2(1)(a) 143
  s3 144
  s4 144, 151, 172
  s5 144, 145
  s6 145
Civil Jurisdiction and Judgments Act 1982 24
Civil Procedure Act 1997
  s7 118
Companies Act 1985
  s691 207
  s725(1) 52
  s744 207, 224
Consumer Credit Act 1974 62, 188
County Courts Act 1984 261
  s52 38, 118
  s53 118
  s69 14, 15, 67, 77, 153, 173
Courts and Legal Services Act 1990
  s58 16

Foreign Judgments (Reciprocal Enforcement) Act 1933 194

Human Rights Act 1998 46, 67, 70, 123, 206
  s4 44, 50, 67
  s9(3) 67

Judgments Act 1838 261
  s17 174

Late Payment of Commercial Debts (Interest) Act 1998 14, 15, 62, 67, 68, 70, 77, 173, 174
Limitation Act 1980 9, 28, 77
  s2 9, 11
  s5 9, 11
  s14 10
  s14A 10, 11
  s14B 10

Mental Health Act 1983 10, 47, 207
  Part VII 4, 47, 48

Occupiers' Liability Act 1957 309, 314, 321

Road Traffic Act 1988 27

Sale of Goods Act 1979 77
Social Security (Recovery of Benefits) Act 1997 243
  s8 243
  Sch2 243
Solicitors' Act 1974
  s87 21
Supreme Court Act 1981
  s33 38, 118
  s34 118
  s35A 14, 15, 67, 72, 77, 153, 157, 162, 173, 308, 310
  s51 92

Torts (Interference with Goods) Act 1977
  s4 118

International legislation

Brussels Convention 1968 24, 54, 122, 194
European Convention on Human Rights 1950 64, 67, 123
  Art6 64, 151
  Art6(1) 28, 29, 91, 122, 123, 134, 151, 183
Lugano Convention 24, 122, 194

Table of Statutory Instruments and Codes of Practice

Civil Procedure Rules 1998 (SI 1998/3132) 1, 2, 3, 4, 7, 13, 27, 31, 32, 34, 40, 43, 46, 55, 59, 73, 89, 91, 94, 97, 141, 185, 196, 197
Part 1
    r1.1 133, 137
    r1.1(1) 1
    r1.1(2) 1
    r1.1(2)(a)–(c) 270
    r1.2 2
    r1.3 2, 3, 12, 24
    r1.4 89
    r1.4(1) 3
    r1.4(2) 3-4
    r1.4(2)(b) 103
    r1.4(2)(e) 6, 196, 201
    r1.4(2)(i) 96
Part 2
    r2.8 57
Part 3 45, 89, 90, 114
    r3.1(2) 89
    r3.1(2)(c) 104
    r3.1(4) 269
    r3.1(5) 89, 90, 269
    r3.1(6A) 90
    r3.4(2) 90
    r3.6 81
    r3.8 92
    r3.8(3) 83
    r3.9 81, 92
    r3.9(e) 269
    r3.9(1) 93
    r3.9(1)(f) 93
    PD 90
Part 5 PD
    para2.1 66
    para2.2 65
Part 6 51
    r6.3(1) 52
    r6.5 53, 74
    r6.6 229
    r6.7 52
    r6.7(1) 52, 229
    r6.12 229
    rr6.13–6.16 54, 229
    r6.19 54
    r6.20 55
    rr6.24–6.26 54
    PD
        para3.2 52
    PD 6B 54
Part 7 69, 205
    r7.4 55
    r7.5(2) 55
    r7.6(3) 55

Civil Procedure Rules 1998 – *continued*
    PD
        para2 43
        para2.4 43
        para3.1 3
        para3.6 46
        para5.1 45
Part 8 2, 3, 48, 62, 65, 83-7, 165, 183
    r8.2 3
    r8.5(1)–(2) 3
Part 10 58
Part 11 25
Part 12 62
Part 13 113
    r13.2 113
    r13.3(1) 113
    r13.5 114
Part 14 59
    PD
        para6.1 62
Part 15 59
Part 16 65, 66
    r16.2(1) 45
    r16.3(2) 45
    r16.4(1) 66
    r16.4(2) 67
    r16.5 90
    r16.5(1)–(4) 74
    r16.5(5) 74, 75
    r16.5(6)–(8) 74
    r16.7(1) 76
    PD
        para7.3(1)–(2) 66
        paras7.4–7.5 66
        paras8.1–8.2 66
        para13.1 76
        para13.3(1)–(3) 77
Part 17 79
    r17.2 80
Part 18 80, 97, 107, 117
    r18.1(1) 80
    PD
        para1 118
        para5.5(1) 118
Part 19 49, 50
    r19.2(2)–(4) 50
    r19.4(2) 50
    r19.5(2)–(3) 50
Part 20 76, 83-7, 95, 97, 107, 122, 155, 161, 173, 222, 223, 224, 225, 226, 227, 234, 237, 249, 251, 309, 310, 311, 312, 313, 314, 316, 320, 322, 323
    r20.2(1)–(2) 83
    r20.4 84
    r20.6 84

Civil Procedure Rules 1998 – *continued*
   r20.7 85
   r20.9(2) 85
   r20.11 86
   r20.13 86
   PD
     para5.3 86
     paras7.1–7.6 86
Part 21 47
   r21.6 48
   PD
     para2.1 47
Part 22 46, 74
   r22.1(2) 79
   PD
     para3.8(1)–(3) 47
     para3.10 47
Part 23 107, 108
   r23.2 107
   r23.6 107
   PD 108
     para3 108
     para6 109
     para9.1 108
Part 24 96, 114, 115, 116, 122, 194, 197, 198
   r24.2 114
   r24.2(b) 115
   PD
     para1.3(1)–(3) 114
     para2(3) 116
     para4 116
     paras5.1–5.2 116
Part 25 118, 122
   r25.1 119
   r25.1(1) 118-19
   r25.1(1)(k) 119
   r25.12 122
   PD 25B (Interim Payments)
     para2.1 120
Part 26 93
   r26.2 93
   r26.3(6A) 94
   r26.7(3) 97
   r26.8(1) 97
   PD
     para2.4 96
     paras6.5–6.6 96
     para7.7 95
     para8.1(1) 97
     para11 97
Part 27 97, 98
   r27.14 98
   PD
     paras7–8 105
     Appendix A 98
Part 28 95, 99, 238, 255
   r28.4 99
   Appendix 252
   PD
     para3.9 150
     para3.12 99
     para4.2(1)–(2) 99

Civil Procedure Rules 1998 – *continued*
     para4.5 100
     para5 100
     para5.4(1) 100
     paras6–7 101
     Appendix 99
Part 29 102
   r29.5 104
   PD
     para2.2 43
     para2.6 94
     para4.10 102
     para5.1 102
     para5.6 104
Part 30 44
   r30.3(2) 44
Part 31 97, 125, 146, 169, 232
   r31 34
   r31.2 126
   r31.3 127
   r31.3(1) 127
   r31.4 126
   r31.6 126, 134, 135, 232
   r31.6(b)–(c) 232
   r31.7 126
   rr31.8–31.9 126
   r31.10(5) 128
   r31.11 128
   r31.12 132
   r31.16 133
   r31.16(3) 38
   r31.16(3)(d)(iii) 109
   r31.17 133
   r31.19 130, 235
   r31.20 131
   rr31.21–31.22 132
   PD
     para2 127
     para3.2 127
     para4.4 128
Part 32 98, 137
   r32.2(1) 137
   r32.4(2) 137
   r32.5(3) 139, 170
   r32.9 140
   r32.10 140
   r32.1(1)–(3) 137
   r32.14 47
   rr32.18–32.19 146
   PD
     paras17–20 138
Part 33 137, 143
   r33.2 169
   r33.2(1)–(2) 143
   r33.2(3) 143-4
   r33.2(4) 144
   r33.4 144
   r33.5 145
   r33.6 145, 169
Part 35 98, 146
   r35.1 34
   r35.1(1) 147
   r35.3 146

Civil Procedure Rules 1998 – *continued*
   r35.4 147
   r35.7 149
   r35.10 148
   r35.10(4) 147
   r35.12 149
   r35.15 151
   PD
     paras2.1–2.2 148
     para3 147
   Part 36 40, 90, 98, 121, 122, 153, 154-65, 242, 244, 293, 294, 295, 296, 297, 320, 322
    r36.4 242
    r36.5 160
    r36.5(8) 161
    r36.6 156
    r36.6(2)(d) 122
    r36.7 242
    r36.10 155
    r36.10(1) 155
    r36.10(2) 155
    r36.10(2)(b) 155
    r36.10(3)–(5) 155
    r36.20 157, 158, 164, 173, 293
    r36.21 155, 156, 161, 162, 163, 164, 174, 177, 295, 322
    r36.21(2) 269
    r36.21(6) 162
    PD 160
     para3.4 156
     para5 156
  Part 37
   r37.2 90
  Part 38 165
  Part 39 123, 168
   PD
    para3.2 168
    para3.9 169
  Part 40
   r40.6 154
  Part 43 236, 249
   r43.2(1) 174
   r43.2(1)(k) 271
  Part 44 174
   r44.3(a) 269
   r44.3(1) 174
   r44.3(2)(a) 173, 174
   r44.3(4)(c) 164
   r44.3(6)(d) 174
   r44.3(6)(g) 174
   r44.3(8) 182
   r44.3B 182
   r44.3B(1)(c) 271
   r44.4 176
   r44.5 177
   r44.8 111
   r44.12A 183
   r44.15 21
   PD
    para8.5 110
    para14 112
  Part 45 46, 62, 112, 192

Civil Procedure Rules 1998 – *continued*
  Part 46 178
  Part 47
   r47.8 180
   r47.9 181
   r47.13 181
   r47.19(1) 182
   r47.20 181
   PD 182
    paras47–48 181
  PD 43–48 Costs 26, 105, 106, 239, 240, 241, 262, 263, 264, 265, 266, 268
   para4 179
   para4.6 179, 180
   para6.6 106, 175
   para8.4 296
   paras11.1–11.3 177
   para14 183
   para32 183
  Part 49 46
  Part 52 112, 181
   r52.3(6) 112
   r52.11 112
   PD 183
  Part 58 44
  Part 71 187
   rr71.3–71.4 187
   PD 187
    para1 187
    Appendices A–B 187
  Part 72 191
   r72.6(2) 192
   r72.8 192
   PD
    para1 191
  Part 73 190, 191
   r73.8 191
   PD
    para1.2 190
  Part 74 194
  Sch1 185
   RSC 4
    Ords46–47 188
  Sch2 185
   CCR 4
   Ord26
    r1 188
   Ord27 192
Pre-action Protocols 36, 37, 38
  PD 269-78
   para2 36
   para4 37
   para4.7 37
   para4A 21
  Contruction and Engineering Disputes 271, 277
  Defamation 271, 277
  Disease and Illness 272
  Housing Disrepair 272
  Judicial Review 271
  Personal Injury 269, 271
  Professional Negligence 273-8

Civil Procedure Rules 1998 – *continued*
  Resolution of Clinical Disputes 269, 271, 277
Conditional Fee Agreements Regulations 2000 (SI 2000/692) 16, 19, 20
  reg2(1) 16, 17
  reg2(2) 17
  reg3 183
  reg3(1) 17
  reg3(2) 17
  reg3(2)(b) 183
  reg3(3) 17
  reg3A 16
  reg3A(1)–(3) 18
  reg3A(4) 18-19
  reg3A(5) 19
  reg3A(5A) 19
  reg3A(6) 19
  reg4(1) 17
  reg4(2) 17-18
  reg4(3)–(6) 18
  reg5(1)–(2) 18

Conditional Fee Agreements (Miscellaneous Amendments) Regulations 2003 (No.1) (SI 2003/1240) 16
Conditional Fee Agreements (Miscellaneous Amendments) Regulations 2003 (No.2) (SI 2003/3344) 16
County Courts (Interest on Judgment Debts) Order 1991 (SI 1991/1184) 174

Solicitors' Costs Information and Client Care Code 15
Solicitors' Practice Rules 1990 21
  r1 24
  r8 21
  r15 15, 31

Regulation 44/2001 24, 54, 194
  Art2 25, 292
  Art5 292
  Art5(1) 25
  Art5(3) 25
  Art6 25, 292
  Arts22–24 25, 292
  Arts38–56 194
  Art60 25

Table of Abbreviations

ADR	alternative dispute resolution
CCA	County Courts Act 1984
CCR	County Court Rules 1981
CEDR	Centre for Dispute Resolution
CFA	conditional fee agreement
CFA Regulations 2000	Conditional Fee Agreements Regulations 2000
CLS	Community Legal Service
CLSF	Community Legal Service Fund
CPR	Civil Procedure Rules 1998
ECHR	European Convention for the Protection of Human Rights and Fundamental Freedoms
ECtHR	European Court of Human Rights
HCEO	High Court Enforcement Officer
LA	Limitation Act 1980
LSC	Legal Services Commission
PD	Practice Direction
RCJ	Royal Courts of Justice
RSC	Rules of the Supreme Court 1965
SCA	Supreme Court Act 1981

Chapter 1
Introduction to Civil Litigation

1.1	The Woolf reforms	1
1.2	The Rules	4
1.3	An overview of a civil claim	4
1.4	Case analysis	7
1.5	Useful websites	7

1.1 The Woolf reforms

The nature of civil litigation in England and Wales changed fundamentally on 26 April 1999, when the Civil Procedure Rules 1998 (CPR 1998) (SI 1998/3132) came into force. These Rules are the courts' attempt to implement the 'Woolf Reforms', as set out in Lord Woolf's report, *Access to Justice*, which was published in 1996. The philosophy behind this report was that the litigation system at the time was too expensive, too slow and incomprehensible to many litigants. Even the simplest case could take years to get to trial, with the costs often exceeding the amount in dispute. Furthermore, because the system was almost entirely adversarial, it did not necessarily operate in the interests of justice as a whole.

Lord Woolf hoped that his proposed reforms, now enshrined in the CPR 1998, would lead to a civil justice system that was just in the results it delivered, fair in the way it treated litigants, and easily understood by users of that legal system. It was hoped that the new system would also provide appropriate procedures at a reasonable cost which could be completed within a reasonable time-scale. In particular, he thought it necessary to transfer the control of litigation from the parties to the court. The court would then determine how each case should progress by making appropriate directions, setting strict timetables and ensuring that the parties complied with them, backed up by a system of sanctions which the court could impose itself without the need for an application by any party. The overriding objective of the reforms is set out in r 1.1 of CPR 1998:

> (1) These Rules are a new procedural code with the overriding objective of enabling the court to deal with cases justly.
> (2) Dealing with a case justly includes, so far as is practicable—
>   (a) ensuring that the parties are on an equal footing;
>   (b) saving expense;
>   (c) dealing with the case in ways which are proportionate—
>   (i) to the amount of money involved;
>   (ii) to the importance of the case;
>   (iii) to the complexity of the issues; and
>   (iv) to the financial position of each party;
>   (d) ensuring that it is dealt with expeditiously and fairly; and
>   (e) allotting to it an appropriate share of the court's resources, while taking into account the need to allot resources to other cases.

In *Maltez v Lewis* (1999) *The Times*, 4 May, the claimant's application was for a direction that the defendants be debarred from instructing leading or senior counsel for a copyright dispute between the parties as the claimant had only been in a position to instruct a junior counsel of seven years' experience. The court held that it was the fundamental right of citizens to be represented by counsel or solicitors of their own choice. The court did not have a power to require a party to change their solicitors, but the court was able to ensure compliance with the overriding objective. For example, if one party had instructed a big firm of expensive solicitors and the other party could only afford to instruct a small firm then the court could and should ensure that a level playing field was achieved. That might occur on disclosure (see **Chapter 10**) by allowing the smaller firm more time, or in the preparation of trial bundles (see **Chapter 13**) the court could direct that the larger firm prepared them. The court had a duty to ensure a fair trial and was used to dealing with one side being more expertly represented than the other. The court could ensure compliance with the overriding objective where the representatives could be said to be unequal. The court has power to prevent a party being unfairly required to pay excessive costs because the other party has instructed unreasonably expensive advisers (see generally **Chapter 13**).

In addition, note that in his *Final Report*, Lord Woolf suggested that:

> Where one of the parties is unable to afford a particular procedure, the court, if it decides that that procedure is to be followed, should be entitled to make its order conditional upon the other side meeting the difference in costs of the weaker party, whatever the outcome.

The overriding objective must be borne in mind at all times when conducting civil litigation, both by the court, because r 1.2 states:

> The court must seek to give effect to the overriding objective when it—
> (a) exercises any power given to it by the Rules; or
> (b) interprets any rule.

and by the parties and their legal advisers, because r 1.3 states:

> The parties are required to help the court to further the overriding objective.

In a sense, all the other rules in the CPR 1998 are designed to try to achieve the overriding objective. It is important to note that solicitors and their clients have a positive duty, pursuant to r 1.3, to help the court to further the overriding objective. As the Commercial Court Guide (para A1.6) states, 'The Court expects a high level of co-operation and realism from the legal representatives of the parties. This applies to dealings (including correspondence) between legal representatives as well as dealings with the Court'.

In the case of *Hannigan v Hannigan* [2000] 2 FCR 650, the Court of Appeal was faced with a claim that should have been started under Part 8 using Form N208, but in fact was commenced on a pre-CPR form with the same number. The defendants sought to strike out the claim. The claimant conceded eight failings, namely:

(a) the claim was issued on the wrong form;
(b) the statement of case was not verified by a statement of truth;
(c) there was a failure to include the Royal Coat of Arms;
(d) the first defendant was incorrectly named;
(e) Mrs Hannigan's witness statement was signed in the name of her firm rather than by her personally;
(f) her witness statement did not have the requisite legend in the top right-hand corner;
(g) her witness statement failed to have marginal notes or a 3.5cm margin; and

(h) the exhibit to her witness statement failed to have the requisite legend in the top right-hand corner, or a front page setting out a list of the documents and the dates of all the exhibits. It also failed to have the documents paginated.

The district judge said that the proceedings were 'fundamentally flawed' and the circuit judge held that 'there is too much wrong with these proceedings to exercise a discretion in the appellants' favour'. In the Court of Appeal, Brooke LJ said:

> [32] ... It has not been suggested that the claimant's solicitors did not set out all the information required of a claimant using the Part 8 procedure (see CPR 8.2) or that the written evidence on which she intended to rely was not filed with the form which was used as a claim form or served on the defendant with that document (see CPR 8.5(1) and (2)). The problem was the technical one that her solicitors did not use CPR practice form N208 (the Part 8 claim form) to start the claim contrary to para 3.1 of the first Practice Direction supplementing CPR Part 7, and that they also made the other technical mistakes.
>
> [33] I am in no doubt that the manner in which the judge exercised his discretion was seriously flawed, because he wholly failed to take into account the fact that in these proceedings, sealed by the county court within the relevant limitation period, the defendants were given all the information they required in order to be able to understand what order Mrs Hannigan was seeking from the court and why she was seeking it.
>
> ...
>
> [36] ... The interests of the administration of justice would have been much better served if the defendants' solicitors had simply pointed out all the mistakes that had been made in these very early days of the new rules and Mrs Hannigan's solicitor had corrected them all quickly and agreed to indemnify both parties for all the expense unnecessarily caused by his incompetence. CPR 1.3 provides that the parties are required to help the court to further the overriding objective, and the overriding objective is not furthered by arid squabbles about technicalities such as have disfigured this litigation and eaten into the quite slender resources available to the parties.

Before the introduction of the CPR 1998, the speed at which cases progressed was largely determined by the parties' solicitors. Under the CPR 1998, the court has a duty to manage cases and will therefore determine the pace of the litigation. Rule 1.4 states:

> (1) The court must further the overriding objective by actively managing cases.
> (2) Active case management includes—
> > (a) encouraging the parties to co-operate with each other in the conduct of the proceedings;
> > (b) identifying the issues at an early stage;
> > (c) deciding promptly which issues need full investigation and trial and accordingly disposing summarily of the others;
> > (d) deciding the order in which issues are to be resolved;
> > (e) encouraging the parties to use an alternative dispute resolution procedure if the court considers that appropriate and facilitating the use of such procedure;
> > (f) helping the parties to settle the whole or part of the case;
> > (g) fixing timetables or otherwise controlling the progress of the case;
> > (h) considering whether the likely benefits of taking a particular step justify the cost of taking it;
> > (i) dealing with as many aspects of the case as it can on the same occasion;
> > (j) dealing with the case without the parties needing to attend at court;
> > (k) making use of technology; and

4   Civil Litigation

(l) giving directions to ensure that the trial of a case proceeds quickly and efficiently.

Case management by the court is considered in further detail in **Chapter 8**.

1.2 The Rules

The CPR 1998 apply to all proceedings in the county courts, High Court and the Civil Division of the Court of Appeal, except:

[exceptions where CPR rules do not apply]

(a) insolvency proceedings;
(b) family proceedings;
(c) adoption proceedings;
(d) proceedings within the meaning of Pt VII of the Mental Health Act 1983;
(e) non-contentious probate proceedings;
(f) proceedings where the High Court acts as a Prize Court (eg, Admiralty proceedings).

Therefore, the CPR 1998 apply to virtually all types of civil litigation proceedings in England and Wales.

In order to understand and interpret the Rules correctly, it is necessary also to look at the Practice Directions which supplement the Rules.

In some cases, the Practice Direction (PD) for a particular Rule is more expansive than the Rule itself. In a sense, the Practice Direction puts flesh on the bare bones of the Rule.

Reference is made to the Rules and Practice Directions throughout this book. Sometimes a Rule or Practice Direction has been quoted in full; at other times it is paraphrased. When conducting civil litigation, it is essential always to check the wording of any relevant Rule or Practice Direction as there are frequent amendments. The 'official' version of the CPR 1998 is contained in a three-volume looseleaf folder – the 'Blue Book'. Because it is a looseleaf service, it can be kept up to date as the Rules and Practice Directions are amended or added to. The Rules can also be accessed on the Internet, via the website of the Department for Constitutional Affairs (www.dca.gov.uk). The Court Service website (www.courtservice.gov.uk) provides access to court forms, leaflets and details of current court fees (amongst other things).

When the CPR 1998 were drafted to replace the old High Court and county court rules, there was insufficient time to draft new Rules for every aspect of the civil litigation process. For that reason, some of the 'old' Rules have been retained and are contained in two Schedules to the CPR 1998. Schedule 1 contains the Rules of *[apply only to High Court]* the Supreme Court 1965 (RSC 1965). Unless otherwise stated, these apply only to proceedings in the High Court. Schedule 2 contains the old County Court Rules 1981 (CCR 1981). Again, unless otherwise stated, these apply only to proceedings *[apply only to County court]* in the county court.

1.3 An overview of a civil claim

P291. — Appendix C(1) sets out a flowchart showing the structure of a case that proceeds from the pre-action steps right through to a trial and the matters that may arise thereafter. We shall call these the five stages of litigation.

① Pre-commencement
② Commencement of the action
③ Interim matters
④ Trial
⑤ Post-trial.

ie. settled out of court.
most clients do not get to this stage

1.3.1 Stage 1: pre-commencement of proceedings

With a new client it is vital to identify the client's objectives. Ask yourself: what is the client really seeking to achieve, legally or otherwise?

It is vital to ensure you consider who will constitute all the potential parties to any negotiations and court proceedings. Issues of professional conduct may arise (eg, a conflict of interest (see **2.1** and **2.6.2**)). Moreover, the general rule is that 'all persons to be sued should be sued at the same time and in the same action': see *Morris v Wentworth-Stanley* [1999] QB 1004. Once all potential defendants have been identified and located, consideration must be given as to whether each is worth pursuing (see **2.3**).

At the end of the first interview summarise the steps you and the client will take and the reasons for these. The key task for a solicitor is to set about collecting relevant evidence. Never delay taking a statement from the client and potential witnesses. Memories fade and evidence has a nasty habit of vanishing. So, if a person has a story to tell or documents that might help, get that information quickly.

Of course, the client will need to know from the outset how his legal costs are to be calculated and paid for. As to the important topic of funding, see **2.5**.

You also need to address the questions of limitation and jurisdiction. You must work out when the limitation period expires and ensure that a careful diary note is kept of this. If, for example, a client is involved in a commercial dispute, you should check to see if the contract provides for any litigation to be conducted in England and Wales or elsewhere (see further **2.2** and **2.7**).

A client should not just launch into litigation. That is the last resort. Pre-action protocols govern the steps parties should take before commencing a court case. The parties should establish what issues are in dispute, share information that is available to each of them concerning those issues and endeavour to resolve those matters. Failure to follow a protocol step or its spirit, without good reason, will usually incur a sanction for that party if litigation is commenced (eg, a successful claimant might be penalised by the award of less interest).

A Practice Direction deals with the implementation of pre-action protocols generally and certain protocols have been published relating to specific types of litigation (see further **3.7** and **Appendix A(24)**). In outline the main steps that should be taken under pre-action protocols are as follows.

1.3.1.1 Alternative Dispute Resolution (ADR)

Parties and their legal representatives are encouraged to enter into discussions and/or negotiations prior to starting proceedings. Whilst the protocols do not usually specify how or when this should be done, the parties must give serious consideration to using any suitable form of available ADR (see **2.8** and **Chapter 15**). If proceedings are commenced, the parties must remember that by r 1.4(2)(e) active case management by the court will include encouraging them to use an ADR procedure if the court considers that appropriate. See, for example, **8.5.1** and **13.3.4** (as to costs).

1.3.1.2 The standard letter of claim

Immediately after collecting sufficient evidence to substantiate a realistic claim, and before addressing issues of quantum in detail, the potential claimant should send to the proposed defendant a letter detailing the claim. Enough information must be given so that the prospective defendant can commence investigations and at least put a broad valuation on the claim. The prospective claimant should set out any proposals he has for ADR.

1.3.1.3 The letter of response

The prospective defendant should acknowledge safe receipt of the letter of claim and after investigating the matter should state whether or not liability is admitted. Reasons should be given if liability is denied. Where primary liability is admitted but contributory negligence is alleged, details of that should be provided. Note that the potential claimant should also respond to any such allegation before issuing proceedings. ADR should also be addressed.

1.3.2 Stage 2: commencement of the claim

Proceedings are commenced by lodging at a county court or High Court a completed claim form. A specimen can be seen at **6.2.1**. To activate the claim, this must be served on the defendant. Full details of the claim, called particulars, must also be served on the defendant. If the defendant wishes to contest the claim, he must file at the court and serve on the claimant a defence. This triggers in the county court the allocation of the case to a particular 'track'. A claim of up to £5,000 will usually be allocated to the small claims track. Typically, these claims concern consumer disputes and the court does not expect parties to be legally represented. Claims exceeding £5,000 and up to £15,000 are usually allocated to the fast track. Whilst parties will usually have legal representation on this track, the court will tightly control costs, as well as the type and amount of evidence each party can rely on. In particular, the expectation is that a single joint expert should be used by the parties where expert evidence is necessary, and the trial must be conducted within one day (effectively five hours). Claims exceeding £15,000 are usually allocated to the multi-track. As a claim cannot be started in the High Court unless it exceeds £15,000, all claims in that court are dealt with on the multi-track.

1.3.3 Stage 3: interim matters

Once on a track, the court carefully manages a case. Directions will be given to the parties as to the steps that must be taken to prepare for trial. A strict timetable will be imposed as to when each step must be taken. On the small claims track and fast track the expectation is that these directions can be given without any court hearing. In multi-track cases of any complexity it is usual for the parties to meet with a judge at a so-called case management conference in order clearly to define the issues in dispute and determine what steps need to be taken and when, in order to prepare for trial. The most common case management directions are for:

(a) standard disclosure (ie, the parties list the documents in their possession that they intend to rely on, or which are adverse to their case, or support an opponent's case (see **Chapter 10**)); and

(b) the exchange of evidence before trial that the parties intend to rely on (eg, expert's reports and statements of non-expert witnesses (see **Chapter 11**)).

Whatever the track, the parties will be working towards either a known trial date, or at least a period of time in the future when the trial will occur.

As to case management generally, see **Chapter 8**.

In addition to case management directions, parties may during this stage apply to the court for any specific orders that might be required (eg, to force an opponent who has neglected to take a required step in accordance with the timetable to do so on pain of having his case thrown out by the court). See further **Chapter 9**.

1.3.4 Stage 4: trial

A trial on the small claims track is informal and conducted at the discretion of the judge. The formal rules of evidence apply on the fast track and multi-track. At the end of a fast track trial, the judge will usually have resolved all issues (ie, liability, quantum (if relevant) and costs). As to costs, the judge will decide if any party should pay the other's costs and, if so, how much. This is known as a summary assessment of costs. The parties must provide each other and the court with a detailed breakdown of costs for this purpose. On the multi-track, the trial judge will decide who should pay costs. The general rule is the loser pays the winner's costs. If the parties cannot subsequently agree on the amount of those costs, they are determined at a later date by a different judge, known as a costs judge, via a process called detailed assessment. See generally 13.3.

1.3.5 Stage 5: post-trial

A party awarded damages and/or costs will expect to be paid by the date set by the court. What if that does not happen? The party will have to apply to the court to enforce the judgment. Most commonly, this involves instructing court officials to attend the debtor's premises and to take his belongings to be sold at public auction. The proceeds are then paid to the party. It is therefore vital, as indicated at **1.3.1** above, to ensure that at stage 1 steps are taken to check that any potential defendant is actually worth suing.

1.4 Case analysis

The key to resolving any legal dispute, either by negotiation or litigation, is to identify from the outset the relevant issues and the evidence available to establish those. For example, in a negligence claim the client must satisfy the opponent or a judge that each of the elements of the tort existed (ie, duty of care, breach of that duty, a causal link between the breach and damages said to have resulted, as well as damages that are not too remote). As a case develops, you should continually review which issues remain in dispute and how those are to be proved.

Chapters 2 and 3 will discuss the steps you will need to take in order to complete your case analysis.

1.5 Useful websites

The starting point for any exploration of the Web in this area should probably be at the Department for Constitutional Affairs website that hosts the Civil Procedure Rules (www.dca.gov.uk/civil/procrules_fin/index.htm). Court forms and guides are on the Court Service site (www.courtservice.gov.uk). From there you can use the related websites page to find other useful links, eg Community Legal Service (www.justask.org.uk/index.jsp), European Court of Justice (www.europa.eu.int/cj/en/index.htm), etc. Of course, these websites will then give you other links, and you will soon find an incredibly diverse range of sites dealing with a whole range of legal matters.

Chapter 2
Considerations at the First Interview and Funding the Claim

2.1	Purpose of the first interview	9
2.2	Limitation	9
2.3	Viability and burden of proof	11
2.4	Remedy sought	12
2.5	Funding	15
2.6	Ethics and conflict of interest	23
2.7	Foreign element and choice of forum	24
2.8	Alternatives to a civil claim	26
2.9	Human rights	28
2.10	Pre-action checklist	29

2.1 Purpose of the first interview

The first interview between the solicitor and client is very important from both parties' points of view. The client will be anxious that the solicitor appreciates his problem, and will want to be assured that there is a satisfactory solution to it. At the same time, the solicitor needs to be able to extract relevant information from the client in order to be able to give preliminary advice on such issues as liability and quantum.

Ideally before the first interview, or at least immediately after it, a conflict of interest check should be done (see 2.6.2).

There is no comprehensive list of those matters which need to be dealt with at first interview because each case is different. However, the matters set out below and summarised at **2.10** do require consideration.

2.2 Limitation

The Limitation Act 1980 (LA 1980) (as amended) prescribes fixed periods of time for issuing various types of proceedings. If this period of time elapses without proceedings being issued, the case becomes 'statute-barred'. The claimant can still commence his claim, but the defendant will have an impregnable defence. If the defendant wishes to rely on this it must be specifically stated in his defence (see **Chapter 6**).

2.2.1 Claims founded on contract or tort (LA 1980, ss 2 and 5)

The basic rule is that the claimant has six years from the date when the cause of action accrued to commence his proceedings.

In contract the cause of action accrues as soon as the breach of contract occurs.

In tort, the cause of action accrues when the tort is committed. In the tort of negligence, as damage is an essential element, the cause of action accrues only when some damage occurs. This may be at a date considerably later than when the breach of duty itself occurred.

This basic rule is modified in the case of certain specific types of claim. As to personal injury cases, see *Personal Injury and Clinical Negligence Litigation*.

2.2.2 Latent damage

In a non-personal injury claim based on negligence, where the damage is latent at the date when the cause of action accrued, s 14A of the LA 1980 provides that the limitation period expires either:

(a) six years from the date on which the cause of action accrued; or

(b) three years from the date of knowledge of certain material facts about the damage, if this period expires after the period mentioned in (a). The definition of 'material facts' is similar to the 'date of knowledge' definition in the LA 1980, s 14.

In theory, these rules could mean that a defendant is indefinitely open to the risk of proceedings being issued in latent damage cases. In order to avoid this, there is a long-stop limitation period of 15 years from the date of the alleged breach of duty (LA 1980, s 14B). This long-stop can bar a cause of action at a date earlier than the claimant's knowledge; indeed, it can even bar a cause of action before it has accrued.

2.2.3 Persons under disability

A person under a disability is either a child (ie, someone who has not yet attained the age of 18), or a patient (ie, a person of unsound mind within the meaning of the Mental Health Act 1983 and who is incapable of managing and administering their property and affairs).

Where the claimant is a person under a disability when a right of action accrues, the limitation period does not begin to run until the claimant ceases to be under that disability. Therefore, for example, if the claimant's cause of action accrues at the age of 16 years, the limitation period does not commence until the claimant is 18 years old and, accordingly, the claimant has until his twenty-first birthday to commence the claim (ie three years from his eighteenth birthday).

2.2.4 Contractual limitation

In a contract case it is very important to check whether there is a contractual limitation period specified in the contract. This is because any such provision is usually shorter than the statutory limitation periods referred to above, and the claim should therefore be commenced within the contractually specified period.

2.2.5 Solicitor's role

From the outset, a solicitor must ascertain when the limitation period began and when it will expire. The matter must be continually reviewed in the light of any new facts. Careful diary notes must be kept to remind the solicitor that time is marching on and the expiration of the limitation period draws closer. Proceedings must be issued before the limitation period expires otherwise the solicitor is likely to face a negligence claim.

2.2.6 Summary

Type of claim	Statutory limitation period
Contract (excluding personal injury)	6 years (LA 1980, s 5)
Tort (excluding personal injury and latent damage)	6 years (LA 1980, s 2)
Latent damage	6 years or 3 years from date of knowledge (LA 1980, s 14A)

2.3 Viability and burden of proof

2.3.1 Viability

The overall viability of pursuing a claim against a potential defendant needs to be considered at the earliest possible stage with the client.

Viability involves a number of issues of which the claimant needs to be aware.

2.3.1.1 Identify all potential defendants and their status

As we saw at **1.3**, the general rule is that all persons to be sued should be sued at the same time and in the same claim. Your case analysis must identify against whom each cause of action lies. Very often, there is only one potential defendant but, for example, where an employee or agent commits a tort when acting in the course of his employment it is usual to sue both the employee or agent and the employer. This is because the latter is vicariously liable for the former. Likewise, a consumer may, in certain circumstances, have a cause of action against both the retailer and manufacturer of a defective product.

Not only must you identify the prospective defendants, you must also ensure they are sued in their correct capacity. Broadly, you should consider if the potential defendant is an individual, partnership or limited company. Sometimes it is not as obvious as it seems. For example, assume your client entered into a contract negotiated with a Mr Jones. We need to ask, in what capacity did Mr Jones do that? Did he act as an individual on his own behalf? Was he acting as an agent for someone else and, if so, did our client know that? Is he one of, say, 10 partners in a firm called Jones & Co, and did he contract on behalf of the partnership? Is he a director in a limited company called Jones Ltd, and did he contract on behalf of that company? Just exactly with whom did the client contract? Will he end up negotiating with, and potentially litigating against, Mr Jones, Mr Jones' principal, Jones & Co (a firm) or Jones Ltd? See further **4.4**.

2.3.1.2 Defendant's solvency

There is little point in suing a defendant who is on the verge of either bankruptcy or liquidation. Enforcement of any judgment obtained would be impossible. If there is doubt as to the liquidity of the prospective defendant then further enquiries should be made. For example, if the proposed defendant is a company, a company search should be carried out. For an individual, a bankruptcy search should be done. In any case an inquiry agent could be instructed, although the costs of doing this must be considered.

12   Civil Litigation

2.3.1.3 Defendant's whereabouts

Clearly, the defendant needs to be traceable and his whereabouts known in order to communicate the claim and, if necessary, serve proceedings. Again, an inquiry agent may be able to help.

2.3.1.4 The claim itself

This involves balancing the merits of the claim itself against the overall cost of pursuing it and the prospects of a successful outcome. The client may believe he has a good claim but will be concerned as to the costs of litigation. Finance is discussed below (see **2.5**), but the client must be advised at this stage on the law, and any possible defences to the claim should be anticipated. The client must be told of the overriding objective and the requirement in r 1.3 that parties must help the court further the overriding objective.

2.3.1.5 Alternative remedies

The solicitor should consider whether there are any alternative remedies available to the client for resolving the problem and advise the client accordingly. For example, the client may wish to use one of the forms of alternative dispute resolution (see **Chapter 15**).

2.3.2 Burden of proof

There are two questions of proof which need to be considered.

2.3.2.1 Legal burden

The party asserting a fact must prove it unless it is admitted by his opponent. For example, a claimant who alleges negligence must prove all the elements of the tort (ie, a duty existed between the parties, the defendant breached that duty and the claimant sustained damage as a result). Similarly, a claimant alleging breach of contract must prove that a contract existed between the parties, the defendant broke the relevant express and/or implied terms of the contract and the claimant suffered loss as a result.

2.3.2.2 Balance of probabilities

In civil cases, the claimant is required to prove a fact on a balance of probabilities. This simply requires the judge to be persuaded that the claimant's version of events is more likely to be true than the defendant's.

2.4 Remedy sought

There are a number of alternative remedies which a claimant can pursue against the defendant, assuming liability can be established. The most common remedy sought is damages.

2.4.1 Damages

The rules as to quantum of damages in civil cases depend on the type of claim being pursued.

2.4.1.1 Contract

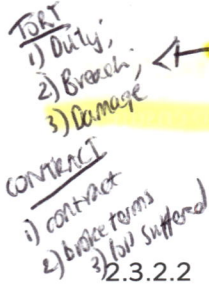

A claim for damages arises when one party to the contract has failed to perform an obligation under the contract. The purpose of damages in such a situation is to place the injured party in the position he would have been in if the contract had been properly performed. [eg. recovery of cost for defective good]

For example, damages can be recovered for either the repair of defective goods, or repayment of the purchase price. In addition, there may be a claim for general damages in respect of physical discomfort and/or inconvenience. However, damages for injured feelings or mental distress are not generally recoverable. There is an exception, where the subject matter of the contract was to provide enjoyment, peace of mind or freedom from distress (eg, a contract for a holiday). In such cases, damages for mental distress and loss of enjoyment are recoverable.

The test for the recovery of damages for breach of contract is that they must not be too remote from the breach (ie, did the loss flow naturally from the breach, or was the loss within the reasonable contemplation of the parties at the time the contract was made as being the probable result of the breach?).

2.4.1.2 Tort

A claim for damages arises where injury, loss or damage is caused to the claimant or the claimant's property. The aim of damages is, so far as possible, to place the claimant in the position he would have been in if the damage had not occurred. Damages are therefore compensatory in nature and, as a result, the claimant can seek compensation for any direct loss and consequential loss, provided the rules on remoteness are not broken. The rules on remoteness require that in order to be recoverable the loss must be a reasonably foreseeable consequence of the tort.

2.4.1.3 Reduction in damages – duty to mitigate

If C failed to mitigate loss, damages can be reduced, in either contract or tort.

Any potential claim for damages for either breach of contract or tort may be reduced if it can be shown that the claimant has failed to mitigate his loss. In *Frost v Knight* (1872) LR 7 Ex 111 the court observed that this duty means looking at what the claimant 'has done, or has had the means of doing, and, as a prudent man, ought in reason to have done, whereby his loss has been, or would have been, diminished'. So a claimant cannot recover by way of damages 'any greater sum than that which he reasonably needs to expend for the purpose of making good the loss' (*Darbishire v Warran* [1963] 1 WLR 1067). The duty only arises on the breach of contract or commission of the tort. If a defendant alleges that the claimant has failed to take all reasonable steps to mitigate his loss, he should raise that in pre-action correspondence (see **Chapter 3**) and state it in his defence (see **6.3**). The burden of proof will be on the defendant at any trial.

2.4.2 Debt

A debt action is a particular type of contract claim. Instead of claiming damages for breach of contract, the claimant is claiming a sum which the defendant promised to pay under the contract.

For example, in a sale of goods case, if the buyer wrongfully rejects the goods (and the seller accepts this as repudiation of the contract) the seller has a claim for damages for breach of contract. However, if the buyer takes delivery but then fails to pay, then the action is for debt. The significance is that in the latter case the claimant has no duty to mitigate his loss.

2.4.3 Specified and unspecified claims for money

The CPR 1998 provide no definition of a claim for a specified or unspecified sum of money. The N1A Notes for a claimant on completing the claim form (see copy at **Appendix A(1)**) refer to a claim for a *fixed amount of money* as being a specified amount. On that basis a specified claim is in the nature of a debt (ie, a fixed amount of money due and payable under and by virtue of a contract). The amount will be known already (from, say, an invoice), or it should be capable of being determined by mere mathematics (from, say, a contractual formula). Examples might include the price of goods sold, commission said to be due under express contractual terms or consideration said to have totally failed.

If the court will have to conduct an investigation to decide on the amount of money payable, the claim is best seen as being for an unspecified amount, even if the claimant puts some figures forward for the amount claimed. For example, in a damages claim for breach of contract the claimant may have had to repair or replace goods. Whilst a figure might be placed on the cost of such, it will be for the trial judge to determine if it is reasonable. Thus, damages claims should usually be regarded as unspecified.

What if a claim is a mixture of specified and unspecified amounts? For example, the recovery of consideration paid that has totally failed (a specified amount) plus damages for breach of contract (unspecified amounts). In these circumstances the entire claim is treated as an unspecified claim.

2.4.4 Interest

Where the remedy sought by the claimant is either damages or the repayment of a debt, the court may award interest on the sum outstanding. The rules vary according to the type of claim. A claimant seeking interest must specifically claim interest in the particulars of claim.

2.4.4.1 Breach of contract (including debt claims)

In contract cases, there are three alternative claims to interest:

(a) The contract itself may specify a rate of interest payable on any outstanding sum. This will be the rate which was negotiated between the parties. The court will usually apply this rate.

(b) If there is no contractual rate then the court has a discretion to award interest either under s 35A of the Supreme Court Act 1981 (SCA 1981) in respect of High Court cases or under s 69 of the County Courts Act 1984 (CCA 1984) in respect of county court cases. The current rate of interest awarded by the courts is 8% per annum.

(c) It may be possible to claim interest under the Late Payment of Commercial Debts (Interest) Act 1998 (see below).

The earliest interest may be awarded from is the date on which the cause of action accrued. As to a claim in contract or tort, see **2.2.1**. The court may order that it is paid up until the date of judgment. As to interest after judgment, see **14.2**.

Since a debt claim is for a specified amount of money, interest must be claimed precisely, giving as a lump sum the amount of interest which has accrued from breach of contract up to the date of issue of the proceedings and a daily rate thereafter. In a damages claim, the request for interest is not set out in detail as the claim is for an unspecified amount of money.

> **Example: specified claim**
>
> You act for Mr Tibbs, a local builder. He is in dispute with one of his customers, Mrs Little. He entered into a written contract to convert her basement into a bedroom last year. He finished the work on 7 July 2004 but, despite reminders, she has not paid him the contract price of £13,000. The written contract between Mr Tibbs and Mrs

Little provides that interest is payable on late payment. This is due at the rate of 20% per annum from and including the day of completion of the works. If a claim form is issued on 31 August 2004, how much interest should be claimed?

Mr Tibbs is entitled to interest on £13,000 for 56 days (namely, 25 days in July and 31 days in August). For each day, he is entitled to interest of £7.12 (that is £13,000 × 20% divided by 365 days. The answer of £7.1232876 is rounded down in the circumstances). So, on the claim form he should claim £398.72 by way of interest.

Late Payment of Commercial Debts (Interest) Act 1998

This Act gives a statutory right to interest on commercial debts which are paid late if the contract itself does not provide for interest in the event of late payment. The term 'commercial debt' includes debts arising from the supply of goods and services. As the Act is only concerned with commercial debt, it does not apply to unspecified claims or a specified amount owed by a consumer.

Interest under the Act can be claimed at a rate of 8% above the Bank of England's base rate. The interest accrues from the expiry of any period of credit under the contract. If the contract does not provide for any such period, interest can be claimed from 30 days after the latest of:

(a) delivery of the bill;
(b) delivery of the goods;
(c) performance of the service.

An example appears in the claim form at **6.2.1**.

2.4.4.2 Tort

The court has a general discretion to award interest on damages in any negligence claim. This power is derived from SCA 1981, s 35A in respect of High Court claims and CCA 1984, s 69 in respect of county court claims. Generally speaking, if interest has been properly claimed the court will normally exercise its discretion to award interest for such period as it considers appropriate. The current rate of interest awarded by the courts is 8% per annum.

2.5 Funding

On taking instructions, the solicitor should give his client the best information he can about the likely cost of the matter, in accordance with r 15 of the Solicitors' Practice Rules 1990 and the Solicitors' Costs Information and Client Care Code. This includes advising the client on the different types of funding available.

In litigation cases, it is usually not possible to agree a fee or give an estimate of costs at the outset. But the client should be told how the solicitor's fee will be calculated (eg, who is going to do the work and the hourly charging rate of that person). Often a payment on account will be required immediately and interim bills may be delivered as the case progresses. The client should be advised of any foreseeable disbursements (eg, court fees) and that he can set a limit on the costs to be incurred.

The solicitor should also consider whether the client's liability for costs may be covered by insurance, and whether the likely outcome of the matter justifies the expense involved.

In addition, the solicitor should advise the client of the risk that he may be ordered to pay the opponent's costs if the case is lost.

16   Civil Litigation

2.5.1 Solicitor and client costs and costs between the parties

In litigation cases, the solicitor should explain to the client the distinction between solicitor and client costs (ie, the sum the client must pay to his own solicitor) and costs that may be awarded between the parties in litigation.

If the client loses the case, he will have to pay his own solicitor's costs and, in addition, he will normally have to pay his opponent's costs. The opponent's costs are not necessarily all the costs incurred by the opponent. The court will assess what costs the client must pay towards the opponent's costs (unless there is agreement on this amount between the parties). The client will only have to pay to his opponent such costs as are ordered by the court or agreed between the parties.

If the client wins the case, he will still have to pay his own solicitor's costs. Indeed, if he is paying privately, he will usually have already paid these costs. He will normally receive from the opponent his costs. Again, this will be such sum as is approved by the court or agreed between the parties as being payable on a 'between the parties' basis. The client will, of course, use the costs that he receives to help towards payment of his own solicitor's bill. But if his own solicitor's charges are more than the costs between the parties that he receives, the client will have to make up the shortfall.

However, if the client wins the case but recovers no costs from his opponent (for example, if the opponent goes bankrupt or simply disappears) the client still has to pay his own solicitor's costs.

2.5.2 Conditional fee agreements

A conditional fee agreement (CFA) is one under which the solicitor receives no payment (or less than normal payment) if the case is lost, but normal, or higher than normal, payment if the client is successful.

A CFA is enforceable only if it meets the requirements of s 58 of the Courts and Legal Services Act 1990. This provides that a CFA:

(a) may be entered into in relation to any civil litigation matter, except family proceedings;

(b) must be in writing; and

(c) must comply with the Conditional Fee Agreements Regulations 2000, SI 2000/692 (the CFA Regulations 2000), as amended by the Conditional Fee Agreements (Miscellaneous Amendments) Regulations 2003 (Nos 1 and 2) (SIs 2003/1240 and 2003/3344).

The CFA Regulations 2000 contain detailed requirements with which every CFA (save one governed by reg 3A: a CFA 'Simple', see below) must meet, namely:

Regulation 2

(1) A conditional fee agreement must specify—

   (a) the particular proceedings or parts of them to which it relates (including whether it relates to any appeal, counterclaim or proceedings to enforce a judgement or order),

   (b) the circumstances in which the legal representative's fees and expenses, or part of them, are payable,

   (c) what payment, if any, is due—

      (i) if those circumstances only partly occur,

      (ii) irrespective of whether those circumstances occur, and

Considerations at the First Interview and Funding the Claim 17

(iii) on the termination of the agreement for any reason, and

(d) the amounts which are payable in all the circumstances and cases specified or the method to be used to calculate them and, in particular, whether the amounts are limited by reference to the damages which may be recovered on behalf of the client.

(2) A conditional fee agreement to which regulation 4 applies must contain a statement that the requirements of that regulation which apply in the case of that agreement have been complied with.

Regulation 3

(1) A conditional fee agreement which provides for a success fee—

(a) must briefly specify the reasons for setting the percentage increase at the level stated in the agreement, and

(b) must specify how much of the percentage increase, if any, relates to the cost to the legal representative of the postponement of the payment of his fees and expenses.

(2) If the agreement relates to court proceedings, it must provide that where the percentage increase becomes payable as a result of those proceedings, then—

(a) if—
 (i) any fees subject to the increase are assessed, and
 (ii) the legal representative or the client is required by the court to disclose to the court or any other person the reasons for setting the percentage increase at the level stated in the agreement,

he may do so,

(b) if—
 (i) any such fees are assessed, and
 (ii) any amount in respect of the percentage increase is disallowed on the assessment on the ground that the level at which the increase was set was unreasonable in view of facts which were or should have been known to the legal representative at the time it was set,

that amount ceases to be payable under the agreement, unless the court is satisfied that it should continue to be so payable, and

(c) if—
 (i) sub-paragraph (b) does not apply, and
 (ii) the legal representative agrees with any person liable as a result of the proceedings to pay fees subject to the percentage increase that a lower amount than the amount payable in accordance with the conditional fee agreement is to be paid instead,

the amount payable under the conditional fee agreement in respect of those fees shall be reduced accordingly, unless the court is satisfied that the full amount should continue to be payable under it.

(3) In this regulation 'percentage increase' means the percentage by which the amount of the fees which would be payable if the agreement were not a conditional fee agreement is to be increased under the agreement.

Regulation 4

(1) Before a conditional fee agreement is made the legal representative must—

(a) inform the client about the following matters, and

(b) if the client requires any further explanation, advice or other information about any of those matters, provide such further explanation, advice or other information about them as the client may reasonably require.

(2) Those matters are—

(a) the circumstances in which the client may be liable to pay the costs of the legal representative in accordance with the agreement,

18 Civil Litigation

(b) the circumstances in which the client may seek assessment of the fees and expenses of the legal representative and the procedure for doing so,

(c) whether the legal representative considers that the client's risk of incurring liability for costs in respect of the proceedings to which agreement relates is insured against under an existing contract of insurance,

(d) whether other methods of financing those costs are available, and, if so, how they apply to the client and the proceedings in question,

(e) whether the legal representative considers that any particular method or methods of financing any or all of those costs is appropriate and, if he considers that a contract of insurance is appropriate or recommends a particular such contract—

(i) his reasons for doing so, and

(ii) whether he has an interest in doing so.

(3) Before a conditional fee agreement is made the legal representative must explain its effect to the client.

(4) In the case of an agreement where—

(a) the legal representative is a body to which section 30 of the Access to Justice Act 1999 (recovery where body undertakes to meet costs liabilities) applies, and

(b) there are no circumstances in which the client may be liable to pay any costs in respect of the proceedings,

paragraph (1) does not apply.

(5) Information required to be given under paragraph (1) about the matters in paragraph (2)(a) to (d) must be given orally (whether or not it is also given in writing), but information required to be so given about the matters in paragraph (2)(e) and the explanation required by paragraph (3) must be given both orally and in writing.

(6) This regulation does not apply in the case of an agreement between a legal representative and an additional legal representative.

Regulation 5

(1) A conditional fee agreement must be signed by the client and the legal representative.

(2) This regulation does not apply in the case of an agreement between a legal representative and an additional legal representative.

A CFA to which reg 3A of the CFA Regulations 2000 applies is often known as a 'CFA Simple'. The CFA Simple is defined in reg 3A as:

(1) A conditional fee agreement under which, except in the circumstances set out in paragraph (5), the client is liable to pay his legal representative's fees and expenses only to the extent that sums are recovered in respect of the relevant proceedings, whether by way of costs or otherwise.

(2) In determining for the purposes of paragraph (1) the circumstances in which a client is liable to pay his legal representative's fees and expenses, no account is to be taken of any obligation to pay costs in respect of the premium of a policy taken out to insure against the risk of incurring a liability in the relevant proceedings.

(3) Regulations 2, 3 and 4 do not apply to a conditional fee agreement to which this regulation applies.

(4) A conditional fee agreement to which this regulation applies must—

(a) specify—

(i) the particular proceedings or parts of them to which it relates (including whether it relates to any appeal, counterclaim or proceedings to enforce a judgment or order); and

Considerations at the First Interview and Funding the Claim 19

(ii) the circumstances in which the legal representative's fees and expenses, or part of them, are payable; and

(b) if it provides for a success fee—

(i) briefly specify the reasons for setting the percentage increase at the level stated in the agreement; and

(ii) provide that if, in court proceedings, the percentage increase becomes payable as a result of those proceedings and the legal representative or the client is ordered to disclose to the court or any other person the reasons for setting the percentage increase at the level stated in the agreement, he may do so.

(5) A conditional fee agreement to which this regulation applies may specify that the client will be liable to pay the legal representative's fees and expenses whether or not sums are recovered in respect of the relevant proceedings, if the client—

(a) fails to co-operate with the legal representative;

(b) fails to attend any medical or expert examination or court hearing which the legal representative reasonably requests him to attend;

(c) fails to give necessary instructions to the legal representative;

(d) withdraws instructions from the legal representative; and

(e) is an individual who is adjudged bankrupt or enters into an arrangement or a composition with his creditors, or against whom an administration order is made; or

(f) is a company for which a receiver, administrative receiver or liquidator is appointed.

(5A) A conditional fee agreement to which this regulation applies may specify that, in the event of the client dying in the course of the relevant proceedings, his estate will be liable for the legal representative's fees and expenses, whether or not sums are recovered in respect of those proceedings.

(6) Before a conditional fee agreement to which this regulation applies is made, the legal representative must inform the client as to the circumstances in which the client or his estate may be liable to pay the legal representative's fees and expenses, and provide such further explanation, advice or other information as to those circumstances as the client may reasonably require.

2.5.2.1 Drafting the CFA

It is of course essential that the CFA is carefully drafted. Consider, for example, the importance of a clear definition of the term 'win'. Does the client win if he succeeds on all aspects of his claim, or is it enough that he recovers some damages (even if they represent only a small percentage of his claim)? The Law Society provides assistance in the form of a model CFA for personal injury cases, which can be adapted for other types of work. Precedents are also available in practitioner works.

What if the Regulations are not met? For example, the agreement fails to record the amount of the success fee that relates to postponement of payment? In those circumstances the CFA is unenforceable and no fees can be recovered from the client: see *Spencer v Gordon Wood (t/a Gordon's Tyres)* [2004] LTL, 15 March.

2.5.2.2 The success fee

Where it is agreed that the solicitor should receive higher than normal payment if the case is won, the increase in his normal fees (known as a success fee) cannot exceed 100% of the solicitor's normal charges.

If the client wins the case and his opponent is ordered to pay his costs, these may include the success fee. The opponent will, however, only be required to pay the success fee to the extent that it is reasonable (see further **13.3.8**). Where part (or all) of the success fee is disallowed, the solicitor is not entitled to recover the remainder from his client unless the court orders otherwise. It is vital that the factors taken into account are carefully recorded so that, if necessary, the solicitor can justify the level at which the success fee was set.

Whenever he enters into a CFA, the solicitor takes a financial risk. The solicitor who regularly acts on this basis will stay in business only if the success fees he recovers on his 'wins' outweigh the fees sacrificed on his 'losses'. It is therefore essential that before entering into a CFA or agreeing the level of the success fee with a client, the solicitor performs a thorough risk assessment. Relevant factors would include:

(a) the chances of the client succeeding on liability;
(b) the likely amount of the damages;
(c) the length of time it will take for the case to reach trial;
(d) the number of hours the solicitor is likely to have to spend on the case.

The solicitor may need to spend some time gathering evidence and information about the client's case before he can perform a full risk assessment. For example, it may be appropriate to obtain an expert opinion and/or interview witnesses (see **Chapter 3**). It is, of course, essential to discuss with the client what work will have to be performed before a decision can be reached about whether the solicitor is prepared to enter into a CFA, and how that work is to be funded.

2.5.2.3 Funding disbursements and liability for the other side's costs

If the CFA client loses the case, he will not usually have to pay his own solicitor's fees but will nevertheless be liable for his opponent's costs. In addition, the client will, during the course of the litigation, have to fund disbursements such as the fees of counsel and expert witnesses, as well as items such as travelling expenses. Many CFA-funded clients are not in a position to pay these disbursements and/or may be concerned by the fact that they will not know until the end of the litigation whether they are liable to their opponent for costs and, if so, for how much.

In such circumstances, the client may benefit from purchasing after-the-event insurance, which provides cover for the other side's costs and his own disbursements in the event of losing the case. The premium payable depends on the strength of the client's case and the level of cover required. If the client wins, the premium, like the success fee, is recoverable from his opponent to the extent that it is reasonable. As stated above, the CFA Regulations 2000 require the solicitor to discuss with his client whether insurance is appropriate before the CFA is entered into.

Of course, obtaining after-the-event insurance to cover the client's disbursements in the event that he loses, does not solve the problem of how those disbursements are to be paid for during the course of the litigation. There are various solutions. As far as counsel's fees are concerned, counsel may be willing to enter into a CFA with the client. However, such an arrangement cannot be entered into with an expert witness. This is to avoid any possibility that the expert's evidence, which should be impartial, will be influenced if he is instructed on a 'no win, no fee' basis.

If necessary, many after-the-event insurers will arrange a loan to the client or his solicitors to fund both the disbursements and the cost of the after-the-event insurance premium. The loan may even be on terms that it is not repayable in the event that the client loses. If he wins, the interest on the loan is not recoverable from his opponent. It is usually deducted from the damages recovered.

2.5.2.4 Notifying the other side of a CFA or insurance cover

If the client enters into a CFA before proceedings have been issued or has insurance cover, he should inform other potential parties to the dispute that he has done so (see para 4A of the Practice Direction on Pre-action Protocols). This may well be in the letter of claim or subsequent correspondence.

Once proceedings are issued, the client must file with the court and serve on all parties a Notice of Funding in Form N251 (a copy appears in **Appendix A(7)**). This informs the other parties of:

(a) the date on which the CFA was entered into;
(b) the date of any relevant insurance policy and the name of the insurer.

If the information is not provided, the client will not be able to claim the success fee or insurance premium from his opponent if he wins the case (see r 44.15). Note that the success fee of a CFA or amount of an insurance premium does not have to be and should not be disclosed.

Where the client is a claimant and the CFA or insurance cover was entered into before the issue of proceedings, Form N251 must be filed when the claim form is issued. Where the client is a defendant and the CFA or insurance cover is entered into before the defendant files any documents with the court, Form N251 must be filed with the first such document. Otherwise, where the CFA or insurance cover is entered into later, Form N251 must be filed within seven days of the date of the CFA or insurance cover being taken out.

If, during the course of the proceedings, there is any change to this information, a notice of the change must be filed and served on all parties within seven days.

2.5.3 Contingency fees

The Solicitors' Practice Rules 1990 define a contingency fee as any sum (whether fixed or calculated as a percentage of damages) which is payable only in the event that the client succeeds in contentious proceedings.

Rule 8 of the Solicitors' Practice Rules 1990 effectively prohibits all contingency fees in contentious proceedings except CFAs. In particular, it should be noted that it is not lawful to enter into an agreement with the client whereby if the case is won, the solicitor is rewarded by receiving a percentage of the damages recovered.

So what constitutes contentious proceedings? This is defined by s 87 of the Solicitors' Act 1974 as, 'business done, in or for the purpose of proceedings *begun* before a court'. So it is possible to agree a contingency fee for all the usual pre-action work (eg, investigation of issues, the initial letters of claim and response, negotiations, etc). If the matter is settled without a claim form being issued, a contingency fee is lawful and payable provided the contingency has been met. However, it is unlawful and so unenforceable once proceedings have begun.

2.5.4 Insurance

Regardless of whether the client is going to enter a CFA, the solicitor should always check to see if the client has the benefit of a before-the-event insurance policy which might fund the litigation. Such insurance is commonly purchased as part of household or motor insurance policies.

In the case of *Sarwar v Alam* [2001] EWCA Civ 1401, [2002] 1 WLR 125, the Court of Appeal laid down the following guidance:

> In our judgment, proper modern practice dictates that a solicitor should normally invite a client to bring to the first interview any relevant motor insurance policy, any household insurance policy and any stand alone before-the-event insurance policy belonging to the client and/or any spouse or partner living in the same household as the client.

Where before-the-event insurance cover is not available, the client may wish to consider purchasing after-the-event insurance even if he does not fund the litigation by way of a CFA. As discussed above, one of the disadvantages of litigation is that, if the case is lost, the loser will generally have to pay the winner's costs, and this liability cannot be quantified until the end of the proceedings. By purchasing after-the-event insurance, the litigant removes this uncertainty (provided the cover bought is sufficient). Moreover, if he wins the case, he is likely to be able to recover the premium paid from the other side. Given these advantages, a solicitor who fails to discuss the possibility of such insurance with a client at the outset of litigation may well be negligent.

2.5.5 Trade unions and professional organisations

If a client is a member of a trade union or professional organisation, it may be possible to arrange for his union or organisation to be responsible for payment of his solicitor's costs.

2.5.6 Public funding

In limited circumstances, clients may receive public funding for civil litigation and the solicitor should always consider whether this might be available. Most civil litigation matters within the scope of this book will not, however, benefit from public funding and what follows is, therefore, no more than a broad outline.

Prior to 1 April 2000, public funding (previously called legal aid) was provided by the Legal Aid Board. As a result of the Access to Justice Act 1999, the Legal Aid Board was replaced by the Legal Services Commission (the LSC) which runs public funding schemes for both criminal and civil litigation. The civil litigation scheme is administered by the Community Legal Service (the CLS), which operates the Community Legal Service Fund (the CLSF).

The effect of the new arrangements is to reduce substantially the scope of public funding in litigation. CLS funding will not usually be available for cases that could be financed by a CFA. With very limited exceptions, claims in negligence for personal injury, death or damage to property (including intellectual property) are excluded. Nor is funding available for matters arising out of the carrying on of a business, including claims brought or defended by sole traders.

In addition to these restrictions, public funding is only open to clients whose income and capital falls within financial eligibility limits. These limits vary depending on whether the client is seeking full representation in proceedings, or merely wants assistance from a solicitor to investigate a proposed claim.

Furthermore, where the client is financially eligible and the claim is of a type covered by the CLSF, public funding will be offered only if a merits test is also satisfied. This involves considering the client's prospects of success and applying cost benefit criteria (ie, weighing the likely cost of the proceedings against their benefit to the client). Put simply, a client who has a strong claim that will not be expensive to pursue, but which would result in substantial damages, has a much better chance of securing funding than one whose prospects of winning are marginal or who wishes to pursue a claim which would involve costs that are disproportionate to its likely benefits.

Where a party is in receipt of public funding, he may be required to make a contribution from his disposable capital or his income towards the costs. Where a contribution is required from income, this is payable on a monthly basis for as long as the case is funded by the LSC. Any change in the client's circumstances must be notified to the LSC as it may affect the amount of the contribution or the client's entitlement to funding.

2.5.6.1 The statutory charge

Where a publicly funded client recovers money as a result of the proceedings, he may have to repay some or all of his legal costs to the LSC out of the money recovered. This is known as the statutory charge and it will apply only to the extent that the client does not succeed in recovering his costs from his opponent.

The same principle applies where the dispute involves property rather than money. Any property that is retained or transferred to the client is subject to the statutory charge.

The solicitor must ensure that the client has understood the statutory charge prior to accepting an offer of public funding.

2.6 Ethics and conflict of interest

A detailed consideration of this area is contained in *Pervasive and Core Topics*, Part II, **Professional Conduct**.

The solicitor acting in civil proceedings must, in particular, have regard to the following rules of professional conduct.

2.6.1 Duty of confidentiality

The solicitor is under a duty to maintain the confidentiality of his client's affairs at all times, unless the client's prior authority is obtained for disclosure.

2.6.2 Conflict of interest

A solicitor cannot act for two or more clients where there is a conflict of interest between them, or a significant risk of such a conflict arising. A check for potential conflicts should be carried out before the client is interviewed for the first time and immediately thereafter.

In civil cases, such a situation could arise, for example, where a solicitor is instructed to act by two partners in a firm which has been sued for damages for fraudulent misrepresentation, where the allegation is that only one of the partners made the fraudulent misrepresentation. The potential conflict arises because there is clearly a risk that the 'innocent' partner may have a right of action against the 'guilty' partner.

2.6.3 Solicitor's duty as an officer of the court

As well as owing duties to the client, the solicitor also has an overriding duty not to mislead the court. The duty to the court means that the solicitor must disclose all relevant legal authorities to the court, such as statutory provisions or case law, even if these are not favourable to his case. The advocate is also under a duty to help the court achieve the overriding objective.

Under r 1.3 of CPR 1998, the parties, and therefore their solicitors, are required to assist the court in advancing the overriding objective. This creates a potential risk of conflict between the solicitor's duty to the court under CPR 1998, r 1.3 and his duty to act in the best interests of his client pursuant to r 1 of the Solicitors' Practice Rules 1990. However, r 1 of the Solicitors' Practice Rules 1990 makes it clear that a solicitor, in acting in the best interests of his client, must take account of his obligations to the court under the overriding objective.

2.6.4 Who is my client and am I authorised to act?

A solicitor warrants his authority to take any positive step in court proceedings, for example, to issue a claim form or serve a defence on behalf of the client. So a solicitor must always be able to answer the questions posed above. For example, assume you attend a new client called Mrs Freeman. She wants to claim under a contract she entered into with Megawindows (Mythshire) Limited.

First, we need to ask: in what capacity are we acting for Mrs Freeman? Is she an individual who entered into the contract on her own behalf? Was she acting as an agent for her principal? Is she a trustee acting on behalf of a trust? Is she, say, one of a hundred partners in a firm, and did she contract on behalf of the partnership such that the partnership is our client? Is she a director in a limited company, and did she contract on behalf of that company such that the company is our client?

Secondly, if we are not acting for her as an individual in her own right, we need to consider if she is the correct person to give us instructions on behalf of her principal, the trust, the partnership or limited company. Note that a solicitor may be ordered to pay personally the costs that are incurred where any steps are taken without authority, even if he does not know that he lacks authority. For example, where the client gives instructions on behalf of a non-existent company, or is a person not properly authorised to give instructions on behalf of a company.

2.7 Foreign element and choice of forum

If a solicitor is instructed by a client who is based abroad, or is instructed to take proceedings against a party based abroad, one of the first things which must be considered is the question of jurisdiction – in which country's courts can proceedings be commenced?

Different rules apply depending on whether the foreign country involved is in the EU or outside it.

2.7.1 EU and Lugano Convention Member States

The question of jurisdiction as between Member States of the EU, with the exception of Denmark, is governed by Council Regulation 44/2001 ('the Regulation'). Denmark is governed by an earlier, similar provision called the Brussels Convention 1968. Norway, Poland, Switzerland and Iceland are governed by the Lugano Convention. These are incorporated into English law by virtue of the Civil Jurisdiction and Judgments Act 1982. The 1982 Act also regulates jurisdiction as between the various parts of the UK (given that Scotland and Northern Ireland are separate jurisdictions).

2.7.1.1 The basic rule (Article 2)

The basic rule under the Regulation is that the defendant must be sued in his local courts. For an individual, that means the place where he is domiciled. For a company, it means its statutory seat or central administration or principal place of business (Article 60). The statutory seat of a UK company is its registered office address.

So, the basic rule states that if you want to sue someone domiciled in France, you must do so in the French courts.

2.7.1.2 Co-defendants and third parties (Article 6)

If a defendant is domiciled in an EU country, he can be sued there; and then other parties can be joined into the claim even though they are domiciled elsewhere in the EU.

2.7.1.3 Contract cases (Article 5(1))

The Regulation confers jurisdiction in contract cases on the courts of the State where the contract was to be performed. This is an alternative to suing the defendant where he is domiciled. In a sale of goods case, unless the parties have agreed otherwise, the place of performance of the obligation in question is deemed to be the State where, under the contract, the goods were delivered or should have been delivered. In the case of the provision of services, unless the parties have agreed otherwise, the place of performance of the obligation in question is deemed to be the State where, under the contract, the services were provided or should have been provided.

Many contracts contain jurisdiction clauses stating that, for example, the contract is governed by the law of England and Wales and any dispute must be resolved in the courts of England and Wales. In such a case, unless both parties agree to waive the jurisdiction clause, proceedings must take place in this country, irrespective of the defendant's domicile or where the obligation in question under the contract was to be performed (Article 23).

2.7.1.4 Tort cases (Article 5(3))

The Regulation confers jurisdiction in tort cases on the courts of the State where the tort was committed, or the State where the harm caused by the tort occurred. Again, this is an alternative to suing a defendant where he is domiciled. So, if an Italian driver causes a road traffic accident in England, he can be sued in England or in Italy.

2.7.1.5 Exclusive jurisdiction (Article 22)

In some cases, such as disputes over land, the Regulation confers jurisdiction on the courts of one State and proceedings must be taken there.

2.7.1.6 Submission to the jurisdiction (Article 24)

If a defendant is sued in England and believes that the English courts do not have jurisdiction, he should simply acknowledge service of the claim and apply under Part 11 of CPR 1998 for an order declaring that the court does not have jurisdiction. If he takes any further steps in the proceedings (eg, by filing a defence), he will be taken to have submitted to the jurisdiction of the English courts. The application must be made within 14 days of filing the acknowledgement of service.

Appendix C(2) sets out a flowchart dealing with the order in which the matters set out at **2.7.1.1** to **2.7.1.6** should be applied in determining jurisdiction.

2.7.2 The rest of the world

2.7.2.1 Defendant served in this country

The English courts can hear any proceedings if the claim form was served on the defendant whilst he was present in England and Wales (no matter how briefly). The defendant could then, however, object to the proceedings continuing in England on the ground that the English courts are not the most appropriate ones for resolving the dispute.

So, if an Englishman has an accident in New York caused by the negligence of a local New Yorker and then is able to serve the defendant with a claim form whilst he is in England on holiday, the defendant could object to the proceedings continuing in England on the basis that New York State was a more convenient forum.

2.7.2.2 Applying for permission to serve out of the jurisdiction

If, on the other hand, the defendant cannot be served with the proceedings in England and Wales, the permission of the court needs to be obtained to serve him outside the jurisdiction (see **4.5.5**).

2.8 Alternatives to a civil claim

There are several alternatives to court proceedings which may produce the remedy the client wants, possibly at less cost. These alternative procedures should always be considered at first interview and regularly reviewed.

2.8.1 Arbitration

Arbitration is an adjudication operating outside the normal court process by which a third party reaches a decision which is binding on the parties. Many business contracts contain an arbitration clause requiring the parties to refer their disputes to arbitration rather than litigation. In the absence of such a clause, the parties in dispute may agree to arbitration once the dispute has arisen and may choose their own arbitrator with the relevant expertise. Arbitration itself is largely governed by statute, namely the Arbitration Act 1996 (provided the agreement to arbitrate is in writing).

The main advantages of the parties agreeing to arbitration instead of litigation are that:

(a) arbitration may be quicker than litigation;
(b) the procedures are less formal and occur in private;
(c) the solutions reached are often more practical than those a court has power to order; and
(d) at the same time those decisions are binding on the parties.

The winning party to an arbitration can apply to the High Court for permission to enforce the arbitration award as if it were a court judgment (Arbitration Act 1996, s 66).

On the other hand, the main disadvantages of using arbitration are that certain remedies, such as injunctions, are not available and, depending on the procedures adopted, the dispute may not receive the depth of investigation it would have done in the courts. Further, it is not always necessarily cheaper than litigation.

2.8.2 Alternative dispute resolution

Alternative dispute resolution (ADR) is a means of resolving disputes by using an independent third party to help the parties to reach a solution. The third party may suggest a solution to the parties but cannot impose one. ADR is voluntary; the parties choose the process and either of them can withdraw at any time before a settlement is reached. If either party does not like the proposed solution they do not have to accept it.

There are various types of ADR, such as mediation, expert appraisal or expert determination.

Under the CPR 1998, the courts actively encourage parties to use some form of ADR. ADR is considered in more detail in **Chapter 15**.

2.8.3 Trade schemes

Some professional bodies and trade associations operate schemes under which a potential claimant may be able to pursue a remedy outside the courts. This is often cheaper and quicker than court proceedings.

2.8.4 Negotiating settlements

A solicitor should always consider with the client whether it is possible to negotiate a settlement with the opponent. Negotiations should be commenced as soon as possible and a genuine attempt made to limit the areas of dispute between the parties. Once all reasonable attempts to settle have been exhausted, there may well be no alternative but to issue proceedings. However, the matter must always be kept under review.

Negotiations are considered in more detail in **Chapter 12**.

2.8.5 Insurance

Many defendants to civil claims are insured. Drivers of motor vehicles are required by law to possess insurance which covers them for at least the minimum insurance (basically third party) under the Road Traffic Act 1988. Most professional bodies, such as The Law Society, require that their practising members be insured against negligence claims by clients.

The existence of insurers does not in any way affect the conduct of the proceedings and the insurers are not a party to the claim as there is no cause of action against them. However, the majority of insurance policies require the insured to notify the insurers of any potential claim in order that they can consider taking over the claim on behalf of the insured. Where an insurance company is involved, they, or their solicitors, will usually deal with any negotiations or subsequent court proceedings.

In certain circumstances, a judgment against an insured defendant can be enforced against the insurers. Notice of the proceedings must be served on the insurers either before or within seven days of commencing proceedings to invoke these provisions.

28 Civil Litigation

2.8.6 Motor Insurers Bureau

The Motor Insurers Bureau (MIB) operates two schemes which allow the victims of either uninsured or untraced drivers to recover compensation for certain losses sustained. The MIB is a scheme set up by the insurance companies and is also financed by them.

2.8.7 Criminal Injuries Compensation Authority

The Criminal Injuries Compensation Authority (CICA) is a body set up by the Government to provide the victims of criminal acts with ex gratia compensation for any personal injuries sustained as a result of those acts.

2.8.8 Criminal compensation order

The criminal courts have powers to order compensation in respect of any personal injury, loss or damage resulting from a criminal offence when imposing sentence at the conclusion of criminal proceedings.

2.9 Human rights

The two areas most likely to lead to a human rights challenge which have been considered in this chapter are the rules relating to limitation and funding.

2.9.1 Limitation

Arguably, any time-limit on bringing court proceedings interferes with the right to a fair and public hearing under Article 6(1) of the European Convention for the Protection of Human Rights and Fundamental Freedoms ('the ECHR'). However, it is important to remember that Article 6(1) also uses the words 'within a reasonable time' and every legal system in the world seems to recognise the concept that there comes a time when a potential defendant is entitled to assume that no claim will be made against him.

In *Stubbings and Others v The United Kingdom* [1997] 1 FLR 105, the applicants alleged that a ruling by the House of Lords that their claims were statute-barred under the Limitation Act 1980 amounted to a breach of Article 6(1). The European Court of Human Rights ('the ECtHR') disagreed and held that it would not be appropriate to interfere with the limitation period unless it restricted or reduced the individual's access to the domestic court in such a way or to such an extent that the very essence of the right to access was impaired. A limitation period would only be incompatible with Article 6(1) if it did not have a legitimate aim or purpose and if there was not a reasonable relationship of proportionality between the purpose sought and the means employed to achieve it. The ECtHR recognised several legitimate aims in limitation periods: they provide legal certainty and finality; protect potential defendants from stale claims which might be difficult to challenge; and prevent the injustice that might arise if the court was required to rule on events which took place so long ago that the evidence has become unreliable.

In the light of the decision in *Stubbings*, challenges to the Limitation Act 1980 are likely to be rare.

2.9.2 Funding

Fears have been expressed in some quarters that the abolition of public funding for most types of litigation will make it more difficult for those of limited means to bring a court case to trial. It is arguable that the increased availability of conditional fee agreements, legal expenses insurance and the establishment of the CLS will have increased rather than restricted access to justice. Even if this is so, there will undoubtedly be particular individuals who are disadvantaged under the new regime, and we may well see challenges from such individuals contending that they have been denied effective access to the courts.

The ECtHR has made it clear that the ECHR does not guarantee public funding in civil cases (*Winer v UK* (1986) 48 DR 154). Nor is public funding the only legitimate way in which governments may arrange to provide effective access to the courts (*Andronicou and Constantinou v Cyprus* (1998) 25 EHRR 491). On the other hand, the right to access must be 'practical and effective'. Thus, where legal representation is indispensible to enable the litigant to present his case satisfactorily, the lack of a funding regime which provides for such representation will be a breach of Article 6(1) (*Airey v Ireland* (1979–80) 2 EHRR 305).

2.10 Pre-action checklist

When acting for a new client, consideration should be given to the following:

(1) check any professional conduct points;
(2) identify the client's objectives;
(3) identify all potential parties;
(4) check financial viability;
(5) check jurisdiction;
(6) ascertain the limitation period;
(7) sort out funding;
(8) collect evidence;
(9) explore possible methods of ADR;
(10) comply with pre-action protocol requirements.

Chapter 3
Early Action

3.1	Writing to the client	31
3.2	Interviewing witnesses	31
3.3	Preserving documents	32
3.4	Obtaining expert evidence	33
3.5	Site visits	34
3.6	Instructing counsel	35
3.7	Pre-action protocols	36
3.8	Sending the letter of claim	37
3.9	Pre-action disclosure	38
3.10	Settlement	39
3.11	Researching the law	40
3.12	Summary of pre-action steps	41

After the first interview with the client, there are a number of practical preliminary steps the solicitor can take to advance the client's claim. The main requirements will be to confirm the client's instructions and to obtain relevant evidence to support the client's version of events. The solicitor will also have to bear in mind the necessity to comply with the requirements of the pre-action protocols under the CPR 1998.

As we have seen at 1.4, case analysis is the key to representing a client effectively. So when you take a statement (otherwise known as a proof of evidence) from the client, you should make a careful note of the main points and ask questions to obtain further information in order to develop that analysis. The key to obtaining a full and accurate set of instructions from the client is to probe but not prompt. Bear in mind that the statement should be in the client's own words. Let the client tell his story and try to ensure he develops this chronologically. Some clients will fail to do this, and you should make a note of any gaps and fill these in by questioning. If any part is ambiguous, get it clarified. You must end up with a clear picture as to what the client's case is about. You can then advise as to its strengths and weaknesses, and consider what further evidence needs to be obtained. You will not be in a position to negotiate effectively with the other side or present your client's case to a court if you do not properly understand that case.

3.1 Writing to the client

The solicitor should always confirm his instructions in writing, both in relation to the nature of the case itself and, specifically, any advice given on the question of funding the claim. If a statement has been taken from the client, this should be sent to the client for approval and signature. The letter should explain the next steps which are to be taken by the solicitor and remind the client of any matters which he has agreed to undertake. The solicitor should, of course, comply with all the requirements of r 15 of the Solicitors' Practice Rules 1990.

3.2 Interviewing witnesses

The solicitor should arrange to take a statement from any witnesses as soon as possible, whilst matters are still fresh in their minds. There is no 'property' in a witness, and the solicitor may request an interview with anyone who may have information about the case. However, there is little that can be done if a witness absolutely refuses to give a statement. A witness may do this, for example, because he does not wish to say anything against his employer, or simply because he does not wish to get involved.

At the eventual trial of the case, a person can be compelled to attend as a witness, but the solicitor will be reluctant to advise his client to call someone as a witness if he has not obtained a statement from him beforehand, because, of course, he will have no idea what the witness is going to say in the witness-box. Therefore, it is most important to persuade potential witnesses to give a statement if at all possible. If the witness refuses, the solicitor could use a witness summary (see **11.5**).

The solicitor will normally write to the witnesses initially and arrange a convenient time for an interview to take place. This may be at the solicitor's office, or the solicitor may have to go out to the witness's home or place of work.

When interviewing witnesses, the solicitor should be wary of people who try too hard to be helpful, and he should try to ensure that the witness's story will stand up to cross-examination. It is better that any weakness in the case is identified at this stage rather than later on when a great deal of time and money has been spent on the case. The initial statement (which is usually called a proof of evidence) should be as comprehensive as possible, including background information which may not be directly relevant to the claim but which may assist in understanding the case. A formal statement (known as a witness statement) containing only the evidence which the witness will give at the hearing will be prepared at a later stage, and this later statement is the one which will be served on the other parties before the hearing (see **11.2**). At this stage, therefore, there is no need to worry unduly if the statement contains matters which will not be admissible in evidence at the trial, although, before proceedings are commenced, the solicitor must ensure that he has, or will have, enough admissible evidence to prove his client's case at trial.

3.3 Preserving documents

The solicitor should ask the client to bring all relevant documents to him as soon as possible. A solicitor is under an obligation, both as a matter of professional conduct and under the CPR 1998, to ensure that the client understands the rules relating to disclosure of documents (see **Chapter 10**). A client who has little or no experience of the civil litigation process may be unaware, for example, that he is under an obligation during the course of the proceedings to disclose documents to the other side, even if those documents harm his case. Furthermore, if the solicitor reads the documents at an early stage, this should ensure that there is nothing to take him by surprise later on in the proceedings which may throw a different light on the case. In a case involving a contractual dispute, it is obviously imperative that the solicitor should see the contract as soon as possible to be able to advise the client properly. For example, the contract may include a jurisdiction clause, an arbitration clause or a provision imposing a limitation period for claims arising under the contract.

The client should also be made aware that the term 'documents' includes any method of recording information, such as video tapes and computer disks, and is not merely limited to written documents. It is advisable to explain to the client his disclosure obligations from the outset and to confirm this in writing.

3.4 Obtaining expert evidence — PART 35 CPR.

3.4.1 Instructing an expert

There are numerous instances where a solicitor may need to obtain expert evidence to advance a client's claim. For example, consulting engineers are regularly requested to report on accidents at the workplace and on road traffic accidents. Similarly, if expert evidence is required on building work, it is likely that the solicitor's firm already has contacts with suitable architects and surveyors. If counsel is involved at an early stage, he may be able to recommend suitable experts for the case. Alternatively, a suitable expert may be found via The Law Society (who maintain a register of experts), or the Academy of Expert Witnesses or other similar organisations.

Specialist expertise is the vital quality required of an expert witness, but it is not the only quality. An ability to present a convincing report which can be easily understood, and to perform well as a witness, particularly under cross-examination, are equally important. There is no fixed test to qualify as an expert witness and anyone who has special expertise in an area can be considered as an expert. Expertise does not depend on qualifications alone, although frequently the expert will be highly qualified in his field. Expertise may have been acquired through years of practical experience. For example, an experienced carpenter with no formal qualifications could nevertheless be an expert on the proper seasoning of wood and so assist in deciding whether, say, an oak dining table was of satisfactory quality.

The usual method of instructing an expert is by letter, the content of which will vary depending on what is required of the expert.

It will be necessary to provide an expert with all the relevant documents and statements from witnesses. It may also be necessary to arrange for an inspection of relevant machinery or site. The solicitor may need to take urgent steps to ensure that material to be inspected is preserved or, where this is not possible, to obtain the best alternative evidence, such as photographs or a video.

Where the client is to pay the expert's fees (eg, if they are not covered by insurance or public funding), the solicitor should obtain an estimate of the likely fees and then clear this with the client. In such cases, the solicitor will prefer to obtain money on account to cover the expert's fees. Where this is not done, the solicitor takes a risk, since he is responsible to the expert for payment of his charges.

It is not only when acting for the prospective claimant that the solicitor will be obtaining expert evidence. The potential defendant is also entitled to have expert evidence available. Proper facilities for inspection and observation should be granted for this.

3.4.2 Experts' reports

When the expert's report is received, the solicitor should check it carefully. Mistakes can be made, even by an expert. The solicitor should send a copy to the client so that he also may check it and inform the solicitor of any errors.

Medical reports, in particular, can be difficult to follow. Resist the temptation simply to concentrate on the conclusion. Consult a medical dictionary where necessary.

Whoever the expert is, never be afraid to return to him for clarification of the report. If the solicitor does not understand it, there is a good chance that no one else will, and that will defeat the object of obtaining the report.

3.4.3 Opinion

A significant advantage which the expert has over the ordinary witness (see **11.8**) is that the expert can give opinion evidence. For example, a surveyor may form the view that an earlier surveyor had been negligent in not observing certain defects in the structure of a building. All of these are matters of opinion, but nevertheless the expert is permitted to state them. Section 3(1) of the Civil Evidence Act 1972 provides that:

> ... where a person is called as a witness in any civil proceedings, his opinion on any relevant matter on which he is qualified to give expert evidence shall be admissible in evidence.

3.4.4 Restrictions on the use of expert evidence

The CPR 1998 have introduced very significant restrictions on the use of expert evidence. Although a party to proceedings is free to obtain as much expert evidence as he wishes, the extent to which such evidence can be used in court is strictly controlled. By r 35.1 of CPR 1998, expert evidence shall be restricted to that which is reasonably required to resolve the proceedings. The court can therefore limit the number of expert witnesses who can give evidence, or order that a single joint expert be appointed, or restrict expert evidence to a written report rather than oral evidence in court. A solicitor advising a client on whether to obtain expert evidence should always bear in mind that the costs of doing so will be recoverable from the opponent (assuming the case is won) only if the court gives permission for the expert evidence to be used.

As a general rule, if the area of expertise is settled, such that any two or more experts are likely to give the same opinion, a single joint expert is appropriate. Where a range of views is likely then normally it serves the overriding objective for the court to allow each party to have their own expert so that the court has such a range of views.

The use of expert evidence in proceedings is considered further in **Chapter 11**.

3.5 Site visits

Site visits may be needed, for the purpose of taking photographs or making plans. Plans and photographs are unlikely to be disputed if they are accurate, but in the event of a dispute the person who prepared the plan or took the photographs may have to give evidence, so they should be prepared by someone other than the solicitor who will be acting as an advocate at the hearing. If a formal plan is required (eg, in a boundary dispute) then this should normally be prepared by a surveyor. In some cases, a visit to the site of the incident, such as in a factory accident case, may be useful. On other occasions, it might help to visit the client's place of business to gain a better understanding of the nature of that business.

If the inspection will be expensive, the solicitor should obtain prior authorisation from the client.

3.6 Instructing counsel

3.6.1 Use of counsel

It is not necessary to instruct a barrister (also known as counsel) in every case. As a highly trained lawyer, the solicitor should have confidence in his own knowledge and ability. The solicitor will be capable of forming an assessment of both the chance of success and the level of damages. Too frequent use of counsel may result in the solicitor's costs being disallowed on an assessment of costs at the end of a case.

Nevertheless, judicious use of counsel is sensible. If the issues are difficult, it is wise to instruct counsel to advise on liability.

Similarly, counsel's opinion on quantum may be needed at an early stage if the case is not straightforward. For example, if it appears that some element of the client's claim might arguably be too remote, it might be appropriate to check with counsel. Even in these cases, however, the solicitor should have formulated his own view and counsel should be assisting with this. The solicitor should not be abrogating responsibility.

3.6.2 Method

Instructing counsel requires the preparation of a formal document (called 'Instructions to counsel'). It will bear the heading of the claim (or proposed claim) and should contain a list of the enclosures being forwarded to counsel. The enclosures will obviously vary with the case but will typically include copies of the client's statement, any other proofs of evidence, any existing statements of case, any experts' reports, and any relevant correspondence. It is not necessary to send counsel the whole file; some judgement should be exercised in deciding which papers counsel needs to have available.

The body of the instructions to counsel will identify the client and set out briefly both sides of the case. Counsel can refer to the enclosures for detail, but the instructions should contain sufficient information to enable the barrister to identify the major issues. The solicitor should indicate his own view of the case and draw counsel's attention to those areas on which particular advice is required.

The instructions will end with a formal request to counsel to carry out the required task.

The instructions must carry a back sheet endorsed with the title of the claim, what the instructions are (eg, Instructions to counsel to advise on quantum), counsel's name and chambers, and the solicitor's firm's name, address and reference.

Sometimes, counsel may not be able to proceed without a conference (the name given to a meeting with counsel) with the solicitor and the client. This could occur, for example, because the facts of the case are too detailed and complicated to be able to cover all the aspects in the instructions. Alternatively, it may be that counsel's advice will, to some extent, depend on his assessment of the client as a potential witness, and this will have to be done face to face.

If a conference is needed, counsel is still instructed in the usual way, but arrangements are then made with counsel's clerk for the solicitor and the client to visit counsel in chambers (the name given to a barrister's office) to discuss the case. Counsel will not normally expect to provide a written opinion after the conference, so the solicitor must take comprehensive notes at the conference. If a written opinion is required, this should be made clear in the instructions, but the costs of both will not be recoverable from the other side unless the court thinks it was reasonable to do so.

Traditionally, instructions to counsel are prepared using the third person ('Counsel is instructed to ...', and 'Instructing Solicitors seek Counsel's advice on ...'). Many firms now adopt a more modern approach, setting out the instructions as if writing a letter. It is a matter for each firm to decide which approach they prefer. Nevertheless, the instructions should still be in a formal document, accompanied by a covering letter to counsel's clerk.

3.7 Pre-action protocols

Pre-action protocols are intended to be an important aspect of the CPR 1998. However, there are still only protocols for personal injury, clinical negligence, construction and engineering, judicial review, defamation and professional negligence claims. (The details of these protocols, save the last, are outside the scope of this book.) It is expected that protocols for other areas of work will be introduced. It is vital to check to see whether any approved protocol applies to a client's case. Note, however, that there is also a Practice Direction on protocols which contains general guidance that should be followed in all cases. A copy of that appears at **Appendix A(24)** and the professional negligence protocol appears at **Appendix A(25)**.

The aims of pre-action protocols are:

(a) to initiate and increase pre-action contact between the parties;
(b) better and earlier exchange of information;
(c) better pre-action investigation by both sides;
(d) to put the parties in a position where they may be able to settle cases fairly and early without litigation;
(e) to enable proceedings to run to the court's timetable and efficiently, if litigation does become necessary.

Protocols deal with matters such as notification to the defendant of a possible claim as soon as possible, the form of the letter of claim, disclosure of documents, and the instruction of experts, if relevant.

Compliance with a protocol should help the parties involved make an informed decision on the merits of the case and lead to a greater number of settlements without the need for court proceedings.

Paragraph 2 of the Practice Direction – Protocols states that the court will expect the parties to have complied with the substance of any protocol that applies to their dispute. Where non-compliance has led to proceedings that might otherwise not have been commenced, or has led to unnecessary costs being incurred, the court may impose sanctions. These can include an order:

(a) that the party at fault pay some or all of his opponent's costs (perhaps on an indemnity basis – see **13.3.3**);
(b) depriving a claimant who is at fault of some or all of the interest he may subsequently be awarded on any damages he recovers; or
(c) requiring a defendant who is at fault to pay interest on some or all of any damages that are subsequently awarded to the claimant at a rate of up to 10% per annum above base rate.

Early Action   37

In exercising these powers, the court should aim to place the innocent party in no worse a position than he would have been in had the protocol been complied with. As to sanctions, see **8.3**.

Paragraph 4 of the Practice Direction – Protocols makes it clear that in cases not covered by a protocol the court will nonetheless expect the parties, in accordance with the overriding objective, to act reasonably in exchanging information and documents and in trying to avoid the need for proceedings. Paragraph 4.7 states, 'If the claim remains in dispute, the parties should promptly engage in appropriate negotiations with a view to settling the dispute and avoiding litigation'.

3.8 Sending the letter of claim   — example p 305.

When the solicitor is satisfied that the client has a valid claim, he should write a letter to the prospective defendant setting out full details of the claim. If the claim is of a type which is governed by a pre-action protocol, then the letter should contain all the information required by the protocol. Indeed, in the case of professional negligence, a preliminary notice of claim should be sent first.

The letter is normally addressed to the potential defendant in person but, if the solicitor is already aware that the defendant has solicitors acting for him, it should be addressed to the solicitors, as it is a breach of the rules of professional conduct to write directly to a defendant in those circumstances. If the potential defendant is likely to be insured in respect of the claim, the solicitor should ask that the letter be passed on to the insurers and enclose a copy for that purpose.

The letter should normally require a response within a specified period of time, failing which the solicitor should warn the defendant that proceedings will be issued without further notice. The Practice Direction – Protocols says that the parties should:

> follow a reasonable procedure, suitable to their particular circumstances, which is intended to avoid litigation. The procedure should not be regarded as a prelude to inevitable litigation. It should normally include (a) the claimant writing to give details of the claim; (b) the defendant acknowledging the claim letter promptly; (c) the defendant giving within a reasonable time a detailed written response; and (d) the parties conducting genuine and reasonable negotiations with a view to settling the claim economically and without court proceedings. (para 4.2)

The prospective claimant's letter of claim should:

(a) give sufficient but concise details to enable the recipient to understand and investigate the claim without extensive further information;
(b) enclose copies of the essential documents on which the claimant relies;
(c) ask for a prompt acknowledgement of the letter, followed by a full written response within a reasonable stated period – for many claims the Practice Direction suggests that this will be one month;
(d) state whether court proceedings will be issued if the full response is not received within the stated period;
(e) identify and ask for disclosure of any essential documents the prospective defendant can supply;
(f) state, if appropriate, that the claimant wishes to enter into any form of ADR;
(g) draw the defendant's attention to the court's powers to impose sanctions for failure to comply with the Practice Direction; and

38 Civil Litigation

(h) enclose a copy of the Practice Direction if the defendant is likely to be unrepresented.

A possible version of a letter of claim appears in the case study at **Appendix D(1)**.

How should the prospective defendant respond if he disputes all or part of the claim? The letter of response should:

(a) give detailed reasons why the claim is not accepted, identifying which of the claimant's contentions, if any, are accepted and which are disputed;

(b) enclose copies of the essential documents on which the defendant relies;

(c) enclose copies of documents asked for by the claimant, or explain why they are not enclosed;

(d) identify and ask for disclosure of any essential documents in the claimant's possession; and

(e) state whether the defendant is prepared to enter into any method of ADR.

Where the defendant requests the disclosure of documents, the claimant should provide these within a reasonably short time, or explain in writing why he is not doing so.

If the potential defendant does not respond to the letter of claim, the next step will be to issue proceedings. Sometimes, however, the intended defendant will reply asking for further time to investigate the matter. If such a request is made, the existing protocols indicate that no proceedings should be issued for a reasonable period. It is to be hoped that in that period the parties will be able to negotiate a settlement, or may refer the matter to ADR; otherwise it will usually be necessary to issue proceedings.

3.9 Pre-action disclosure

In a relatively small number of cases it may be necessary for a prospective claimant to see documents held by a potential defendant.

An application for disclosure of documents prior to the start of proceedings is permitted under s 33 of the SCA 1981 or s 52 of the CCA 1984. The application must be supported by evidence and the procedure is dealt with in r 31.16(3) of CPR 1998. The court may make an order for disclosure only where:

(a) the respondent is likely to be a party to subsequent proceedings;

(b) the applicant is also likely to be a party to the proceedings;

(c) if proceedings had started, the respondent's duty by way of standard disclosure set out in rule 31.6, would extend to the documents or classes of documents of which the applicant seeks disclosure; and

(d) disclosure before proceedings have started is desirable in order to—
   (i) dispose fairly of the anticipated proceedings;
   (ii) assist the dispute to be resolved without proceedings; or
   (iii) save costs.

An order under this Rule must specify the documents or class of documents which the respondent must disclose and require him, when making such disclosure, to specify any of those documents which he no longer has, or which he claims the right or duty to withhold from inspection. The order may also specify the time and place for disclosure and inspection to take place.

The most common examples of pre-action disclosure where the claimant is deciding whether or not to make a claim are to be found in personal injury litigation, for example, where the other side holds the records of an accident.

However, pre-action disclosure may also be ordered in significant commercial cases to try to resolve a dispute without proceedings or to save costs: see *Burrells Wharf Freeholders Ltd v Galliard Homes Ltd* [1999] 2 EGLR 81.

Disclosure and inspection of documents is dealt with fully in **Chapter 10**.

3.10 Settlement

3.10.1 Negotiations

A solicitor may soon find that he is in a position to commence negotiations with his opposite number, or with the opponent directly (provided he is not represented) or with an insurance company (eg, in a professional negligence case). The opportunity to negotiate will continue throughout the pre-action stages, the proceedings and even during the trial itself.

Any negotiations which take place as a part of a genuine attempt to settle a claim are impliedly 'without prejudice'. However, it is preferable to mark any correspondence accordingly, or to clarify at the start of a meeting/telephone negotiation that this is the basis on which you are proceeding.

So, a concession made by a party when genuinely trying to settle a case cannot be used against him at the trial.

> **Example**
>
> A is suing B for a debt of £150,000. A's solicitor writes to B's solicitor on a without prejudice basis saying A will accept £120,000 if that sum is paid immediately. B rejects this compromise.
>
> B cannot refer to this letter at trial and A can still try to obtain judgment for the full amount of the claim.

This rule exists to encourage litigants to reach a settlement, if possible. It means that all negotiations which are genuinely aimed at a settlement are excluded from being given in evidence. The rule applies whether the negotiations are oral or in writing, and thus applies to an attendance note of a without prejudice conversation as well as to correspondence. As Oliver LJ stated in *Cutts v Head* [1984] Ch 290:

> That the rule rests, at least in part, upon public policy is clear from many authorities, and the convenient starting point of the inquiry is the nature of the underlying policy. It is that parties should be encouraged so far as possible to settle their disputes without resort to litigation and should not be discouraged by the knowledge that anything that is said in the course of such negotiations (and that includes, of course, as much the failure to reply to an offer as an actual reply) may be used to their prejudice in the course of the proceedings. They should, as it was expressed by Clauson J in *Scott Paper Co v Drayton Paper Works Ltd* [1927] 44 RPC 151, 156, be encouraged fully and frankly to put their cards on the table ... The public policy justification, in truth, essentially rests on the desirability of preventing statements or offers made in the course of negotiations for settlement being brought before the court of trial as admissions on the question of liability ... The rule applies to exclude all negotiations genuinely aimed at settlement whether oral or in writing from being given in evidence.

Although as a matter of good practice the words 'without prejudice' should appear on this type of correspondence, the presence or absence of the words is not conclusive. What is important is that the letter is a genuine attempt to settle the case. If there is a dispute as to whether or not a communication is privileged in this way, the court can examine the document (obviously in advance of the trial so that the trial judge does not see it) to see whether or not its purpose was to settle the dispute. If it was, it is privileged; if not then, even if it carries the words 'without prejudice', it is not.

Once a settlement is concluded, any 'without prejudice' correspondence can be produced in court to show the terms agreed between the parties. This might be necessary if, for example, a dispute arose as to enforcement of an agreed settlement.

If a party wishes to reserve the right to draw the trial judge's attention to a without prejudice offer to settle a case on the question of costs then he should mark the offer: 'without prejudice except as to costs' (see *Cutts v Head* [1984] Ch 290 and **3.10.2** below).

Details about the solicitor's authority to negotiate are to be found at **12.1**.

3.10.2 Pre-action offers under Part 36

As we have seen, before litigation starts the parties are encouraged to negotiate and settle the claim. It is open to the parties to make 'without prejudice' offers to settle (see **3.10.1**). Part 36 of CPR 1998 formally recognises this and gives *teeth* to such offers which are made 'without prejudice save as to costs' (ie, once a trial judge has dealt with the issues of liability and quantum, he can be addressed on Part 36 points when dealing with the question of costs). A prospective claimant can offer to settle a monetary claim for a specified sum, or on express terms for any non-monetary claim. If the potential defendant does not accept this and litigation occurs, and at trial the claimant is awarded a greater sum or more advantageous terms than he proposed, then the defendant is likely to suffer a heavy financial penalty.

A potential defendant can also make a Part 36 offer. However, once involved in litigation and where he faces a claim for money, Part 36 requires that any offer is made via the court by depositing the proposed sum with the court (a Part 36 payment). If a defendant wishes to convert a pre-action Part 36 offer into a Part 36 payment he must do so within 14 days of service of the claim form. If the claimant does not accept any defendant's Part 36 pre-action offer and/or Part 36 payment but then at trial is not awarded more than the proposed amount, the claimant is likely to suffer a heavy financial penalty. For full details see **12.4**.

3.11 Researching the law

Researching the law will often not be necessary. The solicitor will be familiar with the relevant law in the areas in which he practises. Nevertheless, from time to time, unfamiliar points arise which need to be researched.

On a point of law, reference should be made to the recognised practitioner works in the relevant subject; but as textbooks rapidly become out of date, it is essential to check a current authority.

If the point to be researched is procedural then the solicitor needs to refer to the CPR 1998 and Practice Directions themselves, together with any relevant case law on their interpretation and any recognised practitioners' works. For this purpose, it can be useful to look at one of the hard-copy versions of the CPR 1998 which are annotated and contain references to relevant cases and SIs where appropriate.

3.12 Summary of pre-action steps

(1) Check any professional conduct points.
(2) Identify the client's objectives.
(3) Explore possible methods of ADR.
(4) Identify all potential parties. → *Part 20 counterclaim?*
(5) Check financial viability of defendant. → *Will they be able to pay damages; debt claimed?*
(6) Check jurisdiction.
(7) Ascertain the limitation period (statutory and contractual, if applicable).
(8) Discuss and agree funding with client.
(9) Collect evidence:
  (a) interview witnesses and take proofs of evidence;
  (b) scrutinise and preserve documents and other evidence;
  (c) obtain experts' reports, if appropriate;
  (d) take photographs / visit site, etc.
(10) Conduct any necessary legal research and send letter of advice to client.
(11) Keep client informed.
(12) Comply with pre-action protocol requirements.
(13) Is an application for pre-action disclosure required?
(14) Consider making a Part 36 offer.

Chapter 4
Commencing Proceedings

4.1	Choice of court	43
4.2	Court personnel	45
4.3	Issuing proceedings	45
4.4	Parties to the proceedings	47
4.5	Service	50
4.6	Time for service of claim form	55
4.7	Service of particulars of claim	55

4.1 Choice of court

Although the CPR 1998 apply to both the High Court and county courts, in some cases a client will have a choice as to which court to start proceedings in. The general rule is that county courts have unlimited jurisdiction to hear all tort and contract cases. This is because PD 7, para 2 provides that proceedings may not be started in the High Court unless the value of the claim is more than £15,000. So, if the value of the case is £15,000 or below, it must be started in a county court. If the value of the case exceeds £15,000 then it can, if the client so wishes, be started in the High Court. In some cases, the High Court has exclusive jurisdiction, but these types of cases are beyond the scope of this book.

Where a claimant has the choice of issuing in the High Court or county court then, by PD 7, para 2.4, a claim should be started in the High Court if by reason of:

(1) the financial value of the claim and the amount in dispute, and/or
(2) the complexity of the facts, legal issues, remedies or procedures involved, and/or
(3) the importance of the outcome of the claim to the public in general,

the claimant believes that the claim ought to be dealt with by a High Court judge.

A claim should therefore be commenced in the High Court only if that is where the case should be tried. Unless the case is complex or important to the general public (not just the parties themselves), it is unlikely to be tried in the Central Office of the Royal Courts of Justice if the claim is less than £50,000 (see PD 29, para 2.2). As a rough rule of thumb, therefore, you should issue in the county court for claims below £50,000 and consider if the High Court is more suitable for claims of £50,000 or above.

There are approximately 200 county courts situated throughout England and Wales and, in most cases, the claimant can issue proceedings in any court he chooses. Similarly, if the claimant is issuing proceedings in the High Court, he has the choice of issuing in any of the District Registries of the High Court, which are usually situated in the same building as the county court, or the Central Office of the High Court in London. The High Court has three divisions, namely:

(a) the Queen's Bench Division, which includes the Admiralty Court and the Commercial Court;
(b) the Chancery Division, which includes the Companies Court and the Patents Court; and
(c) the Family Division.

44 Civil Litigation

Which Court? High Court: Which Division?

If the claimant is claiming damages for breach of contract or tort, the claim should be commenced in the Queen's Bench Division. The Queen's Bench Division produces a *Guide to Litigation*, which is particularly aimed at those litigating in the Central Office.

The Commercial Court is part of the Queen's Bench Division. The Commercial Court sits in London and there are separate mercantile lists in Birmingham, Bristol, Cardiff, Chester, Leeds, Liverpool, Manchester and Newcastle for cases relating to commercial transactions. The Commercial Court produces a *Commercial Court Guide*, which gives guidance on the day-to-day practice in that court. Also see CPR 1998, Part 58.

The Chancery Division of the High Court deals with such matters as trusts, contentious probate business, partnership claims, disputes about land, and landlord and tenant disputes. A claim should be commenced in the Chancery Division if the claimant is claiming an equitable remedy such as specific performance, or if it is an intellectual property claim, such as copyright or passing-off. As with Queen's Bench proceedings, a Chancery claim can be commenced either in the Central Office in London or in a District Registry. Chancery matters can also be commenced in a county court.

The Family Division deals with High Court family matters which are outside the scope of this book.

Part 30 of CPR 1998 deals with the powers of the High Court and county court to transfer matters from one court to another. Such a transfer could be:

(a) from a county court to the High Court;
(b) from the High Court to a county court;
(c) from one county court to another county court;
(d) from a District Registry to Central Office, or from Central Office to a District Registry;
(e) from one Division of the High Court to another Division;
(f) to or from a specialist list (eg, the Commercial Court).

In deciding whether to make a transfer order, the matters to which the court must have regard under r 30.3(2) include:

(a) the financial value of the claim and the amount in dispute, if different;
(b) whether it should be more convenient or fair for hearings (including the trial) to be held in some other court;
(c) the availability of a judge specialising in the type of claim in question;
(d) whether the facts, legal issues, remedies or procedures involved are simple or complex;
(e) the importance of the outcome of the claim to the public in general;
(f) the facilities available at the court where the claim is being dealt with and whether they may be inadequate because of any disabilities of a party or potential witness;
(g) whether the making of a declaration of incompatibility under section 4 of the Human Rights Act 1998 has arisen or may arise.

There are also provisions for automatic transfer to the defendant's home court in certain circumstances (see **8.5**), and provisions for transfer from Central Office to a county court if the claim is worth less than £50,000 (see above).

4.2 Court personnel

The great bulk of both county court and High Court work is dealt with by district judges and, for matters proceeding in the Central Office in London, masters. These deal with the great majority of interim applications (see **Chapter 9**) and also have jurisdiction to hear trials where the amount involved does not exceed £15,000. Trials for amounts in excess of that figure are, in a county court, heard by circuit judges and, in the High Court, by High Court judges. Under Part 3 of CPR 1998, the judges have extensive case management powers (see **Chapter 8**).

4.3 Issuing proceedings

A party who wishes to start proceedings must complete a claim form, which should either be handed in or sent to the court office. Proceedings are commenced when the court 'issues' the claim form by sealing it with the court seal (although for limitation purposes, the relevant date is the date when the court receives the claim form: see PD 7, para 5.1). A copy of a claim form appears at **Appendix A(1)**.

4.3.1 Completing the claim form

In addition to the points set out here, the Court Service provides detailed guidance notes on the completion of the claim form which appear at **Appendix A(1)**.

4.3.1.1 Claimant and defendant details

The person who makes the claim is described as the claimant and the person against whom it is made is the defendant.

The claim form must include an address at which the claimant resides or carries on business.

Where the defendant is an individual, the claimant should (if he is able to do so) include in the claim form an address at which the defendant resides or carries on business. This applies even if the defendant's solicitors have agreed to accept service of the claim form on the defendant's behalf.

Where one of the parties is not an individual over the age of 18, or is not suing or being sued in his personal capacity, special considerations may apply (see 4.4). The Court Service guidance notes set out how these should be reflected in the claim form.

4.3.1.2 Brief details of claim

The claim form must contain a concise statement of the nature of the claim and specify the remedy that the claimant is seeking (see r 16.2(1) and the notes on completing the claim form).

4.3.1.3 The amount claimed/value

Rule 16.3(2) requires that if the claim is for money, the claim form must either state the amount claimed or, if the claim is for an unspecified amount of money, whether or not the claimant expects to recover:

(a) not more than £5,000; or
(b) more than £5,000 but not more than £15,000; or
(c) more than £15,000; or

(d) that the claimant cannot say how much he expects to recover.

This information assists the county court in appropriately allocating the claim to the multi-track, fast track or small claims track. Allocation of cases in the county court is dealt with in detail in **Chapter 8**.

4.3.1.4 High Court cases

PD 7, para 3.6 provides that if a claim for an unspecified sum of money is started in the High Court, the claim form must:

(a) state that the claimant expects to recover more than £15,000; or
(b) state that some enactment provides that the claim may only be commenced in the High Court and specify that enactment; or
(c) state that the claim is to be in one of the specialist High Court lists (see CPR 1998, Part 49) and specify that list.

The Notes for Claimant on completing the claim form (see **Appendix A(1)**) suggest a form of words such as: 'I wish my claim to issue in the High Court because' followed by one of the above grounds (eg, 'I expect to recover more than £15,000'). Arguably, the Notes are aimed at litigants in person, and most solicitors, when relying on the value exceeding £15,000 as giving the High Court jurisdiction, will simply put, 'The Claimant expects to recover more than £15,000'.

4.3.1.5 The court fee

The claimant is obliged to pay a fee on issue of the claim form, based on the value of the claim. The amount of the fee should be stated on the front of the form. Details of court fees are contained in the Guide to Supreme Court Fees and the Guide to County Court Fees (which are available on the Court Service website (www.courtservice.gov.uk)).

4.3.1.6 Solicitor's costs

If the claim is for a specified amount of money, and was issued by a solicitor, the form should also include a figure for solicitor's costs. These are fixed costs payable by the defendant, in addition to the court fee, should he admit the claim. Fixed costs are dealt with in Part 45 of CPR 1998.

4.3.1.7 Issues under the Human Rights Act 1998

The claimant is obliged to state whether the claim does or will include any issues under the Human Rights Act 1998.

4.3.1.8 The particulars of claim

The details of the claimant's claim, known as the particulars of claim, must be set out either in the claim form itself or in a separate document that is either served with the claim form or within 14 days of service of the claim form. Care is needed in the drafting of the particulars of claim, and this issue is considered in **Chapter 6**.

4.3.1.9 The statement of truth

The CPR 1998 require that various documents, including the claim form, are verified by a statement of truth (see CPR 1998, Part 22). If the particulars of claim are served separately they must also be so verified and the statement of truth in the claim form should be amended to read, 'the facts stated in this claim form are true'.

The statement of truth may be signed by the claimant, by his legal representative or by his litigation friend (see **4.4.1**). Where signed by the legal representative, the statement of truth will refer to 'the claimant's belief', whereas a client refers to his own belief. A legal representative who signs must do so in his own name, rather than in the name of his firm (PD 22 at para 3.10).

Where a legal representative signs a statement of truth, para 3.8 of PD 22 states that this will be taken as his statement:

(1) that the client on whose behalf he has signed had authorised him to do so,
(2) that before signing he had explained to the client that in signing the statement of truth he would be confirming the client's belief that the facts stated in the document were true, and
(3) that before signing he had informed the client of the possible consequences to the client if it should subsequently appear that the client did not have an honest belief in the truth of those facts.

(The consequences referred to in para 3.8(3) above are that proceedings for contempt of court may be brought against the client: see r 32.14.)

If a statement of case (which includes a claim form) is not verified by a statement of truth, it remains effective unless the court strikes it out, which the court may do on its own initiative or on the application of another party. If the statement of case is not struck out, the claimant will not, however, be allowed to rely on its contents as evidence (for example, on an interim application: see **Chapter 8**).

4.4 Parties to the proceedings

If the claimant and defendant are both individuals of full age suing or being sued in their personal capacity then there are no special considerations. In other cases, there may be special considerations because of the nature of the party concerned, for example, in cases where the claimant or defendant is a child, a patient, a partnership or a limited company. These special rules are considered below.

4.4.1 Children and patients

A child is a person aged under 18 and a patient is a person who is incapable of managing and administering his own affairs because of a mental disorder, as defined by the Mental Health Act 1983. Part 21 of CPR 1998 contains special provisions relating to these types of litigant.

4.4.1.1 The requirement for a 'litigation friend'

The Rules require a patient to have a litigation friend to conduct proceedings, whether as claimant or defendant, on his behalf. A child must also have a litigation friend to conduct proceedings on his behalf unless the court orders otherwise. In the case of patients, the litigation friend will usually be a person authorised under Pt VII of the Mental Health Act 1983 to conduct legal proceedings in the name of a patient; and in the case of a child, the litigation friend will normally be a parent or guardian.

By PD 21, para 2.1:

> It is the duty of a litigation friend fairly and competently to conduct proceedings on behalf of a child or patient. He must have no interest in the proceedings adverse to that of the child or patient and all steps and decisions he takes in the proceedings must be taken for the benefit of the child or patient.

In relation to proceedings against a child or patient, a person may not, without permission of the court, make an application against a child or patient before proceedings have started, or take any step in proceedings except:

(a) issuing and serving a claim form; or

(b) applying for the appointment of a litigation friend under r 21.6.

4.4.1.2 Steps to be taken by a litigation friend

A person authorised under Pt VII of the Mental Health Act 1983 to act as a litigation friend on behalf of a patient must file an official copy of the document which is his authority to act. Otherwise, a litigation friend acting on behalf of a patient or child must file a certificate of suitability. If acting on behalf of a claimant, this must be done when making the claim; and if acting on behalf of a defendant, when first taking a step in the proceedings. The certificate of suitability must state that the proposed litigation friend:

(a) consents to act;

(b) believes the party to be a child or patient (with reasons and medical evidence);

(c) can fairly and competently conduct proceedings on behalf of the party;

(d) has no adverse interest;

(e) if acting as a litigation friend for a claimant, undertakes to pay any costs which the claimant may be ordered to pay in the proceedings. (A counterclaim – see **Chapter 7** – is treated like a claim for the purposes of the costs undertakings.)

The litigation friend must serve the certificate of suitability on every person on whom the claim form should be served, and must then file a certificate of service when filing the certificate of suitability.

4.4.1.3 Cessation of appointment of a litigation friend

In relation to a child, the appointment of a litigation friend ceases when the child becomes 18. The appointment of a litigation friend for a patient does not cease when the party ceases to be a patient. It continues until the appointment is ended by a court order sought by the former patient, the litigation friend, or any party.

4.4.1.4 Settlement of cases brought by or against a child or patient

Special provisions apply where a case involving a child or patient is settled. Such a settlement is not valid unless it has been approved by the court. Before the court approves a settlement, it will need to know:

(a) whether and to what extent the defendant admits liability;

(b) the age and occupation (if any) of the child or patient;

(c) that the litigation friend approves of the proposed settlement.

The application to the court must, in most cases, be supported by a legal opinion on the merits of the settlement and the instructions on which it was based. Although the application will be heard in private, the formal approval of the settlement will usually be given publicly in open court – see *Beathem v Carlisle Hospitals NHS Trust* (1999) *The Times*, 20 May.

If a claim by or against a child or patient is settled before proceedings are begun and proceedings are issued solely to obtain the court's approval of the settlement, the claim must include a request to the court for approval of the settlement and must be made under Part 8 of CPR 1998 (see **7.3**).

Commencing Proceedings 49

If money is recovered by or on behalf of or for the benefit of a child or patient, or money paid into court is accepted by or on behalf of a child or patient, the money should be dealt with in accordance with the directions of the court. The court will usually direct that the money be paid into the High Court for investment. In relation to a child, the money must be paid out when the child becomes 18.

4.4.2 Partnerships

4.4.2.1 Where a partnership is the claimant

Partnerships may sue in the name of the firm or by naming individual partners. It is usually easier and more convenient to use the firm name (eg, 'ABC & Co (a firm)').

4.4.2.2 Where a partnership is the defendant

Partnerships may be sued in the name of the firm or in the names of the individual partners. The names of the partners may be discovered by checking the firm's notepaper or the list of partners kept at the firm's principal place of business. In practice, it is usually simpler and more efficient to sue a partnership in the name of the firm, especially as service on the firm can be effected by serving any one of the partners, or by serving the firm at its principal place of business (see **4.5**).

[margin note: Joint/Several Liability s9 PA 1890]

4.4.3 Sole traders

4.4.3.1 Where a sole trader is the claimant

Sole traders should sue in their own name and not in any business name. However, there is no objection to adding any trading name (eg, 'Amy Freeman trading as Freeman's Designs').

4.4.3.2 Where a sole trader is the defendant

Sole traders carrying on business with a name other than their own can be sued in that name. In that case, the proceedings can be served on the sole trader either at his residence, or at his place of business. If the trader is sued under his trade name, he will be referred to in the heading to the claim as, for example, 'Anthony Tucker T/A Marble Designs' (T/A is an acceptable abbreviation of 'trading as'). If the claimant does not know the name of the sole trader, he may sue naming the defendant under his business name (eg, 'Welcome Homes' (a trading name)).

4.4.4 Limited companies

4.4.4.1 Where a limited company is the claimant

A company can sue under its corporate name.

4.4.4.2 Where a limited company is the defendant

A company can be sued under its corporate name.

Before commencing proceedings against a company, the claimant should carry out a company search to confirm the corporate status and continued existence of the proposed defendant company, to confirm the correct name of the company and to ascertain the registered address of the company if it is intended to serve the company at its registered office.

4.4.5 Addition and substitution of parties (Part 19 of CPR 1998)

On occasions, it will be necessary for another party to be added to a claim or for a party to be replaced by another. For example, A may take proceedings against B for damages for negligence, and subsequently may discover that C was also negligent. A may then want to add C to the proceedings as a second defendant.

Or, A may sue B (an individual) for a debt, but A then discovers that his contract was not with B trading on his own account but with a company controlled by B. A will want to substitute the company for B as defendant.

As stated in r 19.4(2), an application for permission to remove, add or substitute a party may be made by:

(a) an existing party; or
(b) a person who wishes to become a party.

The application may be made without notice and must be supported by evidence.

Nobody may be added or substituted as a claimant unless he has given his consent in writing and that consent has been filed with the court.

Rule 19.2 states:

(2) The court may order a person to be added as a new party if—
 (a) it is desirable to add the new party so that the court can resolve all the matters in dispute in the proceedings; or
 (b) there is an issue involving the new party and an existing party which is connected to the matters in dispute in the proceedings, and it is desirable to add the new party so that the court can resolve that issue.
(3) The court may order any person to cease to be a party if it is not desirable for that person to be a party to the proceedings.
(4) The court may order a new party to be substituted for an existing one if—
 (a) the existing party's interest or liability has passed to the new party; and
 (b) it is desirable to substitute the new party so that the court can resolve the matters in dispute in the proceedings.

Special provisions apply where parties are to be added or substituted after the end of the relevant limitation period. Rule 19.5 states:

(2) The court may add or substitute a party only if—
 (a) the relevant limitation period was current when the proceedings were started; and
 (b) the addition or substitution is necessary.
(3) The addition or substitution of a party is necessary only if the court is satisfied that—
 (a) the new party is to be substituted for a party who was named in the claim form in mistake for the new party;
 (b) the claim cannot properly be carried on by or against the original party unless the new party is added or substituted as claimant or defendant; or
 (c) the original party has died or had a bankruptcy order made against him and his interest or liability has passed to the new party.

Part 19 also contains provisions enabling the Crown to be joined as a party to proceedings in which the court may wish to make a declaration of incompatibility in accordance with s 4 of the Human Rights Act 1998.

4.5 Service

Once a claim form has been issued by the court, it must be served on the other parties if the claimant is to pursue the claim.

Commencing Proceedings 51

The rules governing service of court documents are set out in Part 6 of CPR 1998. A claim form may be served by any of the methods outlined below (also see **4.5.5**).

4.5.1 Methods of service generally available

4.5.1.1 Personal service

This is effected by leaving the document with the party (if an individual), a person holding a senior position (if the party is a company or other corporation), or a partner or person having control or management of the partnership business at its principal place of business (if the partners have been sued in the name of their firm). If the document is served after 5 pm on a business day, or at any time during a weekend or on a bank holiday, Christmas Day or Good Friday, it will be deemed to have been served on the next business day. See further **4.5.2**.

Where a partner or partnership manager is personally served, notice in Form N215 must also be served. A copy is in **Appendix A(8)**.

4.5.1.2 First-class post

This is deemed effective the second day after the document was posted to the address for service of the person to be served. See further **4.5.2**. The Rules do not allow for service by second-class post or any other postal method, such as recorded delivery.

4.5.1.3 Leaving the document

This is deemed effective on the day after the document was left at the address for service of the person to be served. See further **4.5.2** and **4.5.4**.

4.5.1.4 Through a document exchange (DX)

This is deemed effective on the second day after it was left at the document exchange. The address for service of the party to be served must include a DX box number on his statement of case or his headed notepaper or that of his solicitor. This method of service cannot be used if the party or his solicitor has indicated in writing that he is unwilling to be served by DX.

4.5.1.5 By fax

This is deemed effective on the day of transmission if transmitted before 4 pm on a business day, or the next business day if transmitted otherwise (see **4.5.2**). The party to be served or his legal representative must have indicated in writing to the party serving a willingness to accept service by fax and the fax number to which the document should be sent. A fax number set out on a statement of case or a response to a claim filed at the court is assumed so to indicate, but the mere presence of a fax number in a party's standard business letterhead is not (*Molins plc v GD SpA* (2000) *The Times*, 1 March). However, the fax number on a party's solicitors' headed notepaper is treated as agreement to service by this method unless the solicitors indicate otherwise in writing. It is advisable in all cases to send a hard copy in case the fax was not received.

4.5.1.6 By other electronic means

This is deemed effective the second day after transmission. A party to be served by e-mail (or similar electronic method) must have expressly indicated in writing the e-mail address (or electronic identification) to which it should be sent. An e-mail address (or electronic identification) set out on a statement of case or a response to a claim filed with the court is treated as sufficient written indication. However, note that PD 6, para 3.2 adds that where a party seeks to serve a document by electronic means he should first seek to clarify with the party who is to be served whether there are any limitations to the recipient's agreement to accept service by such means, including the format in which documents are to be sent and the maximum size of attachments that may be received.

4.5.1.7 Service on limited companies

Where the party to be served is a limited company, s 725(1) of the Companies Act 1985 provides an alternative method of service in addition to the CPR (see *Murphy v Staples UK Limited* [2003] 3 All ER 129). The Act provides that documents may be left at or posted to the registered office of the company. Whilst second-class post can be used when serving under s 725(1), it is not recommended.

4.5.2 Calculating the deemed date of service (r 6.7)

If you re-read **4.5.1**, you may be struck by the fact that personal service and fax service refer to 'business days' when calculating deemed service, whilst all the others do not. This oddity was addressed by the Court of Appeal in *Anderton v Clwyd County Council* [2002] EWCA Civ 933, [2002] 3 All ER 813. The court held that where r 6.7(1) does not refer to business days, then Saturdays, Sundays, bank holidays, etc are to be included when calculating the date of deemed service.

> Examples
>
> If the document is personally served before 5 pm on Friday, 3 September 2004, it is deemed to be served that day. But if it is served on that Friday after 5 pm it is deemed to be served on the next business day, namely Monday 6 September.
>
> If the document is sent by first class post on Friday, 3 September 2004, it is deemed to be served the second day after it was posted, namely Sunday, 5 September.
>
> If the document is delivered to or left at a permitted address on Friday, 3 September 2004 it is deemed to be served the day after it was delivered or left, namely Saturday, 4 September.
>
> If the document is left at the DX on Friday, 3 September 2004, it is deemed to be served the second day after it was left, namely Sunday, 5 September.
>
> If the document is faxed before 4 pm on Friday, 3 September 2004, it is deemed to be served that day. However, if it is faxed after 4 pm it is deemed to be served on the next business day, namely Monday, 6 September.
>
> If the document is sent by another electronic method such as email on Friday, 3 September 2004, it is deemed to be served the second day after it was transmitted, namely Sunday, 5 September.

4.5.3 Service by the court or a party

Documents will usually be served by the court and the court will choose the appropriate method of service, which will normally be by first-class post. A party who prepares a document which will be served by the court must provide the court with enough copies for the court to serve it on all other parties, together with a copy for the court's file.

Rule 6.3(1) provides that the court will not effect service where:

(a) a Rule or Practice Direction provides otherwise; or

(b) the court orders otherwise; or

(c) the party on whose behalf the document is to be served notifies the court that he wishes to serve it himself;

Commencing Proceedings 53

(d) the court has failed to serve the document and has sent a notice of non-service to the party on whose behalf the document was to be served.

Where the court has been unable to effect service, it will notify the party who requested service. The notice will state the method of service attempted and service then becomes the responsibility of that party.

Where a party serves the document, it should file a certificate of service in Form N215. A copy is at **Appendix A(8)**.

4.5.4 Addresses for service (r 6.5)

All parties must give an address for service within England and Wales. If the party is legally represented, the address for service is his solicitor's address.

Where no solicitor is acting, and the party has not given an address for service, then service must be effected at the place shown in the following table:

NATURE OF PARTY TO BE SERVED	PLACE OF SERVICE
Individual	• Usual or last known residence
Proprietor of business	• Usual or last known residence or • Place of business or last known place of business
Individual who is suing or being sued in the name of a firm	• Usual or last known residence or • Principal or last known place of business of the firm
Corporation incorporated in England and Wales other than a company	• Principal office of the corporation or • Any place within the jurisdiction where the corporation carries on its activities and which has a real connection with the claim
Company registered in England and Wales	• Principal office of the company or • Any place of business of the company within the jurisdiction which has a real connection with the claim
Any other company or corporation	• Any place within the jurisdiction where the corporation carries on its activities or • Any place of business of the company within the jurisdiction

Notes:
1. If a solicitor is authorised to accept service on behalf of a party and has so notified the other party in writing, the document must be served on the solicitor.
2. A company registered in England and Wales may also be served at its registered office.

54 Civil Litigation

4.5.5 Special rules relating to service of the claim form

The claim form should be served in one of the ways set out above, but rr 6.13–6.16 contain some special provisions.

If there is a solicitor's firm which has written confirming that it will accept service of proceedings on behalf of the defendant, the claimant's solicitors cannot properly effect service of the proceedings on the defendant direct: see *Nanglegan v Royal Free Hampstead NHS Trust* [2001] EWCA Civ 127, [2001] 3 All ER 793.

In *Smith v Probyn* (2000) *The Times*, 29 March, the parties' solicitors had corresponded prior to a claim form being issued but the defendant's solicitors were never asked if they were authorised to accept service. Equally, the defendant's solicitors had never intimated in any way that they were instructed to accept service. Just before the four-month deadline to serve the claim form expired, the claimant's solicitors sent it in the document exchange to the defendant's solicitors. Morland J held that there had been no effective service of the claim form. He also refused retrospectively to extend the time for service as it could not be said that the claimant had taken all reasonable steps to serve it but had been unable to do so (see **4.6**). Likewise, it will not be effective service to send the claim form to the defendant's insurers rather than the defendant. The court does not have any power to correct the consequences of service on the wrong party: see *Elmes v Hygrade Food Products plc* [2001] EWCA Civ 121, [2001] LTL, 27 February.

If the claim form is served by the court, the court must send the claimant a notice which will include the date when the claim form is deemed to be served.

Where the claim form is served by the claimant, he must file a certificate of service within seven days of service of the claim form, and may not obtain judgment in default (see **5.6**) unless he has filed the certificate of service (r 6.14). A copy is at **Appendix A(8)**.

The other special provisions concern service of the claim form by a contractually agreed method (r 6.15) and service of a claim form on the agent of an overseas principal (r 6.16).

4.5.6 Service out of the jurisdiction

4.5.6.1 EU countries

No special permission is required to serve a defendant based in Scotland, Northern Ireland or any other EU country, provided the English courts have jurisdiction under Council Regulation 44/2001 or, in the case of Denmark, the Brussels Convention (see **Chapter 2**).

The claim form must, however, contain a statement of the grounds on which the claimant is entitled to serve it outside the jurisdiction (r 6.19). The usual form of words is set out in PD 6B – Service out of the jurisdiction.

The time for responding to the claim form will usually be extended to 21 days.

There are special provisions as to the methods of service that are acceptable where the claim form is to be served outside the jurisdiction (see rr 6.24–6.26).

4.5.6.2 Non-EU countries

The claimant must obtain permission to serve proceedings on a defendant outside the EU, for example an American company (but note that if such a company has an office in England and Wales, it could be served there just as if it were an English company).

The grounds for obtaining permission are set out in r 6.20 of CPR 1998. Examples of the grounds set out in r 6.20 are where the claim is brought to enforce a contract which is governed by English law, or where the breach of contract occurred in England and Wales.

The application must be supported by evidence and is made without notice.

If an order permitting service outside the jurisdiction is made, the time-limit for responding to the claim will again be extended.

Service is usually effected through the judicial authorities of the State in question or the British Consul.

4.6 Time for service of claim form

If a claim form is to be served within the jurisdiction, r 7.5(2) provides that it must be served within four months of being issued, although the court has a discretion to extend this period. It is essential to apply for an extension before the four-month period expires, since if the claimant does not apply for an extension until after that date, r 7.6(3) provides that the court may extend time for service only if:

(a) the court has been unable to serve the claim form; or
(b) the claimant has taken all reasonable steps to serve the claim form but has been unable to do so; and
(c) in either case, the claimant has acted promptly in making the application.

In *Vinos v Marks & Spencer plc* [2001] 3 All ER 784, the claim form was served nine days after the expiry of the four-month period. The claimant's solicitors had no explanation for this other than that it was an oversight and their application for an extension was dismissed. The Court of Appeal upheld the decision, holding that the wording of r 7.6(3) was such that an extension could not be granted in these circumstances as neither grounds (a) nor (b) applied.

This decision has been followed in other cases. For example, extensions have been refused where the claimant's solicitor was mistaken as to the date on which the claim form was issued (*Satwinder Kaur v CTP Coil Ltd* [2000] LTL, 10 July). Where the claimant's solicitors mistakenly served the defendant when they should have served the claim form on the defendant's solicitors who were nominated to accept service, an extension was refused (*Nanglegan v Royal Free Hampstead NHS Trust* [2001] EWCA Civ 127, [2001] 3 All ER 793). Also see the cases cited at **4.5.5**.

4.7 Service of particulars of claim

What if a claim form is served marked 'particulars of claim to follow' but the particulars are not subsequently served on the defendant within 14 days pursuant to r 7.4? In *Totty v Snowden; Hewett v Wirrall and West Cheshire Community NHS Trust* [2001] EWCA Civ 933, [2002] 1 WLR 1384, the Court of Appeal held that the courts have a discretion to grant an extension of time to a claimant who has served a claim form within the time prescribed by the Rules but who either has not served particulars of claim, or alternatively has failed to serve particulars of claim that comply with the formal requirements within the prescribed 14-day period.

Chapter 5

Responding to Proceedings and Judgment in Default

5.1	Introduction	57
5.2	Computation of time (r 2.8)	57
5.3	Acknowledgement of service (Part 10)	58
5.4	The defence (Part 15)	59
5.5	Admissions (Part 14)	59
5.6	Default judgments (Part 12)	62
5.7	Human rights	64

5.1 Introduction

It is important to note that the defendant need only respond once he has been served with the particulars of claim. Where he is served with a claim form with particulars of claim 'to follow, he need do nothing. He will receive Form N1C (Notes for Defendants) explaining this. See the copy at **Appendix A(2)**.

When either the court or the claimant serves the particulars of claim on the defendant, they must also send the defendant Form N9 (the response pack). A copy of this form appears at **Appendix A(3)**. The response pack explains to the defendant how he should respond to the claim and the time-limits for doing so. There are three ways in which a defendant may respond, namely:

(a) by filing an acknowledgement of service;
(b) by filing a defence;
(c) by filing an admission.

Before considering these steps in turn, it is important to be clear about the rules relating to the calculation of the time for doing any act, such as filing an acknowledgement of service. As we shall see at **5.6**, if the defendant does not respond within the appropriate time period, the claimant may enter judgment in default against the defendant. It is therefore essential that a party and his legal adviser are clear about the meaning of the various time periods prescribed in the rules.

5.2 Computation of time (r 2.8) — "CLEAR DAYS"

Rule 2.8 sets out how to calculate any period of time for doing an act which is specified in the Rules, a Practice Direction, or by a judgment or order of the court.

If the time for doing an act ends on a day when the court office is closed, the time does not actually expire until the end of the first day on which the court office is next open.

Any order imposing a time-limit should, wherever practicable, give a calendar date (eg Monday, 20 October) and a time of day (eg, 4 pm) for compliance.

Any period of time expressed as a number of days will be a period of 'clear days' as defined by r 2.8.

Example 1

On 1 October, the defendant is served with the particulars of claim.

The defendant has 14 days (not including the day of service of the particulars of claim) within which to either acknowledge service or file a defence.

The deadline for doing so is therefore 15 October.

Example 2

An application to the court has been fixed for hearing on a Monday.

Generally, the notice of the application must be served on the other party at least three days prior to the hearing.

The notice must be served on the preceding Tuesday (ie, where notice of a hearing is being given, both the day on which notice is served and the day of the hearing are excluded in calculating the clear days.) However, it should be noted that in computing a period of five days or less, any weekend or bank holiday must be ignored.

Example 3

Month means a calendar month.

So if a claim form for service within the jurisdiction is issued on 13 October, it must be served no later than 13 February.

5.3 Acknowledgement of service (Part 10)

When served with the particulars of claim, the defendant usually has a choice of what to do: he may either simply acknowledge service, or he may file a defence. The defendant may acknowledge service if he is unable to file a defence in time, or if he wishes to contest the court's jurisdiction. The time for acknowledging service is 14 days from service of the particulars of claim (which may have been set out on the claim form, served with it, or served subsequently).

The acknowledgement of service form is part of the response pack (Form N9). On the form, the defendant should set out his name in full; and if his name has been incorrectly set out in the claim form, it should be correctly set out on the acknowledgement of service form, followed by the words 'described as' and the incorrect name (eg, John Patrick Smith described as Pat Smith). The defendant's address for service, which must be within England or Wales, must be stated. This will either be the defendant's residence or business address, or, if the acknowledgement of service form is signed by his solicitor, his solicitor's address. The defendant must state on the form whether he intends to defend all of the claim, part of the claim, or wishes to contest jurisdiction. The form must be signed by the defendant or his solicitor. The defendant must file the completed acknowledgement of service form at the court where the claim was issued. The court will then forward a copy to the claimant.

If a defendant wishes to dispute the jurisdiction of the court, he must indicate this on the acknowledgement of service. After filing the acknowledgement of service, he must then challenge the jurisdiction by making an application within the time-limit for filing a defence (see 5.4) or he will be treated as having submitted to the jurisdiction. The application to the court to dispute the court's jurisdiction must be supported by evidence as to why England and Wales is not the proper forum for the case. If the court grants the defendant's application and finds that the claim should not have been brought in England and Wales, service of the claim form will usually be set aside. In effect, that brings the proceedings to an end.

Responding to Proceedings and Judgment in Default   59

If the court refuses the defendant's application then the original acknowledgement of service ceases to have effect and the defendant must file a further acknowledgement within 14 days or such other period as the court may direct.

5.4 The defence (Part 15) → Part 16 sets out what defence must contain.

Time limits

* If NO Ack. Service = 14 days of service of Particulars
* If Ack. Service = 28 days of service of Particulars

The defendant, if he wishes to defend the claim, must file at court a defence within 14 days of service of the particulars of claim or, if the defendant has acknowledged service, within 28 days of service of the particulars of claim. There are forms which the defendant can use which will have been served as part of the response pack. In the case of a claim for a specified amount, the appropriate form is Form N9B; and in the case of a claim for an unspecified amount or a non-money claim, the appropriate form is Form N9C. In practice, these forms will usually be used by defendants who are acting in person. Where solicitors are acting for a defendant, the defence is usually prepared as a separate document (see **Chapter 6**).

> **Example**
>
> Assume particulars of claim are deemed to have been served on Monday, 6 September 2004 (as to deemed service, see **4.5.2**). By what date must the defendant acknowledge service and indicate an intention to defend or file a defence? He must do so within 14 days of service, not including the day of deemed service. So he must act by Monday, 20 September (otherwise the defendant can enter default judgment on Tuesday, 21 September: see **5.6**). If he chooses to file an acknowledgment in time, he then has until Monday, 4 October to file his defence.

The time for filing a defence may be extended by agreement between the parties for a period of up to 28 days. — Part 15.5(1)   If the parties do reach such an agreement, the defendant must give the court written notice of the agreement. — Part 15.5(2)

Any further extension can only be authorised by the court. The court will usually grant an extension but, if the claimant has complied with the pre-action protocols, such extension will probably be for a short period of time and will be granted at the defendant's expense. If, however, the claimant did not comply with the pre-action protocols, the court is likely to conclude that the defendant should be granted a significant extension of time. If the claimant has unreasonably refused to grant a voluntary extension of time and/or has opposed the defendant's application to the court unreasonably, the court may well order the claimant to pay the defendant's costs of seeking the extension.

When the defence is filed, a copy must be served on all other parties. The court will effect service, unless the defendant's solicitor has told the court that he will do so.

The contents of a defence, as required by the CPR 1998, are dealt with in **Chapter 6**.

5.5 Admissions (Part 14)

If a defendant wishes to admit either the whole or part of the claim, he should complete the appropriate sections of the response pack. The way in which the defendant should complete the forms and the consequences of doing so vary depending on the nature of the claim and whether the admission is in full or only in part.

5.5.1 Admissions in full of a claim for a specified amount

If a defendant admits the whole of a claim for a specified amount, he should serve the appropriate form of admission (Form N9A) on the claimant. This should be done within 14 days of service of the particulars of claim. On Form N9A, the defendant has to give certain personal details, together with details of his income and expenditure, and he should also make an offer of payment, which can be an offer to pay either in full by a certain date, or by monthly instalments.

Upon receipt of the form, the claimant may then file a request for judgment. If the claimant accepts the defendant's offer to pay either by a certain date or by monthly instalments, then the claimant simply accepts the defendant's offer and files a request for judgment.

If the claimant rejects the defendant's offer to pay by a certain date or to pay by instalments then the court will decide the appropriate order. If the claim is for not more than £50,000, a court officer may decide the rate of payment without any court hearing or, alternatively, the rate of payment will be decided by a judge. Where the rate of payment is to be decided by a judge, the proceedings must be automatically transferred to the 'defendant's home court', if the defendant is an individual. So where is the 'defendant's home court'? For a county court claim, it is the county court for the district in which the defendant resides or carries on business. For a High Court claim, it is the District Registry for the district in which the defendant resides or carries on business, or, where there is no such District Registry, the Royal Courts of Justice.

The judge may make the decision without any hearing, but if there is to be a hearing, the parties must be given at least seven days' notice. In deciding the time and rate of payment, the court will take into account:

(a) the defendant's statement of means;
(b) the claimant's objections to the defendant's request; and
(c) any other relevant factors.

5.5.2 Part admission of a claim for a specified amount

If a defendant admits only part of a claim for a specified amount, he must do so by filing Form N9A at the court within 14 days of service of the particulars of claim. The court will then give notice of the admission to the claimant, who must say whether he:

(a) accepts the offer in full satisfaction of his claim; or
(b) accepts the offer but not the defendant's proposals for payment; or
(c) rejects the offer and wishes to proceed with his claim.

The claimant has 14 days in which to file his notice and serve it on the defendant. If he does not do so, the claim will be stayed until he does file his notice.

If the claimant accepts the offer, he will request judgment.

If the defendant has not requested time to pay, the claimant's request can stipulate the time for payment and the court will enter judgment accordingly.

If the defendant has requested time to pay, the procedure in **5.5.1** applies.

If the claimant rejects the offer, the case continues as a defended action.

5.5.3 Admissions of a claim for an unspecified amount (no offer made)

Where the defendant admits liability for a claim for an unspecified amount and makes no offer of payment, he must do so within the usual time for making an admission. The court will serve a copy of the admission on the claimant, who may then apply for judgment.

The court will then enter judgment for the damages to be assessed. The hearing at which the damages are assessed is often called a 'disposal hearing'. Where needed, the court will give directions to the parties as to the steps to be taken to prepare for the disposal hearing, and may also allocate the case to a track if that is appropriate (see **Chapter 8**).

5.5.4 Admissions of a claim for an unspecified amount (offer made)

Where the defendant admits liability for a claim for an unspecified amount and offers a sum of money in satisfaction of the claim, he must do so in the usual time for making an admission.

The court will serve a notice on the claimant requiring him to return the notice stating whether or not he accepts the amount in satisfaction of the claim. If he does not file the notice within 14 days, his claim will be stayed until he does file the notice.

If the claimant does not accept the amount offered, he will enter judgment for damages to be assessed at a disposal hearing.

If the claimant accepts the offer and the defendant has not asked for time to pay, the claimant may enter judgment for the amount offered and will stipulate when payment should be made.

If the defendant has asked for time to pay the usual procedure applies (see **5.5.1**).

5.5.5 Challenging the court's decision

Where the court has decided the time and rate of payment and the decision was made either:

(a) by a court officer; or
(b) by a judge without any hearing,

either party may apply for a redetermination by a judge. Such application must be made within 14 days of service of the determination on the applicant.

The case must be transferred to the defendant's home court if the claim is for a specified amount and the defendant is an individual (unless the case was started in a specialist list) (see **5.5.1**).

If the original decision was made by a court officer, the redetermination will be made by a judge without a hearing unless the application notice requests a hearing.

If the original decision was made by a judge, the redetermination must be at a hearing unless the parties agree otherwise.

5.5.6 Interest

Judgment where the defendant admits liability for the whole amount of a claim for a specified amount will include interest at the date of judgment if:

(a) interest has been properly claimed in the particulars of claim; and
(b) where the claim is for statutory interest it does not exceed 8% per annum; and
(c) the claimant's request for judgment includes a calculation of interest from issue to judgment.

62 Civil Litigation

If the above conditions are not satisfied, the judgment will be for an amount of interest to be decided by the court and the court will give directions as to how this should be achieved. For example, condition (b) will not be met if the claim was for a commercial debt and interest was claimed under the Late Payment of Commercial Debts (Interest) Act 1998 (see **2.4.4**).

5.5.7 Varying the rate of payment

By para 6.1 of PD 14, either party may apply to vary the time and rates of payment of a judgment on admissions if there has been a change of circumstances.

5.6 Default judgments (Part 12)

5.6.1 Introduction

Once the proceedings have been served upon the defendant, it may be that the defendant takes no action. The defendant may fail to return the acknowledgement of service or file a defence. In those circumstances, the claimant can obtain judgment in default against the defendant. This means that the claimant obtains judgment without there being a trial of the issues involved in the case.

5.6.1.1 Cases where default judgment is not available

The claimant may not enter a default judgment in the following types of cases:

(a) if the claim is for delivery of goods under an agreement regulated by the Consumer Credit Act 1974;

(b) if it is a Part 8 claim (see **Chapter 7**);

(c) if it is a mortgage claim;

(d) if it is a claim for provisional damages;

(e) if it is in a specialist court.

5.6.2 Procedure

The claimant applies for default judgment by filing a request using the relevant form if he is claiming money (whether or not it is a claim for a specified amount) or goods (if the claim form gives the defendant the option of returning the goods). There are different forms, depending on whether the claim is for a specified or an unspecified amount. (See Forms N205A, N205B, N225 and N227.)

The claimant must satisfy the court that:

(a) the particulars of claim have been served on the defendant;

(b) the defendant has not acknowledged service/filed a defence and the relevant time period has expired;

(c) the defendant has not satisfied the claim;

(d) the defendant has not admitted liability for the full amount of the claim.

5.6.3 Claims for specified amounts

A request for default judgment for a specified amount may indicate the date for full payment, or the times and rate at which it is to be paid by instalments. If it does not, the court will normally give judgment for immediate payment. Additional fixed costs are payable by the defendant (see CPR 1998, Part 45).

5.6.4 Claims for unspecified amounts

A request for default judgment for a claim for an unspecified amount is a request for the court to decide the amount of the claim and costs. This will involve a full hearing before a trial judge to decide the amount of the claim (again often called a disposal hearing), and it may, therefore, be necessary to allocate the claim to a track and give directions (see **Chapter 8**).

5.6.5 Interest

The default judgment may, in the case of a claim for a specified amount, include interest from the date of judgment if:

(a) the particulars of claim include the necessary details;
(b) any claim for statutory interest does not exceed 8% per annum;
(c) the request for judgment includes a calculation of the amount of interest from the date from which it was calculated in the claim form to the date of request.

Otherwise the court will decide the amount of interest and will give directions for this.

> **Example: specified claim**
>
> Assume proceedings were issued on 8 September 2004. Interest is claimed under statute at 8% per annum from when the cause of action arose to the day of issue. The daily rate of interest is £5.35. If default judgment is entered on 29 September, how much additional interest should be claimed? As 21 days have passed since issue, so a further £112.35 should now be claimed when entering default judgment.

5.6.6 Co-defendants

Where there are co-defendants, the claimant may enter a default judgment against one or more of the co-defendants while proceeding with his claim against the other defendants, provided the claim can be dealt with separately from the other defendants. Otherwise, the court will not deal with the default judgment until it deals with the claim against the other defendants.

5.6.7 Setting aside a default judgment

A defendant against whom a default judgment has been entered may apply to have it set aside. Such applications are considered in **Chapter 9**.

5.6.8 Summary

A defendant might respond to a specified claim in any of the following ways:

(a) admit the full amount and pay it. Alternatively he can ask for time to pay, which, if rejected by the claimant, will be determined by the court; or
(b) admit part of the claim and offer to pay it. Alternatively, he can ask for time to pay. If the claimant accepts the part admitted in full and final settlement but rejects the proposal as to payment, the court will determine the time for payment. However, if the claimant does not accept the part admitted in full and final settlement, the case will continue as a defended claim.

A defendant might respond to a claim for an unspecified amount of money in any of the following ways:

(a) admit liability but make no offer of payment. The court will enter judgment for damages to be assessed at a disposal hearing; or

(b) admit liability and make an offer to pay a sum of money. Additionally he may ask for time to pay that amount. If the claimant accepts the offer but rejects any proposal as to payment, the court will determine the time for payment. However, if the claimant does not accept the offer, he will enter judgment for damages to be assessed at a disposal hearing.

Where a claimant enters default judgment on a specified claim, the judgment will be for a final sum of money as calculated by the claimant and he can immediately proceed to enforcement.

Where a claimant enters default judgment on a claim for an unspecified amount of money, the judgment will be for damages to be assessed by the court at a disposal hearing.

See further the flow diagrams in **Appendix C**.

5.7 Human rights

There is potential for an argument that the fact that a claimant can get a default judgment and thereby bring the case to an end deprives the defendant of his right to 'a fair and public hearing' under Article 6 ECHR. The counter-argument is that the defendant still has the power to apply to set aside that judgment if he has a defence with real prospects of success. English default judgments have been recognised and enforced by the courts of other EU States. That said, however, in most other European jurisdictions a claimant cannot obtain judgment merely because the defendant has failed to respond to the court proceedings. Instead, the claimant has to prove his claim judicially by presenting evidence to the court, and so there is a possibility that the default judgment procedure could be held to be a breach of the ECHR.

Chapter 6

Statements of Case

6.1	Introduction	65
6.2	Contents of the particulars of claim	66
6.3	The defence	74
6.4	Reply to defence	76
6.5	The role of statements of case	77
6.6	Amendments to statements of case (Part 17)	79
6.7	Requests for further information (Part 18)	80

6.1 Introduction

Statements of case are the formal documents in which the parties set out their respective cases. They are served between the parties (as well as being filed at court) so that each party knows the case he will have to meet at the hearing. The statements of case are central to the litigation, since at trial the court will only decide those issues which are raised in the statements of case. They therefore must be carefully drafted and continually reviewed as the case develops. The trial court will not allow a party to pursue an issue which, on a fair reading of the statement of case, is not stated: see *Royal Brompton Hospital NHS Trust v Hammond & Others* [2000] LTL, 4 December.

The claimant's first statement of case is the particulars of claim. As has been seen in **Chapter 4**, this may be contained within the claim form itself, or be set out in a separate document served either with the claimant's claim form or within 14 days thereafter.

The defendant's statement of case is called a defence. Frequently, the only statements of case in a claim will be the particulars of claim and the defence. In some cases, however, a claimant may wish to serve a reply to the defence, and in other cases a defendant may wish to make his own claim against the claimant by way of a counterclaim (see **Chapter 7**).

The rules relating to statements of case are contained in Part 16 of CPR 1998 and the accompanying Practice Directions. Part 16 does not apply if the claimant has used the Part 8 procedure (see **Chapter 7**).

6.1.1 Formalities

By PD 5, para 2.2, every document prepared by a party for filing or use at the court must:

(a) unless the nature of the document renders it impracticable, be on A4 paper of durable quality having a margin not less than 3.5cm wide;
(b) be fully legible and should normally be typed;
(c) where possible, be bound securely in a manner which would not hamper filing, or otherwise each page should be endorsed with the case number;
(d) have the pages numbered consecutively;
(e) be divided into numbered paragraphs;
(f) have all numbers, including dates, expressed as figures; and

(g) give in the margin the reference of every document mentioned that has already been filed.

By PD 5, para 2.1, where a firm of solicitors prepares a statement of case, the document should be signed in the name of the firm.

In addition, statements of case should set out the material facts in chronological order and on a point-by-point basis to allow for a point-by-point response.

6.2 Contents of the particulars of claim

6.2.1 What must be included?

Rule 16.4(1) states that the particulars of claim must include:

(a) a concise statement of the facts on which the claimant relies;
(b) if the claimant is seeking interest, a statement to that effect and the details set out in paragraph (2) (see below);
(c) if the claimant is seeking aggravated damages or exemplary damages, a statement to that effect and his grounds for claiming them;
(d) if the claimant is seeking provisional damages, a statement to that effect and his grounds for claiming them; and
(e) such other matters as may be set out in a practice direction.

The primary function of the particulars of claim is to state concisely the facts upon which the claimant relies. The claimant should state all facts necessary for the purpose of showing that he has a complete cause of action.

PD 16 goes into more detail as to what must be, or may be, included in the particulars of claim. There are particular requirements for certain types of cases (eg, recovery of land and hire purchase claims).

More generally, where a claim is based upon a written agreement, then by para 7.3 of PD 16:

(1) a copy of the contract or documents constituting the agreement should be attached to or served with the particulars of claim and the original(s) should be available at the hearing, and
(2) any general conditions of sale incorporated in the contract should also be attached (but where the contract is, or the documents constituting the agreement are bulky this practice direction is complied with by attaching or serving only the relevant parts of the contract or documents).

Therefore, where the claim arises out of a breach of a written contract, a copy of the relevant contract should be attached to, or served with, the particulars of claim.

By para 7.4:

Where a claim is based upon an oral agreement, the particulars of claim should set out the contractual words used and state by whom, to whom, when and where they were spoken.

and by para 7.5:

Where a claim is based upon an agreement by conduct, the particulars of claim must specify the conduct relied on and state by whom, when and where the acts constituting the conduct were done.

Paragraphs 8.1–8.2 of PD 16 set out further matters which must be specifically set out in the particulars of claim. For example, by para 8.2:

The claimant must specifically set out the following matters in his particulars of claim where he wishes to rely on them in support of his claim:

(1) any allegation of fraud,
(2) the fact of any illegality,
(3) details of any misrepresentation,
(4) details of all breaches of trust,
(5) notice or knowledge of a fact,
(6) details of unsoundness of mind or undue influence,
(7) details of wilful default, and
(8) any facts relating to mitigation of loss or damage.

Rule 16.4(2) sets out the details which must be supplied where, as will usually be the case, the claimant is seeking interest. In such cases, the claimant must:

(a) state whether he is doing so—
 (i) under the terms of a contract;
 (ii) under an enactment and if so which; or
 (iii) on some other basis and if so what that basis is; and
(b) if the claim is for a specified amount of money, state—
 (i) the percentage rate at which interest is claimed;
 (ii) the date from which it is claimed;
 (iii) the date to which it is calculated, which must not be later than the date on which the claim form is issued;
 (iv) the total amount of interest claimed to the date of calculation; and
 (v) the daily rate at which interest accrues after that date.

If the claimant is claiming interest pursuant to statute, then in the High Court this would be under s 35A of the SCA 1981 and in the county court under s 69 of the CCA 1984. Alternatively, a claimant may be entitled to claim interest pursuant to a particular clause in a contract. A claimant would normally seek to do this where the contractual interest rate is higher than the current statutory interest rate of 8%. Where the contract does not provide for payment of interest, the claimant may nevertheless be entitled to claim a higher rate of interest than the statutory rate if the Late Payment of Commercial Debts (Interest) Act 1998 applies (see **2.4.4**). A claimant who claims for interest under contract or the 1998 Act may well seek statutory interest under s 35A of the SCA 1981 or s 69 of the CCA 1984 in the alternative, just in case the court refuses to award interest under the contract or the 1998 Act.

If a party wishes to rely on any provision of, or right arising under, the Human Rights Act 1998, or seeks a remedy available under that Act, he must state that fact. Precise details of the Convention right which it is alleged has been infringed and particulars of the infringement must be set. In addition, the relief sought must be specified along with any declaration of incompatibility in accordance with s 4 of the Act or damages in respect of a judicial act to which s 9(3) of the Act applies. If a declaration of incompatibility is sought, precise information of the legislative provision alleged to be incompatible and details of the alleged incompatibility must be given. Where the claim is founded on a finding of unlawfulness by another court or tribunal, details of the finding must be set out. If the claim is founded on a judicial act which is alleged to have infringed a Convention right of the party, the party must state the judicial act complained of and the court or tribunal which is alleged to have made it.

There now follow two examples of particulars of claim, both concerning a breach of contract claim. In the first example the claim is for a specified amount of money. Interest is claimed under the Late Payment of Commercial Debts (Interest) Act 1998 where a base rate of 3% per annum has been assumed. For an example of particulars of claim in a negligence claim, see **Appendix D(2)**.

6.2.1.1 Example of particulars of claim in a county court debt claim (particulars of claim set out on claim form)

Claim Form

In the Reading County Court

Claim No. RO45439
Issue date 1 October 2004

Claimant
Brewsters Limited,
Unit 12, Brownside Industrial Estate,
Reading,
Berkshire
RG2 6DS
Tel: 0118 598 3990

SEAL

Defendant(s)
Gates Launderettes Limited,
73 Cider Street,
Slough,
Berkshire
SL1 1PP
Tel: 01753 547790

Brief details of claim
The claim is for an unpaid debt of £63,450 in respect of 3 industrial drycleaners and 6 industrial washing machines supplied by the Claimant to the Defendant.

Value

Defendant's name and address
Gates Launderettes Limited,
73 Cider Street,
Slough,
Berkshire
SL1 1PP

	£
Amount claimed	63,450.00
Court fee	600.00
Solicitor's costs	100.00
Total amount	64,150.00

The court office at Reading County Court, 161-163 Friar Street, Reading RG1 1HE
is open between 10 am and 4 pm Monday to Friday. When corresponding with the court, please address forms or letters to the Court Manager and quote the claim number.
N1 Claim form (CPR Part 7) (01.02)   *Printed on behalf of The Court Service*

	Claim No.	RO45439

Does, or will, your claim include any issues under the Human Rights Act 1998? ☐ Yes ☐ No

Particulars of Claim (attached)(to follow)

1. By clause 1 of a written agreement (the 'Agreement') dated 14 May 2004 the Claimant agreed to sell to the Defendant machinery, namely 3 Chloridal dry cleaning machines and 6 Isadal washing machines for an agreed price of £63,450.00. A copy of the Agreement is attached.

2. By clause 4 of the Agreement payment of the agreed price was due within 7 days of delivery.

3. In pursuance of clause 6 of the Agreement the machinery was delivered to the Defendant's premises at 6, Station Road, Reading on 16 August 2004.

4. In breach of the Agreement the Defendant has failed to pay the agreed price or any part thereof.

5. The Claimant claims the sum of £63,450.00 and interest under the Late Payment of Commercial Debts (Interest) Act 1998.

AND THE CLAIMANT CLAIMS:

1. The sum of £63,450.00.

2. Interest pursuant to the Late Payment of Commercial Debts (Interest) Act 1998. For the purposes of the Act both parties acted in the course of a business. The statutory interest began to run from 24 August 2004 (the 8th day after delivery) at 8% over base rate, namely 11% per annum. Interest due to the date of issue totals £554.48 (24 August to 1 October 2004 being 29 days) and is continuing until judgment or sooner payment at the daily rate of £19.12

DATED: 1 October 2004

Statement of Truth

*(I believe)~~(The Claimant believes)~~ that the facts stated in these particulars of claim are true.
* I am duly authorised by the claimant to sign this statement

Full name _Brian Charlton_

Name of claimant's solicitor's firm _Collaws_

signed _Brian Charlton_ position or office held _Managing Director_

*(Claimant)~~(Litigation friend)(Claimant's solicitor)~~ (if signing on behalf of firm or company)

*delete as appropriate

Collaws,
14 Ship Street,
Weyford,
Guildshire WE1 8HQ
Ref: BM/ABC/Brewsters
DX 1599 Weyford
Fax: 01904 876554

Claimant's or claimant's solicitor's address to which documents or payments should be sent if different from overleaf including (if appropriate) details of DX, fax or e-mail.

Statements of Case 71

6.2.1.2 Example of particulars of claim in a High Court claim for breach of contract

IN THE HIGH COURT OF JUSTICE 2004 I No 876

QUEEN'S BENCH DIVISION

READING DISTRICT REGISTRY

BETWEEN

INDUSTRIAL MANUFACTURING LIMITED   Claimant

and

HEATECHS LIMITED   Defendant

PARTICULARS OF CLAIM

1. At all material times the Defendant carried on business as a manufacturer and supplier of central heating boilers and systems.

2. By a written contract made on 22 April 2004 between the Claimant and Defendant, the Defendant agreed to sell to the Claimant a central heating gas boiler and integrated water pump described in clause 1 as a Heatechs Powerheat Unit Model 312K ('the Unit') for the sum of £60,000 plus £10,500 VAT. A copy of the contract is attached.

3. The Claimant bought the Unit from the Defendant who sold it in the course of its business. It was an implied condition of the contract that the Unit should be of satisfactory quality.

4. Further, during a telephone conversation at about 11.30 am on 19 April 2004, the Claimant by its contracts manager, Ian Jones, expressly or by implication made known to the Defendant (represented by their sales manager, Polly Rees) the particular purpose for which it required the Unit, namely for the purpose of installation in the Claimant's factory 'as part of a heating system required to be in continuous use for six days per week'. It was an express and/or implied condition of the contract that the Unit to be delivered by the Defendant should be reasonably fit for that purpose.

5. In purported performance of the contract the Defendant delivered the Unit on 24 June 2004 and it was installed by the Claimant on or about 2 July 2004.

6. In breach of the express and/or implied conditions the Unit delivered by the Defendant was not of satisfactory quality and was not reasonably fit for its purpose.

PARTICULARS OF BREACH

(a) The integrated water pump failed to operate.

(b) The impeller retaining nut on the integrated water pump was insufficiently secure owing to a defective thread.

7. As a consequence of the breaches of conditions the boiler in the Unit became or had become drained of water on 2 August 2004 and overheated as a result. When the pump effectively re-engaged cold water flowed into the boiler causing it to explode and rupture on 2 August 2004 and the pipe connections to distort. As a result the boiler house had to be pumped out and repaired and a new boiler installed. During this time the Claimant lost five days of production.

8. By reason of the above the Claimant has suffered loss and damage.

PARTICULARS OF LOSS AND DAMAGE

[Margin note: What the Claimant is claiming]

Cost of replacement boiler	£70,500
Installation of new boiler	£4,700
Cost of pumping out boiler house and repairing damaged premises	£17,625
Consequential losses as the result of production losses (estimated)	£25,000

9. In respect of damages awarded the Claimant is entitled to interest pursuant to s 35A of the Supreme Court Act 1981 at such rates and for such period as the Court thinks just.

AND THE CLAIMANT CLAIMS:

(1) Damages.

(2) Interest pursuant to s 35A of the Supreme Court Act 1981.

Dated 10 December 2004.

Singleton Trumper & Co

STATEMENT OF TRUTH

I believe that the facts stated in these Particulars of Claim are true. I am duly authorised by the Claimant to sign this statement.

Signed: *D Smith*
DAVID SMITH
Director

The Claimant's Solicitors are Singleton Trumper & Co of Bank Chambers, Streatham, Reading RD62 5PA where they will accept service of proceedings on behalf of the Claimant.

To the Defendant

To the Court Manager.

6.2.2 Particulars of breach and damage

It is necessary to include detailed particulars of some aspects of the claim. For example, particulars of the breach of a contract or duty must always be stated so that the defendant knows exactly the manner in which he is alleged to have been in breach. Similarly, the detail of the claim for damages is often most conveniently set out in 'particulars of loss and damage'.

6.2.2.1 The summary for relief

The relief or remedy claimed must be specifically stated in the particulars of claim. Traditionally, it is also often repeated in summary form towards the end of the particulars of claim, immediately before the date, and will vary depending upon the subject matter of the claim.

In a debt claim, the summary will often include the claim for the amount of the debt, the exact amount of interest claimed up to the date of issue of the proceedings and the daily rate of interest claimed thereafter. In a damages claim, it will include the claim for damages plus interest.

6.2.3 The statement of truth

If the particulars of claim are not part of the claim form itself, they must be verified by a statement of truth (see **4.3**).

6.2.4 Practical points

Whilst CPR 1998 provide for the content and format of statements of case, practitioners will adopt their own style within that framework. For example, in the 'Industrial Manufacturing Limited v Heatechs Limited' particulars of claim at **6.2.1.2** above, paragraph 3 states that the sale was in the course of the defendant's business. This is because the claimant wishes to rely upon the terms implied by the Sale of Goods Act 1979 which apply only where the sale was made in the course of the defendant's business. However, many practitioners do not consider it necessary to state this explicitly as they rely upon the description of the defendant's business in the opening paragraph and the subsequent entry into the contract as satisfying this requirement. When looking at precedents, you will see that this additional paragraph appears in some but not others — neither is wrong, they are merely alternatives.

Another point to consider is the chronology of the material facts in the same example. We refer first (in paragraph 2) to the contract which was made on 22 April 2004 and later (in paragraph 4) to a conversation which took place on 19 April 2004. This is because the conversation became incorporated into the contract as a condition. This is the traditional way of setting out such material. However, an alternative would be to deal with the conversation first, then the contract, and, thirdly, refer back to the conversation when stating the relevant condition of the contract.

A vital point to remember is that there must be a link or thread between the key parts of the particulars of claim. So, in a breach of contract claim:

(a) the express and/or implied terms relied on must be the same ones said to have been breached by the defendant;

(b) the factual consequences of the breach should be the same ones said to constitute the damage and loss.

74   Civil Litigation

You can see this in the *Industrial Manufacturing Limited v Heatechs Limited* example at **6.2.1.2**. Namely:

(a) the terms relied on are set out in paragraphs 3 and 4, whilst exactly the same terms are said to have been broken in paragraph 6;

(b) the factual consequences of the breach are set out in paragraph 7 (boiler exploded, boiler house pumped out and repaired, new boiler installed and five days of production lost) and these are then quantified and particularised in paragraph 8.

6.3 The defence

As seen in **Chapter 5**, the defendant has a limited amount of time in which to file a defence with the court, depending upon whether or not an acknowledgement of service has been filed.

Rule 16.5 sets out what must be contained in the defence:

(1) In his defence, the defendant must state—
  (a) which of the allegations in the particulars of claim he denies;
  (b) which allegations he is unable to admit or deny, but which he requires the claimant to prove; and
  (c) which allegations he admits.

(2) Where the defendant denies an allegation—
  (a) he must state his reasons for doing so; and
  (b) if he intends to put forward a different version of events from that given by the claimant, he must state his own version.

(3) A defendant who—
  (a) fails to deal with an allegation; but
  (b) has set out in his defence the nature of his case in relation to the issue to which that allegation is relevant,
  shall be taken to require that allegation be proved.

(4) Where the claim includes a money claim, a defendant shall be taken to require that any allegation relating to the amount of money claimed be proved unless he expressly admits the allegation.

(5) Subject to paragraphs (3) and (4), a defendant who fails to deal with an allegation shall be taken to admit that allegation.

(6) If the defendant disputes the claimant's statement of value under rule 16.3 he must—
  (a) state why he disputes it; and
  (b) if he is able, give his own statement of the value of the claim.

(7) If the defendant is defending in a representative capacity, he must state what that capacity is.

(8) If the defendant has not filed an acknowledgement of service under Part 10, he must give an address for service.

(Part 22 requires a defence to be verified by a statement of truth)

(Rule 6.5 provides that an address for service must be within the jurisdiction)

The defence must provide a comprehensive response to the particulars of claim and, therefore, in respect of each allegation in the particulars of claim, there should be an admission, a denial, or (where the defendant has no knowledge of the matter stated) a requirement that the claimant prove the point (a non-admission). Any denial must be explicit and a defendant must state his reasons for denying the allegation in the particulars of claim. If the defendant wishes to put forward a different version of events from that given by the claimant, the defendant must state his own version. A bare denial is not acceptable. Moreover, by the so-called rule of implied admissions, a defendant who fails to deal with an allegation is taken to admit it (see r 16.5(5) above).

In order to ensure that every allegation in the particulars of claim is dealt with and nothing is admitted through omission (see r 16.5(5)), the defence usually answers each paragraph of the claim in turn. This is the approach adopted in the defence to the breach of contract claim between 'Industrial Manufacturing Limited and Heatechs Limited' in the example set out at **6.3.1** below, and in the defence to the negligence claim between 'Simpson and Templar' in **Appendix D(3)**.

6.3.1 Example of a defence in a High Court claim for breach of contract *see also p 309*

IN THE HIGH COURT OF JUSTICE　　　　　　　　　　　　　　　　2004 I 876
QUEEN'S BENCH DIVISION
READING DISTRICT REGISTRY
BETWEEN

	INDUSTRIAL MANUFACTURING LIMITED	Claimant
	and	
	HEATECHS LIMITED	Defendant

DEFENCE

1. The Defendant admits paragraphs 1 to 4 of the Particulars of Claim.

2. The delivery of the Unit referred to in paragraph 5 of the Particulars of Claim was wholly in accordance with the terms of the contract and constituted full and complete performance thereof by the Defendant. No admission is made as to the installation of the Unit by the Claimant as the Defendant has no knowledge of that matter.

3. The Defendant denies it was in breach of contract as alleged in paragraph 6 of the Particulars of Claim, or at all. The Defendant asserts that the Unit supplied was of satisfactory quality and fit for its purpose. In particular, the impeller retaining nut on the water pump was sufficiently secure and did not have a defective thread.

4. The Defendant makes no admission as to the matters stated in paragraph 7 as the Defendant has no knowledge of these matters.

5. As to paragraph 8 it is not admitted that the Claimant has suffered the alleged or any loss and damage as the Defendant has no knowledge of these matters.

6. If, which is not admitted, the Claimant suffered the loss and damage alleged in paragraph 8, it is denied that such occurred as a result of the alleged or any breach of condition by the Defendant. Any such loss or damage was caused by the Claimant's installation and/or subsequent use of the Unit.

7. In all the circumstances it is denied that the Claimant is entitled to the relief claimed or any relief.

Dated the 6th January 2005.　　　　　　　　　　　　　　　　　　　*Haughton & Co*

STATEMENT OF TRUTH

I believe that the facts stated in this Defence are true. I am duly authorised by the Defendant to sign this statement.

Signed: *D Bennett*
D. BENNETT
Managing Director

The Defendant's Solicitors are Haughton & Co, 19 High Pavement, Reading RD61 4UZ, where they will accept service of proceedings on behalf of the Defendant.

To the Court Manager

To the Claimant.

When answering each paragraph of the claim, the defendant should clearly deny any allegations which are disputed and make clear admissions in respect of the factual issues which are not in dispute (eg, paragraph 1 in the example at **6.3.1** above). Any allegations of loss or damage which are disputed should be 'not admitted' in the defence, such as in paragraph 4 of the example. The defendant should also include any additional facts in the defence which make his side of the story clearer. See paragraphs 3 and 6 of the example.

The consequence of making admissions in the defence is that the claimant does not have to prove the point at trial. Such admissions are most often made in respect of facts which came into existence prior to the breach of contract or negligent act, such as the date, the parties and the terms of the contract.

If a defendant wishes to make a counterclaim against a claimant, the counterclaim should form part of the same document. Counterclaims are a form of Part 20 claim and are considered in more detail in **Chapter 7**. For an example, see **Appendix D(3)**.

If a defendant wishes to rely upon the expiry of a limitation period, he must give details in his defence (PD 16, para 13.1).

A party is required to verify that the facts stated in the defence are true by way of a statement of truth (see **4.3**).

6.4 Reply to defence

A claimant may wish to file a reply to the defence but is under no obligation to do so. He should do so if he needs to allege facts in answer to the defence which were not included in the particulars of claim. By r 16.7(1), a claimant who does not file a reply to the defence is not taken to admit the matters raised in the defence. There is therefore no corresponding rule of implied admission which we saw when looking at the defence itself (see **6.3**). In practice, replies to defences are most common where the defendant has made a counterclaim, in which case the claimant must file a defence to the counterclaim and then will often incorporate a reply as well.

For an example of a Reply (to Defence) which also includes a Defence to a Part 20 Counterclaim, see **Appendix D(4)**.

6.5 The role of statements of case

6.5.1 The basics

In the case of *McPhilemy v Times Newspapers Limited and Others* [1999] 3 All ER 775, Lord Woolf MR said:

> The need for extensive [statements of case] including particulars should be reduced by the requirement that witness statements are now exchanged. In the majority of proceedings identification of the documents upon which a party relies, together with copies of that party's witness statements, will make the detail of the nature of the case the other side has to meet obvious.

When thinking about the five stages of litigation (see **1.3**) it can be seen that statements of case are dealt with at stage 2. The detailed evidence is dealt with subsequently at stage 3. So a statement of case should be thought of as putting together the bare bones of the case. The 'flesh' will be put on by way of evidence later.

For example, the particulars of claim in respect of a breach of contract claim should deal with the essential facts that will establish the cause of action, namely:

(a) status of the parties (eg, defendant's business when relying on sale during course of that business to establish terms implied by Sale of Goods Act 1979);

(b) chronological story (eg, request for a sample; pre-contract statements, etc);

(c) contract: date; type; parties; subject matter; consideration;

(d) express terms relied on;

(e) implied terms relied on;

(f) chronological story (eg, delivery, payment, etc);

(g) breach particularised;

(h) consequences of breach;

(i) damage and loss particularised;

(j) interest (contract; Late Payments of Commercial Debts (Interest) Act 1998; SCA 1981, s 35A, or CCA 1984, s 69: see **2.4.4**).

It is important to bear in mind that the witness statements served later in the proceedings by the claimant and on which he intends to rely at trial will flesh out the detail as to the formation of the contract, etc. Any technical matters will, of course, be dealt with by expert evidence (see **11.13**).

In relation to either the particulars of claim or the defence, by para 13.3 of PD 16, a party may:

(1) refer in his statement of case to any point of law on which his claim or defence, as the case may be, is based,

(2) give in his statement of case the name of any witness he proposes to call, and

(3) attach to or serve with this statement of case a copy of any document which he considers is necessary to his claim or defence, as the case may be (including any expert's report to be filed in accordance with Part 35).

As a general rule there is no need to state any law. It will normally be a defendant, however, who will wish to raise a point of law (eg, that the claim discloses no cause of action (such as a promise unsupported by consideration) or a defence under the Limitation Act 1980 (see **6.3**)).

Whilst excessive factual details should not be given in a statement of case, a party can state 'the name of any witness he proposes to call'. So a party can choose to indicate if he has any particular witness in mind who will prove a particular fact.

There is little advantage in this unless perhaps the details have already been revealed pre-action, or it helps to particularise the party's case (eg, in an industrial accident claim, part of the defendant's case may be that the machinery in question was regularly checked and so he should state by whom and when).

A party can attach to a statement of case any document he considers 'necessary' to his claim or defence. This provision ensures that the court has the fullest possible knowledge of relevant facts from the outset. So, if a party has voluntarily disclosed a document pre-action, or has received a document from the other side that assists his case, and it is admissible, then it may be appropriate to attach a copy.

6.5.2 Defining the issues

How do the statements of case define the issues between the parties? If the particulars of claim have set out the factual allegations and the defence answered each allegation by way of admission, non-admission or denial, then by comparing the two documents we can identify the issues in dispute (namely, those not admitted and denied). So if we compare these documents in the Industrial Manufacturing Limited v Heatechs Limited example at **6.2.1.2** and **6.3.1**, we have the following agreed issues and issues in dispute:

Example 1 – Agreed issues

Particulars of claim	Defence	Issue
Paragraph 1	Paragraph 1	Defendant a manufacturer and supplier of central heating boilers and systems.
Paragraph 2	Paragraph 1	Written contract made on 22 April 2004 for the Unit.
Paragraph 3	Paragraph 1	Implied term that Unit to be of satisfactory quality.
Paragraph 4	Paragraph 1	Express or implied term that Unit to be reasonably fit to heat Claimant's factory continuously six days a week.
Paragraph 5	Paragraph 2	Unit delivered to Claimant on 24 June 2004

Example 2 – Issues in dispute

Particulars of claim	Defence	Issue
Paragraph 5	Paragraph 2	Claimant installed Unit on 2 July 2004.
Paragraph 6	Paragraph 3	Defendant breached contract as water pump failed to operate and impeller retaining nut had defective thread.
Paragraph 7	Paragraph 4	On 2 August 2004 boiler overheated and exploded.
Paragraph 8	Paragraph 5	Claimant suffered loss due to Defendant's breach.
Paragraph 8	Paragraph 5	Claimant's loss consists of cost of replacement boiler and its installation, cost of pumping out and repairing boiler house and loss of profit.
Paragraph 8	Paragraph 6	Claimant caused own loss by way installed and/or subsequently used Unit.

6.6 Amendments to statements of case (Part 17)

In a perfect world, nobody would ever have to amend their statements of case. However, sometimes mistakes are made, and on other occasions fresh information comes to light after the statement of case has been served. Part 17 of CPR 1998 provides the ways in which statements of case can be amended.

6.6.1 Amendments before service

A party may amend his statement of case at any time before it has been served.

6.6.2 Amendments with permission

After a party has served his statement of case he can amend it only with either:

(a) the written consent of all of the parties; or
(b) the permission of the court.

On making an application for permission to amend the statement of case, the applicant should file a copy of the statement of case with the proposed amendments along with the application notice (see **Chapter 9**).

If the court grants permission for the amendment, the applicant must file the amended statement of case and serve the order and the amended statement of case on all other parties.

The statement of case will be endorsed with the words:

> Amended [describe the type of statement of case] by Order of [name of master/ district judge] dated [ ].

The amended statement of case need not show the original text unless the court directs otherwise.

6.6.3 Directions following amendment

If the court gives permission to amend the statement of case, it may give directions regarding amendments to any other statement of case and service of the amended statements of case. It is common, for example, for a defendant to be allowed to amend his defence if the court has given the claimant permission to amend his particulars of claim.

6.6.4 Application to amend the statement of case outside the limitation period

If a claim is made after the relevant limitation period has expired, the defendant has an absolute defence (see 2.2). So, if the amendment will add or substitute a new claim, the new claim must arise out of the same facts or substantially the same facts as the claim which the applicant has already made in the proceedings.

If the amendment is to correct a mistake as to the name of a party, the mistake must be genuine and one which would not have caused reasonable doubt as to the identity of the party in question.

If the amendment alters the capacity in which a party brings his claim, the new capacity must be one which that party had when the proceedings commenced or has since acquired.

6.6.5 Statements of truth

By r 22.1(2), amendments to the statement of case have to be verified by a statement of truth unless the court orders otherwise.

6.6.6 Costs

A party applying for an amendment will usually be responsible for the costs of and caused by the amendment being allowed (see **9.3**).

6.6.7 Amendments without permission

Where a party has amended his statement of case without requiring the court's permission (ie, in the case of an amendment by consent or before service), the court may disallow the amendment (r 17.2). A party may apply to the court asking it to exercise its discretion to disallow within 14 days of service of the amended statement of case.

6.7 Requests for further information (Part 18)

6.7.1 The request

A party to the proceedings, or the court itself, may wish another party to give further information about its case. By r 18.1(1), the court may at any time order a party to:

(a) clarify any matter which is in dispute in the proceedings; or
(b) give additional information in relation to any such matter,

whether or not the matter is contained or referred to in a statement of case.

If one of the parties requires further information then, before applying to the court for an order, that party should first serve a written request on the other party stating a date for the response, which must allow a reasonable time for the response.

A request should be concise and strictly confined to matters which are reasonably necessary and proportionate to enable the applicant to prepare his own case or to understand the case he has to meet. The most common request is by a defendant seeking further information from a claimant who has failed to give sufficient particulars of breach and/or damage (see **6.2.2**).

Requests must be made as far as possible in a single comprehensive document and not piecemeal.

If the text of the request is brief and the reply is likely to be brief, then the request may be made by letter. If so, the letter must state that it contains a request made under Part 18 and must not deal with any other matter. Otherwise, the request should be made in a separate document.

Any request must:

(a) be headed with the name of the court and the title and number of the claim;
(b) state in its heading that it is a Part 18 request, identify the applicant and the respondent, and state the date on which it is made;
(c) set out each request in a separate numbered paragraph;
(d) identify any document and (if relevant) any paragraph or words in that document to which the request relates;
(e) state the date for a response.

If the request is not in the form of a letter, the applicant may, if this is convenient, put the request on the left-hand side of the document so that the response may appear on the right-hand side. If so, the applicant should serve two copies of the request on the respondent.

6.7.2 Response to the request

The response must be in writing, dated and signed by the respondent or his solicitor. If the original request was made in a letter, the response can also be in the form of a letter or a formal reply. If in a letter, it should state that it is a response to the request and should not deal with any other matters. The response should set out the same information as the request and then give details of the response itself. The respondent must file at court and serve on all parties a copy of the request and his response.

The response must be verified by a statement of truth. [PART 22.1(b)]

6.7.3 Cases where the respondent does not respond to the initial request

If the respondent objects to all or part of the request, or cannot comply with the request, he should inform the applicant, giving reasons and, where relevant, giving a date by which he will be able to comply with the request. He may do so by letter or by formal response. If the respondent considers that a response will involve disproportionate expense, he should explain briefly in his reply why he takes this view.

6.7.4 Applications for court orders

[Remedy for application.] If no response is received or the response is considered to be inadequate, then the applicant can apply for an order from the court (see **Chapter 9**). The court will grant an order only if it is satisfied that the request is confined to matters which are reasonably necessary and proportionate to enable the applicant to prepare his case or understand the case he has to meet.

Chapter 7

Part 20 Proceedings and Part 8 Claims

7.1	Introduction	83
7.2	Procedure	84
7.3	Part 8 claims	87

7.1 Introduction

We have looked at the rules relating to a claimant bringing a claim against a defendant. Part 20 of CPR 1998 deals with other types of claim which may be brought in the proceedings. The types of claim covered by Part 20 are set out in r 20.2:

(1) A Part 20 claim is any claim other than a claim by a claimant against a defendant and includes—

    (a) a counterclaim by a defendant against the claimant or against the claimant and some other person;

    (b) a claim by a defendant against any person (whether or not already a party) for contribution or indemnity or some other remedy; and

    (c) where a Part 20 claim has been made against a person who is not already a party, any claim made by that person against any other person (whether or not already a party).

(2) In this Part 'Part 20 claimant' means a person who makes a Part 20 claim.

Frequently, a defendant who has been sued by a claimant wants to make a claim against that person.

Example

A supplies goods to B.

B has paid 50% of the price, but the other 50% is unpaid.

B sues A for damages for breach of contract based on the allegation that the goods were not of satisfactory quality.

A defends the claim (on the basis that the goods were of satisfactory quality) and also counterclaims for the balance of 50% which is still outstanding.

This counterclaim is a Part 20 claim.

Another common scenario is where the defendant wishes to pass the blame, either in whole or in part, on to a third party. The defendant may be seeking a full indemnity from the third party, or a contribution towards any damages he has to pay the claimant. A claim for an indemnity often arises where there is a contractual relationship between the defendant and the third party, and the defendant alleges that the third party is obliged by the terms of the contract to indemnify him if he is found liable in respect of the claimant's claim against him. Sometimes a right to an indemnity may arise from statute or by implication of law. An example of a claim for an indemnity is where a consumer sues a retailer in respect of goods which he alleges are not of satisfactory quality, and the retailer alleges that there was an inherent defect in the goods and attempts to pass on liability to the manufacturer. The retailer will claim an indemnity from the manufacturer in respect of any sums that he is ordered to pay to the consumer.

A claim for a contribution often arises where there are joint wrong-doers, and the defendant claims that the third party is partly responsible for the harm that the claimant has suffered. An example of a claim for a contribution is where the claimant claims damages from the defendant as a result of a road traffic accident, and the defendant alleges that another driver was partly to blame for the accident. A defendant will then claim a contribution from the other driver towards the damages which he is ordered to pay to the claimant.

These types of claims are further examples of Part 20 claims.

7.2 Procedure

7.2.1 Counterclaims (r 20.4)

If a defendant wishes to make a counterclaim against a claimant, he should file particulars of the counterclaim with his defence. This should form one document, with the counterclaim following on from the defence.

If a defendant does this, he does not need permission from the court to make the counterclaim. However, if a defendant decides to make a counterclaim after he has already filed his defence, he will need the court's permission. The application for permission should be made on notice.

If he wishes to dispute the counterclaim, the claimant (who does not have the option of acknowledging service) has to file a defence to counterclaim within the usual 14-day period. This will usually be a reply (to the defence) and defence (to the counterclaim). Note also that the title to the proceedings then changes (see 7.2.8 and **Appendix D(3)**). If the claimant fails to file a defence to the counterclaim, the defendant may enter judgment in default on the counterclaim. Therefore, if the claimant requires more time to file a defence to the counterclaim, he should request an extension of time from the defendant. As already seen (see **5.4**), the parties can agree an extension of up to 28 days in addition to the initial 14-day period. — Part 15.5

A defence and Part 20 counterclaim, along with the reply and defence to that Part 20 counterclaim, can be found in the case study at **Appendix D(3) and (4)**. Note that in order to keep this case study simple and for illustrative purposes only, the potential liability of the Claimants' builders, if they did leave glass on the Claimants' driveway, is ignored.

7.2.2 Contribution or indemnity between co-defendants (r 20.6)

If one defendant wishes to seek a contribution or indemnity from another defendant, after filing his acknowledgement of service or defence, he may proceed with his claim against his fellow defendant by:

(a) filing a notice containing a statement of the nature and grounds of his claim; and

(b) serving the notice on the co-defendant.

No permission is required if he files and serves the notice with the defence or, if the defendant against whom the claim is made is added later, within 28 days of that defendant filing his defence. Permission is required to file and serve the notice at all other times.

7.2.3 Other Part 20 claims (r 20.7)

In other Part 20 claims, such as a claim against a third party, the defendant may make a Part 20 claim without the court's permission by issuing a Part 20 claim form before or at the same time as he files a defence. A copy of a Part 20 claim form appears at **Appendix A(6)**. Particulars of the Part 20 claim must be contained in or served with the claim form.

If a Part 20 claim is not issued at that time, the court's permission will be required. The application for permission can be made without notice, unless the court directs otherwise.

7.2.4 Applications for permission to make a Part 20 claim

When the court's permission is required, because the counterclaim or other type of Part 20 claim was not made at the time of filing the defence, then the application notice should be filed with a copy of the proposed Part 20 claim. The application for permission must be supported by evidence stating:

(a) the stage which the proceedings have reached;
(b) the nature of the claim to be made by the Part 20 claimant, or details of the question or issue which needs to be decided;
(c) a summary of the facts on which the Part 20 claim is based; and
(d) the name and address of the proposed Part 20 defendant.

If there has been any delay in making the application, the evidence must also explain the delay. Where possible, the applicant should provide a timetable of the proceedings to date.

Rule 20.9(2) sets out the matters the court takes into account in deciding whether to grant permission, and these include:

(a) the connection between the Part 20 claim and the claim made by the claimant against the defendant; some other party is claiming from him; and
(b) whether the Part 20 claimant is seeking substantially the same remedy which
(c) whether the Part 20 claimant wants the court to decide any question connected with the subject matter of the proceedings—
  (i) not only between existing parties but also between existing parties and a person not already a party; or
  (ii) against an existing party not only in a capacity in which he is already a party but also in some further capacity.

The court may permit the Part 20 claim to be made, dismiss it, or require it to be dealt with separately from the claim by the claimant against the defendant.

7.2.5 Service (r 20.8)

If the defendant did not need permission in order to make the Part 20 claim then:

(a) in the case of a counterclaim, he must serve it on every other party when he serves his defence;
(b) except for claims for contributions or indemnities from co-defendants, he must serve the Part 20 claim on the new party within 14 days of issue.

If a defendant had to make an application for permission to issue a Part 20 claim, the court will give directions as to service when granting permission to make the claim.

If a defendant serves a Part 20 claim form on a person who is not already a party (such as a third party), he must also serve:

(a) forms for defending or admitting or acknowledging service of the claim;
(b) copies of every statement of case which has already been served; and
(c) such other documents as the court may direct.

The defendant must also serve copies of the Part 20 claim form on all existing parties to the proceedings.

7.2.6 Judgment in default on Part 20 claims (r 20.11)

Special rules apply where the Part 20 claim is not a counterclaim or a claim by a defendant for an indemnity or contribution against a co-defendant. In other Part 20 cases, if the party against whom a Part 20 claim is made fails to acknowledge service or file a defence, then:

(a) he is deemed to admit the Part 20 claim and will be bound by any decision in the proceedings between the claimant and the defendant which affects the Part 20 claim; and
(b) if a default judgment is entered against the Part 20 claimant, he may also enter judgment in respect of the Part 20 claim by filing a request in the relevant practice forms. However, the Part 20 claimant will need permission to enter default judgment (which can be obtained without notice unless the court directs otherwise) if he has not satisfied any default judgment obtained against him; or he is seeking any remedy other than a contribution or an indemnity.

7.2.7 Directions (r 20.13)

If a defence is filed to a Part 20 claim (other than a counterclaim), the court will arrange a hearing to give directions as to the future conduct of the case. In giving directions, the court must ensure that, as far as practicable, the Part 20 claim and the main claim are managed together. At the directions hearing, the court may (see para 5.3 of PD 20):

(1) treat the hearing as a summary judgment hearing,
(2) order that the Part 20 proceedings be dismissed,
(3) give directions about the way any claim, question or issue set out in or arising from the Part 20 claim should be dealt with,
(4) give directions as to the part, if any, the Part 20 defendant will take at the trial of the claim,
(5) give directions about the extent to which the Part 20 defendant is to be bound by any judgment or decision to be made in the claim.

7.2.8 Title of the proceedings

Paragraphs 7.1–7.6 of PD 20 give information as to how parties to Part 20 claims should be described in the title of the proceedings. The title of every Part 20 claim should include both the full name of each party and his status in the proceedings (ie, claimant, defendant, Part 20 claimant, Part 20 defendant). For example, if a counterclaim is made against a claimant, then the claimant will thereafter be described as claimant/Part 20 defendant and the defendant will be described as defendant/Part 20 claimant. If there is more than one Part 20 claim then the parties should be described, for example, as Part 20 claimant (first claim) or Part 20 claimant (second claim).

7.3 Part 8 claims

7.3.1 Introduction

The Part 8 claim procedure may be used by claimants where the claimant is seeking the court's decision on a question which is unlikely to involve a substantial dispute of fact, or if a Rule or Practice Direction requires or permits the use of the Part 8 procedure.

PD 8 lists various types of claim for which the procedure may be used, which include:

(a) a claim by or against a child or patient which has been settled before the commencement of proceedings and the sole purpose of the proceedings is to obtain the approval of the court to the settlement; and

(b) a claim for a summary order for possession against named or unnamed defendants, occupying land or premises without the licence or consent of the person claiming possession.

7.3.2 Procedure

The claimant issues a Part 8 claim form (Form N208) which must state:

(a) the question the court is to decide or the remedy the claimant is seeking;
(b) any enactment under which the claim is being made;
(c) the representative capacity (eg, litigation friend) of any of the parties.

Instead of serving particulars of claim, the claimant must file and serve any written evidence, usually in the form of witness statements, with the claim form.

The defendant must then file and serve an acknowledgement of service not more than 14 days after service of the claim form. Again, instead of serving a defence, the defendant has to file and serve his written evidence with the acknowledgement of service.

If the defendant fails to file an acknowledgement of service, the claimant is unable to obtain a default judgment, and the defendant may still attend the hearing of the claim. However, the defendant may not take part in the hearing unless the court gives permission.

The court may give directions, including a hearing date, when the claim form is issued, or otherwise as soon as practicable after the defendant has acknowledged service or the time for acknowledging service has expired.

All Part 8 claims will be allocated to the multi-track.

Chapter 8

Case Management and Allocation of Cases

8.1	Introduction	89
8.2	The court's powers	89
8.3	Striking out and other sanctions	90
8.4	Relief from sanctions	92
8.5	Allocation	93
8.6	Allocation to a county court track	96
8.7	Costs estimates	105

8.1 Introduction

One of the key elements of the CPR 1998 is the notion of case management. As we saw in **Chapter 1**, r 1.4 imposes a duty on the court to manage cases actively.

Part 3 of CPR 1998 gives the court a wide range of case management powers. It should be noted that these powers are in addition to any powers given to the court by any other Rule or Practice Direction, or by any other enactment or any powers it may otherwise have.

8.2 The court's powers

Rule 3.1(2) sets out a non-exclusive list of the court's powers, which include instructions that the court can:

(a) extend or shorten the time for compliance with any Rule, Practice Direction or court order (even if an application for extension is made after the time for compliance has expired);
(b) adjourn or bring forward a hearing;
(c) require a party or a party's legal representative to attend the court;
(d) hold a hearing and receive evidence by telephone, or by using any other method of direct oral communication;
(e) direct that part of any proceedings (such as a counterclaim) be dealt with as separate proceedings;
(f) stay the whole or part of any proceedings or judgment either generally or until a specified date or event;
(g) consolidate proceedings;
(h) try two or more claims on the same occasion;
(i) direct a separate trial of any issue;
(j) decide the order in which issues are to be tried;
(k) exclude an issue from consideration;
(l) dismiss or give judgment on a claim after a decision on a preliminary issue;
(m) take any other step or make any other order for the purpose of managing the case and furthering the overriding objective.

The court may make any order subject to conditions and can specify the consequence of non-compliance. Such conditions can include a requirement to pay a sum of money into court. In particular, by r 3.1(5), the court may order a party to pay a sum of money into court if that party has, without good reason, failed to comply with a Rule, Practice Direction or a relevant pre-action protocol. In exercising its power under r 3.1(5), however, the court must have regard to both the amount in dispute and the costs which the parties have incurred or which they may incur.

By r 3.1(6A), the money paid into court stands as security for any sum payable by that party to any other party in the proceedings, subject to the right of a defendant under r 37.2 to treat all or part of any money paid into court as a Part 36 payment (see **12.4**).

The court can normally exercise any of its powers of case management on its own initiative. However, before doing so, it must give any person likely to be affected by the order an opportunity to make representations within a specified time and in a specified manner.

If the court proposes to hold a hearing before making an order on its own initiative, it must give the parties at least three days' notice of the hearing.

The court may make a provisional order without notice to the parties. However, any party may then apply to set aside, vary or stay the order within seven days of service of the order on that party (or such other period as the court may specify). The order must notify the parties of this right.

8.3 Striking out and other sanctions

Rule 3.4(2) gives the court a specific power to strike out all or part of a statement of case.

The court can exercise this power if it appears to the court:

(a) that the statement of case discloses no reasonable grounds for bringing or defending the claim;

(b) that the statement of case is an abuse of the court's process or is otherwise likely to obstruct the just disposal of the proceedings; or

(c) that there has been a failure to comply with a rule, practice direction or court order.

8.3.1 Inadequate statements of case

PD 3 gives examples of the types of statement of case which may fall to be struck out within (a) above. These include particulars of claim which set out no facts indicating what the claim is about – for example, 'money owed £5,000' – and particulars of claim which contain a coherent set of facts, but those facts, even if true, do not disclose any legally recognisable claim against the defendant. As far as defences are concerned, it gives examples of a defence which consists of a bare denial or otherwise sets out no coherent statement of facts, or a defence which, whilst coherent, would not, even if true, amount in law to a defence to the claim.

The following is an example of how a judge might use this power.

> Example
>
> A claimant issues proceedings for the recovery of a debt. A defence is filed which simply consists of a bare denial that the money is due. The defence has therefore failed to comply with r 16.5 of CPR 1998 (see **Chapter 6**). The judge, when looking at the case, may, as part of his case management powers under Part 3, make an order that unless the defendant files a full defence setting out his reasons for denying that the debt is owed within seven days of service of the order, the defence will be struck out.

Note that the court may, as in the example given, make such an order of its own volition or, alternatively, the claimant in such a case may make an application to the court for an order in similar terms.

If, in the example given above, the defendant did not comply with the order then the claimant would be able to obtain judgment simply by filing a request for judgment. As this was a debt claim, the claimant would be able to obtain judgment for the amount of the debt, together with interest and costs. If it had been a claim for an unspecified sum, the judgment would be for an amount to be decided by the court at a disposal hearing. Note that the request must state that the right to enter judgment has arisen because the court's order has not been obeyed.

Continuing with the above example, if judgment is entered in these circumstances against the defendant, the defendant can apply to the court under r 3.6 for the judgment to be set aside. Such an application must be made not more than 14 days after the judgment has been served. If the judgment had been entered incorrectly (eg, prematurely), the court must set aside the judgment. However, if the judgment was entered correctly, r 3.9 (relief from sanctions) applies.

8.3.2 Non-compliance with a Rule, Practice Direction or court order

The striking-out sanction is not confined to cases where the statement of case is defective. As stated in **8.3**, the court can also strike out a party's statement of case and enter judgment against him for 'failure to comply with a Rule, Practice Direction or court order'.

Striking out is, however, only one of a number of sanctions that the court can apply (see **8.3.3**). How does the court decide what is appropriate? The starting point for decisions on sanctions for default is *Biguzzi v Rank Leisure plc* [1999] 1 WLR 1926. This was an early post-CPR case where the Court of Appeal emphasised the importance of compliance with the CPR 1998 and court orders, but recognised that, whilst it would, on occasions, be appropriate to deal with non-compliance by striking out, there were less drastic but equally effective ways of dealing with default. In many cases, the use of these other powers would produce a more just result.

Given that there is a range of sanctions that the court can apply, when will it apply the ultimate sanction of striking out? In each case, the court will have to consider all the circumstances, and in particular the factors set out in r 3.9 (relief from sanctions: see **8.4**). However, the case law emphasises that the overriding objective of dealing with cases justly and the duty to ensure fairness will be a central consideration in the exercise of the court's discretion (see, eg, *Necati v Commissioner of Police for the Metropolis* [2001] LTL, 19 January). The court should also bear in mind the observations of the Court of Appeal in *Arrow Nominees Inc v Blackledge* [2000] 1 BCLC 709, that striking out a case purely on the basis of a breach of the rules or an order of the court may infringe Article 6(1) of the ECHR unless the breach itself meant that it may no longer be possible to have a fair trial.

None of the above should, however, be read as a reluctance on the part of the courts to strike out a party's statement of case in appropriate circumstances. Where delay or non-compliance means that it is no longer possible to have a fair trial (see *Habib Bank Ltd v Abbeypearl Ltd and Others* [2001] EWCA Civ 62, [2001] 1 All ER 185), or where the default is so bad that it amounts to an abuse of the court (see *UCB Corporate Services Ltd v Halifax* (SW) Ltd [1999] 1 Lloyd's Rep 154), strike out may be the appropriate response.

8.3.3 Sanctions other than striking out

8.3.3.1 Costs

A common sanction is to require the party in default to pay the other party's costs occasioned by the delay on an indemnity basis. The court will make a summary assessment of those costs at the time of the hearing and may order those costs to be paid immediately. The solicitor handling the case would then have to explain to his client why he had been ordered to pay those costs. See generally **9.3** and **13.3.3**.

Where the court forms the view that the fault lies not with the party himself but with his legal representative, the court may make a wasted costs order. This obliges the legal representative to pay costs incurred by a party as a result of any improper, unreasonable or negligent act or omission on the part of the legal representative (SCA 1981, s 51). Before making such an order, the court must allow the legal representative a reasonable opportunity to attend a hearing and give reasons why the order should not be granted.

8.3.3.2 Interest

Alternatively, the court may make orders affecting the interest payable on any damages subsequently awarded to the claimant. If the party at fault is the claimant, the court may reduce the amount of interest payable on his damages. If the party in default is the defendant, the interest payable on the claimant's damages at the end of the case may be increased.

8.3.3.3 Limiting the issues

The appropriate sanction may be to limit the issues that are allowed to proceed to trial. See, for example, *AXA Insurance Co Ltd v Swire Fraser* (2000) *The Times*, 19 January.

8.3.3.4 The unless order

The 'unless order' is not, strictly speaking, a sanction but rather a suspended sanction. The court makes an order that unless a party complies with a particular court order or rule within a specified time, his claim or defence will be struck out.

> **Example**
>
> Although an order of the court required the defendant, D, to serve his witness statements on his opponent, C, by 7 November 2004, D did not do so. In order to force D to comply, C applies for and obtains an unless order requiring D to serve the witness statements by a new deadline (usually seven or 14 days from the date of the unless order), failing which his defence will be struck out.

8.4 Relief from sanctions

A party's ability to obtain relief from the sanctions imposed by the court is dealt with by rr 3.8 and 3.9.

Where a party has failed to comply with a Rule, Practice Direction or court order, any sanction for failure to comply imposed by the Rule, Practice Direction or court order has effect unless the party in default applies for and obtains relief from the sanction. Note that where the sanction is the payment of costs, the party in default may obtain relief only by appealing against the order for costs.

Where a Rule, Practice Direction or court order requires a party to do something within a specified time, and specifies the consequence of failure to comply, can the time for doing the act in question be extended by agreement between the parties? No, says r 3.8(3).

Where a party applies for relief from any sanction for failure to comply with any Rule, Practice Direction or court order, the court will consider all the circumstances, including the following (r 3.9(1)):

(a) the interests of the administration of justice;
(b) whether the application for relief has been made promptly;
(c) whether the failure to comply was intentional;
(d) whether there is a good explanation for the failure;
(e) the extent to which the party in default has complied with other rules, practice directions, court orders and any relevant pre-action protocol;
(f) whether the failure to comply was caused by the party or his legal representative;
(g) whether the trial date or the likely trial date can still be met if relief is granted;
(h) the effect which the failure to comply had on each party; and
(i) the effect which the granting of relief would have on each party.

Although it is a relevant consideration on an application for relief whether the failure to comply is the failure of the party or his legal representative (r 3.9(1)(f)), the court will generally not be keen to spend time considering separately the conduct of the legal representatives from that which the party himself must be treated as knowing, encouraging or permitting (*Daryanani v Kumar & Co and Another* [2000] LTL, 15 March). After all, the other side will be equally affected whether the shortcomings are those of the party or his representatives. On the other hand, the issue of where the fault lies will be very relevant to the question of whether a wasted costs order is appropriate (see **8.3.3.1**).

An application for relief from sanctions must be supported by evidence.

Sanctions may also be imposed by the court for non-payment of any court fees. Where a party fails to pay a fee on filing an allocation questionnaire (see **8.5**), or a pre-trial checklist, listing questionnaire (see **8.6.2.6**), the court will serve notice requiring payment of the fee by a specified date. If the claimant does not pay the fee, or make an application for exemption from or remission of the fee within the specified time period, the claim will be struck out with costs.

8.5 Allocation

Part 26 of CPR 1998 deals with the preliminary stage of case management when cases are allocated to a particular track. This stage of case management arises where a defence has been filed.

Rule 26.2 provides for the automatic transfer of certain types of cases which are defended. If the claim is for a specified amount of money and the defendant is an individual, then, if the claim was not commenced in the defendant's 'home court', the court will transfer the proceedings to the defendant's home court when a defence is filed (see **5.5.1**). This Rule also applies in certain circumstances when a defendant admits the claim (see **5.5**), or on an application to set aside a default judgment (see **9.5.1**).

In most cases, the crucial preliminary case management issue is that of allocation.

Where the claim is defended then, on receipt of the defence, the court will serve each party with an allocation questionnaire. This is in Form N150 and a copy of this form appears in **Appendix A(12)**.

The questionnaire must be returned by the parties to the court by the date stipulated in the questionnaire, which must be at least 14 days after service of the questionnaire. The claimant must pay a fee when filing his allocation questionnaire. Where there are two or more defendants, the questionnaire will be sent when all the defendants have filed their defence, or (provided at least one defendant files a defence) when the period for filing the last defence has expired, whichever is the sooner. If the matter is going to be automatically transferred to the defendant's home court then the court at which the proceedings were commenced will serve an allocation questionnaire before the proceedings are transferred.

8.5.1 Completing the allocation questionnaire   p234

The allocation questionnaire (Form N150) is a key document in the progress of a case and must be completed carefully by each party and filed by the set date. The parties should consult one another and co-operate in completing the allocation questionnaire, although this must not delay its filing. Indeed, r 26.3(6A) provides that the date for filing cannot be varied by agreement between the parties.

The first question on the form (paragraph A) asks the parties if they wish there to be a one-month stay of proceedings so that they can attempt to settle the case. One of the key elements of the CPR 1998 is that parties should be given encouragement to settle their disputes without having to go to trial. If all the parties request a stay, the court will usually order a stay of one month. Alternatively, the court, of its own initiative, may order a stay if it considers it appropriate. If a stay is granted and the parties feel they require more time than the initial one month to try to reach a settlement, any of the parties may, by letter to the court, request an extension of time. This will usually be for a maximum of one month, although more than one extension of the stay may be granted. If a settlement is reached, the claimant must tell the court. If a settlement is not reached, the court will allocate the case and give directions in the usual way.

Paragraph B asks the parties whether there is any reason why the case needs to be heard at a particular court. If the claim has been issued in the Central Office of the Royal Courts of Justice (RCJ) then each party should state whether he considers the claim should be managed and tried at the RCJ and, if so, why.

As set out in para 2.6 of PD 29, claims suitable for trial in the RCJ include:

(1) professional negligence claims,
(2) Fatal Accident Act claims,
(3) fraud or undue influence claims,
(4) defamation claims,
(5) claims for malicious prosecution or false imprisonment,
(6) claims against the police,
(7) contentious probate claims.

If a claim does not fall within one of the above categories and has an estimated value of less than £50,000 then it will generally be transferred from the RCJ to a county court. If it has a value of more than £50,000, it will be transferred to a District Registry.

Paragraph C of the allocation questionnaire asks the parties to state whether they have complied with any relevant pre-action protocols and, if not, to explain the reasons why.

Paragraph D asks the parties if they have made an application to the court, including an application for summary judgment (see **Chapter 9**) or to join another party into the proceedings. Any such application should be made as soon as possible.

Paragraph D then asks the parties to name the witnesses of fact they will be calling and what facts they are witnesses to. If a party does not wish to, or cannot, 'name names' at this stage, he can simply indicate the number of witnesses he may call on a particular fact.

This paragraph also deals with expert evidence and asks the parties various questions about whether and, if so, how they wish to use expert evidence at the trial. See further **11.3**.

Lastly, paragraph D asks the parties which track they consider is most suitable for their case.

As already seen in **Chapter 1**, there are three tracks:

(a) small claims;
(b) fast track;
(c) multi-track.

The basic criteria for allocation to a particular track is the value of the claim which is in dispute, disregarding interest, costs and any question of contributory negligence. If there is a counterclaim or other Part 20 claim, in assessing the value the court will not usually aggregate the claims but generally will regard the largest of the claims as determining the financial value of the claim. So, for example, if the original claim was for £10,000, but there is a counterclaim valued at £25,000, the latter figure will usually be the relevant one for allocation purposes (PD 26, para 7.7).

The parties should indicate at paragraph E any dates on which their expert witnesses or any other essential witness will be unavailable to give evidence. It is advisable also to state why the experts are unavailable on those dates (*Matthews v Tarmac Bricks and Tiles Ltd* [1999] CPLR 463).

Paragraph E asks the parties to state how long they estimate the trial or final hearing will take.

In accordance with paragraph F, the parties should attach a list of directions that are appropriate for the management of the case and indicate whether or not these are agreed. For the fast track, the parties should consider the directions outlined in PD 28. For the multi-track the parties are referred to the Queen's Bench Division Practice Form, PF52. See further **Appendix A(20)**.

Paragraph G requires the parties to provide an estimate of costs incurred to date and the overall costs of the case. In fast track and multi-track cases, a detailed estimate is required (see **8.7**).

Paragraph H asks the parties whether they have attached documents to the questionnaire and whether they intend to make any applications in the immediate future. The parties are also asked whether there is any other information which could assist the judge in managing the case.

96 Civil Litigation

8.5.2 Failure to file an allocation questionnaire

If none of the parties has filed an allocation questionnaire within 14 days, the matter will be referred to a judge for directions and the judge will usually order that all claims, defences and counterclaims should be struck out unless an allocation questionnaire is filed within three days of service of the order.

If some, but not all, of the parties have filed an allocation questionnaire, the court will allocate the case on the basis of the information available or, if it does not have enough information, it will list an allocation hearing. Otherwise, the court will hold an allocation hearing on its own initiative only if it considers that it is necessary to do so. Where the court does order an allocation hearing to take place, the parties must be given at least seven days' notice of the hearing. Where an allocation hearing does take place then, by para 6.5 of PD 26, the legal representative who attends should, if possible, be the person responsible for the case and must, in any event, be familiar with the case, be able to provide the court with the information it is likely to need to take its decisions about allocation and case management, and have sufficient authority to deal with any issues that are likely to arise.

Paragraph 6.6 of PD 26 sets out the sanctions which the court will usually impose where a party has been in default in connection with the allocation procedure. In particular, where an allocation hearing takes place because a party has failed to file an allocation questionnaire or to provide further information which the court has ordered, the court will usually order that party to pay, on the indemnity basis (see **13.3.3**), the costs of any other party who has attended the hearing, summarily assess the amount of those costs (see **9.3**), and order them to be paid immediately or within a stated period. The court may order that if the party does not pay those costs within the time stated, that party's statement of case will be struck out.

These are very severe sanctions and emphasise the fact that the allocation stage is extremely important in the overall case management of the proceedings. It is therefore imperative that the parties return the allocation questionnaires, properly completed and within the requisite time period.

By para 2.4 of PD 26, if a court hearing takes place (eg, on an application for summary judgment under Part 24 – see **Chapter 9**) before the claim is allocated to a track, the court may, at that hearing, either dispense with the need for the parties to file allocation questionnaires, treat the hearing as an allocation hearing, make an order for allocation and give directions for case management, or fix a date for allocation questionnaires to be filed and give other directions. This is an example of the general principle in r 1.4(2)(i) that whenever a case comes for hearing before the court, the court should endeavour to carry out as much case management at that hearing as possible.

8.6 Allocation to a county court track

After the filing of the allocation questionnaires or any allocation hearing, or at the end of any stay of proceedings, a county court case will be allocated to one of the three tracks. Generally, the most important factor in allocation will be the financial value of the claim.

- Claims not exceeding £5,000 will normally be allocated to the small claims track.
- Claims between £5,000 and £15,000 will normally be allocated to the fast track.
- Claims exceeding £15,000 will normally be allocated to the multi-track.

Rule 26.8(1) sets out the factors to which the court must have regard, including:

(a) the financial value, if any, of the claim;
(b) the nature of the remedy sought;
(c) the likely complexity of the facts, law or evidence;
(d) the number of parties or likely parties;
(e) the value of any counterclaim or other Part 20 claim and the complexity of any matters relating to it;
(f) the amount of oral evidence which may be required;
(g) the importance of the claim to persons who are not parties to the proceedings;
(h) the views expressed by the parties; and
(i) the circumstances of the parties.

Furthermore, the fast track is the normal track for claims with a value exceeding £5,000, but not £15,000, only if the trial is likely to last for no longer than one day, oral expert evidence at trial will be limited to no more than one expert per party in relation to any expert field and there will be expert evidence in no more than two expert fields. For example, if the court at the allocation stage considered that the trial was likely to last two days then the court will usually allocate it to the multi-track.

In assessing the financial value of a claim, the court will disregard any amount not in dispute, any claim for interest, costs and any allegation of contributory negligence.

The court will not allocate proceedings to a particular track if the financial value of any claim in those proceedings exceeds the limit for that track, unless all the parties consent to the allocation of the claim to that track. So, for example, in a straightforward debt case worth £20,000, if one party asked for it to be allocated to the fast track rather than the multi-track, the court could not do this unless the other party consented (r 26.7(3)).

When it has allocated a claim to a track, the court will serve notification on every party. The court may subsequently re-allocate a claim to a different track either on the application of any party, or on its own initiative.

If a party is dissatisfied with the allocation to a particular track, PD 26, para 11 provides that he may:

(a) appeal, if the order was made at a hearing at which he was present or represented, or of which he was given due notice; or
(b) in any other case (eg, the case was allocated without an allocation hearing), apply to the court to re-allocate the claim.

8.6.1 Allocation to the small claims track (Part 27)

Part 27 of CPR 1998 deals with allocation to the small claims track. The small claims track is designed to provide a procedure whereby claims of not more than £5,000 in value can be dealt with quickly and at minimal cost to the parties.

Note that PD 26, para 8.1(1) provides that:

(a) The small claims track is intended to provide a proportionate procedure by which most straightforward claims with a financial value of not more than £5,000 can be decided, without the need for substantial pre-hearing preparation and the formalities of a traditional trial, and without incurring large legal costs.

(b) The procedures laid down in Part 27 for the preparation of the case and the conduct of the hearing are designed to make it possible for a litigant to conduct his own case without legal representation if he wishes.

(c) Cases generally suitable for the small claims track will include consumer disputes, accident claims, disputes about the ownership of goods, and most disputes between a landlord and tenant other than those for possession.

(d) A case involving a disputed allegation of dishonesty will not usually be suitable for the small claims track.

In most small claims cases, after allocation, the court will order standard directions and fix a date for the final hearing. The court does have the power to hold a preliminary hearing, but this will happen only in a very limited number of cases. Certain parts of the CPR 1998 do not apply to small claims, including Part 18 (Further Information), Part 31 (Disclosure and Inspection), Part 32 (Evidence), most of Part 35 (Experts and Assessors) and Part 36 (Offers to Settle and Payments into Court), unless the court orders otherwise. The intention is to make the procedure as simple as possible because, in most cases, solicitors will not be involved. The reason for this is that, under r 27.14, the costs which can be recovered by a successful party are extremely limited, and therefore it is usually uneconomic for solicitors to represent the parties in a case proceeding on the small claims track.

The standard directions which the court gives in small claims cases are set out in various forms which are in Appendix A to PD 27 of CPR 1998. The directions vary depending on the type of case, so that there are particular directions for claims arising out of holidays or weddings. The most simple forms of directions as set out in Form A are as follows:

1 Each party shall deliver to every other party and to the court office copies of all documents (including any expert's report) on which he intends to rely at the hearing no later than [ ] [14 days before the hearing].

2 The original documents shall be brought to the hearing.

3 [Notice of hearing date and time allowed.]

4 The court must be informed immediately if the case is settled by agreement before the hearing date.

The hearing itself will be informal and, if all parties agree, the court can deal with the claim without a hearing at all. In other words, a court could make a decision based on the statements of case and documents submitted rather than by hearing oral evidence.

As mentioned earlier, the costs which can be recovered in a small claims case are limited by r 27.14. Generally speaking, the only costs recoverable are the fixed costs attributable to issuing the claim, any court fees paid and sums to represent travelling expenses and loss of earnings. On those (rare) occasions where expert evidence is called, a limited amount may be recovered in respect of the expert's fees. The court does have power to award further costs if a party has behaved unreasonably.

It should be noted, however, that where a claim has been allocated to the small claims track but is subsequently reallocated to another track, the costs rules of the new track will apply from the date of reallocation.

8.6.2 Allocation to the fast track (Part 28)

When a case is allocated to the fast track, the court will give directions as to how the case is to proceed to trial. In most cases, the court will allocate the case to this track without a hearing and order standard directions.

8.6.2.1 Timetable of directions

Paragraph 3.12 of PD 28 (The Fast Track) sets out a typical timetable for case preparation of a case allocated to the fast track:

Disclosure [see **Chapter 10**]	4 weeks
Exchange of witness statements	10 weeks
Exchange of experts' reports	14 weeks
Court sends pre-trial checklist, listing questionnaires	20 weeks
Parties file listing questionnaires	22 weeks
Trial	30 weeks

These periods will run from the date of allocation.

The trial date will either be a fixed date or a 'trial period', not exceeding three weeks, within which the trial will take place. At this stage, the court is more likely to fix a 'trial period' rather than a fixed date for trial.

The parties may agree directions between themselves, but if they do so, the directions must be approved by the court (which will not necessarily accept them).

Fast track standard directions, dealing with disclosure, etc, are set out in the Appendix to PD 28. A copy appears at **Appendix A(19)**.

8.6.2.2 Varying directions (r 28.4)

Although the parties can vary certain directions by written agreement, for example for disclosure or exchange of witness statements, an application must be made to the court if a party wishes to vary the dates for:

(a) the return of the allocation questionnaire and the pre-trial checklist, listing questionnaire;
(b) the trial; or
(c) the trial period.

Furthermore, the parties cannot agree to vary any matter if the change would lead to an alteration of any of those dates. For example, it would not be possible to agree to delay the exchange of witness statements until after the date for the return of the pre-trial checklist, listing questionnaire, since this would inevitably lead to the need to alter the trial date or period.

PD 28 states that any party who wishes to have a direction varied should take steps to do so as soon as possible (para 4.2(1)). There is an assumption that if an application to vary directions is not made within 14 days of the service of the order then the parties are content that the directions were correct in the circumstances then existing (para 4.2(2)).

A party dissatisfied with a direction or other order given by the court should either:

(a) appeal, if the direction was given or the order was made at a hearing at which he was present or represented, or of which he had due notice; or

(b) in any other case, apply to the court to reconsider its decision. Such an application would be heard by the same judge or same level of judge as gave the original decision.

8.6.2.3 Variation by consent (PD 28, para 4.5)

Where the agreement to vary relates to an act which does not need the court's consent, the parties need not file their written agreement to vary (which will usually be recorded in correspondence). In any other case, the party must apply to the court for an order by consent. The parties must file a draft of the order sought and an agreed statement of the reasons why the variation is sought. The court may make an order in the agreed terms, or in other terms, without a hearing, but it may well direct that a hearing is to occur.

8.6.2.4 Failure to comply with directions (PD 28, para 5)

If a party fails to comply with a direction, any other party may apply for an order enforcing compliance and/or for a sanction to be imposed (see **8.3.2**).

The application should be made without delay.

PD 28 is quite clear that a failure to comply with directions will not normally lead to a postponement of the trial date (see para 5.4(1)). This will not be allowed unless the circumstances of the case are exceptional.

If it is practical, the court will exercise its powers in a manner that enables the case to come up for trial on the date or within the period previously set. In particular, the court will assess what steps each party should take to prepare the case for trial, direct that those steps be taken in the shortest possible time and impose a sanction for non-compliance. Such a sanction may, for example, deprive a party of the right to raise or contest an issue, or to rely on evidence to which the direction relates.

Further, if the court is of the view that one or more issues can be made ready for trial within the time fixed, the court may direct that the trial will proceed on the issues which are, or will then be, ready. The court can also order that no costs will be allowed for any later trial of the remaining issues, or that those costs will be paid by the party in default. If the court has no option but to postpone the trial, it will do so for the shortest possible time and will give directions for the taking of all outstanding necessary steps as rapidly as possible.

It is clear, therefore, that the trial date is sacrosanct and the parties should ensure that they are ready for trial on the due date.

8.6.2.5 Directions as to exchange of witness statements and exchange of expert reports

We shall look in detail at evidence in **Chapter 11**. However, the evidence of those witnesses on whom a party intends to rely at trial must be exchanged in the form of witness statements and experts' reports. The exchange should normally be simultaneous.

So far as expert evidence is concerned, the direction in relation to the evidence will say whether it gives permission for oral evidence, or written reports or both, and will usually name the experts concerned or the fields of expertise. The court will not make a direction giving permission for an expert to give oral evidence unless it believes that it is necessary in the interests of justice to do so. In fast track cases, therefore, the usual provision will be for expert evidence to be given by means of written reports and experts will not be allowed to give oral evidence at the trial. Furthermore, the court may order that a single joint expert be appointed, rather than allowing each party to appoint their own.

8.6.2.6 The pre-trial checklist, listing questionnaire (PD 28, para 6)

The purpose of the pre-trial checklist, listing questionnaire is to check that directions have been complied with so that the court can fix a date for the trial (or confirm the date if one has already been fixed).

The directions order will specify a date by which the parties should return the pre-trial checklist, listing questionnaire. This date will be not more than eight weeks before the trial date or the trial period. The pre-trial checklist, listing questionnaire will have been sent to the parties at least two weeks before it has to be filed at court. A copy of the pre-trial checklist, listing questionnaire (Form N170) appears at **Appendix A(18)**. Parties are encouraged to exchange copies of the pre-trial checklist, listing questionnaires before filing them with the court. A cost estimate (see **8.7**) should also be filed and served.

If no party files a pre-trial checklist, listing questionnaire, the court will normally direct that any claim, defence or counterclaim will be struck out unless a pre-trial checklist, listing questionnaire is filed within three days. If some, but not all, parties have filed a pre-trial checklist, listing questionnaire, the court will give its normal listing directions or may hold a hearing (see **8.6.2.7** below).

8.6.2.7 Listing directions (PD 28, para 7)

The court will confirm or fix the date, length and place of the trial. The court will normally give the parties at least three weeks' notice of the trial.

The parties should try to agree directions. The agreed directions should deal with, among other things:

(a) evidence;
(b) a trial timetable and time estimate;
(c) preparation of a trial bundle (see below).

The court may fix a listing hearing on three days' notice if either:

(a) a party has failed to file the pre-trial checklist, listing questionnaire; or
(b) a party has filed an incomplete pre-trial checklist, listing questionnaire; or
(c) a hearing is needed to decide what directions for trial are appropriate.

Prior to the trial, the parties should try to agree the contents of the trial bundle (see **13.1.3**) which will contain all documents needed for use at the trial. The standard directions require that this bundle should be lodged with the court by the claimant not more than seven days and not less than three days before the start of the trial. Included in the bundle should be a case summary, not exceeding 250 words, outlining the matters still in issue, and referring, where appropriate, to the relevant documents. This is designed to assist the judge in reading the papers before the trial. The case summary should be agreed by the parties if possible.

8.6.3 Allocation to the multi-track (Part 29)

8.6.3.1 Directions

Cases which have a value of more than £15,000 will, as we have seen, usually be allocated to the multi-track. The multi-track therefore includes an enormously wide range of cases, from the fairly straightforward to the most complex and weighty matters involving claims for millions of pounds and multi-party claims. Case management on the multi-track has to reflect this wide diversity of claims. In straightforward cases, the standard directions which we have already looked at in relation to the fast track may be perfectly adequate, but in more complex cases the court will need to adapt the directions to the particular needs of the case.

When the matter is allocated to the multi-track, the court will either:

(a) give directions for the management of the case and set a timetable for the steps to be taken between the giving of directions and the trial; or

(b) fix a case management conference, or a pre-trial review or both and give such directions relating to the management of the case as it sees fit.

The court will fix the trial date or the period in which the trial is to take place as soon as practicable. There is no deadline, however, of 30 weeks as we saw in the fast track (see **8.6.2.1**).

In a fairly straightforward case, the court may well give directions without holding a case management conference. If it does so, then, by para 4.10 of PD 29, its general approach will be:

(1) to give directions for the filing and service of any further information required to clarify either party's case,

(2) to direct standard disclosure between the parties,

(3) to direct the disclosure of witness statements by way of simultaneous exchange,

(4) to give directions for a single joint expert on any appropriate issue unless there is a good reason not to do so,

(5) ... to direct disclosure of experts' reports by way of simultaneous exchange on those issues where a single joint expert is not directed,

(6) if experts' reports are not agreed, to direct a discussion between experts ...

(7) to list a case management conference to take place after the date for compliance with the directions, and

(8) to specify a trial period.

Alternatively, the parties themselves may agree directions that deal with these matters and should be guided in the Queen's Bench Division by PF52. A copy appears at **Appendix A(20)**. Obviously these will still be subject to the approval of the court.

An order for directions can be found in the multi-track case study at **Appendix D(6)**.

8.6.3.2 The case management conference

In many multi-track cases, the court will hold a case management conference where it feels that more of a 'hands on' approach is needed.

At any case management conference, the court will (by para 5.1 to PD 29):

(1) review the steps which the parties have taken in the preparation of the case, and in particular their compliance with any directions that the court may have given,

(2) decide and give directions about the steps which are to be taken to secure the progress of the claim in accordance with the overriding objective, and

(3) ensure as far as it can that all agreements that can be reached between the parties about the matters in issue and the conduct of the claim are made and recorded.

8.6.3.3 Topics the court will consider at the case management conference

These are likely to include:

(a) Whether each party has clearly stated their case, for example has the claimant made clear the claim he is bringing and the amount he is claiming, so that the other party can understand the case he has to meet? As we saw in **Chapter 1**, r 1.4(2)(b) requires the court to identify the issues in dispute at an early stage.

(b) Whether any amendments are required to the claim form, a statement of case or any other document.

(c) What disclosure of documents, if any, is necessary.

(d) What expert evidence is reasonably required, and how and when that evidence should be obtained and disclosed.

(e) What factual evidence should be disclosed.

(f) What arrangements should be made about the giving or clarification of further information and the putting of questions to experts.

(g) Whether it will be just and will save costs to order a split trial (eg, on liability and quantum) or the trial of one of more preliminary issues.

In all cases, the court will set a timetable for the steps it decides are necessary to be taken.

The case management conference is an extremely important hearing and it is essential that the parties are properly prepared for it. The person who attends the hearing on behalf of a party should be someone who is personally involved in the conduct of the case, and who has the authority and information to deal with any matter which may reasonably be expected to be dealt with at such a hearing, including the fixing of the timetable, the identification of issues and matters of evidence.

The consequences of failing to send a properly prepared legal representative to a directions hearing were considered by the Court of Appeal in *Baron v Lovell* [1999] CPLR 630. The court will usually make an order imposing a sanction (see **8.3.2**) where the inadequacy of the person attending or his instructions leads to the adjournment of the conference. In this case, the court made a wasted costs order against the solicitor concerned personally.

In the case of *Tarajan Overseas Ltd v Kaye* (2002) *The Times*, 22 January, the Court of Appeal stressed that if a judge requires a party to attend a case management conference then the individual must know about the dispute and have authority to make decisions. The Court stressed that it would be 'objectionable ... to make an order that a party should attend with a view to putting pressure on the party concerned to drop the proceedings altogether'. The Court also considered what the judge should do if he had ADR in mind. Tuckey LJ said:

There is no doubt that the court, in exercising its case management powers, can order the attendance of a party: CPR 1998, r 3.1(2)(c). One good reason why this may be appropriate is to facilitate settlement if the court takes the view that the case before it is one which the parties should strive to settle. There would be nothing wrong either in requiring the attendance of a party with a view to making an ADR order which, of course, is not coercive but simply suspends the proceedings to enable the parties to explore (if they agree) the prospect of settlement with the assistance of an experienced mediator. Such an order is one which could be made however, and usually is made, without the attendance of any party.

PD 29 sets out, at para 5.6, guidelines as to how parties should prepare for the case management conference. They should:

(1) ensure that all documents that the court is likely to ask to see (including witness statements and experts' reports) are brought to the hearing,
(2) consider whether the parties should attend,
(3) consider whether a case summary will be useful, and
(4) consider what orders each wishes to be made and give notice of them to the other parties.

A case summary should set out a brief chronology of the claim, the issues of fact which are agreed or in dispute and the evidence needed to decide them. It should not normally exceed 500 words and should be prepared by the claimant and agreed with the other party, if possible. Its purpose is to assist the judge at the case management conference, in particular to determine what issues should be tried and what evidence will be required to do so. Whilst the rule makes it clear that a case summary is not a mandatory requirement, they are, in practice, routinely used.

A case summary for use at a case management conference can be found in the multi-track case study at **Appendix D(5)**. p313.

Any party who wishes to apply for an order which is not usually made at a case management conference should issue and serve his application in plenty of time if he knows that the application will be opposed; and he should warn the court if the time allowed for the case management conference is likely to be insufficient for his application to be heard.

8.6.3.4 Variation of directions (r 29.5)

A party must apply to the court if he wishes to vary the date which the court has fixed for:

(a) a case management conference;
(b) a pre-trial review;
(c) the return of a pre-trial checklist, listing questionnaire;
(d) the trial; or
(e) the trial period.

Just like the fast track, any date set by the court or the rules for doing any act may not be changed by the parties if the change would make it necessary to vary any of the dates mentioned above.

A party who wishes to vary a direction (eg, because of a change of circumstances) must apply as soon as possible. There is an assumption that if an application to vary directions was not made within 14 days of service of the directions order, the parties were content that the directions ordered were correct in the circumstances then existing.

A party who is dissatisfied with the direction may appeal, but if he was not notified of the hearing or was not present when it was made, he must apply for the court to reconsider, and the court will give all parties three days' notice of the hearing.

8.6.3.5 Non-compliance with directions (PD 29, para 7)

If a party fails to comply with a direction, any other party may apply for an order for compliance and/or for the imposition of a sanction. Any delay in making the application will be taken into account by the court.

As we saw in the fast track, the trial date is sacrosanct. The court will not allow failure to comply with directions to lead to the postponement of the trial unless the circumstances are exceptional.

8.6.3.6 The pre-trial checklist, listing questionnaire (PD 29, para 8)

The date for filing the completed pre-trial checklist, listing questionnaire will be not later than eight weeks before the trial date or the start of the trial period and the checklists will have been served on the parties at least 14 days before that date. The parties are encouraged to exchange copies of the checklists before they file them. If none of the parties files a checklist, the court will usually order that the claim, the defence and any counterclaim will be struck out unless any party files a checklist within three days of service of the order.

If only some of the parties have filed a checklist questionnaire, the court will usually fix a listing hearing and give directions.

On receipt of the pre-trial checklists, listing questionnaires, the court may decide that it is necessary to hold a pre-trial review (or may decide to cancel one already listed). The court must give the parties at least seven days' notice of its decision. A pre-trial review will usually occur in any heavy case, particularly when the trial is likely to last longer than 10 days.

As soon as practicable after:

(a) each party has filed a completed pre-trial checklist, listing questionnaire;

(b) the court has held a listing hearing; or

(c) the court has held a pre-trial review,

the court will:

(a) set a timetable for the trial, unless a timetable has already been fixed or the court considers that it will be inappropriate to do so; and

(b) fix the date for the trial or the week within which the trial is to begin (or, if it has already done so, confirm that date).

As with the fast track, the court will also order, on listing, that a trial bundle of documents be prepared.

8.7 Costs estimates

In fast track and multi-track cases, the parties must file and serve with their allocation and pre-trial checklist, listing questionnaires an estimate of costs. These are designed to keep the parties informed about their potential liability in respect of costs and in order to assist the court to decide what, if any, order to make about costs and about case management. Under the Practice Direction – Costs an 'estimate of costs' means an estimate of base costs (including disbursements) already incurred; and an estimate of base costs (including disbursements) to be incurred, which a party intends to seek to recover from any other party under an order for costs if he is successful in the case. Base costs are those which do not include any additional liability (ie, the success fee under a conditional fee agreement and/or the amount of an after the event insurance premium). A party who intends to recover an additional liability need not, and should not, reveal the amount of that liability in the estimate.

The court may direct that an estimate should be prepared in such a way as to demonstrate the likely effects of giving or not giving a particular case management direction which the court is considering, for example a direction for a split trial or for the trial of a preliminary issue.

An estimate of base costs should be substantially in the form illustrated in Precedent H in the Schedule of Costs Precedents annexed to the Practice Direction (a copy of which appears at **Appendix A(13)**).

On an assessment of the costs of a party the court may have regard to any estimate previously filed by that party, or by any other party in the same proceedings. Such an estimate may be taken into account as a factor among others, when assessing the reasonableness of any costs claimed: see PD – Costs (Parts 43 to 48), para 6.6, and *Leigh v Michelin Tyres plc* [2003] EWCA Civ 1766 (discussed at **13.3.2**).

Chapter 9
Applications to the Court

9.1	Introduction	107
9.2	Applications generally	107
9.3	Interim costs	110
9.4	Appeals against an interim order	112
9.5	Particular types of application	113
9.6	Interim remedies	118
9.7	Interim payments	119
9.8	Security for costs	122
9.9	Human rights	122

9.1 Introduction

In this chapter, we shall consider the way in which a party to the case can make an application to the court. We are considering applications made after the issue of proceedings and before the trial. These are known as interim applications.

Part 23 of CPR 1998 sets out the general rules governing applications to the court. These rules are subject to any express provisions which may apply to specific types of application.

We have already considered some possibilities, for example pre-action disclosure (see **3.9**); permission to serve a claim form out of the jurisdiction (see **4.5.6.2**); challenging the court's jurisdiction (see **5.3**); extension of time to serve a claim form or defence (see **4.6** and **5.4** respectively); permission to amend a statement of case (see **6.6.2**); requiring a reply to a Part 18 request (see **6.7.4**); permission to make a Part 20 claim (see **7.2.4**); and relief from a sanction (see **8.4**).

9.2 Applications generally

An application to the court is made by an application notice. Form N244 (see **Appendix A(16)**) should be used.

The party who is making the application is, not surprisingly, known as the applicant, and the person against whom the order is sought is known as the respondent.

9.2.1 Where to make the application

By r 23.2, the application must be made to the court where the claim has been started, or the court to where the claim has been transferred. If the claim has already been listed for trial, it must be made to the court where the trial is to take place. Most applications will be heard by a master in the RCJ or, a district judge in the county court or a High Court District Registry.

9.2.2 Content of the application notice

By r 23.6, an application notice must state what order the applicant is seeking and, briefly, why the applicant is seeking the order.

108 Civil Litigation

If the applicant wishes to rely on matters set out in the application notice as evidence at the hearing, then it must be verified by a statement of truth. This appears at the foot of Part C of Form N244.

9.2.3 Draft order

PD 23 states that, except in the most simple application, the applicant should attach a draft of the order sought. If the case is proceeding in the RCJ and the order is unusually long or complex, it should also be supplied on disk for use by the court office.

9.2.4 Evidence in support of the application

As we shall see at **9.2.9** and **9.6**, certain of the rules set out a specific requirement for evidence in support of a particular application. Apart from that, PD 23 states, at para 9.1, that where there is no specific requirement to provide evidence, it should be borne in mind that, as a practical matter, the court will often need to be satisfied by evidence of the facts that are relied on in support of, or for opposing, the application. The evidence will usually take the form of a witness statement, although a party may also rely on the contents of a statement of case or the application notice itself as evidence, provided it is verified by a statement of truth.

Affidavits (see **11.7**) may be used, but the extra cost of preparing an affidavit over and above that of a witness statement may be disallowed since affidavits are no longer required, except for a limited number of specific applications.

Any evidence relied upon must be filed at the court as well as served on the parties with the application notice. Any evidence in response must be served as soon as possible.

9.2.5 Service of the application notice

Unless the rules relating to a particular type of application specify another time-limit, the application notice must be served at least three clear days before the court is to deal with the application. The court may allow a shorter period of notice if this is appropriate in the circumstances. When served, the application notice must be accompanied by a copy of any supporting written evidence and a copy of any draft order.

9.2.6 Consent orders

If the parties have reached agreement on the order they wish the court to make, they can apply for an order to be made by consent without the need for attendance by the parties. The parties must ensure that they provide the court with any material it needs to be satisfied that it is appropriate to make the order, and usually a letter will suffice.

9.2.7 Orders made without notice

Most applications have to be made on notice (ie, served on the other party so that he can respond and object to the application if he wishes to do so). However, in certain cases it is possible for an application to be made without notice being given to the other side. Paragraph 3 of PD 23 indicates that this may be done in the following circumstances:

(a) where there is exceptional urgency;
(b) where the overriding objective is best furthered by doing so;
(c) by consent of all parties;

(d) with the permission of court;

(e) where a date for a hearing has been fixed and the party wishes to make an application at that hearing but he does not have sufficient time to serve an application notice, he should inform the other party and the court of the intended application as soon as possible and make the application orally at the hearing;

(f) where a court order, Rule or Practice Direction permits.

The most common examples are freezing injunctions and search orders (see **9.6**).

When an order is made on an application without notice to the respondent, a copy of the order must be served on the respondent, together with a copy of the application notice and the supporting evidence. The order must contain a statement of the right of the respondent to make an application to set aside or vary the order. The respondent may then apply to set aside or vary the order within seven days of service of the order on him.

9.2.8 Telephone hearings and video conferencing

PD 23, para 6 sets out provisions which enable the court to deal with applications by way of a telephone hearing. This will normally be by way of a conference call system, whereby all the parties can speak together at the same time. All parties must consent for the hearing to be dealt with in this way. This method of dealing with applications is most useful where one or more of the parties' solicitors are located a considerable distance from the court and it is not feasible to instruct local agents to attend on their behalf.

Where the parties wish to use video conferencing facilities, and those facilities are available in the relevant court, they should apply to the master or district judge for directions.

9.2.9 Preparing supporting evidence

Most solicitors will prepare a witness statement in support of, or in opposition to, an interim application. Whilst the Rule under which the application is made may dictate some of the content of that statement, the following general questions must always be answered:

(a) Who should make the statement? It should be the person best able to address the relevant points from personal knowledge. For example, on an application for pre-action disclosure which relies on ground (d)(iii) of r 31.16(3), the person who can quantify and justify the savings in costs will probably be best placed to make the witness statement.

(b) What needs to be included? List the important points to be brought to the court's attention. Include all the relevant detailed evidence relied on and anticipate your opponent's case, where appropriate.

(c) How should the statement appear? Divide up the important points into numbered paragraphs. Set out the relevant information in chronological order.

(d) What about hearsay evidence (see **11.9**)? When relying on this, state the source of the information. A witness statement must indicate which of the contents derive from the maker's own knowledge and which are either matters of information he has received from a third party or form the basis of his own belief. The source of any matters of information or belief must also be given. For example, a witness may state, 'I am advised by Laura Smith who inspected the machinery immediately after it broke down that ...'.

(e) What is the key to possible success? Focus on detail and exhibit any relevant supporting documents. A witness statement containing highly relevant details and made by a person with first-hand knowledge of the facts will be very persuasive indeed. If any of the facts arise from or are supported by documents, these should be exhibited.

Should points of law be included? Legal arguments are best left to the advocates at the hearing. However, your client may have to express a legal opinion. For example, when applying for summary judgment (see **9.5.2**) there must be a statement of belief that on the evidence the respondent has no real prospect of succeeding and there is no other compelling reason for a trial.

9.3 Interim costs

The costs of the application are at the discretion of the master or district judge who hears the application. The costs will include preparation of the application or opposition to it, as well as attendance at the hearing.

PD 44 sets out, at para 8.5, the different orders which are usually made and the effect of those orders. They are as follows:

Term	Effect
Costs Costs in any event	The party in whose favour the order is made is entitled to the costs in respect of the part of the proceedings to which the order relates, whatever other costs orders are made in the proceedings.
Costs in the case Costs in the application	The party in whose favour the court makes an order for costs at the end of the proceedings is entitled to his costs of the part of the proceedings to which the order relates.
Costs reserved	The decision about costs is deferred to a later occasion, but if no later order is made the costs will be costs in the case.
Claimant's/defendant's costs in case/application	If the party in whose favour the costs order is made is awarded costs at the end of the proceedings, that party is entitled to his costs of the part of the proceedings to which the order relates. If any other party is awarded costs at the end of the proceedings, the party in whose favour the final costs order is made is not liable to pay the costs of any other party in respect of the part of the proceedings to which the order relates.

Term	Effect
Costs thrown away	Where, for example, a judgment or order is set aside, the party in whose favour the costs order is made is entitled to the costs which have been incurred as a consequence. This includes the costs of: (a) preparing for and attending any hearing at which the judgment or order which has been set aside was made; (b) preparing for and attending any hearing to set aside the judgment or order in question; (c) preparing for and attending any hearing at which the court orders the proceedings or the part in question to be adjourned; (d) any steps taken to enforce a judgment or order which has subsequently been set aside.
Costs of and caused by	Where, for example, the court makes this order on an application to amend a statement of case, the party in whose favour the costs order is made is entitled to the costs of preparing for and attending the application and the costs of any consequential amendment to his own statement of case.
Costs here and below	The party in whose favour the costs order is made is entitled not only to his costs in respect of the proceedings in which the court makes the order, but also to his costs of the proceedings in any lower court. In the case of an appeal from a Divisional Court the party is not entitled to any costs incurred in any court below the Divisional Court.
No order as to costs Each party to pay his own costs	Each party is to bear his own costs of the part of the proceedings to which the order relates whatever costs order the court makes at the end of the proceedings.

If the order made at the hearing makes no mention of costs, none are payable in respect of that application.

If the court makes an order for costs in favour of one of the parties to the application (eg, 'claimant's costs', or 'claimant's costs thrown away' or 'defendant's costs of and caused by') then the court will make a summary assessment of costs there and then. Any such costs are payable within 14 days, unless the court orders otherwise (r 44.8). In order for the court to be able to assess the costs at the end of the application, the parties are required, not less than 24 hours prior to the hearing, to file and serve a statement of costs. This provides a breakdown of the costs incurred in relation to the application. A model form of the statement of costs (Form N260) appears at **Appendix A(17)**. If a party fails to comply with this requirement without reasonable excuse, this will be taken into account by the court in deciding what costs order to make. To help the judge carry out a summary assessment, he will take into account the guideline rates for solicitors and counsel: see **Appendix B(2)**.

On a few occasions, the court may award fixed costs rather than making one of the orders set out above (see, eg, **9.5.2**). Part 45 sets out the occasions on which fixed costs may be granted and specifies the amount awarded to the paying party. Where fixed costs are granted there is, of course, no need for a summary assessment.

9.3.1 Conditional fee agreements and the summary assessment of interim application costs

This is dealt with at para 14 of PD 44. The fact that one (or even both) of the parties has entered into a conditional fee agreement (a CFA) will not prevent the costs of the interim application from being summarily assessed if the court has awarded costs in favour of a party.

9.3.1.1 Receiving party CFA funded

Where the receiving party (the party whose costs are to be paid) is CFA funded, the court cannot order payment to be made unless satisfied that the receiving party is immediately liable to his solicitor for the costs of the application under the terms of the CFA. To order otherwise would be contrary to the indemnity principle (see **13.3**). Accordingly, the form of agreement recommended by The Law Society entitles solicitors to payment of costs on all successful interim applications, whatever the outcome of the proceedings at trial.

It should be noted that where the receiving party is on a CFA, the court's summary assessment can deal only with the base costs. The question of whether the paying party should be responsible for the success fee on those costs (and if so to what extent) will not be considered by the court until the conclusion of the case.

9.3.1.2 Paying party CFA funded

A party who is CFA funded may not be in a position to pay interim costs if ordered to do so. Although many CFA clients have the benefit of after-the-event insurance, it is common for such policies not to cover the payment of interim costs awarded to the other side. The court may, therefore, decide to defer the payment of the interim costs until the end of the proceedings. In considering whether to do so, the court should take into account the unfairness of this on the receiving party.

The topic of CFAs is dealt with at **2.5.2**.

9.4 Appeals against an interim order

The procedure for appeals is set out in Part 52. An appeal from a decision of a district judge in a county court is made to a circuit judge, and from a master or district judge in the High Court to a High Court judge.

Permission to appeal is required and will be granted only if the appeal has a real prospect of success, or there is some other compelling reason for the appeal to be heard (r 52.3(6)). Permission may be sought either at the original hearing, or from the appeal court within 14 days of the original decision. If permission is sought at the original hearing but refused, a further application for permission may be made to the appeal judge.

The appeal hearing will usually be limited to a review of the district judge's or master's original decision and no new evidence will be admitted unless the court orders otherwise (r 52.11). The appeal will be allowed if the original decision was either wrong or unjust because of a serious procedural or other irregularity. If the appeal is allowed, the appeal judge may make a variety of orders (eg, setting aside or varying the original order and ordering a re-hearing).

9.5 Particular types of application

9.5.1 Applications to set aside a default judgment (Part 13)

9.5.1.1 The mandatory grounds

Under r 13.2, the court is obliged to set aside a default judgment that was wrongly entered before the defendant's deadline for filing an acknowledgement of service or a defence (whichever is applicable) expired. The court is also obliged to set aside a default judgment entered after the claim was paid in full.

9.5.1.2 The discretionary grounds

Rule 13.3(1) gives the court the power to set aside or vary a default judgment where:

(a) the defendant has a real prospect of successfully defending the claim; or
(b) it appears to the court that there is some other good reason why—
 (i) the judgment should be set aside or varied; or
 (ii) the defendant should be allowed to defend the claim.

The court will take account of the promptness of the defendant's application and it is therefore essential that the defendant should issue the application as soon as he becomes aware of the default judgment. The application to the court must be on notice and must be supported by evidence. Although the rule states that only one of the grounds needs to be satisfied, in practice the defendant will usually have to show a defence with a real prospect of success at trial in order to persuade the court to exercise its discretion.

Example 1

A issues a claim form (with particulars of claim) against B, claiming the price of goods sold and delivered to B. B receives the claim form but forgets to deal with it and A is able to enter default judgment.

B then instructs solicitors. They immediately apply to set the default judgment aside. The evidence in support of the application is a witness statement from B in which he seeks to show that the goods were not of satisfactory quality.

If B can show that he has a real prospect of successfully defending the claim, the default judgment will be set aside. He may, however, have to pay the costs of the application, which will be summarily assessed, as he was to blame for the default judgment being entered. If the evidence in support of his application was very strong, he might argue that the claimant should have consented to the application as it was clear that the court would set aside the default judgment. In that situation, he may not have to pay the costs of the application.

Example 2

Mr and Mrs X buy a dining room table and chairs from Y Ltd. There is a dispute about the quality of the wood used in the construction of the furniture. Mr and Mrs X refuse to pay Y Ltd. Whilst they are away on holiday Y Ltd issue proceedings for the price of the furniture, serve the proceedings and enter default judgment when no acknowledgement or defence is filed within the prescribed time. On their return from holiday Mr and Mrs X open their post and discover the proceedings and default judgment.

Mr and Mrs X have a good reason for asking the court to set aside the default judgment as they were away on holiday when the proceedings were served and default judgment entered. Hence they were unable to respond to the proceedings through no fault of their own. They should immediately ask Y Ltd to agree to the default judgment being set aside, or otherwise make an application to the court. Any application should be supported by evidence to show that they were away on holiday at the material times and that they have acted promptly in making the application once they became aware of the default judgment. Any delay should be explained. They should also state the basis of the defence to the claim and the evidence they have to support that to show that there is a defence with a real prospect of success at trial. As neither party can be said to be at fault in these circumstances it is likely that the court will set aside the default judgment and make an order for costs in the case.

If the original claim was for a specified amount of money and the defendant is an individual then, if the judgment was not entered in the defendant's home court, the application to set aside the default judgment will be transferred to the defendant's home court (see **8.5**).

9.5.1.3 The claimant's duty (r 13.5)

If the claimant has good reason to believe that the defendant did not receive the particulars of claim before the claimant entered judgment, the claimant is under a duty to set aside the default judgment himself or apply to the court for directions. This can normally be done by letter rather than making an on notice application to the court. No steps should be taken to enforce the judgment until the court has considered the matter.

9.5.2 Summary judgment (Part 24)

We saw in the previous chapter that the court has the power, under its case management powers contained in Part 3 of CPR 1998, to strike out a statement of case if it discloses no reasonable grounds for bringing or defending the claim. The court has similar powers under Part 24 of CPR 1998, which deals with applications for summary judgment. The aim behind the Part 24 procedure is to enable a claimant or defendant to obtain judgment at an early stage without the time and expense involved in proceeding to a full trial.

9.5.2.1 Grounds for the application

Rule 24.2 states that:

The court may give summary judgment against a claimant or defendant on the whole of the claim or on a particular issue if—
(a) it considers that—
    (i) that claimant has no real prospect of succeeding on the claim or issue; or
    (ii) that defendant has no real prospect of successfully defending the claim or issue; and
(b) there is no other compelling reason why the case or issue should be disposed of at trial.

Therefore, either party can make an application for summary judgment (or indeed the court could list the case for a Part 24 hearing on its own initiative). According to para 1.3 of PD 24, the application may be based on:

(1) a point of law (including a question of construction of a document),
(2) the evidence which can reasonably be expected to be available at trial or the lack of it, or
(3) a combination of these.

The court can give summary judgment against a claimant in any type of proceedings and against the defendant in most types of proceedings, with some exceptions which are beyond the scope of this book.

What cases are not suitable for summary judgment? In *Swain v Hillman* [2001] 1 All ER 91, Lord Woolf MR said:

> Useful though the power is under Part 24, it is important that it is kept to its proper role. It is not meant to dispense with the need for a trial where there are issues which should be investigated at the trial ... the proper disposal of an issue under Part 24 does not involve the judge conducting a mini trial, that is not the object of the provisions; it is to enable cases, where there is no real prospect of success either way, to be disposed of summarily.

What is a compelling reason for the purposes of r 24.2(b)? In *Secretary of State for Health v Norton Healthcare Ltd and Others* [2004] LTL, 25 February, the claimants alleged that the defendants had operated an unlawful price fixing cartel or under an anti-competition arrangement in supplying a particular drug. The seventh defendant applied for summary judgment on the basis that the claim against it was legally and factually flawed. The application was dismissed. The court held that the public interest in controlling pharmaceutical costs and the investigation of a possible cartel was a compelling reason for a trial. In addition, the claim involved allegations of conspiracy between the parties and those accusations could only be properly examined at trial.

In *Kirschel & Others v Fladgate Fielder (a firm)* [2000] LTL, 22 December, the court refused applications for summary judgment by both parties for the compelling reason that their contrary submissions raised difficult questions of law, two of which did not appear to be covered by authority and so ought to be tried.

A compelling reason for a trial may be to allow the respondent more time to investigate the matter, particularly if he has a good reason for being unable so far to get in touch with a material witness. Alternatively, the respondent may argue that the claim or defence is of such a highly complicated and/or technical nature that it can only be properly understood if the usual procedural steps are taken and the evidence then given at a full trial subject to cross-examination (see *Three Rivers District Council and Others v Governor and Company of the Bank of England (No 3 bis)* [2001] 2 All ER 513, HL).

9.5.2.2 Procedure

The claimant may not apply for summary judgment until the defendant has filed an acknowledgement of service or a defence, unless the court gives permission. The reason for this is that if the defendant fails to file an acknowledgement of service or defence, the claimant can enter a default judgment without having to make an application for summary judgment. If the claimant applies for summary judgment before the defendant has filed a defence, the defendant need not file a defence until after the application for summary judgment has been heard.

The defendant can apply for summary judgment at any time. Irrespective of who makes the application, it should be made without delay and usually prior to, or at the time of, filing of allocation questionnaires (see **8.5.1**).

The respondent to the application must be given at least 14 days' notice of the date fixed for the hearing. A respondent who wishes to rely on written evidence must file and serve this at least seven days before the hearing. An applicant who wishes to rely on written evidence in reply to the respondent's submissions must file and serve it at least three days before the hearing.

The application notice itself must state that it is an application for summary judgment and the application notice or the evidence contained or referred to in it, or served with it, must, as stated in para 2(3) of PD 24:

(a) identify concisely any point of law or provision in a document on which the applicant relies, and/or

(b) state that it is made because the applicant believes that on the evidence the respondent has no real prospect of succeeding on the claim or issue, or (as the case may be) of successfully defending the claim or issue to which the application relates,

and and in either case state that the applicant knows of no other reason why the disposal of the claim or issue should await trial.

If the application notice does not contain all the applicant's evidence, it should identify the written evidence (such as a witness statement or statement of case) the applicant intends to rely on. The application notice should also inform the respondent of his right to file and serve written evidence in reply.

9.5.2.3 Orders the court may make on an application for summary judgment

On a Part 24 application the court may order:

(1) judgment on the claim,
(2) the striking out or dismissal of the claim,
(3) the dismissal of the application,
(4) a conditional order.

(para 5.1 of PD 24)

To grant summary judgment, the court will have to come to the conclusion that the claim or defence has no real prospects of succeeding at trial (and there is no other compelling reason for a trial). For example, in the Court of Appeal case of *Peskin v Anderson and Others* [2001] 1 BCLC 372, Mummery LJ described the claimant's case as a 'flight of fancy [that] does not, on the pleaded facts, even make it to the take off point and should be grounded immediately under CPR Part 24'. Simon Brown LJ added that the claim was 'worthless and must fail'. So, summary judgment should be granted where the claim, etc is 'merely fanciful, imaginary, unreal or intrinsically unrealistic' (*per* Otton LJ in *Sinclair v Chief Constable of West Yorkshire and Another* [2000] LTL, 12 December).

When should the application be dismissed? Pill LJ in *Hussain v Woods and Another* [2001] Lloyd's Rep PN 134 suggested this was appropriate where 'an apparently credible witness says one thing and another apparently credible witness says the opposite, and there is not conclusive circumstantial evidence pointing one way or the other'.

A conditional order is an order which requires a party:

(1) to pay a sum of money into court, or
(2) to take a specified step in relation to his claim or defence, as the case may be,
and provides that that party's claim will be dismissed or his statement of case will be struck out if he does not comply.

(para 5.2 of PD 24)

The court is likely to make a conditional order where it appears to the court possible that a claim or defence may succeed but improbable that it will do so. See PD 24, para 4. This is a situation where the statement of case might be described as 'shadowy and unsatisfactory' (*per* Sir Richard Scott V-C in *Bates v Microstar Ltd*

[2000] LTL, 4 July). For example, where a claimant applies for summary judgment in a debt case, if the court is not satisfied that the defence has a 'real prospect' of success, but none the less considers that success is possible (although improbable), the court may allow the defendant to continue to defend the claim on the condition that he pays the amount of the claim into court or such amount as he can reasonably afford (see **9.9.2**). The money would remain in court pending the final outcome of the case. If the defendant fails to make the payment into court then the defence would be dismissed and judgment entered for the claimant.

But what financial condition will the judge impose on a claimant where the claim may possibly succeed although it probably will not do so at trial? In the case of *Sweetman v Shepherd* (2000) *The Times*, 29 March, the Court of Appeal indicated that in the absence of financial constraints it would expect a claimant to pay into court a sum of about 75% to 80% of those costs which the defendant could reasonably expect to recover at the end of the claim if it were fully contested. The defendant should produce an estimate of those costs (see **8.6**).

9.5.2.4 Directions

When the court determines a summary judgment application it may:

(a) give directions as to the filing and serving of a defence, if one has not already been filed; and

(b) give further directions.

So, where the court dismisses the application or makes an order that does not completely dispose of the claim, the court may well give case management directions as to the future conduct of the case.

9.5.2.5 Costs

The costs order made at the conclusion of the hearing will depend on the type of claim and the outcome of the application. Where a claimant is successful in obtaining summary judgment for a specified sum, the court will usually award fixed costs (see Part 45). The fixed costs are £175 if the judgment exceeds £25 but does not exceed £5,000, and £210 if the judgment exceeds £5,000. In fairly straightforward cases, it is likely that the court will award fixed costs. However, it is open to the successful claimant to ask for costs to be summarily assessed if these are going to be more than the fixed costs. See **9.3**.

What is the effect if a claimant of an unspecified sum is awarded summary judgment? The claimant will have established liability but a later assessment of the quantum of damages will be necessary. The court will normally award the claimant his costs of making the application and summarily assess these. The court will then usually fix a date to assess quantum and deal with the costs of the entire claim ('a disposal hearing'), and may allocate the matter to a track and give case management directions.

What if the defendant secures summary judgment (ie, the claim is struck out)? The court will normally award the defendant his costs of the claim (including pre-action costs) and, unless agreed, these will be subject to a summary assessment.

9.5.3 Application for further information (Part 18)

As we saw in **Chapter 6**, a party may request further information from another party to clarify any matter which is in dispute, or give additional information in relation to any such matter.

If the request is not met, the party can apply for an order from the court.

Provided that the request made complied with para 1 of PD 18 (see **Chapter 6**), and at least 14 days have elapsed and the time stated for a response has expired, the application notice need not be served on the other party and the court may deal with the application without a hearing (PD 18, para 5.5(1)). Otherwise, the application notice must be served on the other party.

9.6 Interim remedies (Part 25)

The court has wide powers to grant parties to a claim, or to a proposed claim, various interim remedies. These are set out in r 25.1.

(1) The court may grant the following interim remedies—
   (a) an interim injunction;
   (b) an interim declaration;
   (c) an order—
      (i) for the detention, custody or preservation of relevant property;
      (ii) for the inspection of relevant property;
      (iii) for the taking of a sample of relevant property;
      (iv) for the carrying out of an experiment on or with relevant property;
      (v) for the sale of relevant property which is of a perishable nature or which for any other good reason it is desirable to sell quickly; and
      (vi) for the payment of income from relevant property until a claim is decided;
   (d) an order authorising a person to enter any land or building in the possession of a party to the proceedings for the purposes of carrying out an order under sub-paragraph (c);
   (e) an order under section 4 of the Torts (Interference with Goods) Act 1977 to deliver up goods;
   (f) an order (referred to as a 'freezing injunction')—
      (i) restraining a party from removing from the jurisdiction assets located there; or
      (ii) restraining a party from dealing with any assets whether located within the jurisdiction or not;
   (g) an order directing a party to provide information about the location of relevant property or assets or to provide information about relevant property or assets which are or may be the subject of an application for a freezing injunction;
   (h) an order (referred to as a 'search order') under section 7 of the Civil Procedure Act 1997 (order requiring a party to admit another party to premises for the purpose of preserving evidence etc);
   (i) an order under section 33 of the Supreme Court Act 1981 or section 52 of the County Courts Act 1984 (order for disclosure of documents or inspection of property before a claim has been made);
   (j) an order under section 34 of the Supreme Court Act 1981 or section 53 of the County Courts Act 1984 (order in certain proceedings for disclosure of documents or inspection of property against a non-party);
   (k) an order (referred to as an order for interim payment) under rule 25.6 for payment by a defendant on account of any damages, debt or other sum(except costs) which the court may hold the defendant liable to pay;
   (l) an order for a specified fund to be paid into court or otherwise secured, where there is a dispute over a party's right to the fund;

(m) an order permitting a party seeking to recover personal property to pay money into court pending the outcome of the proceedings and directing that, if he does so, the property shall be given up to him;

(n) an order directing a party to prepare and file accounts relating to the dispute; and

(o) an order directing any account to be taken or inquiry to be made by the court.

An interim remedy can be obtained before proceedings are issued (eg, for pre-action disclosure of documents – see **10.5**), during proceedings, or even after judgment has been given. A court can grant a remedy before a claim is issued only if the matter is urgent, or it is otherwise desirable to do so in the interests of justice. Unless the court orders otherwise, a defendant may not apply for one of the orders listed in r 25.1 until he has filed an acknowledgement of service or defence.

A court can grant an interim remedy on an application made without notice if it appears to the court that there are good reasons for not giving notice. Examples of applications which will, by their very nature, be made without notice are freezing injunctions and search orders. A freezing injunction restrains a party from removing his assets from the jurisdiction (ie, England and Wales). If notice was given to the respondent of such an application, the respondent could simply transfer his assets prior to the hearing of the application.

A search order is an order compelling the respondent to allow his premises to be searched by the applicant. It is obtained where the applicant believes that the respondent has documents which, it is usually alleged, belong to the applicant. Again, if notice was given to the respondent in advance, it would be a simple matter for the respondent to hide the documents somewhere else. Because freezing injunctions and search orders can be quite draconian in their impact upon the respondent, such applications must be made to a High Court judge and the evidence in support of these applications must be by way of affidavit. Evidence in support of other applications for interim remedies is by the usual methods:

(a) witness statements;
(b) the application notice;
(c) the statement(s) of case.

The contents of (a) and (c) can be relied on as evidence only where they contain a statement of truth. By their very nature, (a) must contain a statement of truth (see **11.3**).

9.7 Interim payments

One particular type of interim remedy is an interim payment (see r 25.1(1)(k) at **9.6** above). An interim payment is an advance payment on account of any damages, debt or other sum (excluding costs) which a defendant may be held liable to pay. The interim payment procedure enables a claimant who has a strong case on liability to avoid the financial hardship and/or inconvenience which might otherwise be suffered because of any delay during the period between the start of the claim and its final determination.

Before making an application to the court, the claimant should try to negotiate with the defendant or the defendant's insurance company to obtain a voluntary interim payment. If one is not forthcoming, and if the claimant feels he has good grounds for making the application, then the application should be made as soon as possible.

A claimant may not seek an interim payment until after the time for acknowledging service has expired. The claimant may make more than one application.

9.7.1 Procedure

An application notice for an interim payment must be supported by evidence and be served at least 14 days before the hearing date.

The evidence required in support of an interim payment application is set out in para 2.1 of PD 25B – Interim Payments. The evidence must deal with:

(a) the amount of the interim payment being sought;
(b) the items or matters in respect of which the interim payment is sought;
(c) the likely amount of the final judgment;
(d) the reasons for believing that the conditions for an interim payment are satisfied (see **9.7.2** below);
(e) any other relevant matters.

Any documents in support of the application should be exhibited.

If the respondent wishes to rely on evidence then this should be served at least seven days before the hearing. If the applicant wishes to use evidence in reply to the respondent's evidence, this should be served at least three days before the hearing.

9.7.2 Grounds for making the order

The grounds for the court making an interim payment are as follows:

(a) the defendant against whom the order is sought has admitted liability to pay damages or some other sum of money to the claimant; or
(b) the claimant has obtained judgment against that defendant for damages to be assessed or for a sum of money (other than costs) to be assessed; or
(c) the court is satisfied that if the claim went to trial the claimant would obtain judgment for a substantial amount of money (other than costs) against the defendant from whom he is seeking an order for an interim payment.

The rules do not require the applicant to show any need for the interim payment, or that he will suffer prejudice if he does not receive it: see *Stringman v McArdle* [1994] 1 WLR 1653. However, if the delay in assessment of damages is unlikely to be substantial, the court may be reluctant to exercise its discretion to make an order unless the claimant has some special reason for requiring it.

A respondent cannot contest the application on the grounds of poverty. However, the respondent will know from the claimant's evidence how much the claimant is seeking. If the respondent wishes the court to take into account his ability to pay that sum (or indeed any sum) when deciding whether or not to exercise its discretion, sufficient details of the respondent's financial position should be disclosed in his evidence in reply to the application.

The applicant must prove the grounds of application relied upon up to the civil standard of the balance of probabilities. There are degrees of probability within the civil standard and ground (c) has been interpreted as meaning that:

the burden is a high one within that standard if only because litigation of its nature involves uncertainties. A [claimant] with what may on paper appear to be a strong case may find it fails at trial. If he does then he will have to repay the whole or, to the extent that he fails, part of the interim payment. But ... the [claimant] may spend it ... If he does it may be difficult ... to recover ... Clearly the burden resting on the applicant in those circumstances is towards the top of the flexible scale. (*per* May LJ in *Gibbons v Wall* (1988) *The Times*, 24 February).

As the burden is so high it is not surprising that the court has interpreted ground (c) as meaning that the applicant *will* succeed. It is not enough that the court thinks it likely that the claimant will succeed at trial: see *British and Commonwealth Holdings plc v Quadrex Holdings Inc* [1989] 3 WLR 723.

An application for an interim payment is often combined with an application for summary judgment (see **9.5.2**). Where the respondent satisfies the court only that it is possible that his claim or defence may succeed but improbable that it will do so, the court might be persuaded to order an interim payment rather than make a conditional order.

If the applicant can establish an entitlement to an interim payment the court then has a discretion as to two questions:

(a) whether to make an order; and
(b) if so, the amount.

As to question (a), an interim payment may be inappropriate if the issues are complicated, or if difficult questions of law arise which may take many hours and the citation of many authorities to resolve: see *British and Commonwealth Holding plc v Quadrex Holdings Inc*, above.

In respect of question (b), the court must not make an interim payment of more than a 'reasonable proportion of the likely amount of the final judgment' after taking into account contributory negligence and any relevant set-off or counterclaim that would reduce any judgment. In other words, the court will seek to calculate what sum is indisputably due to the claimant and then finally consider what sum the defendant is able to pay. For example, in *British and Commonwealth Holding plc v Quadrex Holdings Inc*, the claim was for over £100 million and the judge made an order for an interim payment of £75 million. The Court of Appeal found that such a payment would have a severe adverse impact on the business of the defendant which would be irremediable. In particular, the repayment of that sum if the defendant's defence succeeded at trial would not remedy the damage caused to it by making an interim payment of that size. In the circumstances the court reduced the amount to £5 million.

When deciding the amount to order by way of an interim payment the court may take into account any Part 36 payment (see **12.4**) that the defendant has previously made. The court may well order that the interim payment should be made from the money already in court.

9.7.3 Consequences of an interim payment order

If a defendant has made an interim payment which exceeds his total liability under the final judgment, the court may award interest on the overpaid amount from the date of the interim payment.

The trial judge will not be told about any interim payment until after he has decided all issues of liability and quantum, unless the defendant consents.

If the defendant later wishes to make a Part 36 payment (see **12.4**), r 36.6(2)(d) requires that the Payment Notice must state that he has taken the interim payment into account.

9.8 Security for costs (r 25.12)

A defendant may be confident that he can successfully defend the claimant's claim against him, but he may feel that if he does so and obtains an order for costs against the claimant, the claimant may not pay those costs. In this situation, the defendant may be able to obtain an order for security for costs against the claimant. The usual way in which security is provided is by the claimant paying a sum of money into court. The order will state the amount to be paid into court and the time-limit for making the payment. If the claimant fails to comply with the order the claim can be dismissed.

The procedure for applying for an order for security for costs is dealt with in Part 25 of CPR 1998. The most common grounds for obtaining an order for security for costs are:

(a) that the claimant is resident out of the jurisdiction but not resident in a Brussels Contracting State, a Lugano Contracting State or a Regulation State (see **2.7**);

(b) that the claimant is a company or other body (whether incorporated inside or outside Great Britain) and there is reason to believe that it will be unable to pay the defendant's costs if ordered to do so.

It should be noted that this procedure is available only for defendants (including a Part 20 defendant) to use against claimants.

Note that in the case of *Olatawura v Abiloye* [2002] EWCA Civ 998, [2002] 4 All ER 903, the Court of Appeal ruled that the court can make an order requiring security to be given for costs not just under Part 25 but also when considering an application for summary judgment under Part 24 (see **9.5.2**), as well as under the general powers set out in Part 3 (see **8.3**).

9.9 Human rights

Various aspects of the rules relating to interim applications to the court might have a human rights dimension, these being: orders made without notice; summary judgment; security for costs; and public access.

9.9.1 Orders made without notice

The very fact that an order has been made against a party without telling him of the application and giving him the opportunity to be heard makes it seem that he has not had a fair hearing and his human rights under Article 6(1) ECHR have been infringed. However, there is always a procedure for the respondent to be heard at a later date on whether the order should have been made, or whether it should now be set aside. Given that the courts do need to be able to act urgently to protect a litigant's rights where those rights are in danger, most orders made without notice should be able to withstand a human rights challenge.

9.9.2 Summary judgment

A litigant who has summary judgment entered against him has not been able to have a full trial of his case with oral evidence and cross-examination of witnesses. There has, however, been a hearing on the merits and the court will have read the evidence in the form of witness statements. This is not like a default judgment where the court has entered judgment for the claimant as a purely administrative act without considering any evidence at all. As a result, the summary judgment procedure should withstand any human rights challenge.

A conditional order made on an application for summary judgment might be more open to challenge under the Human Rights Act 1998. This is an order which requires the respondent to pay a sum of money into court as a condition of being allowed to continue to bring or defend the claim. If the money is not paid, the respondent will lose the case. There might be an argument that a litigant of limited means whose case is stifled in this way is not getting a fair trial because a wealthier litigant would still be able to continue with the litigation. It should be noted that the Court of Appeal has stated (albeit not in the context of a summary judgment application) that an order requiring an impecunious party to pay money into the court with which he clearly cannot comply, should not be made (*Chapple v Williams* [1999] CPLR 731). Where, however, the court has imposed a condition which the respondent can reasonably meet, because it has concluded that the respondent's prospects of success are improbable, is there any real injustice?

9.9.3 Security for costs

The objection raised in the previous paragraph that the claim may be unjustly stifled applies equally to an order for security for costs. Indeed, perhaps more so, since there will have been no explicit finding by the court that the claimant's prospects of success are improbable. The ECtHR considered an application for security for costs in *Tolstoy Miloslavsky v UK* (1995) 20 EHRR 442. The applicant had lost a libel case and been ordered to pay substantial damages. The Court of Appeal would permit him to appeal only if he paid into court a significant sum as security for his opponent's costs. He complained that, given his circumstances, the effect was to stifle his appeal. The ECtHR took the view that the Court of Appeal's order had been legitimate in principle and proportionate in the particular circumstances. However, the ECtHR gave weight to the fact that the appeal was thought to have no prospect of success and that there had been a lengthy trial at first instance. By implication, an order for security where the party cannot raise the sum ordered and there is a reasonable prospect of success could well be a breach of Article 6(1) ECHR.

9.9.4 Public access

Article 6(1) ECHR also states that:

> Judgment shall be pronounced publicly but the press and public may be excluded from all or part of the trial in the interests of morals, public order or national security in a democratic society, where the interests of juveniles or the protection of the private life of the parties so require, or to the extent strictly necessary in the opinion of the court in special circumstances whereby publicity would prejudice the interests of justice.

Although this provision could be interpreted as being limited to the final trial of the claim, the Rules Committee interpreted it as extending to interim applications. As a result, Part 39 of CPR 1998 establishes a presumption that the public are entitled to access to any interim application subject to a list of well defined exceptions, such as applications to approve a settlement of a claim brought by a child. In practice, most interim applications continue to be heard in the master's or district judge's room, rather than in a courtroom, but requests from a non-party to sit in will usually be granted.

Chapter 10
Disclosure and Inspection of Documents – CPR 1998, Part 31

10.1	Purpose of disclosure and inspection	125
10.2	Definition of 'disclosure' (r 31.2)	126
10.3	Definition of 'documents' (r 31.4)	126
10.4	Standard disclosure (r 31.6)	126
10.5	Disclosure of copies (r 31.9)	126
10.6	The duty to search (r 31.7)	126
10.7	The right of inspection (r 31.3)	127
10.8	Procedure for standard disclosure	127
10.9	The disclosure statement	128
10.10	Continuing obligation (r 31.11)	128
10.11	Withholding inspection	128
10.12	Disclosing the existence of documents: the list	131
10.13	Failure to disclose (r 31.21)	132
10.14	Subsequent use of disclosed documents (r 31.22)	132
10.15	Applying for specific disclosure (r 31.12)	132
10.16	Pre-action disclosure (r 31.16)	133
10.17	Non-party disclosure (r 31.17)	133
10.18	Human rights	134
10.19	Summary of key points	134
10.20	Disclosure obligations and solicitors' duties	135

10.1 Purpose of disclosure and inspection

> In plain language, litigation in this country is conducted 'cards face up on the table'. Some people from other lands regard this as incomprehensible. 'Why', they ask, 'should I be expected to provide my opponent with the means of defeating me?' The answer, of course, is that litigation is not a war or even a game. It is designed to do real justice between opposing parties and, if the court does not have *all* the relevant information, it cannot achieve this object. (*per* Sir John Donaldson MR in *Davies v Eli Lilly & Co* [1987] 1 WLR 428)

As we saw in **Chapter 3**, the pre-action protocols require the parties to prospective litigation to share information. However, there is no general obligation on a party to show his opponent the contents of documents, and in particular no requirement to show documents that are adverse to his own position. A party can request that an opponent disclose documents that he would normally show during court proceedings, but the only way to compel that disclosure is by way of court order (see **3.9** and **10.16**). Therefore, prior to a claim form being issued, the parties can to a large extent select those documents they wish to show and keep all the others hidden.

The main purpose of the disclosure and inspection stage of the litigation process is to enable the parties to evaluate the strength of their case in advance of the trial. The parties have to reveal to each other the documents which have a bearing on the case. The process is intended to promote settlements and therefore a saving in costs. It ensures that the parties are not taken by surprise at the trial and that the court has all relevant information in order to do justice between the parties. Disclosure is governed by Part 31 of CPR 1998, which applies to all claims save those allocated to the small claims track.

10.2 Definition of 'disclosure' (r 31.2)

'Disclosure' is defined in r 31.2, which states:

A party discloses a document by stating that the document exists or has existed.

This is done by preparing and serving a list of documents on every other party (see 10.8).

10.3 Definition of 'documents' (r 31.4)

'Documents' are defined in r 31.4 as being anything in which information of any description is recorded. 'Documents' therefore include written documents, audiotapes, videotapes, computer disks and photographs.

10.4 Standard disclosure (r 31.6)

When a court makes an order for a party to give disclosure of documents, the order is limited to standard disclosure unless the court directs otherwise. Standard disclosure is defined in r 31.6 and requires a party to disclose:

(a) the documents on which he relies; and

(b) the documents which:
  (i) adversely affect his own case;
  (ii) adversely affect another party's case; or
  (iii) support another party's case; and

(c) the documents which he is required to disclose by a relevant Practice Direction. At the time of writing, there are none.

The duty of disclosure is limited to documents which are or have been in a party's control (see r 31.8). This means that:

(a) the document is or was in his physical possession; or
(b) he has or has had a right to possession of it; or
(c) he has or has had a right to inspect or take copies of it.

Documents held by a party's agent would therefore be within that party's control.

Note that it is open to the parties to agree in writing to dispense with or limit standard disclosure.

10.5 Disclosure of copies (r 31.9)

A party need not disclose more than one copy of a document unless the copy contains 'a modification, obliteration or other marking or feature' on which the party intends to rely, or which supports another party's case, or which could adversely affect his own or another party's case. In that case, the copy document is treated as a separate document.

10.6 The duty to search (r 31.7)

In order to give standard disclosure, a party must make a reasonable and proportionate search for all documents which could adversely affect his own or another party's case, or which support another party's case.

What is reasonable depends on:

(a) the number of documents involved;

(b) the nature and complexity of the proceedings;
(c) the ease and expense of retrieval of any particular document; and
(d) the significance of the document.

[margin note: easier document is to obtain, party is more likely to be expected to find it.]

If a party has limited the search for certain documents, he must state this in his disclosure statement (see **10.9**). PD 31 suggests, at para 2, for example, that it may be reasonable to decide not to search for documents coming into existence before some particular date, or to limit the search to documents in some particular place or places, or to documents falling into particular categories.

[margin note: reasonable if there are a large amount of documents and time needs to be limited]

10.7 The right of inspection (r 31.3)

Rule 31.3(1) gives a party a right of inspection of a disclosed document, except where:

(a) the document is no longer in the control of the party who disclosed it;
(b) the party disclosing the document has a right or a duty to withhold inspection of it; or
(c) a party considers it would be disproportionate to the issues in the case to permit inspection of documents within a category and states in his disclosure statement (see **10.9**) that inspection of those documents will not be permitted on the grounds that to do so would be disproportionate.

[margin note: privileged documents]
[margin note: eg. client confidentiality]

Where a party has a right to inspect a document, that party wishing to inspect must give written notice of his wish to inspect and the party who disclosed the document must permit inspection not more than seven days after the date on which he received the notice. Rather than going to inspect the documents personally, a party may also request a copy of the document, provided the party also undertakes to pay reasonable copying costs. In this case, the party who disclosed the document must supply him with a copy not more than seven days after the date on which he received the request.

10.8 Procedure for standard disclosure

[margin note: multi-track → case management conference → court will decide what disclosure of documents is necessary.]

Where an order for standard disclosure has been made, each party must make and serve a list of documents using Practice Form N265 (a copy of which appears **Appendix A(11)**), which must identify the documents in a convenient order and manner and as concisely as possible. PD 31, at para 3.2, states that it will normally be necessary to list the documents in date order, to number them consecutively and to give each a concise description (eg, letter, claimant to defendant). It also suggests that where there is a large number of documents all falling into a particular category, the disclosing party may list those documents as a category rather than individually.

[margin note: p232]

The list is in three parts. The first part of the list sets out the documents within the party's control and which he does not object to the other party inspecting. The second part of the list sets out other documents of which the party has control but where the party objects to the other party inspecting them. The most common reason for objection is that the party claims privilege from inspection in relation to those documents (see **10.11**).

The third part of the list consists of documents which a party has had but which are no longer in his control. The list must state what has happened to these documents.

See further **10.12**.

10.9 The disclosure statement

It will have been seen from the definition of standard disclosure at **10.4** that a party is under an obligation to disclose documents which might adversely affect his own case or support another party's case. A party is therefore under an obligation to disclose documents which could be very detrimental to that party's chances of success, but which the other party does not know exist until disclosure. It is, therefore, essential that parties comply fully and honestly with the requirements of disclosure. Partly for that reason, the list of documents contains a disclosure statement (see r 31.10(5)). This is a statement made by the party disclosing the documents:

[margin note: PD 31 PARA 4 — See Annex]

(a) setting out the extent of the search that has been made to locate documents of which disclosure is required;

(b) certifying that he understands the duty to disclose documents;

(c) certifying that, to the best of his knowledge, he has carried out that duty.

Where the party making the disclosure statement is a company, firm, association or other organisation, the statement must also identify the person making the statement, the office or position he holds, and explain why he is considered the appropriate person to make the statement.

Proceedings for contempt of court may be brought against a person if he makes, or causes to be made, a false disclosure statement without an honest belief in its truth. The proceedings require the permission of the court unless they are brought by the Attorney-General.

PD 31, at para 4.4, also states that if the disclosing party has a legal representative acting for him, the legal representative must endeavour to ensure that the person making the disclosure statement understands the duty of disclosure (see further at **10.20**).

A solicitor, therefore, is under a clear duty to advise his client as to the requirements of disclosure. The solicitor must ensure as far as possible that all documents which have to be disclosed are preserved and made available for inspection. (See **10.20**.) This is obviously something a solicitor must explain to the client on receiving instructions. It is best practice to confirm that advice in writing.

10.10 Continuing obligation (r 31.11)

Disclosure is an obligation which continues until the proceedings are concluded. If documents to which the duty of disclosure extends come to a party's notice at any time during the proceedings, even though the party has already supplied a list of documents, he must immediately notify every other party.

The process of disclosure does not therefore come to an end simply because a list has been supplied. If a document is created after that date then it too must be disclosed to the other party if it comes within the definition of standard disclosure.

10.11 Withholding inspection

As we have already seen, a party can withhold the right to inspect a document which has been disclosed. The usual reason for this is that a party claims that the documents are privileged from inspection. These privileged documents fall into three classes:

(a) documents protected by legal professional privilege; *advice privilege; litigation privilege*
(b) documents tending to incriminate the party producing them;
(c) documents privileged on the grounds of public policy.

10.11.1 Legal professional privilege

10.11.1.1 Communications passing between a party and his legal advisers or between a party's legal advisers ('advice privilege')

Letters and other communications passing between a party and his solicitor are privileged from inspection provided they are written by or to the solicitor in his professional capacity and for the sole or dominant purpose of obtaining legal advice or assistance for the client. 'Legal advice' is not confined to telling the client the law; it includes information passed by solicitor to client, or vice versa, so that advice may be sought and given, and it includes advice about what should prudently and sensibly be done in the relevant legal context.

Privilege, however, does not extend without limit to all solicitor/client communications. The range of assistance given by solicitors to their clients has greatly broadened in recent times; for example, many solicitors now provide investment advice to clients. The scope of legal professional privilege has to be kept within reasonable bounds. See further *Three Rivers District Council and Others v Governor and Company of the Bank of England (No 10)* [2004] EWCA Civ 218.

The privilege extends to communications between a party and his solicitor's employee or agent, and also to communications between a party and a solicitor in his service, for example a solicitor to a government department or in a legal department of a commercial enterprise. The privilege also covers instructions and briefs to counsel, counsel's opinions, and counsel's drafts and notes.

10.11.1.2 Communications passing between the solicitor and a third party ('litigation privilege')

Communications passing between the solicitor and a third party are privileged from production and inspection only if:

(a) they come into existence after litigation is contemplated or commenced; and
(b) they are made with a view to the litigation, either for the sole or dominant purpose of obtaining or giving advice in regard to it, or for obtaining evidence to be used in it.

Examples of documents which may come within this head of privilege are a report from an expert obtained by a solicitor with a view to advising his client about existing or contemplated litigation, or witness statements obtained by a solicitor for the purpose of existing or contemplated litigation.

10.11.1.3 Communications between the client and a third party ('litigation privilege')

Documents which have passed between the client and a third party are privileged if the sole or dominant purpose for which they were produced was to obtain legal advice in respect of existing or contemplated litigation or to conduct, or aid in the conduct, of such litigation. It must be the case that litigation was reasonably in prospect at the time when the document was brought into existence, and that the sole or dominant reason for obtaining the document was to enable solicitors to advise as to whether a claim should be made or resisted. For example, a report compiled following an accident may be prepared for the purpose of obtaining legal advice as to whether to resist a claim, or it may be prepared with a view to avoiding similar accidents in the future, or it might be prepared for both purposes.

In order to determine whether the document is privileged, one must look at the dominant purpose at the time when it came into existence. If the document is subsequently used by solicitors for the purposes of litigation, that will not mean that it is privileged if the original purpose of the document was something different.

Where a client is not an individual, this form of privilege is also applied to communications between individuals within that organisation. Thus, a memorandum sent by one partner of a firm to another would be privileged if it was prepared for the dominant purpose of obtaining legal advice in respect of existing or contemplated litigation, or to aid the conduct of such litigation.

10.11.1.4 Waiver of privilege

The privilege is the client's and not the solicitor's, and therefore it may be waived by the client but not by the solicitor.

Once a copy of a privileged document is served on the other side, the privilege is waived.

Subsequent to disclosure and inspection, each party is required by the court to serve on the other(s) copies of the witness statements and expert reports upon which he intends to rely at trial (see further **Chapter 11**). This waives the privilege in these documents, unless it had been waived earlier.

Special considerations apply to the letter of instruction given by a solicitor to an expert whose report is relied upon at trial (see **11.13.3**).

10.11.2 Documents tending to incriminate the party who would produce them

A party is entitled to claim privilege for documents which will tend to incriminate either him or his spouse. This rule applies to criminal liability or penal proceedings under the law of any part of the UK. The details are beyond the scope of this book.

10.11.3 Documents privileged on the ground of public policy

If producing a copy of a document would be injurious to the public interest, it may be withheld on the ground of public policy.

The judge has to consider whether the withholding of the documents is necessary for the proper functioning of the public service. Examples of documents which have been withheld from production on this ground are documents dealing with matters of national defence, information as to ill-treatment of children given to the NSPCC, local authority social work records, probation service records, and evidence which might reveal the identity of a police informant.

10.11.4 Challenging a claim to privilege (r 31.19)

A party who wishes to challenge his opponent's claim to privilege can apply for the court to decide whether the claim to privilege should be upheld. In any case where there is a claim to privilege, the court may require the party claiming privilege to produce the document to the court and may invite any person, even if they are not a party, to make representation.

Disclosure and Inspection of Documents – CPR 1998, Part 31   131

10.11.5 Inadvertent disclosure of privileged documents

If privileged documents are mistakenly listed in part 1 of a party's list (instead of part 2), no harm is done if the error is spotted before the other side inspects the document since the list may be amended and re-served.

But what if inspection of privileged material is allowed inadvertently, for example where copies of privileged documents have been sent in error to the other side's solicitor? Under r 31.20, the receiving party is not permitted to use the documents or their contents without the permission of the court. If the receiving party does not seek that permission, the disclosing party may be able to persuade the court to grant an injunction requiring the receiving party and his solicitor to return the documents, without retaining a photocopy and restraining the use of the privileged material in the litigation. The court has a discretion whether to grant an injunction and will do so only if satisfied that the mistake was evident to the solicitor receiving the documents, or, if not, that it would have been obvious to a hypothetical reasonable solicitor that disclosure had occurred as a result of an obvious mistake (*IBM Corporation and Another v Phoenix International (Computers) Ltd* [1995] 1 All ER 413).

Where the mistake is less than obvious, there is no obligation on the solicitor receiving the documents to make enquiries of the sending party: see *Norman Roger Breeze v John Stacy & Sons Ltd* (1999) *The Times*, 8 July.

The Guide to the Professional Conduct of Solicitors, 8th edn (Law Society Publishing, 1999), makes it clear that as soon as a solicitor who receives privileged documents realises that the sender has made an obvious mistake, he should immediately stop reading the documents, inform the other side and return the documents. He may then inform his client what has happened.

10.11.6 Without prejudice correspondence

As mentioned in **Chapter 3**, attempts to settle a case should usually be conducted on a 'without prejudice' basis. Without prejudice correspondence is not privileged from inspection in the same way that solicitor–client correspondence is; both solicitors have seen the letter anyway. If, however, there are, for example, three parties involved in a claim and the without prejudice correspondence has taken place between only two of the parties, such correspondence is privileged from inspection by the third party (see *Rush & Tomkins Ltd v Greater London Council* [1989] AC 1280).

10.12 Disclosing the existence of documents: the list

A party discloses a document by stating that the document exists or has existed. There are two possible ways of disclosing the existence of a document, namely by identifying either:

(a) the actual document itself; or
(b) the type of document.

So, in the first part of the list of documents the actual documents are identified so that the other parties can decide whether or not they wish to inspect them. Remember that these are documents in the party's control which he does not object to being inspected.

In the second part of the list of documents the party should disclose the type of documents for which he is claiming privilege from inspection, for example 'confidential correspondence between the claimant and his solicitors'; 'various experts' reports and witness statements', etc. It is quite proper to do this. The existence of the document has been disclosed and so the duty to give disclosure is thereby discharged. However, the general description as to the type of document ensures that the contents are not indirectly revealed. The objections to inspection must then be stated. A legitimate ground must be claimed. It is *not* a ground of objection that the document is adverse to the party's case. For examples of different possible grounds, see **10.11**. In practice, the most common objection is based on legal professional privilege. For example, as to the confidential correspondence between the claimant and his solicitors, the objection might be stated as 'these documents were created for the purposes of giving or obtaining legal advice and are by their nature privileged from inspection'. If different grounds are relied on for different documents they should be arranged and listed in separate bundles.

In the third part of the list of documents the party must state the actual (non-privileged) documents that he once had, but no longer has, in his control. This often comprises little more than the original letters, written by or on behalf of the party, copies of which have already been detailed in the first part of the list. In respect of each document it is necessary to state when it was last in the party's control and where it is now. The purpose is to enable the parties receiving the list to continue their investigations elsewhere. If they can locate the present whereabouts of the documents they may be able to obtain copies on an application for disclosure by a non-party (see **10.17**).

10.13 Failure to disclose (r 31.21)

A party who fails to disclose a document or fails to allow inspection of a document may not rely on that document unless the court permits. Note, importantly, however, that a party who fails to disclose a document which harms his case may find that his case is struck out as a result of failure to comply with an order for specific disclosure (see **10.15**).

10.14 Subsequent use of disclosed documents (r 31.22)

Where a document has been disclosed to a party, he may use that document only for the purposes of the case in which it has been disclosed unless:

(a) the document has been read or referred to during a public hearing (eg, at trial); or

(b) the court grants permission; or

(c) the party who disclosed the document and the person to whom the document belongs consent.

Where (a) applies, the court may make an order restricting or prohibiting the use of the document.

10.15 Applying for specific disclosure (r 31.12)

If a party is dissatisfied with disclosure provided by the other party and believes it is inadequate then he may make an application for an order for specific disclosure. The application notice must specify the order the applicant wants the court to make, and the grounds of the application must be set out in the application notice or in the supporting evidence. For example, in a claim arising out of the supply of allegedly defective goods sold by the defendant to the claimant, the claimant may suspect that the defendant should have quality control records. If these have not been disclosed then an application for specific disclosure may be justified.

Before making such an application, a party should write to the other side explaining why he believes the documents are disclosable and asking the other party to comply properly with the order for disclosure. If a satisfactory response is not forthcoming then it would be appropriate to issue the application.

An order for specific disclosure can require a party to:

(a) disclose specified documents or classes of documents;
(b) carry out a search as specified by the order and disclose any documents located as a result of that search.

When deciding whether to make an order for specific disclosure, the court will take into account all the circumstances of the case and, in particular, the overriding objective in r 1.1. If the court concludes that the party from whom specific disclosure is sought has failed adequately to comply with the obligation imposed by the order for disclosure, the court will usually make such order as is necessary to ensure that those obligations are properly complied with. For example, the order will often be made in the form of an unless order.

A party can also apply for an order for specific inspection, which would require a party to permit inspection of documents which he omitted from his disclosure statement on the grounds that inspection would be disproportionate (see **10.7**).

10.16 Pre-action disclosure (r 31.16)

As we saw at **3.9**, a party may make an application for pre-action disclosure.

This procedure will normally be used where a party is unsure whether he has a good case against another party and, therefore, does not know whether to issue proceedings. The party could, therefore, apply for pre-action disclosure against the intended defendant so that he can then make an informed decision as to whether or not to issue proceedings against that person.

10.17 Non-party disclosure (r 31.17)

Where proceedings are already in existence, a party to the proceedings can apply for disclosure against a non-party.

The application must be supported by evidence.

The court may order non-party disclosure only if:

(a) the documents in question are likely to support the applicant's case or adversely affect the case of another party; and
(b) disclosure is necessary to dispose fairly of the case or to save costs.

The order must:

(a) specify the documents or classes of documents to be disclosed; and
(b) require the non-party to specify which documents are no longer in his control and which are privileged.

The order may specify a time and place for disclosure and inspection, and may require the non-party to indicate what has happened to the documents which are no longer in his control.

This procedure enables a party to proceedings which are already in existence to obtain disclosure of documents from a non-party if it is going to help resolve the issues in the case.

The most common application of this procedure would be where a party indicates in his list of documents that he no longer has a document in his possession. He also indicates that X now has possession of that document. The other party may then write to X asking for a copy of the document. If X refuses to supply that copy voluntarily, the other party could then apply for an order for non-party disclosure against X.

10.18 Human rights

Article 6(1) ECHR requires the disclosure of relevant documents to all parties in civil proceedings (see, eg, *McGinley and Egan v UK* (1998) 27 EHRR 1). Is it therefore possible that some of the rules relating to privilege could be open to attack as interfering with the right to a fair hearing under Article 6(1)? It is almost inconceivable that the rules on legal professional privilege could be successfully attacked on this basis, and the privilege against self-incrimination is such a well recognised bastion of human rights that it is bound to be supported.

However, withholding documents on the grounds that they are covered by public interest immunity has always been a controversial part of the common law and is virtually certain to be the subject of human rights litigation.

10.19 Summary of key points

Broadly, standard disclosure involves a party taking the following steps.

(1) Identify the issues in dispute between the parties.

(2) Decide who should carry out the search for r 31.6 documents and how this should be done, eg whether there should be any limitations placed on the search in relation to the age, location and/or categories of documents.

(3) Carry out a reasonable and proportionate search for r 31.6 documents, namely those that record information which the party:
   (a) intends to rely on; or
   (b) adversely affects that party's case; or
   (c) adversely affects another party's case; or
   (d) supports another party's case.

(4) Prepare a list of documents in Form N265. On the second page, decide where each r 31.6 document should appear.
   (a) The document should appear in the first part of the list if it is in the party's control and is not privileged from inspection. The actual document should be described (ie the name of the author (and recipient, if appropriate) and date: for example, 'Letter from Claimant to Defendant dated 8 September 2004').
   (b) The document should appear in the second part of the list if it is currently privileged from inspection. The actual document must not be described, as that will allow the other parties to identify it. Two things must be done. First, describe the document generally, for example: 'instructions to counsel', 'proof of evidence', 'correspondence between the claimant and the claimant's solicitors', 'expert's report', etc. This discloses the existence of the document and so standard disclosure is given. However, secondly, the relevant

privilege from inspection must be claimed. For example (correspondence between the claimant and the claimant's solicitors), 'to give legal advice' or (expert's report) 'obtained by the claimant when this litigation was reasonably contemplated for the sole purpose of taking legal advice'.

(c) A document that is not privileged from inspection but is no longer in the party's control should appear in the third part of the list, for example, 'Bundle of invoices concerning the onward sale of the goods in question, all dated 2003, destroyed in a flood at the claimant's premises on 6 February 2004'.

10.20 Disclosure obligations and solicitors' duties

Principle 21.01 of *The Guide to the Professional Conduct of Solicitors* provides that 'Solicitors who act in litigation, whilst under a duty to do their best for their client, must never deceive or mislead the court'.

A solicitor must ensure that his client understands the duties to conduct a reasonable and proper search and then give full and frank disclosure. The client must also appreciate that disclosure is an ongoing obligation. As an officer of the court a solicitor has a duty to ensure disclosure is properly given and that the court is not misled. Moreover, the client should sign the disclosure statement only after receiving legal advice. Remember that statement includes the following:

> I certify that I understand the duty of disclosure and that to the best of my knowledge I have carried out that duty. I further certify that the list of documents set out in or attached to this form, is a complete list of all documents which are or have been in my control and which I am obliged under the order to disclose. I understand that I must inform the court and the other parties immediately if any further document required to be disclosed by Rule 31.6 comes into my control at any time before conclusion of the case.

So during the first three Stages of Civil Litigation the client must be made aware of the extent of his disclosure obligations and the importance of not destroying documents that might have to be disclosed.

Woods v Martin's Bank [1959] 1 QB 55 imposes a duty on a solicitor to the court to examine his client's documents himself in order to ensure that proper disclosure is made. *Myers v Elman* [1940] AC 282 provides that if the client will not permit this, or insists on giving imperfect disclosure, the solicitor must withdraw from the case, as otherwise he will be participating in a deception of the court in breach of principle 21.01.

A solicitor should advise a client that if he destroys disclosable documents deliberately and contumaciously or such that a fair trial is rendered impossible, his statement of case is likely to be struck out.

Chapter 11
Evidence

11.1	Introduction	137
11.2	Witness evidence	137
11.3	Form of witness statements	138
11.4	Use of witness statements at trial	139
11.5	Witness summaries (r 32.9)	140
11.6	Sanctions for non-service of witness statements (r 32.10)	140
11.7	Affidavits	141
11.8	Opinion evidence	141
11.9	Hearsay evidence	142
11.10	Use of plans, photographs and models as evidence (r 33.6)	145
11.11	Notice to admit facts (r 32.18)	146
11.12	Notice to admit or prove documents (r 32.19)	146
11.13	Expert evidence (Part 35)	146
11.14	Assessors (r 35.15)	151
11.15	Human rights	151

11.1 Introduction

The rules on evidence are contained primarily within Parts 32 and 33 of CPR 1998. These rules do not change the law on the admissibility of evidence save for the fact that the court, as might be expected through its court management powers, can control the evidence brought before the court.

Rule 32.1 states:

(1) The court may control the evidence by giving directions as to—
   (a) the issues on which it requires evidence;
   (b) the nature of the evidence which it requires to decide those issues; and
   (c) the way in which the evidence is to be placed before the court.
(2) The court may use its power under this rule to exclude evidence that would otherwise be admissible.
(3) The court may limit cross-examination.

In exercising its powers under this Rule, the court will bear in mind the overriding objective in r 1.1 and will attempt to define and identify the issues between the parties. For example, the court may decide, prior to the trial, that a particular issue which has been raised is no longer important and make an order excluding any evidence which the parties intended to use in relation to that particular issue.

11.2 Witness evidence

Under r 32.2(1), the general rule is that any fact which needs to be proved is to be proved at trial by oral evidence given in public, and at any other hearing by evidence in writing. The Rules also provide that the court may allow a witness to give evidence by any means, including a video link.

As already seen in **Chapter 8**, when giving directions for trial, the court will usually order witness statements to be exchanged. Rule 32.4(2) states that the court will order a party to serve on the other parties any witness statement of the oral evidence which the party serving the statement intends to rely upon in relation to any issue of fact to be decided at the trial. As outlined at **11.6**, where a witness statement is not served, the witness will be allowed to give evidence at trial only with the court's permission.

The court can give directions as to the order in which witness statements are to be served. Usually the court will order simultaneous exchange, but may order one party (usually the claimant) to serve first (sequential exchange). Once a witness statement is served, it ceases to be privileged (see further **10.11.1.4**).

What should you do if, after exchanging witness statements, you object to the relevance or admissibility of material contained in your opponent's statements? Best practice is to notify the other party of your objection immediately and seek to resolve the dispute. Failing that, raise the matter at any pre-trial review or at the beginning of the trial itself.

What if, after the exchange of witness statements, a party wants a witness to give additional evidence? It may well be that a witness needs to deal with events occurring, or matters discovered, after the exchange, or in response to matters dealt with by another party's witness. The answer is to prepare and serve a supplemental witness statement dealing with these points as soon as possible. The other party should be asked to agree to the evidence being adduced at trial. Failing that, an application for permission to rely on the evidence should be made at any pre-trial review or at the beginning of the trial itself.

11.3 Form of witness statements

Rules relating to the form of witness statements are set out in paras 17–20 of PD 32.

The witness statement should be headed in the same way as any other court document and the top right-hand corner should state:

(a) the party on whose behalf the statement is filed;
(b) the initials and surname of the witness;
(c) the number of the statement in relation to that witness;
(d) the identifying initials and number of each exhibit referred to; and
(e) the date the statement was made.

The statement should be in the witness's own words as far as practicable. It should be in the first person and state:

(a) the full name of the witness;
(b) where he lives or, if the statement is made as part of his employment or business, where he works, his position in the business and the name of the business;
(c) his occupation or description; and
(d) (if so) that he is a party or an employee of a party.

In the case of *Alex Lawrie Factors Ltd v Morgan, Morgan and Turner* (1999) *The Times*, 18 August, the Court of Appeal held that the purpose of a witness statement was for the witness to say, in his or her own words, what the relevant evidence was. It was not to be used by the lawyer who prepared it as a vehicle for complex legal argument to which the witness would not be readily able to speak if cross-examined on the document. In this case, the second defendant, Mrs Morgan, was seeking to avoid liability to the claimant under a deed of indemnity. She had averred that the reason why her signature appeared on the deed was due to her former husband's fraudulent actions and misrepresentations. The claimant applied for summary judgment (see **9.5.2**) and, in her evidence in reply, Mrs Morgan stated that she had had the opportunity of studying the decision of the House of Lords in *Barclays Bank plc v O'Brien* [1994] 1 AC 180 in some detail. She made a number of points in reliance on that decision. The judge said that Mrs Morgan was clearly, from her evidence, an intelligent woman. He concluded that her evidence as to how she came to sign the deed of indemnity was simply not credible and he awarded summary judgment.

On the appeal, Mrs Morgan's counsel sought permission to put in new evidence going to her intelligence. The court allowed such because the situation was susceptible of injustice if the matter proceeded on the basis on which the judge had considered it, which would derive from his interpretation of the kind of woman Mrs Morgan must be from a perusal of her evidence. The court said that the case was a very good warning of the grave dangers which could occur when lawyers put into witnesses' mouths a sophisticated legal argument which, in effect, represented the lawyers' arguments in the case, to which the witnesses themselves would not be able to speak if cross-examined. Having had the benefit of further evidence, the court did not consider that this was a case in which it was appropriate to disregard Mrs Morgan's evidence as incredible and it allowed the appeal.

The statement must indicate which of the statements are based on the witness's own knowledge and which are matters of information or belief, and the source of his information and belief. The statement is required to be set out in numbered paragraphs and will generally outline the relevant events chronologically. Dates and any other numbers should be expressed in figures, not words.

Any exhibit used in connection with a witness statement should be verified and identified by the witness and remain separate from the statement. Exhibits should be numbered and, where a witness makes more than one statement in which there are exhibits in the same proceedings, the numbering of the exhibits should run consecutively throughout and not start again with each witness statement.

The witness statement must contain a statement of truth in the following words:

> I believe that the facts stated in this witness statement are true.

The statement of truth must be signed by the witness himself. Proceedings for contempt of court may be brought against a person who makes a false statement in a witness statement without an honest belief in its truth.

11.4 Use of witness statements at trial

Having served a witness statement on the other side, the witness will usually be called to give oral evidence at trial, unless the court orders otherwise or the party uses the statement as hearsay evidence (see **11.9**).

The witness statement will stand as the evidence-in-chief of the witness unless the court orders otherwise. When preparing a witness statement to be used at trial, it is, therefore, essential to ensure that the statement is comprehensive. By r 32.5(3), a witness may amplify his statement or give evidence of matters which have arisen since he served his witness statement, but only if the court gives permission (see **11.2**). The court will do so only if it considers that there is good reason not to confine the evidence of the witness to the contents of his witness statement. Further, the statement should only contain evidence that the witness could give orally at trial (ie, evidence that is admissible and relevant to the issues).

If a party who has served a witness statement does not call the witness or use the statement as hearsay evidence, any other party may use the witness statement as hearsay evidence.

As the witness statement will usually stand as the evidence-in-chief, the witness will normally simply be asked to confirm that it is true and will then be subject to cross-examination by the other side. It is because it is subject to cross-examination that oral evidence from witnesses is considered to be the 'best' form of evidence as it has been tested in court.

11.5 Witness summaries (r 32.9)

Sometimes it will be very difficult to persuade a witness to give a witness statement. As we shall see at **13.1.2**, the means exist to compel a witness to come to court, but it is obviously risky to do that if you do not know what the witness is going to say and, of course, as no witness statement will have been exchanged, permission of the court will be necessary anyway before the witness can give oral evidence.

Example

Fred is suing his former employers for damages arising out of an accident he suffered at work. Fred believes that his former colleague, Mark, could give evidence about poor safety practices within the firm, but Mark has refused to give a witness statement to Fred's solicitors as he is worried that if he does he might be dismissed.

Rule 32.9 provides that Fred's solicitors can apply to court without notice for an order to serve a 'witness summary'. This provision applies where a party is required to serve a witness statement for trial but cannot obtain one. The witness summary must contain:

(a) the evidence which would otherwise go in a witness statement; or
(b) if the party serving the summary does not know what evidence will be given, the areas about which he proposes to question the witness; and
(c) the witness's name and address.

Unless the court orders otherwise, the summary must be served on the other side at the same time as the witness statements.

11.6 Sanctions for non-service of witness statements (r 32.10)

If a party does not serve a witness statement or witness summary within the proper time-limit, the witness cannot give oral evidence unless the court gives permission. What if a party knows that it will not make the deadline to exchange? As soon as that becomes clear, he should contact all other parties and seek an agreement to an extension. He must try to ascertain when the witness's signed statement is going to be available. Any agreement reached must be recorded in writing, but it must be remembered that the parties cannot alter the key case management dates set in fast track or multi-track cases (see **8.6.2.2** and **8.6.3.4**). If no agreement is reached, or if a key case management date will not be met, an immediate application to the court should be made.

What if a party is ready to exchange within the deadline but his opponent is not? If a good reason is given for an extension it should be agreed, subject to the above comments. But what if there has been no request or application for an extension? If the party complies with the direction and serves the statements on the

[Handwritten top: OPTIONS → IF WITNESS STATEMENT NOT SERVED BY A PARTY
① Do Nothing → serve your statements anyway
② Negotiate with other party and agree a later exchange date
③ File with court within time limit
④ Apply to strike out opponent's case for failure to comply with court order]

[Handwritten left margin: Adv. prevents foul play from one party; party can't tailor own statements according to ours. court is made aware of party's failure to comply with court order (eg. case management) ↓ can take this into account at later stage.]

[Handwritten right margin: must have good case or may fail in application ↔ waste time and cost.]

opponent then that party potentially gains an advantage in that he will see the evidence first and could tailor his own evidence accordingly. The usual practice in these circumstances is for the party to file the statements with the court and explain the situation in a covering letter. Subsequently, an application might be made to strike out the opponent's case for failing to complying with the court order (see 8.3).

Will the court allow an application to serve a witness statement late or to rely on a witness at trial without having previously served a statement? All will turn on the circumstances of the case and the application of the overriding objective. What if a party discovers a new, favourable witness after witness statements have already been exchanged? At an interim application before trial, will the court's permission be given to serve the statement in order that the party can rely on the evidence at trial? The court will scrutinise why the discovery was made so late in the day, and only in exceptional cases is it likely that the party will be successful: see *Stroh v London Borough of Haringey* [1999] LTL, 13 July, where the Court of Appeal upheld the refusal of permission as it was clear that the judge had had in mind the overriding objective and he was entitled to conclude that the prejudice to the respondent outweighed the prejudice to the applicant.

What about the first instance case of *Mealey Horgan plc v Horgan* (1999) *The Times*, 6 July, which some argue shows the court will not be too rigid in the application of the Rules here. Arguably, the case turns on its own unique facts. The claimant had received the statements late but, as there were six weeks before the trial date, it was held that, given the nature of the statements, the claimant could still properly prepare for trial, notwithstanding the defendant's delay. It was the lack of any prejudice to the claimant in the case which convinced the court that it would be disproportionate to exclude the defendant's evidence.

11.7 Affidavits

Affidavits are sworn statements of evidence (ie, the maker of the affidavit has to swear before a solicitor (not his own), or other authorised person, that the contents of the affidavit are true). Prior to the CPR 1998 coming into force, affidavits were the usual means of submitting evidence at interim applications. As we have seen, however, evidence at such applications is now given by witness statements, the statement of case itself or the application notice provided it contains a statement of truth.

In the great majority of cases, therefore, there is no need to go to the extra expense (an oath fee) of using sworn affidavits as evidence. Indeed, if you do, it is very unlikely that the court would allow you to recoup the extra cost from the other side.

On some occasions, however, it is still necessary to use affidavits. The Rules provide that if you are applying for a freezing injunction or search order (see 9.6), the evidence in support of such an application must be by way of affidavit rather than a witness statement.

11.8 Opinion evidence

[Handwritten: but, depends on situation]

The general rule is that opinion evidence is not admissible. The function of a witness is to relate the facts to the court so that the court can draw its own conclusions. There are some situations in which it may be difficult for a witness to separate fact and opinion. A typical example is speed. If a witness gives evidence that a vehicle was being driven at 'about 60 mph', that is only the witness's

[Handwritten bottom: opinion is admissible if found unable to differentiate/separate fact and opinion]

opinion. Nevertheless, it is difficult to see how else the witness could express what he saw unless he restricted himself to describing the speed as 'fast'. Accordingly, whilst the cogency of the witness's assessment of the speed might be challenged, it would usually be admissible. Similarly, a witness may be permitted to express a view that 'John was drunk'. Properly, the witness should relate the physical characteristics he observed which led to that conclusion (eg, slurred speech, glazed eyes, an unsteadiness of gait, breath smelling of alcohol, etc). However, the witness's opinion, whilst it might be challenged, will be admissible. This is confirmed by s 3(2) of the Civil Evidence Act 1972, which states that:

> ... where a person is called as a witness in any civil proceedings, a statement of opinion by him on any relevant matter on which he is not qualified to give expert evidence, if made as a way of conveying relevant facts personally perceived by him, is admissible as evidence of what he perceived.

So, when a solicitor prepares a witness statement, it is vital that any relevant opinions expressed are based firmly on what the witness personally perceived.

As is indicated in s 3(2), the other main exception to the inadmissibility of opinion evidence concerns expert evidence (see **11.13**).

11.9 Hearsay evidence

Special considerations apply where hearsay evidence is to be used. Before looking at these, it is necessary to understand what is meant by 'hearsay'.

11.9.1 Definition

Hearsay evidence is defined in s 1(2)(a) of the Civil Evidence Act 1995 as 'a statement made otherwise than by a person while giving oral evidence in the proceedings which is tendered as evidence of the matters stated'.

Hearsay evidence may be an oral or a written statement made outside the courtroom which is repeated to the court in order to prove the truth of the matter stated out of court.

Therefore, in considering whether evidence is hearsay, there are two questions to consider:

(a) Does the evidence consist of an oral or written statement made outside the courtroom?

(b) Is that statement being presented to the court in order to prove that it is true? If the previous statement is being related, for example, to show a person's state of mind or simply to show that the statement was made, it will not be hearsay.

Example 1

Richard is giving evidence. He says in his evidence, 'Dave told me that Peter had stolen a car'. Richard is repeating what someone else said outside the courtroom, so the first part of the definition of hearsay is satisfied. But consider why Richard is giving this evidence. If it is as part of a case against Peter where it is relevant to show that Peter did, indeed, steal a car, then it will be hearsay. On the other hand, if Richard is giving evidence in a defamation claim brought by Peter against Dave then it will not be hearsay, as Richard is not giving the evidence to show that Peter stole a car. Indeed, this would be exactly what Peter does not want to show! Richard is relating the evidence simply to show that the statement was made.

Evidence 143

Example 2

Michael booked a holiday with Fancy Tours Ltd. When booking, the agent assured him that the hotel would be quiet and peaceful, close to the beach and with its own swimming pool. However, the hotel was noisy, some distance away from the beach, and did not have a swimming pool. Michael is now suing for misrepresentation and wishes to repeat in evidence the statements made to him. This will not be hearsay because it is not being related to show the truth of those statements. It is being related to show the effect that the statements had on his state of mind, namely that he relied on them and was misled by the misrepresentations.

Hearsay evidence may be either first-hand or multiple.

Example 1

Sara gives evidence of something that she was told by John (in order to prove the truth of John's statement). Sara's evidence is first-hand hearsay.

Example 2

Sara also gives evidence of something that John was told by Michelle (in order to prove the truth of what Michelle said). This evidence is multiple hearsay.

Example 3

Sara keeps a diary. She records what she saw one day. Sara's diary is used at a trial to prove the truth of its contents. That evidence is first-hand hearsay.

Example 4

Sara keeps a diary. She records what she was told by John one day. Sara's diary is used at a trial to prove the truth of what John said. That evidence is multiple hearsay.

11.9.2 Using hearsay evidence

Section 1 of the Civil Evidence Act 1995 provides that, in civil proceedings, evidence shall not be excluded on the ground that it is hearsay. Therefore, hearsay evidence is admissible in civil proceedings. Section 2 of the Act provides that a party proposing to bring hearsay evidence must notify any other party of that fact and, on request, give particulars of, or relating to, the evidence. This must be read in conjunction with Part 33 of CPR 1998 which sets out the rules relating to how hearsay evidence can be used.

Rule 33.2 states:

(1) Where a party intends to rely on hearsay evidence at trial and either—
   (a) that evidence is to be given by a witness giving oral evidence; or
   (b) that evidence is contained in a witness statement of a person who is not being called to give oral evidence;
   that party complies with section 2(1)(a) of the Civil Evidence Act 1995 by serving a witness statement on the other parties in accordance with the court's order.

(2) Where paragraph (1)(b) applies, the party intending to rely on the hearsay evidence must, when he serves the witness statement—
   (a) inform the other parties that the witness is not being called to give oral evidence; and
   (b) give the reason why the witness will not be called.

(3) In all other cases where a party intends to rely on hearsay evidence at trial, that party complies with section 2(1)(a) of the Civil Evidence Act 1995 by serving a notice on the other parties which—
   (a) identifies the hearsay evidence;
   (b) states that the party serving the notice proposes to rely on the hearsay evidence at trial; and

(c) gives the reason why the witness will not be called.

(4) The party proposing to rely on the hearsay evidence must—

(a) serve the notice no later than the latest date for serving witness statements; and

(b) if the hearsay evidence is to be in a document, supply a copy to any party who requests him to do so.

Therefore, if a party serves a witness statement of Mr X which contains hearsay evidence, but intends to call Mr X to give evidence at trial, then simply serving the statement on the other party complies with the notice requirements of the Civil Evidence Act 1995. However, if a party does not intend to call a witness but instead intends to rely on the statement itself as hearsay evidence, then that party must inform the other side when he serves the witness statement that he is not calling the witness to give oral evidence and give the reason why, if any, the witness will not be called.

Notice of intention to rely on hearsay evidence is only required for evidence to be used at a trial.

11.9.3 Other matters relating to the use of hearsay evidence

11.9.3.1 Weight to be attached to hearsay evidence

Section 4 of the Civil Evidence Act 1995 provides guidelines for the courts to assist them in assessing the weight they should attach to hearsay evidence.

It provides that the court is to have regard to any circumstances from which any inference can reasonably be drawn as to the reliability or otherwise of the evidence, and, in particular, to:

(a) whether it would have been reasonable and practicable for the party adducing the evidence to have called the person who made the original statement as a witness;

(b) whether the original statement was made contemporaneously with the events in question;

(c) whether the evidence involves multiple hearsay;

(d) whether any person involved had any motive to conceal or misrepresent matters;

(e) whether the original statement was edited, or was made in collaboration with someone else or for a particular purpose;

(f) whether the circumstances suggest an attempt to prevent proper evaluation of the weight of the evidence.

11.9.3.2 Right of the opposing party to cross-examine the person who originally made the statement

Section 3 of the Civil Evidence Act 1995 provides that where a party adduces hearsay evidence from a person whom he does not call as a witness, any other party may, with the permission of the court, call that person as a witness and cross-examine him. An application for such permission must be made not later than 14 days after service of the hearsay notice (CPR 1998, r 33.4).

11.9.3.3 Competence (Civil Evidence Act 1995, s 5)

Hearsay evidence is not admissible if the original statement was made by a person who was not competent as a witness because of his mental or physical infirmity or lack of understanding.

11.9.3.4 Credibility (Civil Evidence Act 1995, s 5)

Where hearsay evidence is adduced and the person who made the original statement is not called as a witness, evidence is still admissible to attack or support his credibility, or to show that he has made another, inconsistent statement. The party wishing to call such evidence must give notice to the other party not later than 14 days after service of the hearsay evidence (CPR 1998, r 33.5).

Although notice may have been given under s 5, how will the party actually adduce the discrediting evidence (such as an allegation of bias, previous convictions or a previous inconsistent statement) at trial? It is now too late to include such allegations in any witness statements as they have already been served pursuant to the directions order. The opponent's agreement, or otherwise the court's permission, should be sought to rely on the evidence. An application to the court should be made at any pre-trial review or trial. If done at a pre-trial review then permission should be requested to serve a supplemental witness statement dealing with the evidence.

11.9.3.5 Previous inconsistent statements (Civil Evidence Act 1995, s 6)

A statement made previously by a person who is called as a witness in the proceedings is admissible in evidence, provided the requirements of the Civil Evidence Act 1995 regarding hearsay evidence are complied with. Thus, prior notice of the intention to adduce the statement in evidence must be given to the other party.

However, a party who calls a person as a witness may not adduce evidence of a previous statement by that person except either with permission of the court, or in order to rebut a suggestion of recent fabrication. The requirements of the Civil Evidence Act 1995 regarding the use of hearsay evidence should have been complied with.

The effect of this provision is that, where a party calls a witness to give evidence at the trial, the opposing party may cross-examine the witness about a previous inconsistent statement provided that he has complied with the requirements of the Civil Evidence Act 1995 concerning the use of hearsay evidence.

This provision does not prevent a person's witness statement that has been exchanged in accordance with a case management order from being treated as his evidence-in-chief. Indeed, the judge at the trial can, and usually will, order that a witness statement which was served before the trial shall stand as the evidence-in-chief of that witness. The witness will, of course, be present at the trial, and will be subject to cross-examination. In these circumstances, his witness statement is not treated as hearsay evidence.

11.10 Use of plans, photographs and models as evidence (r 33.6)

Where evidence such as a plan, photograph, model or the records of a business or public authority is to be given in evidence and it is not:

(a) contained in a witness statement, affidavit, or expert's report;

(b) to be given orally at the trial; or

(c) the subject of a hearsay notice;

the evidence will not be admissible unless the party intending to use it has disclosed his intention to use such evidence within the deadline for serving witness statements.

He must disclose his intention at least 21 days before the hearing, if:

(a) there are not to be witness statements; or

(b) he intends to use the evidence solely to disprove an allegation made in a witness statement.

If the evidence forms part of an expert's report, he must disclose his intention when he serves his expert's report.

Where a party has given notice of his intention to put in the evidence, he must give every other party an opportunity to inspect it and to agree to its admission without further proof.

11.11 Notice to admit facts (r 32.18)

In order to try to avoid the expense of proving a particular fact at trial, a party may serve on another party a notice requiring him to admit certain facts or a certain part of his case, as specified in the notice. Form N266 should be used. A copy is set out at **Appendix A(10)**. p 231

Such a notice must be served no later than 21 days before the trial.

If the party upon whom the notice is served refuses to admit the relevant fact(s), the other party will still be required to prove the fact(s) at trial. Where, however, he does so, the court may take this into account when considering the issue of costs. Effectively, this means that the party who served the notice will usually recover the cost of proving the facts in question (even if he loses the case).

11.12 Notice to admit or prove documents (r 32.19)

A party is deemed to admit that any document disclosed in a list of documents served under Part 31 (see **Chapter 10**) is genuine unless he serves notice that he wants the document to be proved at trial.

A notice to prove a document must be served by the later of the following:

(a) the latest date for serving witness statements; or

(b) within seven days of disclosure of the document.

11.13 Expert evidence (Part 35)

As we saw at **3.4**, in many cases a party may wish to instruct an expert and rely upon expert evidence. However, parties do not have an unfettered right to use expert evidence and, as part of its case management powers, the court will restrict expert evidence to that which is reasonably required to resolve the proceedings, bearing in mind the overriding objective and particularly the issue of proportionality. *to deal with cases justly and fairly*

expert evidence can be restricted by case management eg joint expert or 1 expert per party

11.13.1 The duty of an expert

Although in many cases an expert is instructed by one particular party, r 35.3 makes it clear that the duty of an expert is to help the court on the matters within his expertise, and this duty overrides any obligation to the person from whom he has received instructions or by whom he is paid. If the expert is unsure of the nature of these obligations, he may file a request for directions from the court. Experts should, therefore, be completely objective and unbiased in the way in which they provide their opinion for the benefit of the court (see *Stevens v Gullis* [1999] BLR 394).

even if their evidence supports one of the party's cases.

Evidence   147

An expert is not disqualified by the fact of being employed by one of the parties, although the court will need to be satisfied that the expert was sufficiently aware of his responsibilities to the court (*Field v Leeds City Council* [2000] 1 EGLR 54). Given the risk of the appearance of bias, parties will generally prefer to instruct an expert who is independent.

11.13.2 The court's power to restrict expert evidence

Rule 35.1(1) provides that expert evidence must be restricted to that which is reasonably required to resolve the proceedings, and r 35.4 provides that no party may call an expert or put in evidence an expert's report without the court's permission. Permission is usually granted at the directions stage, and the party applying for permission must identify both the field in which he wishes to rely on expert evidence and, where practicable, the expert in that field on whose evidence he wishes to rely. As we saw in **Chapter 8**, this information should normally be provided in the allocation questionnaire.

The options available to the court in giving directions on expert evidence include:

(a) directing that no expert evidence is to be adduced at all, or no expert evidence of a particular type or relating to a particular issue;

(b) limiting the number of expert witnesses which each party may call, either generally or in a given speciality;

(c) directing that evidence is to be given by one or more experts chosen by agreement between the parties or, where they cannot agree, chosen by such other manner as the court may direct.

The court will also decide whether it is necessary for experts to give oral evidence at trial. This is probably going to be the case in multi-track proceedings, but in fast track proceedings, the normal position is that expert evidence will be given in the form of a written report or reports rather than by way of oral evidence (see **Chapter 8**).

The court also has the power to limit the amount of the expert's fees and expenses that the party who wishes to rely on the expert may recover from any other party.

11.13.3 Instructions to an expert witness

One would normally expect the instructions from a solicitor to an expert witness to be privileged from inspection by other parties (see **10.11**). However, r 35.10(4) states:

> The instructions referred to in paragraph (3) [the substance of all material instructions, written or oral, on which the report is based] shall not be privileged against disclosure but the court will not, in relation to those instructions—
>
> (a) order disclosure of any specific document; or
>
> (b) permit any questioning in court other than by the party who instructed the expert,
>
> unless it is satisfied that there are reasonable grounds to consider the statement of instructions given under paragraph (3) to be inaccurate or incomplete.

As we shall see at **11.13.5**, the report itself must contain the substance of all material instructions received.

So has legal professional privilege in relation to instructions to an expert gone? The answer appears to be that it has not. Rule 35.10(4) is qualified by PD 35, para 3, which provides that such cross-examination will be permitted only where it is in the 'interests of justice'. Arguably the instructions remain privileged from

148   Civil Litigation

inspection unless and until the court makes an order under the Rule. Such an order will be made only if there are reasonable grounds for believing that the expert's statement of instructions is inaccurate or incomplete: *Lucas v Barking, Havering and Redbridge Hospitals NHS Trust* [2003] EWCA Civ 1102.

Of course, a party can always waive privilege if he wishes to do so. Indeed, there are many occasions when solicitors might use a standard format for instructions to an expert, especially where recommended by a pre-action protocol. In such a case there should be no objection to the expert exhibiting those to his report. However, there is no question of confidential information concerning the merits of the case having to be disclosed. The court will not readily entertain any applications for disclosure or cross-examination in this context. After reports have been exchanged it should be routine for a party to send a copy of the other side's report to their own expert for comment. Obviously one point that can be looked for is whether any report is based on inaccurate or incomplete instructions. If there are doubts the matter should be raised in correspondence and/or an interim application made for directions concerning the 'suspicious' report.

11.13.4 Form of expert evidence

Expert evidence is to be given in a written report unless the court directs otherwise, and, if the party wishes to rely on the expert evidence at trial, the report must be disclosed to the other party in accordance with the directions given by the court. The usual order is for simultaneous mutual exchange on or before a set date.

When first obtained, an expert's report which has been prepared for the sole or dominant purpose of the litigation is a privileged document. It need be disclosed to the other party only if the party who commissioned it wishes to rely on it at trial. If he decides not to rely on the report (perhaps because it is unfavourable) he does not have to allow the other side to inspect it. It is, however, disclosable in part 2 of the list of documents. See further **Chapter 10**.

11.13.5 Contents of the report

Rule 35.10 and PD 35, paras 2.1 and 2.2 give detailed instructions on the contents of an expert's report. The report must:

(a) be addressed to the court and not to the party from whom the expert has received his instructions;

(b) give details of the expert's qualifications;

(c) give details of any literature or other material which the expert has relied on in making the report;

(d) say who carried out any test or experiment which the expert has used for the report and whether or not the test or experiment has been carried out under the expert's supervision;

(e) give the qualifications of the person who carried out any such test or experiment;

(f) where there is a range of opinion on the matters dealt with in the report, summarise the range of opinion and give reasons for his own opinion;

(g) contain a summary of the conclusions reached;

(h) contain a statement that the expert understands his duty to the court and has complied with that duty and will continue to comply with that duty;

(i) contain a statement setting out the substance of all material instructions. The statement should also summarise the facts and instructions given to the expert which are material to the opinions expressed in the report or upon which those opinions are based;

(j) comply with the requirements of any approved expert's protocol;

(k) make clear which of the facts are within the expert's own knowledge;

(l) where an opinion is qualified, state the qualification.

The report must also be supported by a statement of truth that states:

> I confirm that insofar as the facts stated in my report are within my own knowledge I have made clear which they are and I believe them to be true, and that the opinions I have expressed represent my true and complete professional opinion.

11.13.6 Questions to the expert

After an expert's report has been disclosed, the party who did not instruct the expert may put written questions to the expert about his report.

Such written questions:

(a) may be put once only;

(b) must be put within 28 days of service of the report;

(c) must be to clarify the report, unless the court permits or the other party agrees to allow questions for a different purpose.

The answers will be treated as part of the expert's report.

11.13.7 Discussion between experts (r 35.12)

The court will usually direct a discussion between experts after the exchange of their reports and will require the experts to:

(a) identify and discuss the expert issues in the proceedings; and

(b) where possible, reach agreement on an issue. (Any agreement is not binding on the parties unless they have already expressly agreed to be bound by any such agreement.)

The court may specify the issues which the experts must discuss.

The court will also usually direct that, after the discussion, the experts must prepare a statement for the court which:

(a) shows the issues on which they are agreed and on which they disagree; and

(b) summarises the reasons for disagreement.

The content of the discussion will not be referred to at the trial without the consent of the parties.

The purpose of this rule is to try to ensure that the issues on which the experts do disagree are narrowed down as far as possible. This will save both time and costs at the trial.

An experts' without prejudice meeting statement can be found in the multi-track case study at **Appendix D(7)**.

11.13.8 The single joint expert (r 35.7)

Whether it is appropriate for each party to call its own expert evidence depends on the issues raised in each particular case. However, in a fast track case the general approach of the court is to order a single joint expert unless there is good reason not to do so (see para 3.9 of PD 28). A joint expert is less likely to be ordered in a multi-track case. Even where the court is willing to allow the parties to call their own expert evidence on the issue of liability, it may order a joint expert on any quantum issues that require expert evidence.

Both the Queen's Bench Division and the Chancery Court Guides provide that:

> In very many cases it is possible for the question of expert evidence to be dealt with by a single expert. Single experts are, for example, often appropriate to deal with questions of quantum in cases where the primary issues are as to liability. Likewise, where expert evidence is required in order to acquaint the court with matters of expert fact, as opposed to opinion, a single expert will usually be appropriate. There remains, however, a body of cases where liability will turn upon expert opinion evidence and where it will be appropriate for the parties to instruct their own experts. For example, in cases where the issue for determination is as to whether a party acted in accordance with proper professional standards, it will often be of value to the court to hear the opinions of more than one expert as to the proper standard in order that the court becomes acquainted with the range of views existing upon the question and in order that the evidence can be tested in cross examination.

Where the court orders a single joint expert it will usually direct that:

(a) the parties should prepare joint instructions for the expert;
(b) the expert's fees should be paid jointly by the parties; and
(c) if the parties have been unable by a set date to agree on the identity of the expert, further directions should be obtained from the court.

It is less likely in the case of a single joint expert that the court will think it appropriate to allow oral evidence at trial.

Where there is an order for a single joint expert there is, of course, no need for a direction that reports be exchanged.

There is useful guidance from the Court of Appeal in relation to dealing with problems with a single joint expert in the case of *Daniels v Walker* [2000] 1 WLR 1382:

(a) where the parties cannot agree joint instructions for the expert, it is perfectly proper for one party to give separate or supplemental instructions;
(b) where a party is dissatisfied with the expert's report, he should first submit questions to the expert;
(c) if this does not resolve the problem, the dissatisfied party can apply to the court for permission to call another expert. This application will be granted if the court is satisfied that it would be unjust, having regard to the overriding objective, to refuse to allow the further evidence to be called;
(d) where the dissatisfied party has already obtained its own expert's report, the court should not grant permission for that evidence to be used at trial until the experts have met to resolve their differences. Permission for oral evidence to be given at trial is a last resort.

Further, where a single joint expert is appointed by the parties pursuant to a court order, neither party should meet that expert without the other party being present. See *Peet v Mid-Kent Healthcare Trust (Practice Note)* [2001] EWCA Civ 1703, [2002] 3 All ER 688.

11.14 Assessors (r 35.15)

In some cases of a technical nature, the court may seek the assistance of someone with technical knowledge in the relevant field. Such a person is known as an assessor, and he has a judicial role in that he is instructed to assist the court. He is not an expert witness and cannot be cross-examined by any of the parties. His function is to 'educate' the judge and to enable the judge to reach a properly informed decision.

By r 35.15, the assessor shall take such part in the proceedings as the court may direct. The court may direct the assessor to prepare a report and/or direct the assessor to attend the trial. Any report prepared by an assessor will be sent to the parties.

The use of assessors remains rare.

11.15 Human rights

11.15.1 Hearsay evidence

In *R (Clingham) v Marylebone Magistrates' Court* [2001] LTL, 22 January, the provisions in the Civil Evidence Act 1995 permitting hearsay evidence to be adduced in civil proceedings were challenged as a breach of Article 6(1) ECHR. The complaint was that since the evidence could not be challenged by cross-examination, the trial was unfair. The Divisional Court held that the admission of hearsay evidence did not automatically result in an unfair trial under Article 6(1). It was, of course, important that the court should consider the weight to be attached to the evidence under s 4 of the Act.

11.15.2 Expert evidence

The ability of parties to challenge directions restricting the use of expert evidence has been dented by the case of *Daniels v Walker* (see **11.13.8**). The defendant complained that the refusal to allow him to call his own expert evidence, when dissatisfied with the conclusions reached by a joint expert, had amounted to a breach of his right to a fair trial under Article 6 ECHR. The Court of Appeal decided that since permission to rely on the additional evidence would not have been refused had this been unjust pursuant to the overriding objective, there could be no question of a contravention of the right to a fair trial. Provided, therefore, that the court is careful to apply the overriding objective in reaching decisions about the use of expert evidence, it is likely to be difficult for parties to challenge successfully under Article 6. The same principle would apply to case management decisions about witnesses of fact.

Chapter 12
Settlement

12.1	Negotiations	153
12.2	Pre-action settlements	153
12.3	Settlements reached after the issue of proceedings	154
12.4	Part 36	154
12.5	Claims involving children and patients	165
12.6	Discontinuance (Part 38)	165

Most disputes are resolved not by a judgment of the court but by the parties reaching a settlement. This can happen at any stage from before the issue of proceedings to during the trial. Settlement may be achieved as a result of negotiations, which will often involve the use of the procedures set out in Part 36, or (less commonly) the use of alternative dispute resolution (ADR).

In this chapter, we consider negotiations, the provisions of Part 36 and various ways in which settlements are recorded in writing. ADR is discussed in **Chapter 15**.

12.1 Negotiations

12.1.1 Solicitor's authority

The scope of the solicitor's authority to negotiate on his client's behalf depends on whether or not proceedings have been issued. Prior to issue, the solicitor has no implied authority to settle the client's claim. Acceptance of any offer can, therefore, only be subject to the client's approval. Where the client wishes to accept, it is advisable for the solicitor to obtain written confirmation of this.

Once proceedings have been issued, the solicitor has implied authority to compromise a claim. However, in practice it is, of course, essential to seek the client's express instructions.

12.1.2 Basis on which to conduct negotiations

Negotiations may be conducted either orally or in writing. Whichever method is adopted, care should be taken to ensure that the negotiations proceed on a 'without prejudice' basis. This ensures that the negotiations cannot be referred to in court at a later date except to prove the terms of any settlement reached (see further **3.10.1**).

Negotiation is dealt with further in *Skills for Lawyers*, **Chapter 11**.

12.2 Pre-action settlements

12.2.1 Costs and interest

Where a settlement is reached prior to the issue of proceedings, the claimant will not be entitled to recover his legal costs unless this has been agreed. Neither will he be entitled to interest under s 69 of the CCA 1984, or s 35A of the SCA 1981. There may, however, be an entitlement to interest under contract. Whatever the

154 Civil Litigation

position, it is important that the parties are clear whether any amount for costs and/or interest is included in the terms being proposed.

12.2.2 Recording a pre-action settlement

It is equally important that once settlement terms have been agreed, they are clearly and accurately recorded in writing, so that the agreement can be enforced if one of the parties defaults.

It will often be sufficient for a settlement reached before the issue of proceedings to be recorded in an exchange of correspondence. Commonly, there will be a letter from the potential defendant setting out the terms being offered 'in full and final settlement' of all claims which the prospective claimant may have, and a reply accepting these terms. More complicated settlements may be recorded in a formal settlement agreement.

12.3 Settlements reached after the issue of proceedings

It is preferable for the settlement to be recorded in a court order or judgment, since this will make enforcement easier if the agreement is not honoured. In particular, enforcement proceedings (see **Chapter 14**) may be commenced to recover any money due under the settlement (including costs). The date by which payment of any debt or damages is due must, however, be specified in the judgment or order.

12.3.1 Consent orders or judgments

Where none of the parties is a litigant in person, it will often be possible to avoid an application to the court by drawing up a consent order or judgment for sealing by a court officer under r 40.6. Although in theory the court retains the power not to approve the proposed order, it will in practice be referred to a judge only if it appears to be incorrect or unclear. An example of a consent order appears at **Appendix D(9)**.

12.3.2 *Tomlin* orders

A *Tomlin* order stays the claim on agreed terms that are set out in a schedule to the order (an example of such an order appears at **Appendix B(1)**). The parties may choose to use a *Tomlin* order if:

(a) they wish to keep some or all of the settlement terms confidential; or
(b) the terms agreed include provisions that go beyond the boundaries of the litigation or are beyond the power of the court to order.

The order should contain a 'liberty to apply' clause. This allows a party to enforce the settlement by reviving the claim and seeking an order that the terms should be complied with.

It should be noted that where one party is to pay the other's costs, the court will not be able to assess the amount of those costs (see **Chapter 13**) unless provision is made for this in the order (rather than the schedule). Similarly, any provision for the payment of money out of court needs to be contained in the order.

12.4 Part 36

The purpose of Part 36 is to encourage settlement by imposing pressure on the recipient of a settlement offer to accept it. The pressure lies in the fact that a failure to accept will usually result in a penalty in costs, and sometimes in interest. A Part

36 settlement can be put forward by either a claimant or a defendant (including a Part 20 claimant or defendant), both before and during proceedings.

A claimant has little to lose in making a Part 36 offer. If accepted by the defendant, the matter is at an end. If refused, it may stimulate the defendant to make his own offer and the parties may move towards a settlement.

Why should a defendant make a settlement proposal under Part 36? Well, no defendant can ever be certain that the claim will be dismissed. Doubts over a defence, worry about adverse publicity, concerns about the potential liability for significant costs, etc may well see a defendant make a Part 36 proposal. Moreover, that proposal cannot be made known to the trial judge until he has determined all issues of liability and quantum. So a defendant's defence cannot be adversely affected. Further, if the proposal is refused, it may stimulate the claimant to make his own proposal and the parties may move towards a settlement.

12.4.1 Pre-action offers (r 36.10)

Before proceedings are issued, it is open to the prospective parties to offer to settle. The terms can include both monetary and other proposals. Rule 36.10 provides as follows:

(1) If a person makes an offer to settle before proceedings are begun which complies with the provisions of this rule, the court will take that offer into account when making any order as to costs.

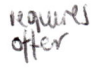

(2) The offer must—
   (a) be expressed to be open for at least 21 days after the date it was made;
   (b) if made by a person who would be a defendant were proceedings commenced, include an offer to pay the costs of the offeree incurred up to the date 21 days after the date it was made; and
   (c) otherwise comply with this Part.

(3) If the offeror is a defendant to a money claim—
   (a) he must make a Part 36 payment within 14 days of service of the claim form; and
   (b) the amount of the payment must be not less than the sum offered before proceedings began.

(4) An offeree may not, after proceedings have begun, accept—
   (a) an offer made under paragraph (2); or
   (b) a Part 36 payment made under paragraph (3), without the permission of the court.

(5) An offer under this rule is made when it is received by the offeree.

12.4.1.1 Differences between claimant's and defendant's pre-action offers

As mentioned in **12.2.1**, a potential claimant who settles before proceedings are commenced is not, as a general rule, entitled to recover costs or interest unless this is agreed to by the defendant. A potential claimant making a pre-action offer under r 36.10 will, therefore, need to make it clear whether he expects to receive interest and costs. Provided a prospective claimant makes an offer in accordance with r 36.10, it will be taken into account under Part 36 if proceedings are issued and a trial takes place (see *Huck v Robson* [2002] EWCA Civ 398, [2002] 3 All ER 263). So potentially an order might be made under r 36.21 (see **12.4.5**).

The position is different for the potential defendant. As an exception to the general rule, a defendant is required by r 36.10(2)(b) to offer to pay the potential claimant's costs up to the expiry of the 21-day period for acceptance. He is not obliged to offer interest, but would be wise to make sure that his position on this is made clear if the prospective claimant has demanded interest.

It should also be noted that once proceedings have been issued, a defendant is obliged to convert his pre-action Part 36 offer into a Part 36 payment if he wishes to preserve his 'Part 36 rights' in respect of that offer (see **12.4.2**). Unless the defendant pays into court a sum at least equal to his pre-action offer within 14 days of service of the claim form, the court will not apply Part 36 to the Part 36 pre-action offer, but only take it into account generally when deciding costs.

Where a potential defendant refuses to accept a Part 36 pre-action offer and is ordered at trial to pay the prospective claimant more than that amount, the court may, and usually will, impose on the potential defendant the penalties in r 36.21 (set out at **12.4.5**).

12.4.2 Defendant's Part 36 payment

Once proceedings have been issued, a defendant may make a Part 36 Payment (ie, he pays a sum of money into court). This applies whether or not he has made a pre-action offer. The defendant is required to file a Part 36 payment notice (also known as a 'notice of payment in'), which he must then serve on the claimant (see **Appendix A(14)**). After service of the payment notice the defendant must file a certificate of service with the court.

The payment notice must comply with the requirements of r 36.6 and para 5 of PD 36. Many of these requirements are aimed at ensuring that the terms on which the payment is offered are clear. Thus the notice must state:

(a) the amount of the payment in;

(b) whether the payment relates to the whole claim or to part of it, or to any issue that arises in it and, if so, which part or issue;

(c) whether it takes into account any counterclaim;

(d) where an interim payment (see **9.7**) has been made, that the payment takes this into account; and

(e) where the payment is stated to be exclusive of interest, whether interest is being offered and, if so, the period(s) and rate(s) for which it is offered.

The payment notice must be signed by the defendant or his solicitor.

PD 36, para 3.4 provides that a defendant who wishes to withdraw or reduce a Part 36 payment must obtain the court's permission to do so. This is usually given where new evidence has come to light which makes it more likely that the claimant will lose on liability, or not receive so much by way of quantum.

12.4.2.1 Acceptance

The claimant has 21 days from service of the notice to accept. If, within this time, the claimant serves the defendant with notice of acceptance, the claim is stayed and the claimant is entitled to the costs of the proceedings on the standard basis (see **13.3.3**) up until that date. The notice of acceptance (see **Appendix A(15)**) must also be filed at court.

Provided the amount offered is reasonable, acceptance has a number of advantages for the claimant. The proceedings are brought to an end without the expense, uncertainty and stress of a trial. The claimant has an entitlement to costs and has the comfort of knowing that the settlement money is immediately available, subject to it being released by the court. In most circumstances, the

Settlement 157

court will do this on receipt of the notice of acceptance, without the need for a court order.

The position is slightly more complicated where the Part 36 payment covers only part of the proceedings. In such cases, acceptance will have the effect of staying only that part of the proceedings and, unless the parties have been able to reach agreement, the court will have to decide on costs.

12.4.2.2 Late acceptance

The claimant may accept after the 21-day period only with the consent of the defendant or the permission of the court. Where the court does grant permission, it will also decide what costs order it should make. It will usually order the claimant to pay the defendant's costs on the standard basis (see 13.3.3) from and including the day after the 21-day period for acceptance expired.

12.4.2.3 Non-acceptance

Where the claimant does not accept the Part 36 payment the proceedings will, of course, continue. If at trial the claimant is awarded more than the amount of the Part 36 payment, the claimant can be seen to have been justified in not accepting it. In those circumstances the court will normally order that the defendant is to pay the claimant's costs.

But what if the claimant is awarded either exactly the same amount as the Part 36 payment, or less? The court will, unless it considers it unjust to do so, make a 'split costs order' pursuant to r 36.20.

Before we look at r 36.20, we need to answer this question: how can the court tell if the claimant has been awarded more or less, or the same amount as the defendant's Part 36 payment? Where the claimant has made a money claim the judgment will be for a capital sum plus interest awarded at the trial judge's discretion, usually from when the cause of action accrued up to trial. If the judge has made an award of interest it is necessary for him to be provided with a calculation of the amount of interest he would have awarded had the judgment been given at the date the Part 36 payment expired.

Example

C instructs solicitors in April 2001. A letter of claim is sent in May 2001 seeking £70,000 damages plus interest in respect of a contract that was broken in July 2000 (when the cause of action accrued).

In July 2003, C commences High Court proceedings which include a claim for interest under s 35A of the SCA 1981. C receives a Part 36 payment notice from D in the sum of £55,000 (inclusive of interest) on 5 January 2004. The last day to accept that sum without needing the court's permission is 26 January 2004. C does not accept the sum.

At trial in July 2005 C is awarded £38,000 plus interest up to that date of approximately £15,200 (five years at 8% per annum). C has been awarded £53,200 in total. But has C beaten D's Part 36 payment made back in January 2004? To decide that we must compare like with like and so calculate the amount of interest at 8% per annum that would be awarded on £38,000 from July 2000 to 26 January 2004. That is approximately three and a half years, totalling £10,640 in interest. Hence, at January 2004 C would have been awarded a total of approximately £48,640 and so has not beaten D's Part 36 payment. Hindsight has shown that C should have accepted the payment in January 2004, and in effect C has wasted the time and money of D and the court ever since.

158   Civil Litigation

So what is a r 36.20 'split costs order'? This means that the defendant is required to pay the claimant's costs of the claim until the end of the 21-day period and the claimant is ordered to pay the defendant's costs from then on. These costs are normally ordered to be paid on the standard basis (see **13.3.3**). Since the run-up to trial and the trial itself are generally the most expensive periods in the litigation, the consequences for a claimant who fails to beat a Part 36 payment can be severe.

Further, if the defendant made a pre-action offer which he converted into a Part 36 payment within 14 days of service of the claim form (see **12.4.1**), the court may order an earlier split in the costs. The defendant may be ordered to pay the claimant's costs up to and including the last day for acceptance of the pre-action offer and the claimant ordered to pay the defendant's costs thereafter. Again, costs will normally be ordered on the standard basis.

In the above example, there are three possible trial outcomes. The table that follows considers each.

Result at trial	Likely costs order (subject to the court's discretion)
C **awarded more** than the payment (ie, C 'beats' Part 36 Payment).	C awarded his costs of the claim to be paid by D on the standard basis.
C awarded the **same or less** than the payment (ie C fails to 'beat' Part 36 Payment).	The court will make a split costs order: D ordered to pay C's costs on the standard basis from April 2001 up to and including 26 January 2004. C ordered to pay D's costs on the standard basis from 27 January 2004 until judgment in July 2005.
C **loses** at trial.	C ordered to pay D's costs of defending the claim on the standard basis.

There is a flowchart summarising the consequences of acceptance and non-acceptance of a Part 36 payment in Appendix C(3).

12.4.2.4   Financial consequences of Rule 36.20 order

Let us consider a very simple example to show the potential financial effect on the parties of a r 36.20 'split costs' order. The first step is to ascertain the last day for acceptance of the defendant's Part 36 payment without needing the permission of the court. In the example we call this the 'split date'.

> **Example**
>
> Assume that C is awarded £45,000 damages (inclusive of interest) at trial. Before the split date C's costs are in the region of £10,000 and D's approximately £8,500. After the split date C's costs are in the region of £15,500 and D's approximately £13,250. Who pays what?
>
> D will pay C:
>
> (a)   the £45,000 damages; and
>
> (b)   C's costs of £10,000 up to the split date; and
>
> (c)   his own costs of £8,500 to his solicitors
>
> After the split date:
>
> (a)   C pays D's costs of £13,250; and
>
> (b)   his own costs of £15,500 to his solicitors.

Settlement

What is the overall effect on C?

	C receives: £	C pays out: £
Damages	45,000	
Costs before split date	10,000	
TOTAL	55,000	
Own legal costs		25,500
D's costs from split date		13,250
TOTAL		38,750
BALANCE	16,250	

C recovers £45,000 damages and £10,000 costs, a total of £55,000.

C pays out his own costs of £25,500 and D's costs of £13,250, a total of £38,750.

C receives the balance of £16,250.

What is the overall effect on D?

	D receives: £	D pays out: £
Damages		45,000
C's costs before split date		10,000
Own legal costs		21,750
TOTAL		76,750
Costs from split date	13,250	
TOTAL	13,250	
BALANCE		63,500

D pays C £45,000 damages and £10,000 costs and D pays his own costs of £21,750, a total of £76,750.

D receives from C costs of £13,250.

D is out of pocket by £63,500.

As to the assessment of the amount of costs payable under a court order see **13.3**.

12.4.2.5 Tactical considerations

From the point of view of a defendant who considers himself at risk on liability, a Part 36 payment can provide a useful mechanism for pressurising the claimant to accept a reasonable settlement and will often be used tactically as part of settlement discussions. Of course, the defendant has to make a careful assessment of how much to pay in. An over-generous payment will be snapped up by a claimant eager to receive more than the true value of the claim. An unrealistically low payment will impose no real pressure, since the claimant will feel confident of beating it at trial. The wise defendant will aim to pitch his payment at a level that is just high enough for the claimant to feel that it would be unsafe not to accept.

Also important is the stage in the proceedings at which a Part 36 payment is made. The earlier this is done, the greater the potential costs protection for the defendant and the greater the pressure placed on the claimant. Thus, the vulnerable defendant should make a payment as soon as he has enough information to judge its amount accurately.

12.4.3 Defendant's Part 36 offer

Once proceedings have started, the only way that a defendant faced with a monetary claim can generally obtain costs protection is by making a Part 36 payment. The court will not usually grant a split costs order against a claimant who has failed to beat an offer which could have been made in the form of a Part 36 payment. However, where the claim is non-monetary (eg, a dispute over ownership of property), the defendant may put forward a Part 36 offer both before and/or during proceedings.

12.4.3.1 Acceptance or non-acceptance of defendant's Part 36 offer

Acceptance by the claimant of the offer within the 21-day period has the same effect as acceptance of a Part 36 payment:

(a) the claimant must file and serve a notice of acceptance;
(b) the proceedings are stayed; and
(c) the claimant receives his costs on the standard basis up to the date of acceptance.

As with a Part 36 payment, late acceptance is possible with the consent of the defendant or the permission of the court. The consequences of non-acceptance are also the same. If the claimant fails to 'beat' the offer at trial, the court will, unless it considers it unjust, make a split costs order.

12.4.3.2 Mixed monetary and non-monetary claims

In the case of a claim that contains both monetary and non-monetary elements, the defendant should make a Part 36 payment in respect of any money being offered and a Part 36 offer as to the non-monetary claim. In such circumstances, the claimant is not entitled to accept the payment but not the non-monetary terms. The defendant is obliged to warn the claimant in the payment notice that if the money is accepted, he is deemed also to have accepted the offer in its entirety.

12.4.4 Requirements in relation to Part 36 offers made during proceedings

The offer must comply with various requirements set out at r 36.5 and PD 36, similar to those relating to a notice of payment in. It must:

(a) be in writing;
(b) state that it is a Part 36 offer;
(c) be expressed to be open for at least 21 days after the date it is received;
(d) state whether the offer relates to the whole claim and whether it takes into account any counterclaim;
(e) be signed by the party or his solicitor.

Where the offer is made by a company or other corporation, it may be signed by someone holding a senior position (such as a director, manager or other officer), provided their position is stated.

It should be noted that the fact that the offer must be expressed to be open for a period of 21 days does not prevent the offeror from withdrawing it within that period provided it has not been accepted. The Court of Appeal so confirmed in *Scammell and Others v Dicker* [2001] 1 WLR 631, concluding that the effect of Part

36 was not to exclude the general law of contract that an unaccepted offer could be withdrawn. However, once an offer is withdrawn, it has no effect at all under Part 36: see r 36.5(8).

12.4.5 Claimant's Part 36 offer

It is not appropriate for a claimant to make a Part 36 payment (unless he wishes to do so in respect of any Part 20 counterclaim: see **7.1**). Instead, once proceedings have started, he may make a Part 36 offer, setting out in writing the terms on which he would be prepared to settle. The offer must comply with the requirements in **12.4.4**. — Part 36.5

A claimant's Part 36 offer in respect of a monetary sum is deemed to be inclusive of interest unless stated otherwise. If interest is required separately, the amount and rate must be stated.

12.4.5.1 Acceptance

If the defendant accepts the Part 36 offer within the time set, the proceedings are stayed on the terms suggested by the claimant and the defendant pays the claimant's costs on the standard basis up until the date of acceptance.

Late acceptance is possible, provided the parties can agree the question of costs. If they cannot, the defendant may accept only with the permission of the court.

12.4.5.2 Non-acceptance

Claimant's failure to beat his Part 36 offer

No specific penalty is imposed on the claimant if he fails at trial to do better than the proposals in his Part 36 offer, although the making of the offer may be taken into account by the court in exercising its general discretion as to costs, especially if the claimant has exaggerated his claim.

Claimant succeeds in beating his Part 36 offer

Where the claimant does better at trial than the proposals in his Part 36 offer, r 36.21 provides that the court will, unless it considers it unjust to do so, order that the claimant:

(a) be awarded interest on the whole or part of any sum awarded to him (excluding interest already awarded) at a rate not exceeding 10% per annum above the Bank of England's base rate for some or all of the period from the expiry of the deadline for acceptance to judgment; and/or

(b) recover his costs on the indemnity basis (see **13.3.3**) from that date; and/or

(c) be awarded interest on those indemnity costs at up to 10% per annum above base rate.

When adjudicating on quantum, the trial judge will usually award interest on damages from when the cause of action accrued.

Before we look at r 36.21, we need to answer this question: how can the court tell if the claimant has been awarded more or less, or the same amount as the claimant's Part 36 offer? Where the claimant has made a money claim the judgment will be for a capital sum plus interest awarded at the trial judge's discretion, usually from when the cause of action accrued up to trial. If the judge has made an award of interest it is necessary for him to be provided with a calculation of the amount of interest he would have awarded had the judgment been given at the date the claimant's Part 36 offer expired.

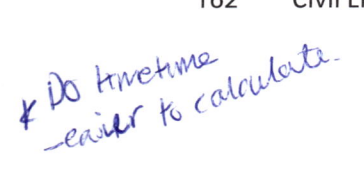

Example

C instructs solicitors in January 2001. A letter of claim is sent in February 2001 seeking £100,000 damages plus interest in respect of a contract that was broken in November 2000 (when the cause of action accrued).

In May 2003, C commences High Court proceedings which include a claim for interest under s 35A of the SCA 1981. C makes a Part 36 offer to D in the sum of £75,000 (inclusive of interest) on 4 August 2003. The last day to accept that sum without needing the court's permission is 25 August 2003. D does not agree to pay the sum.

At trial in November 2005 C is awarded £65,000 plus interest up to that date of approximately £26,000 (five years at 8% per annum). C has been awarded £91,000 in total. But has C beaten his Part 36 offer made back in August 2003? To decide that we must compare like with like and so calculate the amount of interest at 8% per annum that would be awarded on £65,000 from November 2000 to 25 August 2003. That is approximately two and three-quarter years totalling £14,300 in interest. Hence, at August 2003 C would have been awarded a total of approximately £79,300 and so has been awarded more than his Part 36 offer. Hindsight has shown that D should have accepted the offer in August 2003, and in effect D has wasted the time and money of C and the court ever since.

There is a cap on the amount of interest that can be awarded by the trial judge generally and under r 36.21. This is set out in r 36.21(6) which provides that 'where the court awards interest under [r 36.21] and also awards interest on the same sum and for the same period under any other power, the total rate of interest may not exceed 10% above base rate'.

This award of interest under r 36.21 is often called 'enhanced interest'. But how much should the court award? David Foskett QC, when sitting as a deputy High Court judge in the case of *Little and Others v George Little Sebire & Co* [2001] EWCA Civ 894, [2001] STC 1065, indicated that the court should take as the starting point 10% above base. However, Lord Woolf MR in *Petrotrade Inc v Texaco Ltd* [2001] 1 WLR 947 said that he did not endorse that approach. In *Mann and Holt v Lexington Insurance Co* [2001] 1 Lloyd's Rep 1, Waller LJ said in the unreported post-judgment discussion:

> What the rule provides for is a rate not exceeding 10%. The object of the rule must be to provide the court with a weapon to punish parties who have failed to take and accept a Part 36 offer and have really behaved badly in the context of litigation as a whole. The ten per cent must be reserved for the worst cases.

In considering whether it would be unjust to impose these penalties, the court will take into account all the circumstances of the case, including:

(a) the terms of the Part 36 offer;
(b) the stage in the proceedings when any Part 36 offer or payment was made;
(c) the information available to the parties at that time; and
(d) the conduct of the parties with regard to giving or refusing information for the purposes of enabling the offer or payment to be evaluated.

Example 1

C alleges a breach of contract by D, occurring in March 2001.

C issues proceedings in December 2002 claiming damages estimated at £75,000 plus interest. In March 2003, C makes a Part 36 offer of £60,000. The deadline for acceptance is 27 March 2003. D does not accept and the case proceeds to trial and judgment is given on 23 September 2005.

(i) If C wins but fails to beat his Part 36 offer

If D loses at trial and is ordered to pay C damages of £60,000 or less, the court will usually award C his costs of the claim on the standard basis.

(ii) If C wins and beats his Part 36 offer

If D loses at trial and is ordered to pay C damages of more than £60,000, the court will, unless it considers it unjust, impose penalties under r 36.21. The court has a discretion but might order D to pay:

- the usual statutory interest of 8% per annum on the damages awarded from March 2001 (when C's cause of action arose) until 23 September 2005, plus
- enhanced interest on the damages awarded from 27 March 2003 to the date of judgment at no more than 10% per annum above the base rate, but less the 8% per annum already awarded, plus
- the costs incurred by C up to 27 March 2003 on the standard basis, plus
- the costs incurred by C from 28 March 2003 on the indemnity basis, plus
- interest on the indemnity basis costs from 28 March 2003 until the date of judgment on 23 September 2005 at a maximum of 10% per annum above base rate.

(iii) If D wins

D will usually be awarded his costs of defending the claim on the standard basis.

Example 2

Where one party makes an offer or payment under Part 36, the other may well choose to counter with a Part 36 offer or payment of their own. What is the effect of this?

Assume the same facts as in Example 1, save that having rejected C's Part 36 offer, D chooses to make a Part 36 payment of £40,000. C does not accept the Part 36 payment and the claim proceeds to trial.

The table below sets out the likely cost consequences of various possible outcomes at trial:

Result at trial	Likely costs order (subject to the court's discretion)
C is awarded more than £60,000 at trial. C beats own offer.	Penalties under r 36.21 imposed (as in (ii) of Example 1)
C is awarded more than £40,000 at trial but not more than £60,000. C fails to better own offer but beats the payment.	D pays C's costs of the claim on the standard basis (as in (i) of Example 1 above)
C wins at trial but is awarded £40,000 or less. C fails to beat the payment.	D's Part 36 payment has been effective. The court is likely to make a split costs order under which: (a) D will have to pay C's costs of the claim on the standard basis up until the last day that D's Part 36 payment could have been accepted by C without the court's permission; and (b) from that point onwards, C will have to pay D's costs on the standard basis.
C loses at trial.	C will pay D's costs of the claim on the standard basis (see (ii) in Example 1)

12.4.5.3 Tactical considerations

Where the defendant does not accept a Part 36 offer and the claimant beats his own offer at trial, the defendant is likely to pay a heavy price. In contrast, we have seen that a claimant who fails to beat his own offer is usually in no worse position than if his offer had not been made. The result is that, whereas there is no downside for the claimant in making such an offer, a reasonable proposal will place the defendant under considerable pressure.

Since the penalties in r 36.21 are imposed as from the expiry of the deadline for acceptance, the earlier the claimant makes his offer, the greater the pressure on the defendant. It is tactically sensible for a claimant to make an offer as soon as there is enough information to judge its amount and prior to issuing proceedings where practicable.

A defendant faced with a pre-action or post-action Part 36 offer should consider carefully whether it would be appropriate to make a pre-action counter-offer or Part 36 payment during the proceedings.

12.4.6 Assessing the terms of a Part 36 offer or payment

Since penalties may result from a failure to accept a Part 36 offer or payment, it is important that the recipient is clear about the terms being proposed. He is, therefore, entitled within seven days of receiving the offer or notice of payment to request clarification. If the information is not provided within seven days, he may apply to the court for an order that it should be.

The party putting forward the offer or payment should also bear in mind that the court's power to impose penalties or a split costs order is ultimately discretionary.

The Court of Appeal has emphasised the need for a party considering a payment or offer to be provided with the information needed to assess whether to accept it (see *Ford v GKR Construction and Others* [2000] 1 All ER 802). Where there is a failure to provide material information the court may well consider it unjust either to make a split costs order under r 36.20, or to impose penalties on a defendant under r 36.21.

12.4.7 Secrecy

Except in very limited circumstances, neither a Part 36 offer nor a Part 36 payment may be revealed to the trial judge until all questions of liability and quantum have been decided.

What if a Part 36 offer or payment is made known to the trial judge? In *Garratt v Saxby* [2004] LTL, 18 February, the Court of Appeal indicated that the judge had to determine whether the disclosure of the offer made a fair trial possible, or whether justice required the judge to withdraw from the case. The judge in exercising that discretion was entitled to take into account the additional time, cost and difficulty involved for all concerned if the hearing were to be aborted.

12.4.8 Offers other than under Part 36

There is nothing to prevent parties from making offers to settle that do not comply with the procedural requirements of Part 36. Provided the offer is an open one or made 'without prejudice save as to costs', the court is obliged to have regard to it when exercising its discretion as to costs (r 44.3(4)(c)). However, parties should be cautious about making non-Part 36 offers if they wish them to carry Part 36 consequences, since to do so will certainly increase the uncertainty of the outcome. In particular, a defendant who could make a Part 36 payment but chooses merely to put forward an offer, will not usually be treated as if a Part 36 payment was made (*Amber v Stacy* [2001] 2 All ER 88).

12.5 Claims involving children and patients

Where a claim is made by or on behalf of a child or patient, or against a child or patient, no settlement of that claim is valid without the approval of the court. Thus, neither a Part 36 offer nor a Part 36 payment may be accepted without the court's approval.

Approval is required even if a compromise is reached before the issue of proceedings. In such a case the application for approval should be made under Part 8 (see **7.3**).

12.6 Discontinuance (Part 38)

12.6.1 General provisions

A claimant may decide not to pursue his claim, even though no settlement has been reached. For example, he may conclude that his chances of succeeding at trial or of recovering any money from the defendant are so slim that he would be better to discontinue. A claimant may discontinue a claim at any time and, if there are co-defendants, he may do so against all or any of them. The claimant will need the court's permission to discontinue a claim where:

(a) the court has granted an interim injunction; or
(b) any party has given an undertaking to the court.

If an interim payment has been made, the claimant may discontinue only if:

(a) the defendant who made the payment consents in writing; or
(b) the court gives permission.

Where there are two or more claimants, a claimant may discontinue only if:

(a) all the other claimants consent in writing; or
(b) the court gives permission.

12.6.2 Procedure

The claimant must file and serve a notice of discontinuance on all other parties. If the claimant needs the consent of another party in order to discontinue, a copy of that consent must be attached to the notice.

If the claimant discontinues in a case where consent or the court's permission was not required, any defendant may apply to set aside the notice of discontinuance. The application must be made within 28 days.

12.6.3 Liability for costs

A claimant who discontinues is liable for the defendant's costs unless the court orders otherwise. It is therefore vital that a solicitor acting for a potential claimant explains this to the client.

If proceedings are only partly discontinued, the claimant is liable only for the costs of the part of the claim he is discontinuing, and those costs must not be assessed until the rest of the case is over unless the court orders otherwise.

Chapter 13

Final Preparations for Trial, Trial and Assessment of Costs

13.1	Final preparations for trial	167
13.2	Trial	169
13.3	Costs	174
13.4	Human rights	183

13.1 Final preparations for trial

13.1.1 Briefing counsel

If the solicitor intends to brief counsel to deal with the trial, counsel should be instructed well in advance of the trial date. Very often, of course, counsel will already have been instructed in a case to advise, draft a statement of case or appear at a case management conference. Moreover, the trial date or period will have been known since allocation. The brief to counsel should contain copies of all relevant documents which will be required at the trial.

The content of the brief should deal in detail with the facts still in issue and how they are to be proved. Even though the barrister may be familiar with the case, the solicitor should nevertheless take the time to set matters out fully in the brief in case it is passed on to another barrister at a later stage. Occasionally, the barrister originally instructed may be unable to attend the trial, in which case the brief will be handed over to another barrister at short notice.

Practice varies as to whether there will be a conference with counsel before the hearing. This will depend on the extent to which there have already been conferences, and the value, importance and complexity of the case.

When acting for a private or commercial client, it is for the solicitor to negotiate the brief fee with counsel's clerk following delivery of the brief. In a fast track case, one would try to restrict the brief fee to the maximum amount allowed for the advocacy in a fast track case (see **13.3.6**).

In a multi-track case, the fee covers only one day unless agreed otherwise. If the case takes more than one day, counsel will be entitled to charge a 'refresher fee' for each subsequent day. For example, the brief fee (to cover preparation for trial and the first day) might be £5,000 for a fairly complex High Court case, with a refresher fee of £1,500.

A brief to counsel can be found in the multi-track case study at **Appendix D(8)**.

13.1.2 Attendance of witnesses (Part 34)

13.1.2.1 Witnesses in general

All witnesses should be kept fully informed of the expected trial date and, once the date has been fixed, should be told of that date without delay. It is essential that, at an early stage, witnesses are asked whether any particular periods would be inconvenient for them to attend the trial. Details of a witness's availability have to be given to the court on the allocation and pre-trial checklists, listing questionnaires (see **Chapter 8**).

Even where witnesses have been kept fully informed and involved, it is unwise to rely on the assumption that they will attend court voluntarily. Instead, their attendance should be encouraged by serving them with a witness summons. This is a document issued by the court requiring a witness to:

(a) attend court to give evidence; or
(b) produce documents to the court.

A witness summons should be served at least seven days before the date on which the witness is required to attend court. It will then be binding upon the witness, and if the witness fails to attend court, he will be in contempt. If a party wishes to issue a summons less than seven days before the date of the trial, permission from the court must be obtained.

The witness summons will normally be served by the court, unless the party on whose behalf it is issued indicates that he wishes to serve it himself.

At the time of service of a witness summons the witness must be offered or paid:

(a) a sum reasonably sufficient to cover his expenses in travelling to and from the court; and
(b) such sum by way of compensation for loss of time as may be specified by the court.

The danger in not serving a witness with a witness summons is that if he fails to attend the trial, the first question the judge will ask the solicitor or barrister conducting the case is why a witness summons was not served. If a witness summons had been served, there is a greater possibility that the court will be sympathetic enough to grant an adjournment of the trial if that is required because of the crucial nature of the missing witness's evidence.

Police officers must always be served with a witness summons, because they will not give evidence in a civil matter on behalf of either party unless they are under an obligation to do so.

13.1.2.2 Expert witnesses

Practice varies as to whether to serve an expert witness with a witness summons. The safest course is to ask the expert whether he wishes to be put under this obligation to attend. Some expert witnesses do wish to be put under this obligation because they are busy professional people and the compulsion of the order makes it easier for them to break any other appointments.

13.1.3 Preparing trial bundles (Part 39)

Unless the court orders otherwise, the claimant must file the trial bundle not more than seven days and not less than three days before the start of the trial. By para 3.2 of PD 39 – Miscellaneous Provisions Relating to Hearings, unless the court orders otherwise, the trial bundle should include a copy of:

(1) the claim form and all statements of case,
(2) a case summary and/or chronology where appropriate,
(3) requests for further information and responses to the requests,
(4) all witness statements to be relied on as evidence,
(5) any witness summaries,

(6) any notices of intention to rely on hearsay evidence under rule 33.2,
(7) any notices of intention to rely on evidence (such as a plan, photograph etc) under rule 33.6 which is not—
   (a) contained in a witness statement, affidavit or expert's report,
   (b) being given orally at trial,
   (c) hearsay evidence under rule 33.2,
(8) any medical reports and responses to them,
(9) any expert's reports and responses to them,
(10) any order giving directions as to the conduct of the trial, and
(11) any other necessary documents.

Each party should prepare a case summary (often called a 'skeleton argument') to use at trial. This is designed to assist both the court and the parties by indicating what points are or are not in issue, and the nature of the argument about the disputed matters. It should also assist the court in its advance reading. As a general rule a case summary should therefore:

(a) concisely review the party's submissions of fact in relation to each of the issues with reference to the evidence;
(b) concisely set out the propositions of law advanced with reference to the main authorities relied on;
(c) be divided into numbered paragraphs and paginated consecutively; and
(d) identify any key documents which the trial judge should, if possible, read before the trial starts.

Paragraph 3.9 of PD 39 provides that the contents of the trial bundle should be agreed where possible. The parties should also agree where possible that the documents contained in the bundle are authentic even if not disclosed under Part 31, and that documents in the bundle may be treated as evidence of the facts stated in them even if a notice under the Civil Evidence Act 1995 has not been served. Where it is not possible to agree the contents of the bundle, a summary of the points on which the parties are unable to agree should be included.

The party filing the trial bundle should supply identical bundles to all the parties to the proceedings and for the use of the witnesses.

The trial bundle should be accompanied by an estimated length of reading time and an agreed estimate of the likely length of the hearing. If the trial bundle is very large, a 'core' bundle of key documents, to be read by the trial judge, should be prepared.

13.2 Trial

13.2.1 Venue

Most county courts belong to a group, with one court being designated the trial centre. The trial of the case, whether fast track or multi-track, will usually take place at that trial centre, which may therefore not be the same court that managed the case.

13.2.2 Timetable

In most cases, in both the fast track and multi-track, a trial timetable will have been fixed after filing the pre-trial checklists (listing questionnaires). The timetable may, for example, limit the time for cross-examination and re-examination of each particular witness. In a complex and long multi-track case, the timetable is usually set at the pre-trial review. See examples in **Appendix A(19)** and **(20)**.

At the trial, the judge may confirm or vary any timetable given previously, or, if none has been given, set his own.

The judge will generally have read the papers in the trial bundle (which, as we saw at **13.1.3**, will have been filed with the court prior to the hearing).

A fast track trial should usually be completed within one day. However, if it lasts more than one day, the judge will normally sit on the next court day to complete the trial. A typical fast track timetable for a day's trial is as follows:

- Judge's reading time: 20 minutes
- Opening speeches: 10 minutes
- Cross-examination and re-examination of claimant's witnesses: 90 minutes
- Cross-examination and re-examination of defendant's witnesses: 90 minutes
- Defendant's closing submissions: 15 minutes
- Claimant's closing submissions: 15 minutes
- Judge preparing and delivering judgment: 30 minutes
- Summary assessment of costs: 20 minutes

In multi-track cases, the judge will normally sit on consecutive court days until it has been completed.

13.2.3 Order of proceedings

13.2.3.1 Preliminary issues

Before the case formally commences, a party may wish to raise a preliminary issue with the trial judge. These will normally concern procedural matters. But bear in mind that most of these issues should have been dealt with if a pre-trial review occurred.

Possible preliminary issues include:

(a) Permission to amend a statement of case (see **6.6**). This would be a very late application liable to fail, and prior notice to the other side would be essential.

(b) Permission to adduce more evidence by way of examination-in-chief from a witness under r 32.5(3) (see **11.4**). However, the trial judge may prefer to deal with this application immediately after the witness in question has been sworn.

(c) An application to strike out part of an opponent's witness statement (see **11.2**).

13.2.3.2 The claimant

If allowed by the judge, the claimant may make an opening speech setting out the background to the case and the facts which remain in issue. If this is allowed by the timetable set by the court, it must be very concise. The claimant's advocate will use the case summary (or skeleton argument) filed with the trial bundle (see **13.1.3**).

THE EVIDENCE

Examination-in-chief

The claimant and his witnesses will then give evidence. In most cases, the witness statements will stand as the evidence-in-chief. If that is the case then, after being sworn, the witness may simply be asked to confirm that his statement is correct. He will be able to amplify what is in his witness statement only if allowed to do so by the judge. If some form of limited examination-in-chief is allowed by the judge then the usual rule is that a witness cannot be asked leading questions by his own advocate to encourage him to relate the story. It is difficult to define a leading question. Basically, it is one which suggests the answer or assumes a fact which has not yet been proved. For example, a question to the claimant in a breach of contract case, 'did the defendant supply your firm with goods which did not match the sample?' suggests that the goods did not match the sample. It is therefore an objectionable leading question. Instead, the claimant should be asked in general terms, 'describe to the court the condition of the goods when they arrived as compared to the sample provided earlier'.

Cross-examination

The next stage is the cross-examination of the witness. There is no bar on leading questions. The purpose of cross-examination is to discredit the person being cross-examined in order to make their evidence appear less believable either on the case overall, or in relation to a specific element of it. There are many ways in which this may be done. It may involve highlighting inconsistencies in the evidence given by the witness, or the improbability of the witness's version of events. It may involve alleging that the witness is biased in some way. If the witness has previous convictions, it is even possible for the advocate to cross-examine on these to show the witness's character generally in a bad light.

Sometimes, the witness's evidence will be inconsistent with an earlier statement. This will then give the advocate scope to cross-examine on the previous inconsistent statement to show the court how the witness has given different versions of events at different times and therefore should not be believed. See further **11.9.3.5**.

However, cross-examination does not always involve an aggressive attack on the witness and his credibility. Cross-examination can be conducted in a more subtle fashion and often the best results are achieved by a less confrontational approach.

In addition to the above, however, there is one mandatory rule concerning cross-examination. This is that the cross-examining advocate must put his own party's case to the witness he is cross-examining. Thus, the claimant's advocate must put the claimant's case to the defendant in cross-examination. For example, perhaps the claimant has given evidence that he made known to the defendant a particular purpose for the goods he has bought. The defendant denies this in his witness statement/ examination-in-chief. It must be put to the defendant in cross-examination that the defendant did know of this particular purpose.

It is highly unlikely that the witness being cross-examined in this way will change his story as a result of the allegation being put to him. Nevertheless, it is essential that the cross-examining advocate puts his own client's case to the witness in this way as failure to challenge the opponent's evidence implies acceptance of that evidence.

Re-examination

Following cross-examination, the advocate is given the opportunity to ask further questions of his own witness. However, re-examination is strictly limited to matters arising out of the cross-examination. It is not possible to introduce new issues at this stage. Accordingly, if some ambiguity has been left as a result of the cross-examination, this might be an opportunity to resolve it and try to restore the witness's credibility on that point. For example, perhaps cross-examination has established that the witness normally wears glasses but that he was not wearing them on the day of the incident in question. In so far as this detracts from his credibility in implying that perhaps he did not see what he thought he saw, re-examination would be an opportunity to clarify the fact that the witness wears glasses only for reading. As with examination-in-chief, the advocate cannot ask a leading question.

Problem witnesses

One problem that can arise with the evidence of a witness is the possibility of the witness unexpectedly being unfavourable to the party who has called him. For example, a witness might change his story during cross-examination. If he does this, there is little that the advocate who called the witness can do to remedy the situation. It is not possible for a party's advocate to cross-examine a witness he has himself called.

However, sometimes matters proceed further than this and the witness proves not merely to be unfavourable to the party who called him, but actually proves to be hostile in giving his evidence. It is difficult to be precise as to when a witness can be said to have passed from merely being unfavourable to being hostile, but it would probably be apparent from the witness's demeanour and lack of co-operation that he has no desire either to see justice done, or to give his evidence fairly. One indicator would be the extent to which the witness's evidence is inconsistent with the statement previously given to the party calling him. It is then for that party to make an application to the court for the witness to be declared hostile; if he is, the party who called him can then (contrary to the usual rule) cross-examine that witness on the facts of the case and on the previous inconsistent statements. The witness's general character cannot, however, be attacked by the party who called him, neither can the witness be cross-examined about any previous convictions. Having a witness declared hostile should be regarded as a damage limitation exercise. Whilst it may allow the advocate to retain some control over the case, he is clearly not going to win it unless the damage done can be repaired by evidence from another witness. Strictly, by virtue of s 4 of the Civil Evidence Act 1995 (see **11.9.3**), it would be open to the court to attach weight to the previous inconsistent statement as evidence. In practice, however, the court is more likely to take the view that this witness is not someone who can be relied upon.

13.2.3.3 The defendant

The defence will present its evidence in exactly the same way as the claimant.

13.2.4 Children as witnesses

A child who understands the nature of an oath will give sworn evidence. Otherwise, s 96(2) of the Children Act 1989 provides that:

> The child's evidence may be heard by the court if, in its opinion—
> (a) he understands that it is his duty to speak the truth; and
> (b) he has sufficient understanding to justify his evidence being heard.

A child for these purposes is a person under the age of 18.

It is for the judge to decide whether the child can give evidence and, if so, whether it will be given on oath. As a general rule, it will be assumed that children over the age of 14 can give sworn evidence, and the judge will make enquiries of children under that age in order to form an opinion.

The judge will speak to the child to discover whether he appreciates the solemnity of the occasion and the added responsibility to tell the truth which is involved in taking an oath, over and above the ordinary social duty to be truthful. If so, the child can give sworn evidence. If not, but nevertheless the conditions in s 96(2) are satisfied, the child can give unsworn evidence.

13.2.5 Closing speeches

After the evidence has been given, usually the defence advocate will make a closing speech followed by the claimant's advocate.

13.2.6 The judgment

The judge will either deliver his judgment immediately, perhaps after a short adjournment if he requires time to collect his thoughts, or (if the case is complex) judgment may be reserved to be delivered at a later date. If the court gives judgment both on the claim and Part 20 counterclaim then, if there is a balance in favour of one of the parties, the court will order the party whose judgment is for the lesser amount to pay the balance.

A judgment will normally address the following matters:

(a) *Liability.* Has the claimant established a cause of action? The judge will review the evidence and should give reasons.

(b) *Quantum*. In a claim for a specified amount of money, the judge will deal with the figure work, eg any Part 20 counterclaim established may be set off against the claim. With an unspecified claim the judge will deal with the heads of damage.

(c) *Interest.* This topic is dealt with in detail at **2.4.4** (and also see **6.2.1** and **13.2.8** below). Once the trial judge has indicated that he will award interest, the rate of such and the period, it is for the advocates to work out the figures.

(d) *Costs.* By r 44.3(2)(a), the general rule is that the unsuccessful party will be ordered to pay the costs of the successful party, but the court may make a different order. See **13.3**.

13.2.7 Part 36

A claimant should now apply for an order under r 36.21 and a defendant pursuant to r 36.20, if appropriate (see **12.4**).

13.2.8 Interest

13.2.8.1 Interest up to the date of judgment

Interest will normally be awarded, provided it has been claimed in the particulars of claim. In the absence of any contractual provision to the contrary, or entitlement to interest under the Late Payment of Commercial Debts (Interest) Act 1998, interest on the damages will usually be awarded by the judge in his discretion (under SCA 1981, s 35A or CCA 1984, s 69) at the rate of 8% per annum from the date the cause of action arose until the date of judgment. See further **2.4.4**.

Interest is a discretionary matter and the judge might choose to award at a different rate or for a different period. For example, if the claimant has been very slow about pursuing the claim then the judge may disallow interest for a period, even if the claimant eventually succeeds in his claim.

13.2.8.2 Interest after judgment

Once judgment has been given different rules apply. In the High Court, interest is payable under s 17 of the Judgments Act 1838 at a rate of 8% per annum (unless there is a contractual right to more). In a county court, interest is payable at 8% per annum under the County Courts (Interest on Judgment Debts) Order 1991 (SI 1991/1184), provided the judgment was for at least £5,000 (or, if less, that the Late Payment of Commercial Debts (Interest) Act 1998 applies). In neither case is the interest discretionary and it accrues on both the judgment and on costs.

It should be noted that whilst judgment interest cannot accrue on damages until they have been quantified, interest is payable on costs from the date of judgment even if the amount to be paid has yet to be assessed (*Hunt v RM Douglas (Roofing) Ltd* [1990] 1 AC 398). As a result, it is in the interests of the party paying costs to make a payment on account as soon as possible, even if an interim order requiring such a payment is not made by the court (see **13.3.7**).

13.3 Costs

13.3.1 The indemnity principle

Although the court has a wide discretion, the general rule is that the loser in litigation will be ordered to pay the winner's costs (r 44.3(2)(a)). Note that the winner (the receiving party) is entitled to an 'indemnity' in respect of the costs he has incurred. In other words, he cannot make a profit out of the paying party by seeking more than his solicitor and client costs. This is known as the indemnity principle (not to be confused with the indemnity basis: see **13.3.3**).

The word 'indemnity' is misleading. In reality, the receiving party will not receive a full indemnity in respect of his costs. The paying party will invariably challenge particular items, arguing that the work was unnecessary or was performed in an unnecessarily expensive way (eg, at too high a charge-out rate).

13.3.2 General provisions about costs (Part 44)

At the end of the trial, under r 44.3(1) the court has a discretion as to:

    (a)   whether the costs are payable by one party to another;
    (b)   the amount of those costs; and
    (c)   when they are to be paid.

What are costs? By r 43.2(1) 'costs' include fees, charges, disbursements, expenses and remuneration. These therefore include the charges of solicitors, barristers, experts, etc. Are pre-action costs included? Yes – see r 44.3(6)(d). Additionally, the success fee under a conditional fee agreement and/or the insurance premium for after-the-event insurance are within the definition of costs: see further **2.5**.

Is interest payable on costs before judgment? The general rule is that it is not. We have already seen an exception is when r 36.21 applies: see **12.4.5**. Also note that by r 44.3(6)(g) the court has a discretion when awarding costs to award interest on such from any date it sees fit, including before judgment.

Whilst the general rule is that the court will order the unsuccessful party to pay the costs of the successful party, this is only a starting point and the court can make a different order for costs if it thinks it appropriate to do so.

All the circumstances will be considered, including:

(a) the conduct of all the parties;
(b) whether a party has succeeded on part of his case, even if he has not been wholly successful; and
(c) any payment into court or admissible offer to settle made by a party which is drawn to the court's attention (whether or not made in accordance with Part 36).

Note that the conduct of the parties includes:

(a) conduct before, as well as during, the proceedings, and in particular the extent to which the parties followed any relevant pre-action protocol;
(b) whether it was reasonable for a party to raise, pursue or contest a particular allegation or issue;
(c) the manner in which a party has pursued or defended his case or a particular allegation or issue; and
(d) whether a claimant who has succeeded in his claim, in whole or in part, exaggerated his claim.

An example of conduct being taken into account in making a decision on costs is the decision of Jacob J in *Mars UK Ltd v Teknowledge Ltd (No 2)* [1999] Masons CLR 322, ChD. In that case, he indicated that the successful claimant would be likely to receive only 40% of the costs because of the heavy-handed way in which it had rushed into court proceedings against a smaller opponent who had been genuinely attempting to achieve a negotiated settlement.

What if a costs estimate filed by a party with the allocation questionnaire and/or pre-trial checklist, listing questionnaire (see **8.7**) was inaccurate? Should that party be able to recover only the estimated amount? In *Leigh v Michelin Tyres plc* [2003] EWCA Civ 1766, the Court of Appeal indicated that if there was a substantial difference between the estimated costs and the costs claimed then that difference called for an explanation. In the absence of a satisfactory explanation the court might conclude that the difference itself was evidence from which it could conclude that the costs claimed were unreasonable. The court might take the estimated costs into account if the other party showed that it relied on the estimate in a certain way, or in cases where it decided that it would probably have given different case management directions if a realistic estimate had been given. It would not be a correct use of the power conferred by PD – Costs (Parts 43 to 48), para.6.6 to hold a party to its estimate simply to penalise it for providing an inadequate estimate. The costs judge should determine how, if at all, to reflect the costs estimate in the assessment, before going on to decide whether, for reasons unrelated to the estimate, there were elements of the costs claimed which were unreasonably incurred or unreasonable in amount.

The order may reflect the decision on particular issues by providing for payment of, for example:

(a) a proportion of a party's costs;
(b) a specified amount of a party's costs;
(c) costs for a particular period;
(d) costs incurred before the proceedings began;

(e) costs of a particular step;
(f) costs of a distinct part of the proceedings;
(g) interest on costs from or until a certain date, including a date before judgment.

Orders whereby the winner receives only part of his costs are becoming increasingly common, and a party who raises a number of issues but who succeeds on only some of them can no longer expect to recover the whole of his costs. For example, where both claim and counterclaim succeed, the court may well set off the costs payable on each and direct only payment of the balance.

13.3.3 The basis of assessment (r 44.4)

When the court assesses costs, it will assess those costs either on the standard basis or on the indemnity basis. So, what is the difference?

13.3.3.1 The standard basis

The standard basis will apply unless the court orders otherwise. Costs on this basis must be:

(a) proportionately and reasonably incurred; and
(b) proportionate and reasonable in amount.

Any benefit of the doubt is given to the paying party.

For example, in the case of *Craven Textile Engineers Ltd v Batley Football Club Ltd* [2000] LTL, 7 July, the claim was for about £9,000. D's costs were put at £6,000 and C's at £17,000. The Court of Appeal commented that C's costs were 'wholly disproportionate'. Further, C had instructed leading counsel before the Court of Appeal. The Court said that in assessing the costs of the appeal as between the parties, although C had succeeded, it was not proportionate to order D to pay any extra costs incurred by C instructing leading counsel.

However, in the case of *Lownds v Home Office: Practice Note* [2002] EWCA Civ 365, [2002] 1 WLR 2450, the Court of Appeal introduced a new test where the overall costs were considered to be disproportionate. In such cases each item is to be individually considered to decide whether it was necessarily incurred. The conduct of the other party may be relevant in deciding whether a cost is necessary.

13.3.3.2 The indemnity basis

Costs on the indemnity basis are awarded as a penalty, usually to reflect the court's displeasure with the manner in which a party has behaved either pre-action and/or during proceedings. Costs on this basis must be:

(a) reasonably incurred; and
(b) reasonable in amount.

Any benefit of the doubt is given to the party receiving the costs.

13.3.3.3 The difference between the two bases

Where there is no doubt over the reasonableness of costs, the difference between the two bases is that in assessing on the standard basis the court will allow only those costs that are proportionate to the matters in issue.

In assessing what is proportionate the court should have regard to:

(a) the amount of money involved;

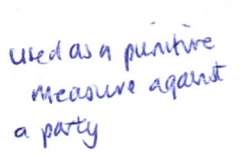

(b) the importance of the case;
(c) the complexity of the issues and the financial position of each party;
(d) the factors in r 44.5 (see **13.3.4** below).

As PD – Costs (Parts 43 to 48), para 11.1 makes clear:

> In applying the test of proportionality the court will have regard to rule 1.1(2)(c). The relationship between the total of the costs incurred and the financial value of the claim may not be a reliable guide. A fixed percentage cannot be applied in all cases to the value of the claim in order to ascertain whether or not the costs are proportionate.

In addition para 11.2 provides that

> In any proceedings there will be costs which will inevitably be incurred and which are necessary for the successful conduct of the case. Solicitors are not required to conduct litigation at rates which are uneconomic. Thus in a modest claim the proportion of costs is likely to be higher than in a large claim, and may even equal or possibly exceed the amount in dispute.

Paragraph 11.3 also recognises that:

> Where a trial takes place, the time taken by the court in dealing with a particular issue may not be an accurate guide to the amount of time properly spent by the legal or other representatives in preparation for the trial of that issue.

The great majority of costs orders are awarded on the standard basis. An award on the indemnity basis is usually reserved for occasions where there has been culpable behaviour on the part of the paying party (for example, pursuing an unjustified claim or defence, or where there has been non-compliance with court orders). We also saw it applied at **12.4.5** in respect of r 36.21. Where the court does not specify in its order which basis is to apply, the standard basis is used.

13.3.4 Relevant factors in assessing the amount of costs (r 44.5)

As well as the basis (ie, standard or indemnity) on which the court is assessing costs, the court must also take into account the following factors in deciding the amount of costs the receiving party is entitled to:

(a) the conduct of all the parties, including conduct before as well as during the proceedings and the efforts made, if any, before and during the proceedings in order to try to resolve the dispute;
(b) the amount or value of any money or property involved;
(c) the importance of the matter to all the parties;
(d) the particular complexity of the matter or the difficulty or novelty of the questions raised;
(e) the skill, effort, specialised knowledge and responsibility involved;
(f) the time spent on the case;
(g) the place where and the circumstances in which work or any part of it was done.

As to factor (a), parties must seriously consider ADR proposals made by the other side. In *Dunnett v Railtrack plc (in Railway Administration)* [2002] EWCA Civ 303, [2002] 2 All ER 850, the Court of Appeal deprived the successful party of its costs because it refused to mediate before the appeal was heard. However, in *Société Internationale de Télécommunications Aéronautiques SC v Wyatt Co (UK) Ltd and Others (Maxwell Batley (a Firm) Pt 20 Defendant)* [2002] EWHC 2401 (Ch), [2002] All ER (D) 189 (Nov), Park J made it clear that requests to mediate must not be used as a weapon to force a settlement and must be a genuine attempt to reach a reconciliation.

As to the last factor, regional hourly guideline figures (for a summary assessment) are normally agreed annually between the Law Society and the Supreme Court Costs Office. Examples appear at **Appendix B(3)**.

13.3.5 Procedure for assessing costs

Where the court orders one party to pay costs to another, the court will either make a summary assessment of costs there and then, or order detailed assessment of the costs by the costs officer. (The costs officer is the district judge or, in London, the costs judge.)

The general rule is that the court should, unless there is good reason not to do so (eg, where the paying party shows substantial grounds for disputing the sum claimed for costs that cannot be dealt with summarily, or there is insufficient time to carry out a summary assessment), make a summary assessment of the costs:

(a) at the conclusion of the trial of a case which has been dealt with on the fast track, in which case the order will deal with the costs of the whole claim; and

(b) at the conclusion of any other hearing, which has lasted not more than one day, in which case the order will deal with the costs of the application or matter to which the hearing related. If this hearing disposes of the claim, the order may deal with the costs of the whole claim;

(c) in certain hearings in the Court of Appeal.

To assist the court to make a summary assessment, the parties must file and serve at least 24 hours before the hearing a breakdown of their costs – see Costs Form N260 Statement of Costs for Summary Assessment at **Appendix A(17)**.

13.3.6 Fast track costs (Part 46)

13.3.6.1 Trial costs

In fast track cases, there is a specified figure for the advocate for preparing for and appearing at the trial.

Value of the claim	Amount of fast track trial costs which the court may award
Up to £3,000	£350
More than £3,000 but not more than £10,000	£500
More than £10,000	£750

The court may not award more or less than the amount shown except in limited circumstances. For example, an additional £250 may be awarded where it is necessary for a legal representative to attend to assist the advocate. Therefore, if a barrister is instructed to conduct the fast track trial and a representative from the solicitor's office attends court with the barrister, £250 may be awarded for that attendance provided the court thinks that it was necessary.

13.3.6.2 Valuing the claim

If the claimant succeeds then the value of the claim is based on the amount awarded, excluding any interest or reduction for contributory negligence.

If the defendant was successful then the value of the claim is based on the amount claimed by the claimant.

Improper or unreasonable behaviour by one of the parties may lead to a departure from the specified figure.

If there is more than one claimant or defendant but the successful parties used only one advocate, there will be only one award. If the successful parties used separate advocates, there will be a separate award for each party.

13.3.6.3 Summary assessment of other fast track costs

The fast track trial costs are in addition to the rest of the costs in bringing the claim. The usual practice on fast track cases is for these to be summarily assessed at the end of the case. In fast track cases, therefore, the party should always file and serve a statement of costs (see **Chapter 9**) at least 24 hours prior to the hearing. Because the costs of the entire case are being summarily assessed by the court there and then, and because counsel will not be familiar with the way in which solicitors' costs are incurred in preparing the case for trial, there is a strong argument for using a solicitor advocate rather than counsel at the trial of a fast track claim. Where the receiving party has funded the litigation by way of a CFA the court will as part of its summary assessment assess whether the paying party should pay some or all of any success fee due to the winner's solicitor and any after-the-event insurance premium that was paid (see **2.5** and **13.3.8**).

13.3.7 Multi-track cases

In multi-track cases there are no specified trial costs. Although the judge does have the power to make a summary assessment of costs, in multi-track cases the court will usually order detailed assessment.

Detailed assessment proceedings are commenced by the receiving party serving on the paying party:

(a) notice of commencement in Form N252 (see **Appendix A(21)**); and
(b) a copy of the bill of costs.

This action must be taken within three months of the date of the judgment or order.

The bill of costs is a rather complex document, which should be prepared in the form described by para 4 of PD – Costs (Parts 43 to 48). A copy of an example of a bill of costs appears at **Appendix A(22)**. Preparing a bill of costs is a specialist task, usually undertaken by either an in-house costs draftsman, or a firm of independent costs draftsmen. A claim can be included for the reasonable costs of preparing and checking the bill.

The first part of the bill sets out background information, including a brief description of the history of the claim and a statement of the grade of fee earner(s) involved (together with the hourly charge-out rate claimed for each). If the litigation was funded by way of a CFA this will be stated, together with the success fee that was agreed. Similarly, if the receiving party has been publicly funded, the relevant details must be set out in the background information.

The main body of the bill comprises a breakdown of the work performed, divided into different categories of work as set out in para 4.6 of PD – Costs (Parts 43 to 48):

(1) attendances on the court and counsel;
(2) attendances on and communications with the receiving party;

(3) attendances on and communications with witnesses including any expert witness;
(4) attendances to inspect any property or place for the purposes of the proceedings;
(5) attendances on and with other persons;
(6) communications with the court and with counsel;
(7) work done on documents: preparing and considering documentation, including documentation relating to pre-action protocols where appropriate, work done in connection with arithmetical calculations of compensation and/or interest and time spent collating documents;
(8) work done in connection with negotiations with a view to settlement (if not already covered under another head);
(9) attendances on and communications with agents and work done by them;
(10) other work done which was of or incidental to the proceedings and which is not already covered above.

The work done within each of these heads is set out chronologically in numbered items. As can be seen from the model bill at **Appendix A(22)**, the information is presented in columns, with the amount claimed for profit costs, disbursements and VAT being shown separately.

'Communications', in the context of para 4.6, means letters out and telephone calls. Most will be classed as routine and charged at a standard rate of six minutes (thus a routine letter drafted by an assistant solicitor charging a rate of £140 per hour would be charged at £14). Where letters out or telephone calls are sufficiently complex and/or lengthy not to be classed as routine, they may be charged according to the time actually spent on them. Letters in are not charged for separately.

Local travelling expenses (generally, within a 10-mile radius of the court) cannot be claimed, but the solicitor is entitled to claim at up to the hourly rate for time spent travelling and waiting (depending on the amount he charged his client).

The cost of postage, couriers, out-going telephone calls, fax and telex messages will in general not be allowed, but the court may exceptionally in its discretion allow such expenses in unusual circumstances or where the cost is unusually heavy.

Note that the bill of costs must not contain any claims in respect of costs or court fees which relate solely to the detailed assessment proceedings. A claim may only be made for the reasonable costs of preparing and checking the bill of costs. The award of costs at a detailed assessment is made at its conclusion.

13.3.7.1 Late commencement of the assessment process

Permission is not required to commence detailed assessment proceedings out of time, but if the receiving party does not commence the process within three months, the court may disallow all or part of the costs, or disallow all or part of any interest accruing on the costs. Since interest will be accumulating on the costs even though they have not yet been quantified, the usual sanction, however, will be to disallow all or part of the interest that would otherwise be payable to the receiving party (r 47.8).

It is open to the paying party to apply for an order that the receiving party lose their right to costs unless detailed assessment proceedings are commenced by a certain date.

13.3.7.2 Challenging the bill

The paying party has 21 days from service of the notice of commencement to serve points of dispute on the receiving party (r 47.9). A specimen can be found at **Appendix A(23)**. If he does not do so, the receiving party can apply for a default costs certificate which will include an order to pay the costs. The default costs certificate will be set aside only if good reason is shown by the paying party. If the paying party serves the points of dispute late (but before the default certificate is issued), the paying party may not be heard further unless the court gives permission.

On service of the points of dispute, the receiving party may serve a reply within 21 days (r 47.13). The receiving party must file a request for an assessment hearing within three months of the expiry of the period for commencing detailed assessment proceedings.

There will then be a detailed assessment hearing, at which the court will decide what costs are to be paid. The receiving party must, within 14 days of the hearing, file a completed bill showing the amount of costs finally due.

The receiving party will normally be entitled to the costs of the detailed assessment proceedings, but the court may take into account:

(a) the conduct of the parties;
(b) the amount of any reduction from the original amount claimed;
(c) the reasonableness of claiming or challenging any particular item.

The court must also take into account any written offer expressed to be 'without prejudice save as to the costs of the detailed assessment proceedings'.

No time is specified for service of such an offer, but any offer made more than 14 days after:

(a) service of the notice of commencement (paying party);
(b) service of the points of dispute (receiving party),

will be given less weight unless good reason is shown.

13.3.7.3 Appeals

Where the assessment was by a judge, the appeals process is governed by Part 52. An appeal from a detailed or summary assessment by a district judge is made to a circuit judge. An appeal from an assessment by a circuit judge is made to a High Court judge. Permission to appeal is required either from the original court, or from the appeal court. If permission is not sought at the original assessment, it must be sought from the appeal court within 14 days. The appeal takes the form of a review of the original decision, rather than a re-hearing.

Part 52 does not apply where the detailed assessment was performed by an officer of the court. In this case, r 47.20 applies (as supplemented by paras 47 and 48 of PD 47). Permission to appeal is not required and the appeal takes the form of a rehearing, either by a costs judge or a district judge of the High Court.

13.3.7.4 Agreeing costs

Rather than go through the detailed assessment procedure, it is always open to the parties to agree the figure for costs payable by one side to another. Very often, the parties will attempt to agree a figure for costs, and proceed to a detailed assessment only if they are unable to reach agreement.

13.3.7.5 Offers to settle a detailed assessment

Costs of a detailed assessment can be significant. A receiving or a paying party can make a written offer to settle under r 47.19(1). The offer must be expressed to be without prejudice save as to the costs of the detailed assessment proceedings. The fact of the offer must not be communicated to the costs judge until the question of costs of the detailed assessment proceedings falls to be decided. The court will take such an offer into account in deciding who should pay the costs of those proceedings. So if a paying party offers to pay a total of £20,000 costs which is refused, but on the detailed assessment the receiving party is awarded less than that amount, the receiving party will usually be ordered to pay the paying party's costs of dealing with the detailed assessment.

13.3.7.6 Interim orders

The detailed assessment of costs procedure initially means that there will be some delay in the successful party receiving their costs from the unsuccessful party. Rule 44.3(8) of CPR 1998 allows the court at trial to order an interim payment of part of these costs, and in *Mars UK Ltd v Teknowledge Ltd (No 2)* [1999] Masons CLR 322, Jacob J indicated that the court should make an order for the interim payment of costs in most cases.

13.3.8 Conditional fee agreements

A winning party who has funded the litigation by a CFA is likely to have agreed to pay his solicitor a success fee, and may also have paid a premium for after-the-event insurance. Where a costs order is made in that party's favour, the costs payable include the success fee and premium. These items are referred to as the 'additional liability' to distinguish them from the base costs.

Rule 44.3B sets out a number of limits on the recovery of the additional liability, including that the following may not be recovered:

(a) Any proportion of the success fee that compensates the solicitor for costs resulting from the postponement of the payment of his fees and expenses. For example, the solicitor will sometimes have funded the disbursements by way of a loan. Any part of the success fee intended to compensate the solicitor for the interest payable on the loan is not recoverable from the paying party.

(b) The success fee applicable to any period during which the required notice of funding had not been filed (see **2.5.2**).

(c) Any success fee if the receiving party has failed to disclose the required risk assessment information (see below).

Where (b) or (c) applies the receiving party may apply for relief from the sanction (see **8.4**).

In addition, the paying party is, of course, liable for the success fee and premium only to the extent that these are reasonable and (where the standard basis applies) proportionate. PD 47 makes clear, however, that the success fee should not be reduced simply because when it is added to the base costs the total appears disproportionate. In considering the success fee the court will take into account the circumstances as they reasonably appeared to the solicitor when the CFA was entered into. Relevant factors include the extent of the risk that the fees and expenses would not be payable, whether the solicitor was liable under the CFA for any disbursements and what other methods of financing the case were available.

Where the court has ordered a detailed assessment, the receiving party must on commencing those proceedings file and serve on the paying party a statement of the reasons for the success fee (in accordance with reg 3 of the CFA Regulations 2000 (SI 2000/692)), together with a copy of the after-the-event insurance certificate giving details of the extent of the cover provided and the premium paid (see para 32 of PD – Costs (Parts 43 to 48)).

Where the court decides to perform a summary assessment of the additional liability, the party must make available:

(a) the Form N251;
(b) all estimates and statements of costs that have been filed during the course of the claim (since the court can take these into account when deciding the reasonableness of the bill); and
(c) a copy of the risk assessment prepared when the CFA was entered into (see para 14 of PD – Costs (Parts 43 to 48)).

Under reg 3(2)(b) of the CFA Regulations 2000, any amount of the success fee which is disallowed on assessment ceases to be payable by the receiving party unless the court orders otherwise.

13.3.9 Costs only proceedings

What if the parties to a dispute:

(a) have reached an agreement on all issues (including which party is to pay the costs);
(b) made or confirmed that agreement in writing;
(c) but have failed to agree the amount of those costs; and
(d) no proceedings have been started?

The answer is provided by r 44.12A. Either party to the agreement may start proceedings by issuing a claim form in accordance with Part 8 (see **7.3**). The claim form must contain or be accompanied by the agreement or confirmation.

13.4 Human rights

The court's ability to restrict the evidence heard at trial and to control the trial timetable raise the possibility of a challenge under Article 6(1) ECHR. As discussed at **11.15.2**, provided the court is careful in exercising its powers to apply the overriding objective, it is likely to be difficult for litigants to challenge such case management decisions successfully.

The right to a fair trial includes an obligation on the part of the court to give reasons for its decisions (see, eg, *Van de Hurk v Netherlands* (1994) 18 EHRR 481). A failure at the end of a trial to give a sufficiently reasoned judgment would, therefore, be a breach of Article 6(1) ECHR.

The approach taken by the ECtHR has already received support from the Court of Appeal in *Hyams v Pender* [2000] 1 WLR 32. The defendant had sought permission to appeal a county court possession order. The application had been decided by the court on paper (ie, without a hearing) and had been refused 'for non-compliance with Practice Direction (Part 52)'. The defendant appealed the refusal to the Court of Appeal, which, whilst dismissing the appeal, stated that the right to reasons meant that the judge should have identified how the Practice Direction had not been complied with.

Chapter 14
Enforcement of Money Judgments

14.1	Introduction	185
14.2	Interest on judgment debts	185
14.3	Tracing the other party	186
14.4	Investigating the judgment debtor's means	186
14.5	Methods of enforcement	187

14.1 Introduction

Once a party has obtained a judgment against his opponent, the opponent will usually pay the amount he has been ordered to pay without any further action being necessary. If, however, the losing party fails to pay the amount he has been ordered to pay, the winning party will have to take steps to enforce the judgment debt. The judgment will not be enforced by the court automatically – unless the winning party takes enforcement action, he will not receive the money that he was awarded. The winning party will have to consider with his solicitor the best method of enforcing payment.

Where the opponent is not insured, the question of enforcement is one which should be considered before proceedings are ever commenced, because it is obviously not worth obtaining a judgment against a party who does not have the means to pay. The solicitor should be satisfied that the defendant's whereabouts are known, that prima facie he has the means to pay the amount in issue, and that he has assets which can be taken from him to enforce payment if necessary.

The CPR 1998 themselves do not yet deal fully with all enforcement methods and so it is occasionally necessary to look at the 'old' High Court and county court rules, contained respectively in Schs 1 and 2 to CPR 1998.

14.2 Interest on judgment debts

14.2.1 High Court judgments

Interest accrues on all High Court judgments from the date judgment is pronounced. The current rate of interest is 8% per annum, although this may be altered from time to time by statutory instrument. The rate applicable to any particular judgment is the rate in force when the judgment was made. Where judgment is entered for damages to be assessed, interest begins to run from the date when damages are finally assessed or agreed (ie, the date of the final judgment). Interest on an order for the payment of costs runs from the date of the judgment, not from the date of the final costs certificate. Therefore, interest is accruing on the costs before the paying party knows how much he has to pay in costs. He can alleviate the situation by making a payment on account of costs.

14.2.2 County court judgments

Interest accrues on county court judgments of £5,000 or more, although the Department for Constitutional Affairs is considering whether to allow interest on judgment debts below £5,000. The current rate of interest is 8% per annum, subject to alteration by statutory instrument, and the rate applicable is the rate in force when the judgment was made.

Where, under the terms of the judgment, payment is deferred, or to be in instalments, interest will not accrue until that date, or until an instalment falls due.

Where enforcement proceedings are taken, the judgment debt ceases to carry interest unless the enforcement proceedings fail to produce any payment, in which case interest will continue to accrue on the judgment debt as if the enforcement proceedings had never been issued. 'Enforcement proceedings' include an application for an order to obtain information from the judgment debtor (see **14.4.2**). If an attachment of earnings order is in force, interest does not accrue.

Care needs to be taken as regards interest in the county court. If enforcement proceedings are taken and anything at all is recovered, the balance of the debt will become interest free.

When applying to enforce interest in the county court, a party must supply a certificate setting out the amount of interest claimed, the sum on which it is claimed, the dates from and to which interest has accrued, and the rate of interest applied.

14.3 Tracing the other party

There are a number of methods of enforcement available, but before commencing enforcement proceedings the other party's whereabouts need to be established. If the other party's whereabouts are not known, consideration should be given to employing an enquiry agent to trace him. If this is to be done, the enquiry agent should be given as much information as possible to assist his enquiries (eg, the other party's last known address, his last known employer, details of any known relatives). A limit should be placed on the costs which may be incurred by the enquiry agent, so that a disproportionate amount of money is not wasted in attempts to trace the defendant, which might be unsuccessful in the end. In practice, these enquiries are likely to have been made at the outset of the case, since there is little point in suing a defendant you cannot trace (see **14.1** above).

14.4 Investigating the judgment debtor's means

The next thing to consider is what assets the judgment debtor has, since the method of enforcement chosen will depend upon what type of assets are available to pay the judgment debt. The winning party may already have enough information about his opponent for a decision to be taken, otherwise further enquiries will have to be made.

There are two main ways to investigate the judgment debtor's assets: the winning party can either instruct an enquiry agent to make investigations; or he can apply to the court for an order to obtain information from the judgment debtor. However, do not forget that pre-action it is usual to make a bankruptcy search against an individual and a company search against a company (see **2.3.1.2**). Those should be updated now.

14.4.1 Instructing an enquiry agent

The enquiry agent should be given as much information as possible to assist his enquiries, and a limit should be placed on the amount of costs to be incurred, to avoid spending a disproportionate amount on these preliminary enquiries. Even so, this method of carrying out the investigations is likely to be considerably more expensive than applying to the court for an order to obtain information from the judgment debtor. However, the enquiry agent may be able to discover assets which are not disclosed at the hearing, and may produce results more quickly, depending on the speed with which the hearing can take place at the court.

14.4.2 Obtaining information from judgment debtor (Part 71)

An order to obtain information from a judgment debtor is a court order requiring the judgment debtor to attend before an officer of the court to be examined on oath as to his means. The judgment creditor obtains the order by making an application without notice. The purpose of the order is to assist the judgment creditor in deciding on the most appropriate method for enforcing the judgment.

14.4.2.1 How to make the application – PD 71

(a) The judgment creditor must complete and file an application notice in Form N316 if the debtor is an individual, and N316A if an officer of a company or other corporation is to be questioned. The application notice must contain a statement of truth.

(b) PD 71, para 1 sets out the matters to be contained in the application notice. These include the name and address of the judgment debtor, the judgment or order the creditor is seeking to enforce and the amount presently owed. If the creditor wishes the examination to be conducted by a judge this must be stated in the application notice, together with reasons. If the creditor wishes the debtor to bring any specific documents to court these must be identified.

(c) Rules 71.3 and 71.4 set out the procedure for service of the order and for payment of the judgment debtor's travelling expenses to court.

14.4.2.2 The hearing

(a) The hearing will usually take place in the court for the area where the debtor resides or carries on business.

(b) The examination will be conducted by an officer of the court, or a judge if considered appropriate.

(c) Where the examination is conducted by a court officer standard questions to be asked are set out in Appendices A and B to PD 71. The judgment creditor may attend the hearing. If the judgment creditor wishes to ask any additional questions these should be set out in the application notice. The officer will make a written record of the responses given by the debtor, who will be invited to read and sign it at the end of the hearing.

(d) Where the hearing is to be conducted before a judge the standard questions are not used. The questions will be asked by the judgment creditor and the hearing will be tape-recorded.

(e) If the debtor fails to attend court, or having attended court refuses to take an oath or affirm or answer questions, a committal order may be made against him.

14.5 Methods of enforcement

There are four common methods of enforcement to choose from:

(a) execution (ie, seizure and sale of the debtor's goods);
(b) charging order (ie, a charge on the debtor's land or securities);

(c) third party debt order (ie, an order requiring a third party who owes money to the debtor to pay it directly to the creditor);

(d) attachment of earnings order (ie, an order requiring the debtor's employer to make deductions from his earnings and pay them to the creditor).

The solicitor must decide, in the light of the information he has obtained about the judgment debtor, which method of enforcement is most suitable.

Each method of enforcement mentioned is now considered in more detail.

14.5.1 Execution (RSC Ord 46 and 47; CCR Ord 26, r 1)

This process enables the sheriff's officer (High Court), or a High Court Enforcement Officer (HCEO) or court bailiff (county court) to seize and sell the debtor's goods to pay the judgment debt and costs and the costs of enforcement. The items seized are sold by public auction. After deducting the expenses of sale, the judgment debt and costs are paid, and any surplus proceeds are returned to the debtor.

14.5.1.1 Choice of court

High Court

A party who has obtained a judgment in the High Court may issue a writ of fieri facias in that court, regardless of the amount to be enforced.

County court

Where a party has obtained judgment in a county court, and the amount to be enforced by execution is £5,000 or more, it must be enforced in the High Court unless the proceedings originated under the Consumer Credit Act 1974.

Where the sum to be enforced is less than £600, it must be enforced in a county court.

In the case of county court judgments of £600 or more but less than £5,000, the judgment creditor can choose whether to issue execution in the High Court or the county court. If he chooses to use the High Court, the county court judgment must first be transferred to the High Court. The advantage of this is that interest then accrues on the judgment debt.

A party with a county court judgment for £5,000 or more will be able to issue a part warrant in that court, for example where an instalment order or the final balance is less than £5,000.

14.5.1.2 Procedure in the High Court

(a) The judgment creditor completes two copies of a writ of fieri facias and a praecipe for a writ of fieri facias.

(b) He delivers these documents to the court office, together with the judgment and the costs officer's certificate where the enforcement relates to costs.

(c) The court seals the writ and returns one copy of it to the judgment creditor.

(d) The judgment creditor forwards the sealed copy writ to the under-sheriff or HCEO for the county where the debtor resides or carries on business.

(e) The under-sheriff sends the writ to his officer for execution.

14.5.1.3 Procedure in the county court

(a) The judgment creditor completes the form of request for a warrant of execution.

(b) The judgment creditor files this at court, together with the fee.

(c) The warrant is executed by the bailiff of the county court for the district where the debtor resides or carries on business.

14.5.1.4 Items exempt from seizure

Certain items cannot be seized. These are:

(a) goods on hire or hire-purchase;

(b) tools, books, vehicles and other items of equipment which are necessary to the debtor for use personally in his job or business;

(c) clothing, bedding, furniture, household equipment and provisions which are necessary for satisfying the basic domestic needs of the debtor and his family;

(d) any money, bank notes, bills of exchange, promissory notes, bonds, specialities, securities for money belonging to the debtor.

'Necessary items' are items which are so essential that without them a debtor could not continue his existing job or business.

Motor vehicles

It should be the exception rather than the rule that a debtor is allowed to retain a motor vehicle as a necessary item. It is for the debtor to satisfy the sheriff/HCEO/bailiff that the vehicle is necessary to allow him to continue his job or business. The fact that a debtor claims to need a vehicle to get to and from his place of work should not by itself be considered grounds to exempt the vehicle. The sheriff/HCEO/bailiff must be satisfied that no reasonable alternative is available.

Household items

Items such as stereo equipment, televisions, videos, or microwave ovens where there is also a conventional cooker, are not considered to be necessary for satisfying the basic domestic needs of the debtor and his family.

It is always helpful to inform the sheriff/HCEO/bailiff of specific items which could be seized, for example tell him the make, type and registration number of the debtor's car.

14.5.1.5 'Walking possession'

In practice, the debtor's goods are not usually removed immediately. The debtor and the sheriff/HCEO/bailiff will enter into an agreement for 'walking possession'. This means that the sheriff/HCEO/bailiff agrees not to remove the goods at once and, in return, the debtor agrees not to dispose of them or permit them to be moved. This gives the debtor a further opportunity to pay the sum due, and he may apply for suspension of the writ or warrant. If this is granted, it means that the writ of fieri facias/warrant of execution is suspended on condition that the debtor pays the sum due by specified instalments.

The sheriff/HCEO/bailiff must not effect a forcible entry to any premises and must not take goods from the debtor's person.

190 Civil Litigation

14.5.2 Charging order on land (Part 73)

A judgment creditor may apply to the court for an order charging the judgment debtor's land with the amount due under a judgment. A charging order can also be made in respect of land which the debtor owns jointly with another person, in which case the order is a charge upon the debtor's beneficial interest, rather than upon the land itself.

14.5.2.1 Restrictions on making a charging order

Where the court has made an order for payment of the sum due by instalments, a charging order will not be made as long as the debtor is up to date with the instalment payments.

14.5.2.2 Registration of the charging order

Once a charging order has been made, it should be registered if possible.

If the judgment debtor is the sole owner of the land, the charging order can be registered at the Land Charges Department as an order affecting land if the title is unregistered, or at HM Land Registry as a notice if the land is registered.

Where the land is jointly owned, the debtor technically has an interest only in the proceeds of sale under the trust for sale, rather than an interest in the land itself. Therefore, in the case of unregistered land, the charging order is not registrable because it is not an order relating to land. In the case of registered land, the charging order can be protected by entry of a caution on the register.

If the creditor does not know whether the land is registered, he should make an Index Map Search before applying for a charging order. If the creditor does not know whether the land is jointly owned, he should make a search of the title in the case of registered land, again before applying for a charging order.

14.5.2.3 Notice

Whether or not the charging order is registered, written notice of it should be given to any prior chargee(s) to prevent any tacking of later advances. A search may be necessary at HM Land Registry (registered land) or the Land Charges Department (unregistered land) to discover the existence of prior incumbrances.

Once this has been done, the creditor has security for the debt, but he still has not obtained the sum due.

14.5.2.4 Order for sale

In order to obtain the money, the creditor can apply to the court for an order for sale of the land charged. The judgment will then be satisfied out of the proceeds of sale.

14.5.2.5 Choice of court

The rules specify the court in which the application should be made. This will usually be the court in which the order being enforced was made.

14.5.2.6 Procedure

(a) The judgment creditor must file an application notice in the prescribed form (N379) containing the information specified in PD 73, para 1.2. This includes details of the judgment debt, the land over which the charging order is sought, and the names and addresses of any other person on whom

Enforcement of Money Judgments 191

the interim order will be served. This will include parties with a prior charge over the property. The application notice must be verified by a statement of truth.

(b) The judgment creditor must also file a draft interim charging order.

(c) The district judge considers the application in the absence of the parties and, if satisfied, makes the interim charging order.

(d) The interim charging order should be registered either at the Land Charges Department, or at HM Land Registry if registration is possible.

(e) The interim charging order, indorsed with a hearing date, together with a copy of the supporting affidavit or witness statement, must be served on the judgment debtor at least 21 days before the return day. Ordinary service is required.

(f) At the hearing the court can make a final charging order confirming the interim charging order, discharge the interim order, deal with issues in dispute between the parties or direct a trial of any such issues – r 73.8.

(g) The creditor now has a charge on the debtor's land which can be enforced by an order for sale of the property.

(h) In order to enforce the charging order by sale of the property charged, fresh proceedings would have to be commenced, normally in the same court that made the final charging order.

14.5.3 Charging order on securities (Part 73)

A judgment creditor can also obtain a charging order on a judgment debtor's beneficial interest in certain specified securities.

The procedure is similar to the procedure for obtaining a charging order on land. An application notice in the prescribed form (N380) must be completed.

14.5.4 Third party debt orders (Part 72)

Where a third party owes money to the judgment debtor, the court can make an order requiring that third party to pay the judgment creditor the whole of that debt, or such part of it as is sufficient to satisfy the judgment debt and costs. This is known as a third party debt order. A bank account or building society account is often the target of such an order. Judgment debtors who are self-employed often have trade debts due to them. It is possible to find out at the hearing of an order to obtain information from a judgment debtor what these debts are and then to take these proceedings accordingly.

The debt must belong to the judgment debtor solely and beneficially. This means, for example, that the judgment creditor cannot get an order over the husband and wife's joint bank account if the husband alone is the judgment debtor. Also, the third party must be within the jurisdiction.

14.5.4.1 Choice of court

The application should be issued in the court which made the order which is being enforced.

14.5.4.2 Procedure

(a) The application is made without notice on the prescribed form (N349). The contents of the application notice are set out in para 1 of PD 72.

(b) The hearing will be before a judge. If successful the judge will make an interim third party debt order. He will also fix a hearing for the final third party debt order, which will be not less than 28 days after the interim order is made.

(c) The interim order is served on the third party not less than 21 days before the hearing date for the final order, and on the judgment debtor within seven days of service on the third party. In practice the interim order will be served as soon as possible as it will not be effective and binding on the third party until served.

(d) Once the third party has been served with the interim order the third party is required to disclose certain information to the judgment creditor pursuant to r 72.6(2).

(e) Before the third party debt order is made final the court will consider any objections made by either the third party, or the judgment debtor or anyone else claiming to have a prior interest in the money: see r 72.8.

(f) Once a final order is made the third party is required to pay the money held to the judgment creditor.

(g) The rules enable the judgment debtor to apply for the order to be discharged in cases of hardship.

14.5.4.3 Third party debt proceedings against a deposit taking institution

A bank or building society account, provided it is in credit, is an ideal target for third party debt proceedings. Once the interim third party debt order is served, the account is frozen (up to the amount outstanding under the judgment or order) and, upon the making of the final order, the money in the account (or amount required to discharge the judgment) must be paid over to the judgment creditor.

There are some special points to bear in mind when third party debt proceedings are taken against a deposit taking institution, namely:

(a) The application notice must state (if known) the name and address of the branch at which the account is believed to be held and the account number.

(b) An order against a building society or credit union cannot require payment which would reduce the balance in the account to a sum less than £1.

(c) Before paying the judgment creditor, the deposit taking institution is entitled to deduct a prescribed sum in respect of administration expenses.

14.5.4.4 Costs

The costs of a successful application are fixed (see Part 45) and may be retained by the judgment creditor out of the money recovered from the third party in priority to the judgment debt. If the application is unsuccessful the court will exercise its discretion in deciding what, if any, costs order to make.

14.5.5 Attachment of earnings (CCR Ord 27)

An attachment of earnings order is an order which compels the judgment debtor's employer to make regular deductions from the debtor's earnings and pay them into court. The High Court has no power to make an attachment of earnings order. If the judgment has been obtained in the High Court, the proceedings will have to be transferred to the county court before this method of enforcement can be used. The amount remaining due under the judgment must be at least £50 for an attachment of earnings application to be made. Also, the debtor must be employed; an order cannot be made if the debtor is unemployed or self-employed.

14.5.5.1 Procedure

(a) The judgment creditor completes the prescribed application form and files it at court.

(b) The court informs the debtor of the application and requires him either to pay the sum due, or to file a statement of means in the prescribed form. The court will make a diary entry for return of the form.

(c) If the debtor returns the form, the court staff will make an attachment of earnings order. The court staff will fix the repayment rate by applying certain guidelines which they are given to the debtor's statement of means. If necessary, the application will be referred to the district judge. The order will specify the 'normal deduction rate' and the 'protected earnings rate'. The latter is the amount which the debtor is allowed to retain out of his earnings in any event. If his earnings for a particular week are equal to or less than the 'protected earnings rate', the creditor will receive nothing that week.

(d) The order will be sent to the parties, and to the debtor's employer, with instructions to deduct the amount ordered from the debtor's pay and forward it to the court. The employer is entitled to deduct an additional sum (currently £1) in respect of his administrative costs for each deduction which he makes in accordance with the order.

(e) If either party objects to the order which has been made, he can apply for the matter to be reconsidered by the district judge. If such an application is made, there will be a hearing before the district judge. In the meantime, the employer will be required to make deductions as ordered unless and until the order is varied.

(f) If the debtor informs the court that he is unemployed or self-employed, the application will be dismissed.

(g) If the debtor does not respond to the initial notice sent to him by the court, an order to produce a statement of means will be served on him personally by the court bailiff. This order is automatically issued by the court. If the creditor has provided the name and address of the debtor's employer, the employer will also be contacted at this stage for a statement of earnings.

(h) If the debtor still does not respond when the order is served on him by the court bailiff, the court will automatically issue a notice to show cause. This will be served on the debtor by the court bailiff, and it will give notice of a hearing before the district judge which the debtor is required to attend. Failure to attend will lead to his committal to prison.

14.5.6 Insolvency

14.5.6.1 Bankruptcy

Where the judgment debt is for £750 or more, the judgment creditor may decide to petition for bankruptcy of the judgment debtor. However, he will not be able to do this if he has already registered a charging order because he is then in the position of a secured creditor, and a secured creditor cannot petition for bankruptcy unless he gives up his security.

Bankruptcy procedure is not dealt with in detail here (for more detail, please refer to *Business Law and Practice*). Briefly, the first step is for the judgment creditor to serve on the judgment debtor a statutory demand in the prescribed form, unless execution has been levied and remains unsatisfied, in whole or in part, in which case there is no need for a statutory demand. Three weeks after service of the statutory demand, the petitioner may file the bankruptcy petition. In addition, an affidavit is required to verify the truth of the petition. The court will issue the petition indorsed with the date and place of hearing. The petition must be served on the debtor at least 14 days before the hearing. At the hearing, the judgment creditor must prove that the debt is still outstanding, and the court will usually then make a bankruptcy order, although the petition may be dismissed, stayed or adjourned. If a bankruptcy order is made, all the debtor's property vests in the trustee in bankruptcy.

14.5.6.2 Winding up

If the judgment debtor is a company, the judgment creditor may consider winding up the company. The procedure for this is very similar to the bankruptcy procedure for individuals.

14.5.7 Enforcement outside the jurisdiction (Part 74)

The methods of enforcing English judgments abroad, or enforcing a foreign judgment in England, depend on the arrangements made with the foreign country in question by EC Council Regulation, Treaty or Convention. These arrangments are as follows.

14.5.7.1 The EU, Brussels and Lugano Conventions

The reciprocal rules relating to enforcement in all EU countries save Denmark are set out in Council Regulation 44/2001 ('the Regulation'). Similar provisions for Denmark are set out in the Brussels Convention, and for Norway, Poland, Switzerland and Iceland in the Lugano Convention ('the Conventions').

In order to enforce a judgment obtained in an EU country (except Denmark) the party must obtain a certificate of enforcement by applying to the relevant court. The application should be accompanied by a copy of the judgment.

Articles 38 to 56 of the Regulation set out the procedure to be followed in making an application.

Similar provisions as to obtaining a certificate of judgment and forwarding it to the court of the country where enforcement is sought apply to judgments in countries governed by the Conventions.

Enforcement proceedings may be stayed on the application of the judgment debtor to the court in which the certificate of enforcement has been sought.

14.5.7.2 Countries outside the EU and the Conventions

Similar provisions to those outlined at **14.5.7.1** above apply to countries covered by the Administration of Justice Act 1920 and the Foreign Judgments (Reciprocal Enforcement) Act 1933. The countries covered by these Acts are mainly Commonwealth States.

For countries not covered by these Acts, such as the USA, enforcement of judgments of the courts of these countries is covered by common law. Usually, the creditor will treat the foreign judgment as a contract containing an implied promise to pay the judgment debt. He will issue proceedings in England alleging breaches of that contract, and if the debtor attempts to defend those proceedings, will apply for summary judgment under Part 24 of CPR 1998.

Enforcement abroad is a matter for the law and courts of the country where the creditor is seeking to enforce an English judgment.

Chapter 15
Alternative Dispute Resolution

15.1	The nature of ADR	195
15.2	Advantages of ADR	196
15.3	Disadvantages of ADR	197
15.4	Types of ADR	198
15.5	Organisations providing ADR	200
15.6	Using ADR	200
15.7	Choosing ADR	201
15.8	Summary	201

This chapter develops further the concept that it may be possible to use less confrontational modes of dispute resolution to reach a quick, cheap and commercially realistic solution. It explains:

(a) how alternative dispute resolution differs from arbitration and litigation;
(b) the advantages and disadvantages of alternative dispute resolution;
(c) the various types of methods available to resolve disputes; and
(d) the organisations which may be able to help if the parties do choose to use some method of dispute resolution instead of arbitration or litigation.

15.1 The nature of ADR

Alternative dispute resolution (ADR) is a means of resolving disputes by using an independent third party who may help the parties to reach their own solution, but who cannot impose a solution. It is voluntary and without prejudice. The parties choose the process and either of them can withdraw at any time before a solution is agreed. If either of them does not like the proposed solution, they do not have to accept it.

15.1.1 How ADR differs from other forms of dispute resolution

Litigation is not voluntary (save in the sense that the claimant chooses to issue a claim in the first place). Once the case is started, usually neither party can withdraw without paying the opponent's costs (see **12.6**). If the parties are unable to negotiate a settlement, the court will impose its own solution. The winner will enforce that solution.

Arbitration is voluntary in the sense that the parties voluntarily entered into an arbitration agreement. When a dispute arises, however, one party can force the other to arbitrate against his will, because of the original contractual agreement to do so. The arbitrator will impose a solution which the winner can enforce. See further **2.8.1**.

Negotiation is both voluntary and non-binding, but it is not the same as ADR. In a negotiation there is no independent third party. The negotiators are identified with their respective 'sides' and may only see the case from their side's point of view. In ADR, there is a third party who is totally independent and who can see both sides' points of view.

15.1.2 The independent third party

The independence of the third party is an essential feature of ADR, as is the fact that he cannot impose a solution. As the parties know that he is independent and cannot do anything to harm them, they are more likely to trust and be open with him. They are less likely to be aggressive towards each other in his presence. They will not want to be seen by him as an obstacle towards a settlement and are likely to be more accommodating in his presence. He may therefore be able to defuse the dispute and make settlement more likely.

The third party can help the parties to settle their dispute in another way. A commercially-minded neutral may come up with ideas which the parties may not have thought of and which solve the problem without either side losing face.

15.2 Advantages of ADR

The CPR 1998 specifically recognise the advantages of ADR. Rule 1.4(2)(e), in giving guidance on how to further the overriding objective of dealing with cases justly, talks about:

> encouraging the parties to use an alternative dispute resolution procedure if the court considers that appropriate and facilitating the use of such procedure.

In a *Practice Statement (Alternative Dispute Resolution) (No 2)* [1996] 1 WLR 1024, Waller J said:

> the settlement of actions by means of ADR (i) significantly helps to save litigants the ever mounting cost of bringing their actions to trial; (ii) saves them the delay of litigation in reaching finality in their disputes; (iii) enables them to achieve settlement of their disputes while preserving their existing commercial relationships and market reputation; (iv) provides them with a wider range of settlement solutions than those offered by litigation; and (v) is likely to make a substantial contribution to the more efficient use of judicial resources ...

Some of these points are amplified below.

15.2.1 Cheapness and speed

Apart from the fact that an independent third party may find it easier to lead the parties to a settlement, ADR has many other attractions. It can be significantly cheaper than both arbitration and litigation. This is because it is quicker. A skilled neutral can, in most cases which are suitable for ADR, help the parties to resolve their dispute in a relatively short period of time.

The parties do, of course, have to pay the third party for his services. They will usually instruct lawyers to help them on the day and they will have to pay those lawyers. If ADR works, however, there will be a significant reduction in the amount of time the lawyers spend in preparing and presenting the case. This will save costs. Even more importantly, the client saves on the indirect costs involved in their employees and executives having to spend time reading court documents, consulting lawyers and attending court.

However, clients should not be given the impression that ADR comes at bargain basement prices. Any lawyer representing the client will want to be fully prepared, and that will take time (including the client's time in dealing with the lawyer's enquiries) and will cost money.

15.2.2 Flexibility

Speed and cheapness are the principal attractions of ADR, but it is also very flexible. The parties can choose one of several forms of ADR. They can choose the procedure to be followed in conjunction with their chosen neutral. They do not have to comply with any statutes or rules of court. There is not even any case law limiting what the parties or the neutral can do.

15.2.3 Preserving a business relationship

ADR shares with arbitration the virtue of privacy. It is also ideal for cases where the parties to the dispute are going to have to continue to deal with each other. The fact that they have chosen a non-confrontational method of solving their problem makes it much easier for them to continue their relationship, since the solution is theirs and has not been imposed upon them.

15.2.4 Commercial reality

A third party unconnected with the dispute may be able to assist the parties to arrive at realistic and workable settlement terms.

15.3 Disadvantages of ADR

15.3.1 It does not bind the parties to the procedure

As a general principle, no one can be forced to resolve a dispute by any form of ADR against their wishes. If one party suggests ADR, the other parties do not have to agree; and even if the parties have started to resolve a dispute by ADR, most ADR agreements allow any party to withdraw at any stage before a solution has been agreed. It will then be necessary to resort to litigation or, if there is an arbitration agreement, to arbitration.

Pre-CPR, the House of Lords, in *Channel Tunnel Group Ltd and France Manche SA v Balfour Beatty Construction Ltd* [1993] 2 WLR 262, indicated that the court does have an inherent jurisdiction to stay litigation which has been commenced in breach of an agreed method of resolving disputes. This is the case even if that method is not technically an arbitration agreement under the Arbitration Act 1996. Post-CPR, the courts have increasing stayed proceedings for ADR to take place (whether or not pursuant to a contractual agreement). In *Cable & Wireless v IBM UK Ltd* [2002] BLR 89, the parties were directed to pursue a previously agreed ADR method. The court held that there were strong case management grounds for allowing the reference to ADR to proceed. Any delay was not such that it would be unfair to impose ADR procedure.

15.3.2 The awards are not so easily enforceable

There is no equivalent of s 66 of the Arbitration Act 1996 (see **2.8.1**) enabling ADR awards to be enforced as if they were court judgments. However, if the parties do agree to terms suggested as a result of ADR, they have entered into a contract. If one of the parties does not carry out that contract, he can be sued for breach of contract and the claimant would usually expect to obtain summary judgment under Part 24 of the CPR 1998 without any difficulty.

It is standard practice in many forms of ADR to provide that no agreement will be binding upon the parties unless it is placed in writing and signed by the parties.

A party who has commenced court proceedings, but then resolved the dispute by ADR, can record the agreement reached in a consent order, which can be enforced by the usual methods.

15.3.3 The facts may not be fully disclosed

The speed of ADR has an associated disadvantage. Because there is no equivalent of disclosure, there is a risk that the parties may resolve the dispute without knowing all the facts. This may lead to the wrong decision. Many businessmen, however, take the view that a quick decision, even if it is not completely accurate, is better than wasting time and money on a protracted dispute in order to get a more correct decision. They often feel that litigation is a lottery anyway.

15.3.4 ADR is not appropriate for all cases

ADR is not appropriate in the following cases:

(a) where the client needs an injunction (after which ADR may then be appropriate);
(b) where there is no dispute. If the case is a simple debt collection matter, the creditor should issue a claim form followed by a Part 24 application, or consider insolvency proceedings;
(c) Where the client needs a ruling on a point of law.

15.4 Types of ADR

15.4.1 Mediation and conciliation

Mediation and conciliation are usually interchangeable terms. For ease of reference the term 'mediation' will be used to cover both processes in this chapter.

In a typical mediation, the third party who has been selected as mediator will have written statements from both parties. Following that, the mediator will discuss the case with them. They will tell him what they think about each party's case on a without prejudice basis. The mediator will not pass on to the other party information which is confidential, unless he is given permission to do so.

These discussions help the mediator to identify the real areas of disagreement and the points which are most important to the respective parties. He can then move the parties towards constructive solutions to the problem.

The method of mediation described above assumes that the mediator and the parties will meet in the same building. This enables things to be dealt with quickly because, if necessary, the parties can meet face to face to iron out their differences. There are, however, other forms of mediation. The parties do not have to meet. The matter can be dealt with by correspondence and telephone conversations.

It is vital that the parties are represented at the mediation by people who have authority to instruct their lawyers to reach agreement.

15.4.2 'Med-arb'

Under this form of ADR, the parties agree to submit their dispute to mediation and that, if this does not work, they will refer the matter to arbitration. They may, if they wish, use the person who has been acting as their mediator as their arbitrator. This will save costs because the arbitrator will already know the facts of the case. There is a risk, however, that, during the mediation, he will have become privy to confidential information belonging to one of the parties. This would compromise his position as arbitrator, so any agreement for 'med-arb' should give either party the right to object to the mediator becoming the arbitrator.

15.4.3 'Mini-trial' or 'structured settlement procedure'

Under this procedure, the parties appoint a neutral who will sit as chairman of a tribunal composed of himself and a senior representative of each of the parties. These representatives may not be immediately connected with the dispute and should have authority to reach such compromise as they see fit. They will then hear and/or read the cases of the two parties (sometimes with an expert), after which they will negotiate with each other with the help of the independent arbiter.

15.4.4 Expert appraisal

The parties can refer all or part of their dispute to an expert in the disputed field for his opinion. His opinion is not binding on the parties, but could influence their approach to subsequent negotiations. It will be for the parties to choose the appropriate procedure, which could even involve a short trial before the expert makes his recommendation.

15.4.5 Judicial appraisal

The Centre for Dispute Resolution (CEDR) has a scheme whereby former judges and senior counsel are available to give a quick preliminary view on the legal position, having heard representations from both parties. It is a matter for agreement between the parties as to whether this opinion is to be binding on them or not.

15.4.6 Expert determination

Expert determination is a halfway house between arbitration and ADR. As in arbitration, the parties select an expert to decide the case for them. They agree to accept his decision and, if one fails to do so, the other can sue for breach of contract. The expert's decision cannot, however, be enforced as a court order and he does not have the powers of an arbitrator under the Arbitration Act 1996. Also, unlike an arbitrator, he can be sued in negligence by a party who thinks his decision was wrong.

15.4.7 Final offer arbitration

The parties can instruct their chosen neutral that they will both make an offer of the terms on which they will settle and that he must choose one of those two offers and no other solution. Neither party can afford to make an unrealistic offer because that will mean that the neutral will choose the opponent's offer, so, at least in theory, the offers are likely to be realistic.

15.4.8 Ombudsman and similar schemes

The number of ombudsmen schemes has grown over the years as the Government, as well as various public and private sector organisations, have sought to resolve complaints without litigation. So you can find schemes covering such diverse matters as financial services, pensions, police, telecommunications, local government, housing, estate agents, legal services, and the like. Full details can be found at the Ombudsman Schemes in the UK website: www.bioa.org.uk/index.html.

Some service and goods providers also offer similar schemes. Probably the best known is the travel industry ABTA arbitration scheme.

15.5 Organisations providing ADR

Anyone can provide help in resolving disputes, but the job is not as easy as it sounds. It should be done by someone who has been trained. The two main organisations that have pioneered ADR in commercial matters in this country are the CEDR and ADR Group.

The CEDR is an independent, non-profit making organisation promoting ADR, which runs training courses and maintains a panel of neutrals.

The ADR Group is a private company which undertakes mediation and training and has established a network of mediators in firms of solicitors throughout the country.

Two other organisations which are very active in the field of ADR, although their principal raison d'être arose from other functions, are the Chartered Institute of Arbitrators and the Academy of Experts.

Lastly, there is Mediation UK, whose general services include all forms of mediation.

Many professional bodies, like the Royal Institution of Chartered Surveyors (RICS), provide ADR services for disputes involving their members.

The judges of the commercial list in the High Court may be prepared to offer their services to help litigants to resolve their disputes without going to trial.

15.6 Using ADR

Parties to a dispute can always reach an ad hoc agreement, when the dispute arises, to use any form of ADR they see fit to solve their problems. It is more proactive, however, to agree in the original contract that, if any dispute does arise between the parties, they will resolve it by some specified form of ADR.

Such contracts may not be effective (see **15.3.1**), because a party cannot be forced to reach a consensual solution, but they do give the parties an opportunity to resolve their disputes peaceably. There is a very strong case for recommending that existing contracts which include an arbitration agreement should be amended, so that the agreement provides for mediation before the parties go to formal arbitration (which they would only do if mediation failed).

15.6.1 Disclosure obligations

An agreement to use ADR should include clauses dealing with some of the potential pitfalls associated with ADR. The parties should decide whether to have a clause requiring full disclosure. The drawback of such a clause is that the more information the parties have to provide for each other, the longer the proceedings may take and the more expensive they will be. Its advantage is that it would be possible to set aside a settlement reached, as a result of ADR, on discovering that one of the parties had concealed vital information. To prevent vexatious applications to set aside any settlement, it might be wise to stipulate in the disclosure clause that a settlement can only be challenged for fundamental non-disclosure of matters which would significantly have affected the result of the ADR process.

15.6.2 Confidentiality

A confidentiality clause in the agreement will encourage full disclosure. The mediator is always under a duty of confidentiality, but the parties will be more likely to disclose information to each other if they know that the other party has agreed not to divulge the information to anyone else. However, if the parties are commercial rivals, who need to keep their methods secret from each other, disclosure and confidentiality clauses are pointless.

15.6.3 Other matters

An ADR agreement should explain how the mediator or other arbiter will be appointed and specify the procedure he should follow. It should also specify that the representatives who attend any ADR process must have full authority to settle the dispute there and then.

15.7 Choosing ADR

A solicitor should discuss with the client the possible uses of ADR whenever a dispute arises in a commercial matter. If the client is willing (or has already agreed) to use ADR, it should be used unless it is obviously inappropriate, for example because an injunction is required, or the other party cannot be trusted to comply with an award or to co-operate in the process. There is no point, however, in proceeding with ADR if it looks like failing. In such cases, at the first sign of non co-operation or lack of trust (eg, where the opponent will not help in the selection of the neutral), litigation or arbitration should be used. This does not mean abandoning ADR. It may be appropriate to continue with ADR in conjunction with litigation, using the latter as a spur to co-operation with the former.

Not surprisingly, given r 1.4(2)(e) (see **15.2**), parties who do choose to litigate may well receive judicial encouragement (and sometimes a degree of pressure) at the case management conference and other hearings to attempt ADR.

15.8 Summary

Alternative dispute resolution involves an independent third party who helps the parties to a dispute to resolve that dispute. The parties are usually free to dispense with his services whenever they see fit. It can provide a quick and cheap means of resolving a dispute in a commercially sensible manner, although the result may not be entirely in accordance with the parties' legal rights and cannot be enforced in the same way as a court judgment or an arbitrator's award.

Solicitors advising clients should be aware of the wide range of ADR techniques and of the organisations that offer help with these techniques. It may be helpful to include ADR agreements in commercial contracts, but careful thought needs to be given to the details of such agreements on matters like disclosure and confidentiality.

Appendix A
Court Forms and Protocols

1. Forms N1 and N1A – Claim Form and Notes for Claimant
2. Form N1C – Notes for Defendant on Replying to the Claim Form
3. Form N9, including Forms N9A–N9D – Response Pack
4. Form N225 – Request for Judgment
5. Form N227 – Request for Judgment by Default
6. Form N211, including Forms N211A and N211C – Part 20 Claim Form
7. Form N251 – Notice of Funding
8. Form N215 – Certificate of Service
9. Form N218 – Notice of Service on Partner
10. Form N266 – Notice to Admit Facts
11. Form N265 – List of Documents
12. Form N150 – Allocation Questionnaire
13. Precedent H – Estimate of Costs
14. Form N242A – Notice of Payment into Court
15. Form N243A – Notice of Acceptance and Request for Payment
16. Form N244 – Application Notice
17. Form N260 – Statement of Costs for Summary Assessment
18. Form N170 – Pre-trial Checklist, Listing Questionnaire
19. Appendix to Part 28
20. QBD PF 52 – Order for Case Management Directions in the Multi-track (Part 28)
21. Form N252 – Notice of Commencement of Assessment of Bill of Costs
22. Precedent A – Bill of Costs
23. Precedent G – Points of Dispute
24. Practice Direction – Protocols
25. Professional Negligence Pre-action Protocol

CPR 1998 Part 16
16.2 → Specifies contents.

Court Forms and Protocols   205

1 Forms N1 and N1A – Claim Form and Notes for Claimant

Claim Form

In the STATE WHICH COURT.

for court use only
Claim No.
Issue date

Claimant
company / individual / partnership
PROVIDE INFORMATION ACCORDING TO CAPACITY IN WHICH YOU ARE SUING...

SEAL

Defendant(s)
AND CAPACITY IN WHICH D IS BEING SUED.

Brief details of claim

Value
Rule 16.3(2)   SPECIFIED → amount claimed
              UNSPECIFIED → Ball Park Figure

See PD 7 para 3.6 If claim is to be started in high Court

Defendant's name and address

	£
Amount claimed	
Court fee	
Solicitor's costs	→ Part 45
Total amount	

The court office at

is open between 10 am and 4 pm Monday to Friday. When corresponding with the court, please address forms or letters to the Court Manager and quote the claim number.

N1 Claim form (CPR Part 7) (01.02)   *Printed on behalf of The Court Service*

	Claim No.	

Does, or will, your claim include any issues under the Human Rights Act 1998? ☐ Yes ☐ No

Particulars of Claim (attached)(to follow)

If served separately, will also need a Statement of Truth Part 22 CPR

Statement of Truth

Required by Rule 22 ✓

*(I believe)(The Claimant believes) that the facts stated in these particulars of claim are true.
* I am duly authorised by the claimant to sign this statement

Full name _____

Name of claimant's solicitor's firm _____

signed _____ position or office held _____

*(Claimant)(Litigation friend)(Claimant's solicitor) (if signing on behalf of firm or company)

*delete as appropriate

Claimant's or claimant's solicitor's address to which documents or payments should be sent if different from overleaf including (if appropriate) details of DX, fax or e-mail.

Notes for claimant on completing a claim form
Further information may be obtained from the court in a series of free leaflets.

- Please read all of these guidance notes before you begin completing the claim form. The notes follow the order in which information is required on the form.
- Court staff can help you fill in the claim form and give information about procedure once it has been issued. But they cannot give legal advice. If you need legal advice, for example, about the likely success of your claim or the evidence you need to prove it, you should contact a solicitor or a Citizens Advice Bureau.
- If you are filling in the claim form by hand, please use black ink and write in block capitals.
- Copy the completed claim form and the defendant's notes for guidance so that you have one copy for yourself, one copy for the court and one copy for each defendant. Send or take the forms to the court office with the appropriate fee. The court will tell you how much this is.

Notes on completing the claim form

Heading

You must fill in the heading of the form to indicate whether you want the claim to be issued in a county court or in the High Court (The High Court means either a District Registry (attached to a county court) or the Royal Courts of Justice in London). There are restrictions on claims which may be issued in the High Court (see 'Value' overleaf).

Use whichever of the following is appropriate:

'In the ....County Court'
(inserting the name of the court)

or

'In the High Court of Justice.........................Division'
(inserting eg. 'Queen's Bench' or 'Chancery' as appropriate)
'..............................District Registry'
(inserting the name of the District Registry)

or

'In the High Court of Justice.........................Division,
(inserting eg. 'Queen's Bench' or 'Chancery' as appropriate)
Royal Courts of Justice'

Claimant and defendant details

As the person issuing the claim, you are called the 'claimant'; the person you are suing is called the 'defendant'. Claimants who are under 18 years old (unless otherwise permitted by the court) and patients within the meaning of the Mental Health Act 1983, must have a litigation friend to issue and conduct court proceedings on their behalf. Court staff will tell you more about what you need to do if this applies to you.

You must provide the following information about yourself **and** the defendant according to the capacity in which you are suing and in which the defendant is being sued. When suing or being sued as:-

an individual:

All known forenames and surname, whether Mr, Mrs, Miss, Ms or Other (e.g. Dr) and residential address (**including** postcode and telephone number) in England and Wales. Where the defendant is a proprietor of a business, a partner in a firm or an individual sued in the name of a club or other unincorporated association, the address for service should be the usual or last known place of residence **or** principal place of business of the company, firm or club or other unincorporated association.

Where the individual is:

under 18 write '(a child by Mr Joe Bloggs his litigation friend)' after the name. If the child is conducting proceedings on their own behalf write '(a child)' after the child's name.

a patient within the meaning of the Mental Health Act 1983 write '(by Mr Joe Bloggs his litigation friend)' after the patient's name.

trading under another name

you must add the words 'trading as' and the trading name e.g. 'Mr John Smith trading as Smith's Groceries'.

suing or being sued in a representative capacity

you must say what that capacity is e.g. 'Mr Joe Bloggs as the representative of Mrs Sharon Bloggs (deceased)'.

suing or being sued in the name of a club or other unincorporated association

add the words 'suing/sued on behalf of' followed by the name of the club or other unincorporated association.

a firm

enter the name of the firm followed by the words 'a firm' e.g. 'Bandbox - a firm' and an address for service which is either a partner's residential address or the principal or last known place of business.

a corporation (other than a company)

enter the full name of the corporation and the address which is either its principal office **or** any other place where the corporation carries on activities and which has a real connection with the claim.

a company registered in England and Wales

enter the name of the company and an address which is either the company's registered office **or** any place of business that has a real, or the most, connection with the claim e.g. the shop where the goods were bought.

an overseas company (defined by s744 of the Companies Act 1985)

enter the name of the company and either the address registered under s691 of the Act **or** the address of the place of business having a real, or the most, connection with the claim.

N1A - w3 Notes for claimant (4.99) — *Printed on behalf of The Court Service*

Brief details of claim

Note: The facts and full details about your claim and whether or not you are claiming interest, should be set out in the 'particulars of claim' *(see note under 'Particulars of Claim')*.

You must set out under **this** heading:
- a concise statement of the nature of your claim
- the remedy you are seeking e.g. payment of money; an order for return of goods or their value; an order to prevent a person doing an act; damages for personal injuries.

Value

If you are claiming a **fixed amount of money** (a 'specified amount') write the amount in the box at the bottom right-hand corner of the claim form against 'amount claimed'.

If you are <u>not</u> claiming a fixed amount of money (an 'unspecified amount') under 'Value' write "I expect to recover" followed by whichever of the following applies to your claim:
- "not more than £5,000" **or**
- "more than £5,000 but not more than £15,000"**or**
- "more than £15,000"

If you are **not able** to put a value on your claim, write "I cannot say how much I expect to recover".

Personal injuries

If your claim is for 'not more than £5,000' and includes a claim for personal injuries, you must also write "My claim includes a claim for personal injuries and the amount I expect to recover as damages for pain, suffering and loss of amenity is" followed by either:
- "not more than £1,000" **or**
- "more than £1,000"

Housing disrepair

If your claim is for 'not more than £5,000' and includes a claim for housing disrepair relating to residential premises, you must also write "My claim includes a claim against my landlord for housing disrepair relating to residential premises. The cost of the repairs or other work is estimated to be" followed by either:
- "not more than £1,000" **or**
- "more than £1,000"

If within this claim, you are making a claim for other damages, you must also write:

"I expect to recover as damages" followed by either:
- "not more than £1,000" **or**
- "more than £1,000"

Issuing in the High Court

You may only issue in the High Court if one of the following statements applies to your claim:-
"By law, my claim must be issued in the High Court. The Act which provides this is ....(specify Act)"
or
"I expect to recover more than £15,000"
or
"My claim includes a claim for personal injuries and the value of the claim is £50,000 or more"
or
"My claim needs to be in a specialist High Court list, namely................................(state which list)".

If one of the statements does apply and you wish to, or must by law, issue your claim in the High Court, write the words "I wish my claim to issue in the High Court because" followed by the relevant statement e.g. "I wish my claim to issue in the High Court because my claim includes a claim for personal injuries and the value of my claim is £50,000 or more."

Defendant's name and address

Enter in this box the full names and address of the defendant receiving the claim form (ie. one claim form for each defendant). If the defendant is to be served outside England and Wales, you may need to obtain the court's permission.

Particulars of claim

You may include your particulars of claim on the claim form in the space provided or in a separate document which you should head 'Particulars of Claim'. It should include the names of the parties, the court, the claim number and your address for service and also contain a statement of truth. You should keep a copy for yourself, provide one for the court and one for each defendant. Separate particulars of claim can either be served
- with the claim form **or**
- within 14 days after the date on which the claim form was served.

If your particulars of claim are served separately from the claim form, they must be served with the forms on which the defendant may reply to your claim.

Your particulars of claim must include
- a concise statement of the facts on which you rely
- a statement (if applicable) to the effect that you are seeking aggravated damages or exemplary damages
- details of any interest which you are claiming
- any other matters required for your type of claim as set out in the relevant practice direction

Address for documents

Insert in this box the address at which you wish to receive documents and/or payments, if different from the address you have already given under the heading 'Claimant'. The address must be in England or Wales. If you are willing to accept service by DX, fax or e-mail, add details.

Statement of truth

This must be signed by you, by your solicitor or your litigation friend, as appropriate.

Where the claimant is a registered company or a corporation the claim must be signed by either the director, treasurer, secretary, chief executive, manager or other officer of the company or (in the case of a corporation) the mayor, chairman, president or town clerk.

Solicitor more likely to put:
"The Claimant expects to recover more than £15,000"

2 Form N1C – Notes for Defendant on Replying to the Claim Form

Notes for defendant on replying to the claim form

Please read these notes carefully - they will help you decide what to do about this claim. Further information may be obtained from the court in a series of free leaflets

- If this claim form was received with the particulars of claim completed or attached, you must reply within 14 days of the date it was served on you. If the words 'particulars of claim to follow' are written in the particulars of claim box, you should not reply until after you are served with the particulars of claim (which should be no more than 14 days after you received the claim form). If the claim was sent by post, the date of service is taken as the second day after posting (see post mark). If the claim form was delivered or left at your address, the date of service will be the day after it was delivered.
- You may either
    - pay the total amount i.e. the amount claimed, the court fee, and solicitor's costs (if any)
    - admit that you owe all or part of the claim and ask for time to pay or
    - dispute the claim
- If you do not reply, judgment may be entered against you.
- The notes below tell you what to do.
- The response pack will tell you which forms to use for your reply. (The pack will accompany the particulars of claim if they are served after the claim form).
- Court staff can help you complete the forms of reply and tell you about court procedures. But they cannot give legal advice. If you need legal advice, for example about the likely success of disputing the claim, you should contact a solicitor or a Citizens Advice Bureau immediately.

Registration of Judgments: If this claim results in a judgment against you, details will be entered in a public register, the Register of County Court Judgments. They will then be passed to credit reference agencies which will then supply them to credit grantors and others seeking information on your financial standing. **This will make it difficult for you to get credit.** A list of credit reference agencies is available from Registry Trust Ltd, 173/175 Cleveland Street, London W1T 6QR.

Costs and Interest: Additional costs and interest may be added to the amount claimed on the front of the claim form if judgment is entered against you. In a county court, if judgment is for £5,000 or more, or is in respect of a debt which attracts contractual or statutory interest for late payment, the claimant may be entitled to further interest.

Your response and what happens next

How to pay

Do not bring any payments to the court - they will not be accepted.

When making payments to the claimant, quote the claimant's reference (if any) and the claim number.

Make sure that you keep records and can account for any payments made. Proof may be required if there is any disagreement. It is not safe to send cash unless you use registered post.

Admitting the Claim

Claim for specified amount

If you admit all the claim, take or send the money, including the court fee, any interest and costs, to the claimant at the address given for payment on the claim form, within 14 days.

If you admit all the claim and you are asking for time to pay, complete Form N9A and send it to the claimant at the address given for payment on the claim form, within 14 days. The claimant will decide whether to accept your proposal for payment. If it is accepted, the claimant may request the court to enter judgment against you and you will be sent an order to pay. If your offer is not accepted, the court will decide how you should pay.

If you admit only part of the claim, complete Form N9A and Form N9B (see 'Disputing the Claim' overleaf) and send them to the court within 14 days. The claimant will decide whether to accept your part admission. If it is accepted, the claimant may request the court to enter judgment against you and the court will send you an order to pay. If your part admission is not accepted, the case will proceed as a defended claim.

Claim for unspecified amount

If you admit liability for the whole claim but do not make an offer to satisfy the claim, complete Form N9C and send it to the court within 14 days. A copy will be sent to the claimant who may request the court to enter judgment against you for an amount to be decided by the court, and costs. The court will enter judgment and refer the court file to a judge for directions for management of the case. You and the claimant will be sent a copy of the court's order.

If you admit liability for the claim and offer an amount of money to satisfy the claim, complete Form

N1C Notes for defendant (11.01) — *Printed on behalf of The Court Service*

N9C and send it to the court within 14 days. The claimant will be sent a copy and asked if the offer is acceptable. The claimant must reply to the court within 14 days and send you a copy. If a reply is not received, the claim will be stayed. If the amount you have offered is **accepted** -

- the claimant may request the court to enter judgment against you for that amount.
- if you have requested time to pay which is not accepted by the claimant, the rate of payment will be decided by the court.

If your offer in satisfaction is **not accepted** -

- the claimant may request the court to enter judgment against you for an amount to be decided by the court, and costs; and
- the court will enter judgment and refer the court file to a judge for directions for management of the case. You and the claimant will be sent a copy of the court's order.

Disputing the claim

If you are being sued as an individual for a specified amount of money and you dispute the claim, the claim may be transferred to a local court i.e. the one nearest to or where you live or carry on business if different from the court where the claim was issued.

If you need longer than 14 days to prepare your defence or to contest the court's jurisdiction to try the claim, complete the Acknowledgment of Service form and send it to the court within 14 days. This will allow you 28 days from the date of service of the particulars of claim to file your defence or make an application to contest the court's jurisdiction. The court will tell the claimant that your Acknowledgment of Service has been received.

If the case proceeds as a defended claim, you and the claimant will be sent an Allocation Questionnaire. You will be told the date by which it must be returned to the court. The information you give on the form will help a judge decide whether your case should be dealt with in the small claims track, fast track or multi-track. After a judge has considered the completed questionnaires, you will be sent a notice of allocation setting out the judge's decision. The notice will tell you the track to which the claim has been allocated and what you have to do to prepare for the hearing or trial. **Leaflets telling you more about the tracks are available from the court office.**

Claim for specified amount

If you wish to dispute the full amount claimed or wish to claim against the claimant (a counterclaim), complete Form N9B and send it to the court within 14 days.

If you admit part of the claim, complete the Defence Form N9B and the Admission Form N9A and send them both to the court within 14 days. The claimant will decide whether to accept your part admission in satisfaction of the claim (see under 'Admitting the Claim - specified amount'). If the claimant does not accept the amount you have admitted, the case will proceed as a defended claim.

If you dispute the claim because you have already paid it, complete Form N9B and send it to the court within 14 days. The claimant will have to decide whether to proceed with the claim or withdraw it and notify the court and you within 28 days. If the claimant wishes to proceed, the case will proceed as a defended claim.

Claim for unspecified amount/return of goods/ non-money claims

If you dispute the claim or wish to claim against the claimant (counterclaim), complete Form N9D and send it to the court within 14 days.

Personal injuries claims:

If the claim is for personal injuries and the claimant has attached a medical report to the particulars of claim, in your defence you should state whether you:
- agree with the report **or**
- dispute all or part of the report **and** give your reasons for doing so **or**
- neither agree nor dispute the report **or**
- have no knowledge of the report

Where you have obtained your own medical report, you should attach it to your defence.

If the claim is for personal injuries and the claimant has attached a schedule of past and future expenses and losses, in your defence you must state which of the items you:
- agree **or**
- dispute **and** supply alternative figures where appropriate **or**
- neither agree nor dispute or have no knowledge of

Address where notices can be sent

This must be either your solicitor's address, your own residential or business address in England and Wales or (if you live elsewhere) some other address within England and Wales.

Statement of truth

This must be signed by you, by your solicitor or your litigation friend, as appropriate.

Where the defendant is **a registered company or a corporation** the response must be signed by either the director, treasurer, secretary, chief executive, manager or other officer of the company **or** (in the case of a corporation) the mayor, chairman, president or town clerk

[Handwritten at top: To be attached to either the claim form AND PoC or PoC and served upon the defendant.]

Court Forms and Protocols 211

3 Form N9, Including Forms N9A–N9D – Response Pack

Response Pack

You should read the 'notes for defendant' attached to the claim form which will tell you when and where to send the forms

Included in this pack are:

- either **Admission Form N9A**
  (if the claim is for a specified amount)
  or **Admission Form N9C**
  (if the claim is for an unspecified amount
  or is not a claim for money)
- either **Defence and Counterclaim Form N9B** (if the claim is for a specified amount)
  or **Defence and Counterclaim Form N9D**
  (if the claim is for an unspecified amount
  or is not a claim for money)
- **Acknowledgment of service**
  (see below)

Complete

If you admit the claim or the amount claimed and/or you want time to pay	▶ the admission form
If you admit part of the claim	▶ the admission form and the defence form
If you dispute the whole claim or wish to make a claim (a counterclaim) against the claimant	▶ the defence form
If you need 28 days (rather than 14) from the date of service to prepare your defence, or wish to contest the court's jurisdiction	▶ the acknowledgment of service
If you do nothing, judgment may be entered against you	

[Handwritten: option 1 ✱]

Acknowledgment of Service

Defendant's full name if different from the name given on the claim form

In the	
Claim No.	
Claimant (including ref.)	
Defendant	

Address to which documents about this claim should be sent (including reference if appropriate)

	if applicable
fax no.	
DX no.	
Ref. no.	
e-mail	

Tel. no.   Postcode

Tick the appropriate box

1. I intend to defend all of this claim ☐
2. I intend to defend part of this claim ☐
3. I intend to contest jurisdiction ☐

If you file an acknowledgment of service but do not file a defence within 28 days of the date of service of the claim form, or particulars of claim if served separately, judgment may be entered against you.

If you do not file an application within 28 days of the date of service of the claim form, or particulars of claim if served separately, it will be assumed that you accept the court's jurisdiction and judgment may be entered against you.

Signed _____
(Defendant)(Defendant's solicitor)
(Litigation friend)

Position or office held _____
(if signing on behalf of firm or company)

Date _____

The court office at
is open between 10 am and 4 pm Monday to Friday. When corresponding with the court, please address forms or letters to the Court Manager and quote the claim number.

N9 Response Pack (5.02)   Printed on behalf of The Court Service

[Handwritten at bottom: If signed by solicitor, will be his solicitors address that is service address.]

212   Civil Litigation

*[handwritten: * option 3]*
[handwritten: different form to send back if claim is for unspecified amount - p216]

Admission (specified amount)

- You have a limited number of days to complete and return this form
- Before completing this form, please read the notes for guidance attached to the claim form

When to fill in this form
Only fill in this form if:
- you are admitting all of the claim **and** you are asking for time to pay; or
- you are admitting part of the claim. (You should also complete form N9B)

How to fill in this form
- Tick the correct boxes and give as much information as you can. **Then sign and date the form.** If necessary provide details on a separate sheet, add the claim number and attach it to this form.
- Make your offer of payment in box 11 on the back of this form. **If you make no offer the claimant will decide how much and when you should pay.**
- If you are not an individual, you should ensure that you provide sufficient details about the assets and liabilities of your firm, company or corporation to support any offer of payment made in box 11.
- You can get help to complete this form at **any** county court office or Citizens Advice Bureau.

Where to send this form
- **If you admit the claim in full**
  Send the completed form to the address shown on the claim form as one to which documents should be sent.
- **If you admit only part of the claim**
  Send the form **to the court** at the address given on the claim form, together with the defence form (N9B).

How much of the claim do you admit?
- [ ] I admit the full amount claimed as shown on the claim form **or**
- [ ] I admit the amount of £ _____

1 Personal details
Surname: _____
Forename: _____
- [ ] Mr [ ] Mrs [ ] Miss [ ] Ms
- [ ] Married [ ] Single [ ] Other *(specify)* _____
Age: _____
Address: _____
Postcode: _____
Tel. no.: _____

In the _____
Claim No. _____
Claimant *(including ref.)* _____
Defendant _____

2 Dependants *(people you look after financially)*
Number of children in each age group
under 11 ___ 11-15 ___ 16-17 ___ 18 & over ___
Other dependants *(give details)* _____

3 Employment
- [ ] I am employed as a _____
  My employer is _____
  Jobs other than main job *(give details)* _____
- [ ] I am self employed as a _____
  Annual turnover is............ £ _____
  - [ ] I am not in arrears with my national insurance contributions, income tax and VAT
  - [ ] I am in arrears and I owe............ £ _____
  Give details of:
  (a) contracts and other work in hand _____
  (b) any sums due for work done _____
- [ ] I have been unemployed for ___ years ___ months
- [ ] I am a pensioner

4 Bank account and savings
- [ ] I have a bank account
  - [ ] The account is in credit by........ £ _____
  - [ ] The account is overdrawn by.... £ _____
- [ ] I have a savings or building society account
  The amount in the account is.......... £ _____

5 Residence
I live in
- [ ] my own house   [ ] lodgings
- [ ] my jointly owned house   [ ] council accommodation
- [ ] rented accommodation

N9A Form of admission (specified amount) (11.01)   Printed on behalf of The Court Service

6 Income

My usual take home pay *(including overtime, commission, bonuses etc)* £ _____ per _____
Income support £ _____ per _____
Child benefit(s) £ _____ per _____
Other state benefit(s) £ _____ per _____
My pension(s) £ _____ per _____
Others living in my home give me £ _____ per _____
Other income *(give details below)*

£ _____ per _____
£ _____ per _____
£ _____ per _____

Total income £ _____ per _____

7 Expenses

(Do not include any payments made by other members of the household out of their own income)

I have regular expenses as follows:

Mortgage *(including second mortgage)* £ _____ per _____
Rent £ _____ per _____
Council tax £ _____ per _____
Gas £ _____ per _____
Electricity £ _____ per _____
Water charges £ _____ per _____

TV rental and licence £ _____ per _____
HP repayments £ _____ per _____
Mail order £ _____ per _____

Housekeeping, food, school meals £ _____ per _____
Travelling expenses £ _____ per _____
Children's clothing £ _____ per _____
Maintenance payments £ _____ per _____
Others *(not court orders or credit debts listed in boxes 9 and 10)*

£ _____ per _____
£ _____ per _____
£ _____ per _____

Total expenses £ _____ per _____

8 Priority debts *(This section is for arrears only. Do not include regular expenses listed in box 7.)*

Rent arrears £ _____ per _____
Mortgage arrears £ _____ per _____
Council tax/Community Charge arrears £ _____ per _____
Water charges arrears £ _____ per _____
Fuel debts: Gas £ _____ per _____
Electricity £ _____ per _____
Other £ _____ per _____
Maintenance arrears £ _____ per _____
Others *(give details below)*

£ _____ per _____
£ _____ per _____

Total priority debts £ _____ per _____

9 Court orders

Court _____ Claim No. _____ £ _____ per _____

Total court order instalments £ _____ per _____

Of the payments above, I am behind with payments to *(please list)*

10 Credit debts

Loans and credit card debts *(please list)*

£ _____ per _____
£ _____ per _____
£ _____ per _____

Of the payments above, I am behind with payments to *(please list)*

11 Offer of payment

☐ I can pay the amount admitted on _____
or
☐ I can pay by monthly instalments of £ _____

If you cannot pay immediately, please give brief reasons below

12 Declaration

I declare that the details I have given above are true to the best of my knowledge

Signed _____

Date _____

Position or office held _____
(if signing on behalf of firm or company)

[handwritten: option 2]
[handwritten: – different form if claim is for unspecified amount.]

Defence and Counterclaim (specified amount)

- Fill in this form if you wish to dispute all or part of the claim and/or make a claim against the claimant (counterclaim).
- You have a limited number of days to complete and return this form to the court.
- Before completing this form, please read the notes for guidance attached to the claim form.
- Please ensure that all boxes at the top right of this form are completed. You can obtain the correct names and number from the claim form. The court cannot trace your case without this information.

How to fill in this form

- Complete sections 1 and 2. Tick the correct boxes and give the other details asked for.
- Set out your defence in section 3. If necessary continue on a separate piece of paper making sure that the claim number is clearly shown on it. In your defence you must state which allegations in the particulars of claim you deny and your reasons for doing so. **If you fail to deny an allegation it may be taken that you admit it.**
- If you dispute only some of the allegations you must
  - specify which you admit and which you deny; and
  - give your own version of events if different from the claimant's.

In the

Claim No.

Claimant (including ref.)

Defendant

- If you wish to make a claim against the claimant (a counterclaim) complete section 4.
- Complete and sign section 5 before sending this form to the court. Keep a copy of the claim form and this form.

Community Legal Service Fund (CLSF)
You may qualify for assistance from the CLSF (this used to be called 'legal aid') to meet some or all of your legal costs. Ask about the CLSF at any county court office or any information or help point which displays this logo.

Community Legal Service

1. How much of the claim do you dispute?

☐ I dispute the full amount claimed as shown on the claim form

or

☐ I admit the amount of £ _____

If you dispute only part of the claim you must **either**:

- pay the amount admitted to the person named at the address for payment on the claim form (see How to Pay in the notes on the back of, or attached to, the claim form). Then send this defence to the court

  or

- complete the admission form **and** this defence form and send them to the court.

  ☐ I paid the amount admitted on (*date*) _____
  or
  ☐ I enclose the completed form of admission
  (*go to section 2*)

2. Do you dispute this claim because you have already paid it? *Tick whichever applies*

☐ **No** (*go to section 3*)

☐ **Yes** I paid £ _____ to the claimant on _____ (*before the claim form was issued*)

Give details of where and how you paid it in the box below (*then go to section 5*)

3. Defence

N9B Defence and Counterclaim (specified amount)(11.02) Printed on behalf of The Court Service

Defence (continued) Claim No. [ ]

4. If you wish to make a claim against the claimant (a counterclaim)

If your claim is for a specific sum of money, how much are you claiming? £ [ ]

I enclose the counterclaim fee of £ [ ]

My claim is for *(please specify nature of claim)*

- To start your counterclaim, you will have to pay a fee. Court staff can tell you how much you have to pay.

- You may not be able to make a counterclaim where the claimant is the Crown (e.g. a Government Department). Ask at your local county court office for further information.

What are your reasons for making the counterclaim?
If you need to continue on a separate sheet put the claim number in the top right hand corner

5. Signed
(To be signed by you or by your solicitor or litigation friend)

*(I believe)(The defendant believes) that the facts stated in this form are true. *I am duly authorised by the defendant to sign this statement

delete as appropriate

Position or office held
(if signing on behalf of firm or company)

Date

Give an address to which notices about this case can be sent to you

Postcode

Tel. no.

if applicable

fax no.

DX no.

e-mail

Admission (unspecified amount, non-money and return of goods claims)

In the	
Claim No.	
Claimant (including ref.)	
Defendant	

- Before completing this form please read the notes for guidance attached to the claim form. If necessary provide details on a separate sheet, add the claim number and attach it to this form.
- If you are not an individual, you should ensure that you provide sufficient details about the assets and liabilities of your firm, company or corporation to support any offer of payment made.

In non-money claims only
☐ I admit liability for the whole claim
(Complete section 11)

In return of goods cases only
Are the goods still in your possession?
☐ Yes ☐ No

Part A Response to claim *(tick one box only)*
☐ I admit liability for the whole claim but want the court to decide the amount I should pay / value of the goods
OR
☐ I admit liability for the claim and offer to pay [   ] in satisfaction of the claim
(Complete part B and sections 1- 11)

Part B How are you going to pay the amount you have admitted? *(tick one box only)*
☐ I offer to pay on (date) [   ]
OR
☐ I cannot pay the amount immediately because *(state reason)*
[   ]

AND
I offer to pay by instalments of £ [   ]
per (week)(month)
starting *(date)* [   ]

1 Personal details

Surname [   ]
Forename [   ]
☐ Mr ☐ Mrs ☐ Miss ☐ Ms
☐ Married ☐ Single ☐ Other *(specify)* [   ]
Age [   ]
Address [   ]
Postcode [   ]
Tel. no. [   ]

2 Dependants *(people you look after financially)*

Number of children in each age group
under 11 [ ]   11-15 [ ]   16-17 [ ]   18 & over [ ]

Other dependants *(give details)* [   ]

3 Employment

☐ I am employed as a [   ]
My employer is [   ]
Jobs other than main job *(give details)* [   ]

☐ I am self employed as a [   ]
Annual turnover is........................... £ [   ]

☐ I am not in arrears with my national insurance contributions, income tax and VAT

☐ I am in arrears and I owe........... £ [   ]

Give details of:
(a) contracts and other work in hand [   ]
(b) any sums due for work done [   ]

☐ I have been unemployed for [ ] years [ ] months
☐ I am a pensioner

4 Bank account and savings

☐ I have a bank account
☐ The account is in credit by........ £ [   ]
☐ The account is overdrawn by.... £ [   ]

☐ I have a savings or building society account
The amount in the account is.......... £ [   ]

5 Residence

I live in
☐ my own property   ☐ lodgings
☐ jointly owned house   ☐ rented property
☐ council accommodation

N9C - w3 Admission (unspecified amount and non-money claims) (8.99) *Printed on behalf of The Court Service*

6 Income

My usual take home pay *(including overtime, commission, bonuses etc)*	£	per
Income support	£	per
Child benefit(s)	£	per
Other state benefit(s)	£	per
My pension(s)	£	per
Others living in my home give me	£	per
Other income *(give details below)*		
	£	per
	£	per
	£	per
Total income	**£**	**per**

7 Expenses

(Do not include any payments made by other members of the household out of their own income)

I have regular expenses as follows:

Mortgage *(including second mortgage)*	£	per
Rent	£	per
Council tax	£	per
Gas	£	per
Electricity	£	per
Water charges	£	per
TV rental and licence	£	per
HP repayments	£	per
Mail order	£	per
Housekeeping, food, school meals	£	per
Travelling expenses	£	per
Children's clothing	£	per
Maintenance payments	£	per
Others *(not court orders or credit debts listed in sections 9 and 10)*		
	£	per
	£	per
	£	per
Total expenses	**£**	**per**

8 Priority debts *(This section is for arrears only. Do not include regular expenses listed in section 7)*

Rent arrears	£	per
Mortgage arrears	£	per
Council tax/Community Charge arrears	£	per
Water charges arrears	£	per
Fuel debts: Gas	£	per
Electricity	£	per
Other	£	per
Maintenance arrears	£	per
Others *(give details below)*		
	£	per
	£	per
Total priority debts	**£**	**per**

9 Court orders

Court	Claim No.	£	per

Total court order instalments	**£**	**per**

Of the payments above, I am behind with payments to *(please list)*

10 Credit debts

Loans and credit card debts *(please list)*

	£	per
	£	per
	£	per

Of the payments above, I am behind with payments to *(please list)*

11 Declaration

I declare that the details I have given above are true to the best of my knowledge

Signed

Date

Position or office held *(if signing on behalf of firm or company)*

Defence and Counterclaim
(unspecified amount, non-money and return of goods claims)

In the	
Claim No.	
Claimant (including ref.)	
Defendant	

- Fill in this form if you wish to dispute all or part of the claim and/or make a claim against the claimant (a counterclaim)
- You have a limited number of days to complete and return this form to the court.
- Before completing this form, please read the notes for guidance attached to the claim form.
- Please ensure that all the boxes at the top right of this form are completed. You can obtain the correct names and number from the claim form. The court cannot trace your case without this information.

How to fill in this form
- Set out your defence in section 1. If necessary continue on a separate piece of paper making sure that the claim number is clearly shown on it. In your defence you must state which allegations in the particulars of claim you deny and your reasons for doing so. **If you fail to deny an allegation it may be taken that you admit it.**
- If you dispute only some of the allegations you must
  - specify which you admit and which you deny; and
  - give your own version of events if different from the claimant's.

- If the claim is for money and you dispute the claimant's statement of value, you must say why and if possible give your own statement of value.
- If you wish to make a claim against the claimant (a counterclaim) complete section 2.
- Complete and sign section 3 before returning this form.

Where to send this form
- send or take this form immediately to the court at the address given on the claim form.
- Keep a copy of the claim form and the defence form.

Community Legal Service Fund (CLSF)
You may qualify for assistance from the CLSF (this used to be called 'legal aid') to meet some or all of your legal costs. Ask about the CLSF at any county court office or any information or help point which displays this logo.

Community Legal Service

1. Defence

N9D Defence and Counterclaim (unspecified amount) (11.02)

Printed on behalf of The Court Service

Defence (continued)   Claim No. [   ]

2. If you wish to make a claim against the claimant (a counterclaim)

If your claim is for a specific sum of money, how much are you claiming? £ [   ]

I enclose the counterclaim fee of £ [   ]

My claim is for *(please specify)*

[   ]

- To start your counterclaim, you will have to pay a fee. Court staff can tell you how much you have to pay.

- You may not be able to make a counterclaim where the claimant is the Crown (e.g. a Government Department). Ask at your local county court office for further information.

What are your reasons for making the counterclaim?
If you need to continue on a separate sheet put the claim number in the top right hand corner

[   ]

3. Signed
(To be signed by you or by your solicitor or litigation friend)

*(I believe)(The defendant believes) that the facts stated in this form are true. *I am duly authorised by the defendant to sign this statement

delete as appropriate

Position or office held
(if signing on behalf of firm or company)

Date [   ]

Give an address to which notices about this case can be sent to you

[Postcode   ]
[Tel. no.   ]

if applicable
fax no.	
DX no.	
e-mail	

Court Forms and Protocols   219

4 Form N225 – Request for Judgment

Request for judgment and reply to admission (specified amount)

In the	
Claim No.	
Claimant (including ref)	
Defendant (including ref)	

- Tick box A or B. If you tick box B you must complete the details in that part and in part C. Make sure that all the case details are given. Remember to sign and date the form. Your signature certifies that the information you have given is correct.
- If the defendant has given an address on the form of admission to which correspondence should be sent, which is different from the address shown on the claim form, you must tell the court.
- Return the completed form to the court.

☐ **The defendant has not filed an admission or defence to my claim**

Complete all the judgment details at C. Decide how and when you want the defendant to pay. You can ask for the judgment to be paid by instalments or in one payment.

B ☐ **The defendant admits that all the money is owed**

Tick only **one** box below and complete all the judgment details at C.

☐ **I accept the defendant's proposal for payment**

Say how the defendant intends to pay. The court will send the defendant an order to pay. You will also be sent a copy.

☐ **The defendant has not made any proposal for payment**

Say how you want the defendant to pay. You can ask for the judgment to be paid by instalments or in one payment. The court will send the defendant an order to pay. You will also be sent a copy.

☐ **I do NOT accept the defendant's proposal for payment**

Say how you want the defendant to pay. Give your reasons for objecting to the defendant's offer of payment in the space opposite. (Continue on the back of this form if necessary.) Send this form to the court **with defendant's admission N9A.** The court will fix a rate of payment and send the defendant an order to pay. You will also be sent a copy.

C Judgment details

I would like the judgment to be paid

☐ (immediately)
☐ (by instalments of £ _____ per month)
☐ (in full by _____)

Amount of claim as admitted (including interest at date of issue)	
Interest since date of claim (if any)	
Period from . . . . to	
Rate . . %	
Court fees shown on claim	
Solicitor's costs (if any) on issuing claim	
Sub Total	
Solicitor's costs (if any) on entering judgment	
Sub Total	
Deduct amount (if any) paid since issue	
Amount payable by defendant	

I certify that the information given is correct

Signed _____   Position or office held _____

(Claimant)(Claimant's solicitor)(Litigation friend)   (if signing on behalf of firm or company)

Date _____

The court office at

is open between 10 am and 4 pm Monday to Friday. When corresponding with the court, please address forms and letters to the Court Manager and quote the Claim number

N225 - w3   Request for judgment and reply to admission (specified amount) (4.99)   *Printed on behalf of The Court Service*

5 Form 227 – Request for Judgment by Default

Request for judgment by default
(amount to be decided by the court)

In the	
Claim No.	
Claimant (including ref)	
Defendant	

To the court

The defendant has not filed (an acknowledgment of service)(a defence) to my claim and the time for doing so has expired.

I request judgment to be entered against the defendant for an amount to be decided by the court and costs.

Signed _____
(Claimant)(Claimant's solicitor)(Litigation friend)

Position or office held _____
(if signing on behalf of firm or company)

Date _____

Note: The court will enter judgment and refer the court file to a judge who will give directions for the management of the case including its allocation to track.

The Court Manager

The court office at

is open between 10 am and 4 pm Monday to Friday. When corresponding with the court, please address forms or letters to the Court Manager and quote the claim number.

N227 - w3 Request for judgment by default (amount to be decided by the court)(4.99) *Printed on behalf of The Court Service*

6 Form N211, Including Forms N211A and N211C – Part 20 Claim Form

Claim Form
(Additional claims-CPR Part 20)

In the	
Claim No.	

SEAL

Claimant(s)

Defendant(s)

Part 20 Claimant(s)

Part 20 Defendant(s)

Brief details of claim

Value

Defendant's name and address

£

Amount claimed	
Court fee	
Solicitors costs	
Total amount	
Issue date	

The court office at

is open between 10 am and 4 pm Monday to Friday. When corresponding with the court, please address forms or letters to the Court Manager and quote the claim number.

N211 - w3 Claim Form (CPR Part 20 - additional claims)(4.99) *Printed on behalf of The Court Service*

	Claim No.	

Particulars of Claim (attached)

PARTICULARS SHOULD BE WRITTEN HERE OR ATTACHED AS SEPARATE DOCUMENT TO CLAIM FORM

Statement of Truth
*(I believe)(The Part 20 Claimant believes) that the facts stated in these particulars of claim are true.
* I am duly authorised by the Part 20 claimant to sign this statement

Full name _____

Name of Part 20 claimant's solicitor's firm _____

signed_____ position or office held_____

*(Part 20 Claimant)('s solicitor)(Litigation friend)   (if signing on behalf of firm or company)

*delete as appropriate

Part 20 Claimant ('s solicitor's) address to which documents or payments should be sent if different from overleaf. If you are prepared to accept service by DX, fax or e-mail, please add details.

Notes for Part 20 claimant on completing a Part 20 claim form

- Please read all of these guidance notes before you begin completing the claim form. The notes follow the order in which information is required on the form. Unless you issue your Part 20 claim before or at the same time as filing your defence to the main claim, (in other words the claim being brought against you as defendant) you will first need to obtain the court's permission to do so.
- Court staff can help you fill in the claim form and give information about procedure once it has been issued. But they cannot give legal advice. If you need legal advice, for example about the likely success of your claim or the evidence you need to prove it, you should contact a solicitor or a Citizens Advice Bureau.
- If you are filling in the claim form by hand, please use black ink and write in block capitals.
- When you have completed the claim form, copy the claim form and the defendant's notes for guidance so that you have one copy for yourself, one copy for the court, one copy for the Part 20 defendant and a copy for each of the other parties to the main claim. Send or take the forms to the court office with the appropriate fee, the court will tell you how much this is.
- Unless the court has ordered otherwise, the Part 20 defendant should be served with the claim form within 14 days of your defence being filed, together with copies of all the statements of case filed in the main claim. The parties to the main claim must also at the same time be served with copies of the Part 20 claim form and particulars of claim, if these are separate from the claim.
- The defendant is added as a party to the main claim once served with the Part 20 claim form.

Notes on completing the claim form

Heading

The name of the court and the claim number will be the same as on the claim form in the main claim. You should copy those details on to your Part 20 claim form.

Claimant and defendant details

You should copy the claimant and defendant details from the main claim into the claimant and defendant boxes. You should enter your name into the Part 20 claimant box and the name of the person you are claiming against into the Part 20 defendant box. Claimants who are under 18 years old (unless otherwise permitted by the court), and patients within the meaning of the Mental Health Act 1983 must have a litigation friend to issue and conduct court proceedings on their behalf. Court staff will tell you more about what you need to do if this applies to you.

You must provide the following information about yourself **and** the Part 20 defendant according to the capacity in which you are suing and in which the defendant is being sued.

When suing or being sued as:-

an individual

All known forenames and surname, whether Mr, Mrs, Miss, Ms or Other (e.g. Dr) and residential address (**including** postcode, telephone and any fax or e-mail number) in England and Wales. Where the defendant is a proprietor of a business, a partner in a firm or an individual sued in the name of a club or other unincorporated association, the address for service should be the usual or last known place of residence **or** principal place of business of the company, firm or club or other unincorporated association.

Where the individual is:

under 18 write '(a child by Mr Joe Bloggs his litigation friend)' after the child's name.

a patient within the meaning of the Mental Health Act 1983 write '(by Mr Joe Bloggs his litigation friend)' after the patients name.

trading under another name

you must add the words 'trading as' and the trading name e.g. 'Mr John Smith trading as Smith's Groceries'.

suing or being sued in a representative capacity

you must say what that capacity is e.g. 'Mr Joe Bloggs as the representative of Mrs Sharon Bloggs (deceased)'.

suing or being sued in the name of a club or other unincorporated association

add the words 'suing/sued on behalf of' followed by the name of the club or other unincorporated association.

a firm

enter the name of the firm followed by the words 'a firm' e.g. 'Bandbox - a firm' and an address for service which is either a partner's residential address or the principal or last known place of business.

a corporation (other than a company)

enter the full name of the corporation and the address which is either its principal office **or** any other place where the corporation carries on activities and which has a real connection with the claim.

a company registered in England and Wales

enter the name of the company and an address which is either the company's registered office **or** any place of business that has a real, or the most, connection with the claim e.g. the shop where the goods were bought.

an overseas company (defined by s744 of the Companies Act 1985)

enter the name of the company and either the address registered under s691 of the Act **or** the address of the place of business having a real, or the most, connection with the claim.

N211A - w3 Notes for claimant (CPR Part 20) (4.99)   *Printed on behalf of The Court Service*

Brief details of claim

Note: The facts and full details about your claim and whether or not you are claiming interest, should be set out in the 'particulars of claim' *(see note under 'Particulars of Claim')*.

You must set out under **this** heading:
- a concise statement of the nature of your claim
- the remedy you are seeking

Value

Note:-
If you are issuing your Part 20 claim in the High Court, you do not have to give a statement of value.

If you are issuing in the county court and claiming a fixed amount of money (a 'specified amount') write the amount in the box at the bottom right-hand corner of the claim form against 'amount claimed'.

If you are <u>not</u> claiming a fixed amount of money (an 'unspecified amount') under 'Value' write "I expect to recover" followed by whichever of the following applies to your claim:
- "not more than £5,000" **or**
- "more than £5,000 but not more than £15,000" **or**
- "more than £15,000"

If your claim is for 'not more than £5,000' and includes a claim for **personal injuries**, you must also write "My claim includes a claim for personal injuries and the amount I expect to recover as damages for pain, suffering and loss of amenity is" followed by either:
- "not more than £1,000" **or**
- "more than £1,000"

If your claim is for 'not more than £5,000' and includes a claim for **housing disrepair** relating to residential premises, you must also write "My claim includes a claim against my landlord for housing disrepair relating to residential premises. The costs of the repairs and other work is estimated to be" followed by either:
- "not more than £1,000" **or**
- "more than £1,000"

"I expect to recover as damages in respect of repairs and other work" followed by either:
- "not more than £1,000" **or**
- "more than £1,000"

If you are <u>not able</u> to put a value on your claim, write "I cannot say how much I expect to recover".

Defendant's name and address

Enter in this box the full names and address of the Part 20 defendant receiving the claim form (ie. one claim form for each Part 20 defendant). If the defendant is to be served outside of England and Wales, you may need to obtain the court's permission.

Particulars of claim

You may include your particulars of claim on the claim form in the space provided or in a separate document which you should head 'Particulars of Claim'. It should include the names of the parties, the court, the claim number and your address for service and also contain a statement of truth. You should keep a copy for yourself, provide one for the court, one for each defendant and one for all other parties in the main claim. Separate particulars of claim **must** be served with the claim form. You should also attach copies of all statements of case already served in the main claim for service on the defendant.

Your particulars of claim must include
- a concise statement of the facts on which you rely
- a statement (if applicable) to the effect that you are seeking aggravated damages or exemplary damages
- details of any interest which you are claiming
- any other matters required for your type of claim as set out in the relevant practice direction

Address for documents

Insert in this box the address at which you wish to receive documents and/or payments, if different from the address you have already given under the heading 'Claimant'. The address you give must be either that of your solicitors or your residential or business address and must be in England or Wales. If you live or carry on business outside England and Wales, you can give some other address within England and Wales.

Statement of truth

This must be signed by you, by your solicitor or your litigation friend, as appropriate.

Where the claimant is a registered company or a corporation the claim must be signed by either the director, treasurer, secretary, chief executive, manager or other officer of the company or (in the case of a corporation) the mayor, chairman, president or town clerk.

Notes for defendant on replying to the Part 20 claim form
Please read these notes carefully - they will help you decide what to do about this claim.

- You must reply to this claim form within 14 days of the date it was served on you. If the claim was
    - sent by post, the date of service is taken as the second day after posting (see post mark).
    - delivered or left at your address, the date of service will be the day after it was delivered.
    - handed to you personally, the 14 days begins on the day it was given to you.
- You may either
    - pay the amount claimed
    - admit the truth of all or part of the claim or
    - dispute the claim
- If you do not reply, the court will consider that you have admitted the claim and judgment may be entered against you.
- The notes below tell you what to do and which forms to use for your reply.
- Court staff can help you complete the forms of reply and tell you about court procedures. But they cannot give legal advice. If you need legal advice, for example about the likely success of disputing the claim, you should contact a solicitor or a Citizens Advice Bureau immediately.

Registration of Judgments: If the claim results in a judgment being made against you in a **county court**, your name and address may be entered in the Register of County Court Judgments. This may make it difficult for you to obtain credit.
Costs and Interest: Additional costs and interest may be added to the amount claimed on the front of the claim form if judgment is entered against you. In a county court, if judgment is for £5,000 or more, or is in respect of a debt which attracts contractual or statutory interest for late payment, the claimant may be entitled to further interest.

Your response and what happens next

How to pay
Do not bring any payments to the court - they will not be accepted.

When making payments to the claimant, quote the claimant's reference (if any) and the claim number.

Make sure that you keep records and can account for any payments made. Proof may be required if there is any disagreement. It is not safe to send cash unless you use registered post.

Admitting the Claim
Claim for a specified amount
Complete Form N9A and send it to the claimant at the address given for payment on the claim form within 14 days. You should at the same time send a copy to all the other parties to the main claim (in other words the claim where the Part 20 claimant is the defendant).

Claim for an unspecified amount
Complete Form N9C and send it to the court within 14 days. A copy will be sent to the claimant.

What happens next
The claimant may apply to the court for judgment to be entered on your admission. The court will arrange a hearing and tell you and the claimant where and when to attend.

Disputing the claim
Complete the form of defence (either N9B if the claim is for a specified amount or N9D if the claim is for an unspecified amount) and return it to the court within 14 days. On receipt of your defence, the court will arrange a hearing and tell you and the claimant when and where to attend. At the hearing the judge will usually give directions as to the future case management of the claim but may make any other order, e.g. striking out all or part of a statement of case.

If you need longer than 14 days to prepare your defence, complete the acknowledgment of service Form N213 and return it to the court. This will allow you 28 days from the date of service of the claim form to file your defence.

Contesting the court's jurisdiction
Complete the acknowledgment of service Form N213 and return it to the court within 14 days. You should make an application to the court within 28 days of service of the claim. An application form (N244) can be obtained from the court and a fee may be payable.

If you do nothing
If you do nothing or you send an acknowledgment of service to the court but fail to send your defence, you will be considered to have admitted the claim and be bound by any judgment or decision made in the main claim where it relates to this claim against you.

Statement of truth
This must be signed by you, by your solicitor or your litigation friend, as appropriate.

Where the defendant is **a registered company or a corporation** the response must be signed by either the director, treasurer, secretary, chief executive, manager or other officer of the company **or** (in the case of a corporation) the mayor, chairman, president or town clerk.

N211C Notes for defendant (CPR Part 20) (10.02) *The Court Service Publications Branch*

7 Form N251 – Notice of Funding

Notice of funding of case or claim

Notice of funding by means of a conditional fee agreement, insurance policy or undertaking given by a prescribed body should be given to the court and all other parties to the case:
- on commencement of proceedings
- on filing an acknowledgment of service, defence or other first document; and
- at any later time that such an arrangement is entered into, changed or terminated.

In the

The court office is open between 10 am and 4 pm Monday to Friday. When writing to the court, please address forms or letters to the Court Manager and quote the claim number.

Claim No.	
Claimant (include Ref.)	
Defendant (include Ref.)	

Take notice that in respect of
- ☐ all claims herein
- ☐ the following claims
- ☐ the case of *(specify name of party)*

[is now][was] being funded by:

(Please tick those boxes which apply)

- ☐ a conditional fee agreement
  Dated
  which provides for a success fee
- ☐ an insurance policy issued on
  Date   Policy no.
  Name and address of insurer
- ☐ an undertaking given on
  Date
  by
  Name of prescribed body
  in the following terms

The funding of the case has now changed:

- ☐ the above funding has now ceased
- ☐ the conditional fee agreement has been terminated
- ☐ a conditional fee agreement
  Dated
  which provides for a success fee has been entered into;
- ☐ an insurance policy
  Date
  has been cancelled
- ☐ an insurance policy has been issued on
  Date   Policy no.
  Name and address of insurer
- ☐ an undertaking given on
  Date
  has been terminated
- ☐ an undertaking has been given on
  Date
  Name of prescribed body
  in the following terms

Signed

Solicitor for the (claimant) (defendant) (Part 20 defendant) (respondent) (appellant)

Dated

N251 Notice of funding of case or claim (06.04)

The Court Service Publications Branch

228   Civil Litigation

[handwritten: Use where partner or partnership manager is personally served]

8 Form N215 – Certificate of Service
[handwritten: Use if party serves the claim form.]

Certificate of service

[handwritten: To be filed within 7 days of service of the claim form.]

In the	
Claim No.	
Claimant	
Defendant	

On the ....*(insert date)*

the .... *(insert title or description of documents served)*

a copy of which is attached to this notice was served on *(insert name of person served, including position i.e. partner, director if appropriate)*

....

Tick as appropriate

☐ by first class post   ☐ by Document Exchange

☐ by delivering to or leaving   ☐ by handing it to or leaving it with

☐ by fax machine (...............time sent)
(you may want to enclose a copy of the transmission sheet)

                                         ☐ by e-mail

☐ by other means *(please specify)*

at *(insert address where service effected, include fax or DX number or e-mail address)*

being the defendant's:

☐ residence   ☐ registered office

☐ place of business   ☐ other *(please specify)* ....

The date of service is therefore deemed to be .... *(insert date - see over for guidance)*

I confirm that at the time of signing this Certificate the document has not been returned to me as undelivered.

Signed ....   **Position or** ....
(Claimant)(Defendant)('s solicitor)('s litigation friend)   **office held**
                                                                   (if signing on behalf
Date ....   *of firm or company)*

N215 - w3 Certificate of service (4.99)   *Printed on behalf on The Court Service*

Notes for guidance
Please note that these notes are only a guide and are not exhaustive
If you are in doubt you should refer to Part 6 of the rules

Where to serve

Nature of party to be served	Place of service
Individual	• Usual or last known residence
Proprietor of business	• Usual or last known residence; or • Place of business or last known place of business
Individual who is suing or being sued in the name of a firm	• Usual or last known residence; or • Principal or last known place of business of the firm
Corporation (incorporated in England and Wales) other than a company	• Principal office of the corporation; or • any place of within the jurisdiction where the corporation carries on its activities and which has a real connection with the claim
Company registered in England and Wales	• Principal office of the company or corporation; or • any place of business of the company within the jurisdiction which has a real connection with the claim

Personal Service - A document is served personally on an individual by leaving it with that individual. A document is served personally on a company or other corporation by leaving it with a person holding a senior position within the company or corporation. In the case of a partnership, you must leave it with either a partner or a person having control or management at the principal place of business. Where a solicitor is authorised to accept service on behalf of a party, service must be effected on the solicitor, unless otherwise ordered.

Deemed Service - Part 6.7(1). A document which is served in accordance with these rules or any relevant practice direction shall be deemed to be served on the day shown in the following table.

Method of service	Deemed day of service
First class post	The second day after it was posted
Document exchange	The second day after it was left at the document exchange
Delivering the document to or leaving it at a permitted address	The day after it was delivered to or left at the permitted address
Fax	If it is transmitted on a business day before 4 p.m., on that day, or otherwise on the business day after the day on which it was transmitted
Other electronic method	The second day after the day on which it was transmitted

- If a document (other than a claim form) is served after 5 p.m. on a business day, or at any time on a Saturday, Sunday or a bank holiday, the document shall, for the purpose of calculating any period of time after service of the document, be treated as having been served on the next business day.

- In this context "business day" means any day except Saturday, Sunday or a bank holiday; and "bank holiday" includes Christmas Day and Good Friday.

Service of documents on children and patients - The rules relating to service on children and patients are contained in Part 6.6 of the rules.

Claim Forms - The general rules about service are subject to the special rules about service of claim forms contained in rules 6.12 to 6.16.

9 Form N218 – Notice of Service on Partner

Notice of service on partner

In the	
Claim No.	
Claimant (including ref.)	
Defendant	

The (claim form) (particulars of claim) served with this notice (is) (are) served on you

(tick only one box)

☐ as a partner of the business

☐ as a person having control or management of the partnership business

☐ as both a partner and as a person having control or management of the partnership business

named in the claim form (particulars of claim).

Signed _____ Date _____

Claimant ('s solicitor)

N218 -w3- Notice of service on partner (4.99)   *Produced on behalf of The Court Service*

A party uses this form to try and get opponent to admit to facts, so then they do not have to prove them at trial.

Court Forms and Protocols 231

10 Form N266 – Notice to Admit Facts

Notice to admit facts

In the	
Claim No.	
Claimant (include Ref.)	
Defendant (include Ref.)	

I (We) give notice that you are requested to admit the following facts or part of case in this claim:

I (We) confirm that any admission of fact(s) or part of case will only be used in this claim.

Signed _____   **Position or office held** _____
(Claimant)(Defendant)('s Solicitor)   (If signing on behalf of firm or company)

Date _____

- -

Admission of facts

I (We) admit the facts or part of case (set out above)(in the attached schedule) for the purposes of this claim only and on the basis that the admission will not be used on any other occasion or by any other person.

← If party admits facts, court will take into account when deciding upon issue of costs

Signed _____   **Position or office held** _____
(Claimant)(Defendant)('s Solicitor)   (If signing on behalf of firm or company)

Date _____

The court office at

is open between 10 am and 4 pm Monday to Friday. Address all communication to the Court Manager quoting the claim number

N266 - w3 Notice to admit facts (4.99)   *Printed on behalf of The Court Service*

11 Form N265 – List of Documents

List of documents: standard disclosure

Notes:
- The rules relating to standard disclosure are contained in Part 31 of the Civil Procedure Rules.
- Documents to be included under standard disclosure are contained in Rule 31.6
- A document has or will have been in your control if you have or have had possession, or a right of possession, of it **or** a right to inspect or take copies of it.

In the	
Claim No.	
Claimant (including ref)	
Defendant (including ref)	
Date	

Disclosure Statement

I state that I have carried out a reasonable and proportionate search to locate all the documents which I am required to disclose under the order made by the court on *(insert date)*

(I did not search for documents -

1. pre-dating

2. located elsewhere than

3. in categories other than

)

I certify that I understand the duty of disclosure and to the best of my knowledge I have carried out that duty. I further certify that the list of documents set out in or attached to this form, is a complete list of all documents which are or have been in my control and which I am obliged under the order to disclose.

I understand that I must inform the court and the other parties immediately if any further document required to be disclosed by Rule 31.6 comes into my control at any time before the conclusion of the case.

(I have not permitted inspection of documents within the category or class of documents (as set out below) required to be disclosed under Rule 31(6)(b)or (c) on the grounds that to do so would be disproportionate to the issues in the case.)

Signed _____ **Date** _____

(Claimant)(Defendant)('s litigation friend)

Position or office held *(if signing on behalf of firm or company)*
Please state why you are the appropriate person to make the disclosure statement.

List of documents:
N265 - w3 standard disclosure (4.99)

continued overleaf
Printed on behalf of The Court Service

Court Forms and Protocols

List and number here, in a convenient order, the documents (or bundles of documents if of the same nature, e.g. invoices) in your control, which you do not object to being inspected. Give a short description of each document or bundle so that it can be identified, and say if it is kept elsewhere i.e. with a bank or solicitor

I have control of the documents numbered and listed here. I do not object to you inspecting them/producing copies.

List and number here, as above, the documents in your control which you object to being inspected. (Rule 31.19)

I have control of the documents numbered and listed here, but I object to you inspecting them:

Say what your objections are

I object to you inspecting these documents because:

List and number here, the documents you once had in your control, but which you no longer have. For each document listed, say when it was last in your control and where it is now.

I have had the documents numbered and listed below, but they are no longer in my control.

234 Civil Litigation

12 Form N150 – Allocation Questionnaire

[handwritten annotations: parties to co-operate; consult each other]

Allocation questionnaire

To be completed by, or on behalf of,

[   ]

who is [1ˢᵗ][2ⁿᵈ][3ʳᵈ][   ][Claimant][Defendant] [Part 20 claimant] in this claim

In the
Claim No.
Last date for filing with court office

Please read the notes on page five before completing the questionnaire.

You should note the date by which it must be returned and the name of the court it should be returned to since this may be different from the court where the proceedings were issued.

If you have settled this claim (or if you settle it on a future date) and do not need to have it heard or tried, you must let the court know immediately.

Have you sent a copy of this completed form to the other party(ies)? ☐ Yes ☐ No

A Settlement

Do you wish there to be a one month stay to attempt to settle the claim, either by informal discussion or by alternative dispute resolution? ☐ Yes ☐ No

B Location of trial

Is there any reason why your claim needs to be heard at a particular court? ☐ Yes ☐ No

If Yes, say which court and why?

[   ]

C Pre-action protocols

If an approved pre-action protocol applies to this claim, complete **Part 1** only. If not, complete **Part 2** only. If you answer 'No' to the question in either Part 1 or 2, please explain the reasons why on a separate sheet and attach it to this questionnaire.

Part 1   The* [   ] protocol applies to this claim.
please say which protocol

Have you complied with it? ☐ Yes ☐ No

Part 2   No pre-action protocol applies to this claim.

Have you exchanged information and/or documents (evidence) with the other party in order to assist in settling the claim? ☐ Yes ☐ No

N150 Allocation questionnaire (10.01)   Printed on behalf of The Court Service

D Case management information

What amount of the claim is in dispute?   £ _____

Applications

Have you made any application(s) in this claim?   ☐ Yes   ☐ No

If Yes, what for? _____   For hearing on _____
(e.g. summary judgment, add another party)

Witnesses

So far as you know at this stage, what witnesses of fact do you intend to call at the trial or final hearing including, if appropriate, yourself?

Witness name	Witness to which facts

Experts

Do you wish to use expert evidence at the trial or final hearing?   ☐ Yes   ☐ No

Have you already copied any experts' report(s) to the other party(ies)?   ☐ None yet obtained   ☐ Yes   ☐ No

Do you consider the case suitable for a single joint expert in any field?   ☐ Yes   ☐ No

Please list any single joint experts you propose to use and any other experts you wish to rely on. Identify single joint experts with the initials 'SJ' after their name(s).

Expert's name	Field of expertise (eg. orthopaedic surgeon, surveyor, engineer)

Do you want your expert(s) to give evidence orally at the trial or final hearing?   ☐ Yes   ☐ No

If Yes, give the reasons why you think oral evidence is necessary:

continue over ▶

Track

Which track do you consider is most suitable for your claim? Tick one box   ☐ small claims track   ☐ fast track   ☐ multi-track

If you have indicated a track which would not be the normal track for the claim, please give brief reasons for your choice

[ ]

E Trial or final hearing

How long do you estimate the trial or final hearing will take?   ____days ____hours ____minutes

Are there any days when you, an expert or an essential witness will not be able to attend court for the trial or final hearing?   ☐ Yes   ☐ No

If Yes, please give details

Name	Dates not available

F Proposed directions *(Parties should agree directions wherever possible)*

Have you attached a list of the directions you think appropriate for the management of the claim?   ☐ Yes   ☐ No

If Yes, have they been agreed with the other party(ies)?   ☐ Yes   ☐ No

G Costs

*Do **not** complete this section if you have suggested your case is suitable for the small claims track **or** you have suggested one of the other tracks and you do not have a solicitor acting for you.*

What is your estimate of your costs incurred to date?   £ [ ]

What do you estimate your overall costs are likely to be?   £ [ ]

In substantial cases these questions should be answered in compliance with CPR Part 43

H Other information

Have you attached documents to this questionnaire? ☐ Yes ☐ No

Have you sent these documents to the other party(ies)? ☐ Yes ☐ No

If Yes, when did they receive them?

Do you intend to make any applications in the immediate future? ☐ Yes ☐ No

If Yes, what for?

In the space below, set out any other information you consider will help the judge to manage the claim.

Signed   Date

[Counsel][Solicitor][for the][1st][2nd][3rd][   ]
[Claimant][Defendant][Part 20 claimant]

Please enter your firm's name, reference number and full postal address including (if appropriate) details of DX, fax or e-mail

		if applicable
	fax no.	
	DX no.	
Tel. no. Postcode	e-mail	
Your reference no.		

Notes for completing an allocation questionnaire

- If the claim is not settled, a judge must allocate it to an appropriate case management track. To help the judge choose the most just and cost-effective track, you must now complete the attached questionnaire.
- If you fail to return the allocation questionnaire by the date given, the judge may make an order which leads to your claim or defence being struck out, or hold an allocation hearing. If there is an allocation hearing the judge may order any party who has not filed their questionnaire to pay, immediately, the costs of that hearing.
- Use a separate sheet if you need more space for your answers marking clearly which section the information refers to. You should write the claim number on it, and on any other documents you send with your allocation questionnaire. Please ensure they are firmly attached to it.
- The letters below refer to the sections of the questionnaire and tell you what information is needed.

A Settlement
If you think that you and the other party may be able to negotiate a settlement you should tick the 'Yes' box. The court may order a stay, whether or not all the other parties to the claim agree. You should still complete the rest of the questionnaire, even if you are requesting a stay. Where a stay is granted it will be for an initial period of one month. You may settle the claim either by informal discussion with the other party or by alternative dispute resolution (ADR). ADR covers a range of different processes which can help settle disputes. More information is available in the Legal Services Commission leaflet 'Alternatives to Court' free from the LSC leaflet line Phone: 0845 3000 343

B Location of trial
High Court cases are usually heard at the Royal Courts of Justice or certain Civil Trial Centres. Fast or multi-track trials may be dealt with at a Civil Trial Centre or at the court where the claim is proceeding. Small claim cases are usually heard at the court in which they are proceeding.

C Pre-action protocols
Before any claim is started, the court expects you to have exchanged information and documents relevant to the claim, to assist in settling it. For some types of claim e.g. personal injury, there are approved protocols that should have been followed.

D Case management information
Applications
It is important for the court to know if you have already made any applications in the claim, what they are for and when they will be heard. The outcome of the applications may affect the case management directions the court gives.

Witnesses
Remember to include yourself as a witness of fact, if you will be giving evidence.

Experts
Oral or written expert evidence will only be allowed at the trial or final hearing with the court's permission. The judge will decide what permission it seems appropriate to give when the claim is allocated to track. Permission in small claims track cases will only be given exceptionally.

Track
The basic guide by which claims are normally allocated to a track is the amount in dispute, although other factors such as the complexity of the case will also be considered. A leaflet available from the court office explains the limits in greater detail.

Small Claims track	Disputes valued at not more than £5,000 except · those including a claim for personal injuries worth over £1,000 and · those for housing disrepair where either the cost of repairs or other work exceeds £1,000 or any other claim for damages exceeds £1,000
Fast track	Disputes valued at more than £5,000 but not more than £15,000
Multi-track	Disputes over £15,000

E Trial or final hearing
You should enter only those dates when you, your expert(s) or essential witness(es) will not be able to attend court because of holiday or other commitments.

F Proposed directions
Attach the list of directions, if any, you believe will be appropriate to be given for the management of the claim. Agreed directions on fast and multi-track cases should be based on the forms of standard directions set out in the practice direction to CPR Part 28 and form PF52.

G Costs
Only complete this section if you are a solicitor and have suggested the claim is suitable for allocation to the fast or multi-track.

H Other Information
Answer the questions in this section. Decide if there is any other information you consider will help the judge to manage the claim. Give details in the space provided referring to any documents you have attached to support what you are saying.

13 Precedent H – Estimate of Costs

SCHEDULE OF COSTS PRECEDENTS
PRECEDENT H

IN THE HIGH COURT OF JUSTICE   2000 - B - 9999

QUEEN'S BENCH DIVISION

BRIGHTON DISTRICT REGISTRY

BETWEEN

	AB	Claimant
	and	
	CD	Defendant

ESTIMATE OF CLAIMANT'S COSTS DATED 12th APRIL 2001

The claimant instructed E F & Co under a conditional fee agreement dated 8th July 2000 in respect of which the following hourly rates are recoverable as base costs

Partner - £180 per hour plus VAT
Assistant Solicitor - £140 per hour plus VAT
Other fee earners - £85 per hour plus VAT

Item No.	Description of work done	V.A.T.	Disbursements	Profit Costs
	PART 1: BASE COSTS ALREADY INCURRED			
	8th July 2000 - EF & Co instructed			
	7th October 2000 - Claim issued			
1	Issue fee	-	£ 400.00	
	21st October 2000 - Particulars of claim served			
	25th November 2000 - Time for service of defence extended by agreement to 14th January 2001			
2	Fee on allocation	-	£ 80.00	
	20th January 2001 - case allocated to multi-track			
	9th February 2001 - Case management conference at which costs were awarded to the claimant and the base costs were summarily assessed at £400 (paid on 24th February 2001)			-
	23rd February 2001 - Claimant's list of documents			
	ATTENDANCES, COMMUNICATIONS AND WORK DONE			
	Claimant			
3	0.75 hours at £180			£ 135.00
4	4.4 hours at £140			£ 616.00
	To Summary	£ -	£ 480.00	£ 751.00

240 Civil Litigation

Item No.	Description of work done	V.A.T.	Disbursements	Profit Costs
5	**Witnesses of Fact** 3.8 hours at £140			£ 532.00
6	Paid travelling on 9th October 2000	£ 4.02	£ 22.96	
7	**Medical expert (Dr. IJ)** 1.5 hours at £140			£ 210.00
8	Dr. IJ"s fee for report		£ 350.00	
9	**Defendant and his solicitor** 2.5 hours at £140			£ 350.00
10	**Court (communications only)** 0.4 hours at £140			£ 56.00
11	**Documents** 0.75 hours at £180 and 22.25 hours at £140			£3,250.00
12	**Negotiations** 2.75 hours at £140			£ 385.00
13	VAT on solicitor's base fees	£ 968.45		
	To Summary	£ 972.47	£ 372.96	£4,783.00
	PART2: BASE COSTS TO BE INCURRED			
14	Fee on listing -		£ 400.00	
15	Attendance at pre-trial review 5 hours at £140			£ 700.00
16	Counsel's base fee for pre-trial review		£ 750.00	
17	Attendance at trial 20 hours at £140			£2,800.00
18	Counsel's base fee for trial including refresher		£3,000.00	
19	Fee of expert witness (Dr. IJ)	-	£ 1,000.00	
20	Expenses of witnesses of fact	-	£ 150.00	
	ATTENDANCES, COMMUNICATIONS AND WORK TO BE DONE			
21	**Claimant** 1 hour at £180			£ 180.00
22	8 hours at £140			£1,120.00
23	**Witnesses of fact** 5 hours at £140			£ 700.00
24	**Medical expert (Dr. IJ)** 1 hour at £140			£ 140.00
25	**Defendant and his solicitor** 2 hours at £140			£ 280.00
	To Summary	£ -	£ 5,300.00	£5,920.00

Item No.	Description of work done	V.A.T.	Disbursements	Profit Costs
26	**Court (communications only)** 1 hour at £140			£ 140.00
27	**Counsel (communications only)** 3 hours at £140			£ 420.00
28	**Documents** 1 hour at £180, 25 hours at £140 and 15 hours at £85			£4,995.00
29	**Negotiations** 5 hours at £140			£ 700.00
30	**Other work** 5 hours at £140			£ 700.00
31	VAT on solicitor's base fees	£2,253.13		
	To Summary	£2,253.13	£ -	£ 6,955.00
	SUMMARY **Part 1** Page 1 Page 2	£ - £ 972.47	£ 480.00 £ 372.96	£ 751.00 £4,783.00
	Total base costs already incurred	£ 972.47	£ 852.96	£5,534.00
	Part 2 Page 2 Page 3	£ - £2,253.13	£ 5,300.00 £ -	£5,920.00 £6,955.00
	Total base costs to be incurred	£2,253.13	£5,300.00	£12,875.00
	Total of base costs	£3,225.60	£6,152.96	£18,409.00
	Grand total			£27,787.56

14 Form N242A – Notice of Payment into Court

Notice of payment into court
(in settlement - Part 36)

MUST BE SERVED ON THE CLAIMANT.

To the Claimant ('s Solicitor)

In the	
Claim No.	
Claimant (including ref)	
Defendant (including ref)	

Take notice the defendant _____ has paid £ _____ (a further amount of £ _____) into court in settlement of
(tick as appropriate)

☐ the whole of your claim
☐ part of your claim *(give details below)*
☐ a certain issue or issues in your claim *(give details below)*

The (part) (issue or issues) to which it relates is(are): *(give details)*

☐ It is in addition to the amount of £ _____ already paid into court on _____ and the total amount in court now offered in settlement is £ _____ *(give total of all payments in court to date)*

☐ It is not inclusive of interest and an additional amount of £ _____ is offered for interest *(give details of the rate(s) and period(s) for which the amount of interest is offered.)*

☐ It takes into account all(part) of the following counterclaim: *(give details of the party and the part of the counterclaim to which the payment relates)*

☐ It takes into account the interim payment(s) made in the following amount(s) on the following date(s):
(give details)

Note: This notice will need to be modified where an offer of provisional damages is made (CPR Part 36.7) and/or where it is made in relation to a mixed (money and non-money) claim in settlement of the whole claim (CPR Part 36.4).

N242A Notice of payment into court (in settlement) (04.03)   The Court Service PublicationsBranch

For cases where the Social Security (Recovery of Benefits) Act 1997 applies

The gross amount of the compensation payment is £_____

The defendant has reduced this sum by £_____ in accordance with section 8 of and Schedule 2 to the Social Security (Recovery of Benefits) Act 1997, which was calculated as follows:

    Type of benefit   Amount

The amount paid into court is the net amount after deduction of the amount of benefit.

← MUST BE SIGNED BY DEFENDANT OR THEIR SOLICITOR.

Signed [ ]   Position held [ ]
Defendant('s solicitor)   (If signing on behalf of a firm or company)

Date [ ]

Name of bank [ ]

Account number [ ]

Sort code [ ]

Note: To the Claimant

If you wish to accept the payment made into court without needing the court's permission you should:
- complete Form 201 and send to the Court Funds Office, 22 Kingsway, London, WC2B 6LE.
  (Copies are available from any court office or from the Court Funds Office or the Court Service website at www.courtservice.gov.uk)
- you must also send copies to the defendant and to the court

15 Form N243A – Notice of Acceptance and Request for Payment

[handwritten note: must be filed at court by claimant if wish to accept]

Notice of acceptance of payment into court (Part 36)

In the	
Claim No.	
Claimant (including ref.)	
Defendant (including ref.)	

Note: to the claimant

If you wish to accept the payment made into court without needing the court's permission you should:
- send this completed notice to the defendant not more than 21 days after you received this notice
- and at the same time send a copy to the court

* Delete as appropriate I accept the payment(s) into court totalling £   *(insert amount accepted)* in settlement of (the whole of)(part of)*(certain issue(s) in)* my claim set out in the notice of payment into court received on   *(insert date)* (together with interim payment(s) of £   already received)

I declare that:-

- [ ] it is not more than 21 days since I received the notice of payment into court

  or

- [ ] it is more than 21 days since I received the notice and I have agreed the following costs provisions with the other party(ies) *(give details below)*

  or

- [ ] the defendant's payment was made less than 21 days before the start of the trial and I have agreed the following costs provisions with the other party(ies) *(give details below)*

And I request payment of the money held in court to be made to

claimant's (solicitor's) full name and address (and ref)

name of bank		sort code	
title of account		account number	
Signed		Position held (If signing on behalf of a firm or company)	
	Claimant('s Solicitor)		
Date			

N243A Notice of acceptance and request for payment (12.99)   *The Court Service Publications Unit*

Court Forms and Protocols 245

see p107.
Why need? Part 23.
*eg. * pre-action disclosure*
& permission to make Part 20 claim.

16 Form N244 – Application Notice

Application Notice

You should provide this information for listing the application	In the	
1. How do you wish to have your application dealt with a) at a hearing? ☐ b) at a telephone conference? ☐ } complete all questions below c) without a hearing? ☐ complete Qs 5 and 6 below	**Claim no.**	
	Warrant no. (If applicable)	
	Claimant (including ref.)	
2. Give a time estimate for the hearing/conference _____(hours)_____(mins) 3. Is this agreed by all parties? ☐ Yes ☐ No	**Defendant(s)** (including ref.)	
4. Give dates of any trial period or fixed trial date _____ 5. Level of judge _____ 6. Parties to be served _____	**Date**	

Note You must complete Parts A **and** B, **and** Part C if applicable. Send any relevant fee and the completed application to the court with any draft order, witness statement or other evidence; and sufficient copies for service on each respondent.

Part A

1. Enter your full name, or name of solicitor

I (We)[1] _____ (on behalf of)(the claimant)(the defendant)

2. State clearly what order you are seeking and if possible attach a draft

intend to apply for an order (a draft of which is attached) that[2]

because[3]

3. Briefly set out why you are seeking the order. Include the material facts on which you rely, identifying any rule or statutory provision

Part B

I (We) wish to rely on: *tick one box*

the attached (witness statement)(affidavit) ☐   my statement of case ☐

evidence in Part C in support of my application ☐

4. If you are not already a party to the proceedings, you must provide an address for service of documents

Signed _____   **Position or office held** _____
(Applicant)('s Solicitor)('s litigation friend)   (if signing on behalf of firm or company)

Address to which documents about this claim should be sent (including reference if appropriate)[4]

	if applicable	
	fax no.	
	DX no.	
Tel. no. _____ Postcode _____	e-mail	

The court office at

is open from 10am to 4pm Monday to Friday. When corresponding with the court please address forms or letters to the Court Manager and quote the claim number.

N244 Application Notice (4.00)   *Printed on behalf of The Court Service*

Part C Claim No. [　　　]

I (We) wish to rely on the following evidence in support of this application:

Statement of Truth

*(I believe) *(The applicant believes) that the facts stated in Part C are true
*delete as appropriate

Signed [　　　]　　**Position or office held** [　　　]

(Applicant)('s Solicitor)('s litigation friend)　(if signing on behalf of firm or company)

Date [　　　]

Handwritten note: MUST VERIFY WITH STATEMENT OF TRUTH IF INTEND TO RELY ON MATTERS AS EVIDENCE AT THE HEARING. PD 22 1.2

17 Form N260 – Statement of Costs for Summary Assessment

Statement of Costs (summary assessment)

In the
Court
Case Reference

Judge/Master

Case Title

[Party]'s Statement of Costs for the hearing on *(date)*   **(interim application/fast track trial)**

Description of fee earners*
- (a) *(name) (grade) (hourly rate claimed)*
- (b) *(name) (grade) (hourly rate claimed)*

Attendances on   *(party)*
- (a) *(number)*   hours at £   £ 0.00
- (b) *(number)*   hours at £   £ 0.00

Attendances on opponents
- (a) *(number)*   hours at £   £ 0.00
- (b) *(number)*   hours at £   £ 0.00

Attendance on others
- (a) *(number)*   hours at £   £ 0.00
- (b) *(number)*   hours at £   £ 0.00

Site inspections etc
- (a) *(number)*   hours at £   £ 0.00
- (b) *(number)*   hours at £   £ 0.00

Work done on negotiations
- (a) *(number)*   hours at £   £ 0.00
- (b) *(number)*   hours at £   £ 0.00

Other work, not covered above
- (a) *(number)*   hours at £   £ 0.00
- (b) *(number)*   hours at £   £ 0.00

Work done on documents
- (a) *(number)*   hours at £   £ 0.00
- (b) *(number)*   hours at £   £ 0.00

Attendance at hearing
- (a) *(number)*   hours at £   £ 0.00
- (b) *(number)*   hours at £   £ 0.00
- (a) *(number)*   hours travel and waiting at £   £ 0.00
- (b) *(number)*   hours travel and waiting at £   £ 0.00

Sub Total £   0.00

N260 Statement of Costs (summary assessment) (10.01)   *Printed on behalf of The Court Service*

248 Civil Litigation

Brought forward £   0.00

Counsel's fees *(name) (year of call)*
         Fee for [advice/conference/documents]   £
         Fee for hearing   £

Other expenses
         [court fees]   £
         Others   £
         (give brief description)

Total   £   0.00

Amount of VAT claimed
         on solicitors and counsel's fees   £
         on other expenses   £

Grand Total   £   0.00

The costs estimated above do not exceed the costs which the *(party)* is liable to pay in respect of the work which this estimate covers.

Dated   Signed

Name of firm of solicitors [partner] for the *(party)*

---

* 4 grades of fee earner are suggested:

(A) Solicitors with over eight years post qualification experience including at least eight years litigation experience.

(B) Solicitors and legal executives with over four years post qualification experience including at least four years litigation experience.

(C) Other solicitors and legal executives and fee earners of equivalent experience.

(D) Trainee solicitors, para legals and other fee earners.

"Legal Executive" means a Fellow of the Institute of Legal Executives. Those who are not Fellows of the Institute are not entitled to call themselves legal executives and in principle are therefore not entitled to the same hourly rate as a legal executive.

In respect of each fee earner communications should be treated as attendances and routine communications should be claimed at one tenth of the hourly rate.

N260 Statement of Costs (summary assessment) (10.01)   *Printed on behalf of The Court Service*

18 Form N170 – Pre-trial Checklist, Listing Questionnaire

Listing questionnaire (Pre-trial checklist)

To be completed by, or on behalf of,

[   ]

who is [1st][2nd][3rd][   ][Claimant][Defendant]
[Part 20 claimant][Part 20 defendant] in this claim

In the

Claim No.

Last date for filing with court office

Date(s) fixed for trial or trial period

This form must be **completed** and **returned** to the court no later than the date given above. If not, your statement of case may be struck out or some other sanction imposed.

If the claim has settled, or settles before the trial date, you must let the court know immediately.

Legal representatives only: You must **attach** estimates of costs incurred to date, and of your likely overall costs. In substantial cases, these should be provided in compliance with CPR Part 43.

For multi-track claims only, you must also **attach** a proposed timetable for the trial itself.

A Confirmation of compliance with directions

1. I confirm that I have complied with those directions already given which require action by me. ☐ Yes ☐ No

   If you are unable to give confirmation, state which directions you have still to comply with and the date by which this will be done.

Directions	Date

2. I believe that additional directions are necessary before the trial takes place. ☐ Yes ☐ No

   If Yes, you should attach an application and a draft order.

   *Include in your application all directions needed to enable the claim **to be tried on the date, or within the trial period, already fixed.** These should include any issues relating to experts and their evidence, and any orders needed in respect of directions still requiring action by any other party.*

3. Have you agreed the additional directions you are seeking with the other party(ies)? ☐ Yes ☐ No

B Witnesses

1. How many witnesses (including yourself) will be giving evidence on your behalf at the trial? *(Do not include experts - see Section C)*

   [   ]

Continued over ➪

N170 Listing questionnaire (Pre-trial checklist) (12.02)

Witnesses continued

2. If the trial date is not yet fixed, are there any days within the trial period you or your witnesses would wish to avoid if possible? *(Do not include experts - see Section C)*

Please give details

Name of witness	Dates to be avoided, if possible	Reason

Please specify any special facilities or arrangements needed at court for the party or any witness (e.g. witness with a disability).

3. Will you be providing an interpreter for any of your witnesses? ☐ Yes ☐ No

C Experts

You are reminded that you may not use an expert's report or have your expert give oral evidence unless the court has given permission. If you do not have permission, you must make an application (see section A2 above)

1. Please give the information requested for your expert(s)

Name	Field of expertise	Joint expert?	Is report agreed?	Has permission been given for oral evidence?
		☐ Yes ☐ No	☐ Yes ☐ No	☐ Yes ☐ No
		☐ Yes ☐ No	☐ Yes ☐ No	☐ Yes ☐ No
		☐ Yes ☐ No	☐ Yes ☐ No	☐ Yes ☐ No

2. Has there been discussion between experts? ☐ Yes ☐ No

3. Have the experts signed a joint statement? ☐ Yes ☐ No

4. If your expert is giving oral evidence and the trial date is not yet fixed, is there any day within the trial period which the expert would wish to avoid, if possible? ☐ Yes ☐ No

If Yes, please give details

Name	Dates to be avoided, if possible	Reason

D Legal representation

1. Who will be presenting your case at the trial? ☐ You ☐ Solicitor ☐ Counsel

2. If the trial date is not yet fixed, is there any day within the trial period that the person presenting your case would wish to avoid, if possible? ☐ Yes ☐ No

If Yes, please give details

Name	Dates to be avoided, if possible	Reason

E The trial

1. Has the estimate of the time needed for trial changed? ☐ Yes ☐ No

If Yes, say how long you estimate the whole trial will take, including both parties' cross-examination and closing arguments ☐ days ☐ hours ☐ minutes

2. If different from original estimate have you agreed with the other party(ies) that this is now the **total** time needed? ☐ Yes ☐ No

3. Is the timetable for trial you have attached agreed with the other party(ies)? ☐ Yes ☐ No

Fast track cases only
The court will normally give you 3 weeks notice of the date fixed for a fast track trial unless, in exceptional circumstances, the court directs that shorter notice will be given.

Would you be prepared to accept shorter notice of the date fixed for trial? ☐ Yes ☐ No

F Document and fee checklist

Tick as appropriate

I attach to this questionnaire -

☐ An application and fee for additional directions   ☐ A proposed timetable for trial

☐ A draft order   ☐ An estimate of costs

☐ Listing fee

Signed

[Counsel][Solicitor][for the][1st][2nd][3rd][   ]
[Claimant][Defendant]
[Part 20 claimant][Part 20 defendant]

Date

Please enter your [firm's] name, reference number and full postal address including (if appropriate) details of DX, fax or e-mail

Postcode

Tel. no.   DX no.   E-mail
Fax no.   Ref. no.

19 Appendix to Part 28

Fast Track Standard Directions

Further Statements of Case

The   must file a   and serve a copy on   no later than   .

Requests for Further Information

Any request for clarification or further information based on another party's statement of case shall be served no later than

[Any such request shall be dealt with no later than   ].

Disclosure of Documents

[No disclosure of documents is required]

[[Each party] [The   ] shall give [to the   ] [to every other party] standard disclosure of documents [relating to   ] by serving copies together with a disclosure statement no later than   ]

[Disclosure shall take place as follows:

[Each party shall give standard discovery to every other party by list]

[Disclosure is limited to [standard] [disclosure by the   to the   ] [of documents relating to damage] [the following documents   ]

[The latest date for delivery of the lists is   ]

[The latest date for service of any request to inspect or for a copy of a document is   ]]

Witnesses of Fact

Each party shall serve on every other party the witness statements of all witnesses of fact on whom he intends to rely.

There shall be simultaneous exchange of such statements no later than   .

Expert Evidence

[No expert evidence being necessary, no party has permission to call or rely on expert evidence].

[On it appearing to the court that expert evidence is necessary on the issue of [   ] and that that evidence should be given by the report of a single expert instructed jointly by the parties, the   shall no later than   inform the court whether or not such an expert has been instructed].

[The expert evidence on the issue of   shall be limited to a single expert jointly instructed by the parties.

If the parties cannot agree by   who that expert is to be and about the payment of his fees either party may apply for further directions.

Unless the parties agree in writing or the court orders otherwise, the fees and expenses of such an expert shall be paid to him [by the parties equally] [   ] and be limited to £   .

[The report of the expert shall be filed at the court no later than   ].

[No party shall be entitled to recover by way of costs from any other party more than £   for the fees or   expenses of an expert].

The parties shall exchange reports setting out the substance of any expert evidence on which they intend to rely.

[The exchange shall take place simultaneously no later than   ].

[The   shall serve his report(s) no later than the   and the   shall serve his reports no later than the   ].

[The exchange of reports relating to [causation] [   ] shall take place simultaneously no later than   . The   shall serve his report(s) relating to [damage] [   ] no later than   and the   shall serve his reports relating to it no later than   ].

Reports shall be agreed if possible no later than [days after service] [   ].

[If the reports are not agreed within that time there shall be a without prejudice discussion between the relevant experts no later than   to identify the issues between them and to reach agreement if possible.

The experts shall prepare for the court a statement of the issues on which they agree and on which they disagree with a summary of their reasons, and that statement shall be filed with the court [no later than   ] [with] [no later than the date for filing] [the listing questionnaire].

[Each party has permission to use [   ] as expert witness(es) to give [oral] evidence [in the form of a report] at the trial in the field of   provided that the substance of the evidence to be given has been disclosed as above and has not been agreed].

[Each party has permission to use in evidence   experts' report(s) [and the court will consider when the claim is listed for trial whether expert oral evidence will be allowed].]

Questions to Experts

The time for service on another party of any question addressed to an expert instructed by that party is not later than   days after service of that expert's report.

Any such question shall be answered within   days of service.

Requests for Information etc.

Each party shall serve any request for clarification or further information based on any document disclosed or statement served by another party no later than   days after disclosure or service.

Any such request shall be dealt with within   days of service.

Documents to be Filed with Listing Questionnaires

The parties must file with their listing questionnaires copies of [their experts' reports] [witness statements] [replies to requests for further information]

Dates for Filing Listing Questionnaires and the Trial

Each party must file a completed listing questionnaire no later than   .

The trial of this case will take place [on] [on a date to be fixed between and   ].

Directions Following Filing of Listing Questionnaire

Expert Evidence

The parties have permission to rely at the trial on expert evidence as follows:

The claimant	Oral evidence
	Written evidence
The defendant:	Oral evidence
	Written evidence

Trial Timetable

The time allowed for the trial is

[The timetable for the trial may be agreed by the parties, subject to the approval of the trial judge].

[The timetable for the trial (subject to the approval of the trial judge) will be that   ].

[The evidence in chief for each party will be contained in witness statements and reports, the time allowed for cross-examination by the defendant is limited to   and the time allowed for cross-examination by the claimant is limited to   ].

[The time allowed for the claimant's evidence is   . The time allowed for the defendant's evidence is   ].

The time allowed for the submissions on behalf of each party is   .

The remainder of the time allowed for the trial (being   ) is reserved for the judge to consider and give the judgment and to deal with costs].

Trial Bundle etc

The claimant shall lodge an indexed bundle of documents contained in a ring binder and with each page clearly numbered at the court not more than 7 days and not less than 3 days before the start of the trial.

[A case summary (which should not exceed 250 words) outlining the matters still in issue, and referring where appropriate to the relevant documents shall be included in the bundle for the assistance of the judge in reading the papers before the trial].

[The parties shall seek to agree the contents of the trial bundle and the case summary].

Settlement

Each party must inform the court immediately if the claim is settled whether or not it is then possible to file a draft consent order to give effect to their agreement.

20 QBD PF52 – Order for Case Management Directions in the Multi-track (Part 28)

IN THE HIGH COURT OF JUSTICE

QUEEN'S BENCH DIVISION

Claim No

Before   [sitting in Private]

Claimant

Defendant

An Application was made by application letter   dated   or by   Solicitor for   and was attended by

The Master [District Judge] read the written evidence filed

[The parties having agreed the directions set out in paragraph(s)   below which are made by consent].

IT IS ORDERED that:

1. Allocation

the case be allocated to the multi-track.

2. Transfer

(1)   the claim be transferred to;

    (a)   the   Division of the High Court,

    (b)   the   District Registry [Mercantile List], or

    (c)   the   County Court [Chancery List][Business List],

(2)   the issue(s)   be transferred to the County Court [Chancery List] [Business List] for determination.

(3)   the   apply by   to a Judge of the Technology and Construction Court [or other Specialist List] for an order to transfer the claim to that court.

(4)   the claim   commenced in the   County Court transferred from that court to the Queen's Bench Division of the High Court.

3. Alternative Dispute Resolution

the claim be stayed until   while the parties try to settle it by mediation or other means. [The parties shall notify the Court in writing at the end of that period whether settlement has or has not been reached, and shall submit a draft consent order of any settlement]. The claim will be listed on   or the court to make further directions unless;

(a) the claim has been settled and the claimant advises the court of the settlement in writing and files a draft consent order, or

(b) the parties apply not later than 3 days before the hearing for further directions without a hearing, or

(c) the parties apply for an extension of the stay and the extension is granted, upon which the hearing will be relisted on the date to which the extension is granted.

4. Probate Cases Only

the Defendant   file his witness statement or affidavit of testamentary scripts and lodge any testamentary script at Room TM7.98 Thomas More Building, Royal Courts of Justice, Strand WC2A 2LL [District Registry/   County Court, at   ] by   .

5. Case Summary

the   by   prepare and serve a Case Summary [not exceeding   words] on all other parties, to be agreed by   and filed by   and if it is not agreed the parties by that date file their own Case Summaries.

6. Case Management Conference etc.

[(a)   there be a [further] Case Management Conference/ Listing Hearing before the Master/ District Judge in [Court/ Room No   ] [Thomas More Building] Royal Courts of Justice] [Court (trial centre)] on   at   of   hours/ minutes duration.] or

[(b) there be a Case Management Conference/ Listing Hearing of   hours/ minutes duration. In order for the Court to fix a date the parties are to complete the accompanying questionnaire and file it by   .] or

[(c) the   apply for an appointment for a [further] Case Management Conference/ Listing Hearing by   .]

At the Case Management Conference, except for urgent matters in the meantime, the Court will hear any further applications for Directions or Orders and any party must file an Application Notice for any such Directions or Orders and serve it and supporting evidence (if any) by   .

7. Amendments To Statements Of Case

(1) the   has permission to amend his statement of case in accordance with the attached draft initialled by the District Judge

(2) the amended statement of case be verified by a statement of truth.

(3) the amended statement of case be filed by   .

(4) the amended statement of case be served by   or service of the amended statement of case be dispensed with.

(5) any consequential amendments to other statements of case be filed and served by   .

(6) the costs of and caused by the amendment to the statement of case be   in any event or are assessed in the sum of £   .

8. Addition of Parties

(1) the   has permission;

    (a) to substitute   as a   , and

    (b) to amend his statement of case in accordance with the attached draft initialled by the District Judge

(2) the amended statement of case be verified by a statement of truth.

(3) the amended statement of case be:

    (a) filed by   and

    (b) served on   by

(4) a copy of this order be served on   by

(5) any consequential amendments to other statements of case be filed and served by   .

(6) the costs of and caused by the amendment to the statement of case be   in any event or are assessed in the sum of £   and are to be paid by   .

9. Consolidation

this claim be consolidated with claim number   , the lead claim to be claim number   . [The title to the consolidated case shall be set out in the Schedule to this order.]

10. Trial of Issue

the issue of   be tried as follows;

(1) with the consent of the parties, before a Master

    (a) on   in Room   at the Royal Courts of Justice,

    (b) with an estimated length of hearing   hours,

    (c) with the filing of listing questionnaires dispensed with,

or

(2) before a Judge

    (a) with the trial of the issue to take place within   after   ('the trial window')

    (b) with the   to apply to the Clerk of Lists at Room W15 by   for a trial date within the trial window

    (c) within the issue

        (i) to be entered in the General List category 'A' 'B' or 'C', with a time estimate of   , and

        (ii) to take place in London

    [(d) the filing of listing questionnaires be dispensed with [unless directed by the Clerk of the Lists] or each party file his completed listing questionnaire by   ], or

(3) before a [District Judge, with the consent of the parties] [Circuit Judge] [High Court Judge] [listing category [A] [B] [C]], at a hearing details of which [accompany this order] [will be sent shortly] with an estimated length of hearing   hours.

11. Further Information

(1) the   provide by   the clarification sought in the Request dated   attached and initialled by the District Judge

(2) any request for clarification   be served by

12. Disclosure of Documents *identifies options court can take as to disclosure.*

(1) no disclosure is required.

(2) each party give by   standard disclosure to every other party by list [by categories].

(3) the   give specific disclosure of documents [limited to the issues of   ] described in the Schedule to this order [initialled by the Master/District Judge] by list [by categories] by

(4) the   give by   standard disclosure by list [by categories] to   of documents limited to the issue(s) of   by list.

13. Inspection of Documents

Any requests for inspection or copies of disclosed documents shall be made within   days after service of the list.

14. Preservation of Property

the   preserve   until trial of the claim or further order or other remedy under rule 25.1(1).

15. Witness Statements

(1) each party serve on every other party the witness statements of the oral evidence which the party serving the statement intends to rely on in relation to [any issues of fact] [the following issues of fact   ] to be decided at the trial, those statements and any Notices of intention to rely on hearsay evidence to be

    (a) exchanged by   or

    (b) served by   by   and by   by

(2) the   has permission to serve a witness summary relating to the evidence of   of   on every party by

16. No Expert Evidence

(1) no expert evidence being necessary, [no party has permission to call or rely on expert evidence] [permission to call or rely on expert evidence is refused].

17. Single Expert

(1) evidence be given by the report of a single expert in the field of   , instructed jointly by the parties, on the issue of   [and his fees shall be limited to £   ].

(2) the claimant advise the court in writing by   whether or not the single expert has been instructed.

(3) if the parties are unable to agree [by that date] who that expert is to be and about the payment of his fees any party may apply for further directions.

(4) unless the parties agree in writing or the court orders otherwise, the fees and expenses of the single expert shall be paid by him [by the parties equally] (or as ordered).

(5) each party give his instructions to the single expert by

(6) the report of the single expert be filed by

(7) the evidence of the expert be given at the trial by written report/ oral evidence of the expert.

18. Separate Experts

[(1) each party has permission to adduce [oral] expert evidence in the field of   [limited to   expert(s) [per party] [on each side]].

(2) the experts reports shall be exchanged by

(3) the experts shall hold a discussion for the purpose of:

    (a) identifying the issues, if any, between them; and

    (b) where possible, reaching agreement on those issues.

(4) the experts shall by   prepare and file a statement for the Court showing:

    (a) those issues on which they did agree; and

    (b) those issues on which they disagree and a summary of their reasons for disagreeing.

(5) no party shall be entitled to recover by way of costs from any other party more than £   or the fees or expenses of an expert.]

or

[(1) the parties   have permission to rely on expert evidence as follows:

Party	Identity of expert	Field of expertise	Issue to be addressed
Claimant			
Defendant			
(other parties			

(2) the number of expert witnesses in each field is limited to   for the   and to   for the   .

(3) the amount of the fees and expenses of the experts in the field[s] of   that the   may recover from the   be limited to £   .

(4) the experts in the field(s) of   prepare reports which are to be served as follows:

   (a) by simultaneous exchange by

   (b) by   by   and by   by

(5) the reports be agreed if possible by

(6) (a) if the reports are not agreed by that date, then the experts in the same field(s) shall, by   , seek to identify, by 'without prejudice' discussion, the issues between them and, where possible, to reach agreement on all/any issue(s),

   (b) the experts shall by   prepare and file a statement showing those issues on which they are agreed, those issues on which they disagree and a summary of the reasons for disagreeing.

(7) the expert evidence relied on by the   in the field of   be given at the trial by written report(s)/written summary of agreement/oral evidence of the expert(s).

(8) no party shall be entitled to recover by way of costs from any other party more than £   for the fees or expenses of an expert.]

19. Trial and Listing Questionnaires

(1) (a) the trial of the claim/issue(s) take place [within   after   ] between   and   ('the trial window'). the experts shall by   prepare and file a statement showing those issues on which they are agreed, those issues on which they disagree and a summary of the reasons for disagreeing.

   (b) the   make an appointment to attend on the Clerk of the Lists/Listing Officer at Room [W14] [W15] in order to fix a trial date within the trial window, such appointment to be [within 14 days after] [on] [not later than   ] and give notice of the appointment to all other parties.

   (c) the claim

      (i) to be entered in the General List category 'A' 'B' 'C', with a time limit of   , and

      (ii) take place in London   , or

(2) (a) Trial Date – the trial take place on a date to be fixed   , a Notice of Hearing will be sent shortly at a venue to be notified or

   (b) Trial Window – the trial take place during the period beginning on   and ending on   at a venue to be notified,

   (c) the present estimate of the time to be allowed for the trial is

(3) Listing Questionnaires–

   [(a) the filing of listing questionnaires be dispensed with [unless directed by the Clerk of the Lists/ Listing Officer]], or

   [(b) each party file his completed listing questionnaire by 4.00 pm on   ],

(4) the parties inform the Court forthwith of any change in the trial time estimate.

20. Pre-Trial Review

[[The trial being estimated to last more than 10 days], There be a Pre-Trial Review on a date to be arranged by the Clerk of the Lists/ Listing Officer in Room [W14] [W15]] [there be a Pre-Trial Review on   at   ] before the Judge at the   Court at which, except for urgent matters in the meantime, the Court will hear any further applications for Directions or Orders.

21. Definition and Reduction of Issues

by   the parties list and discuss the issues in the claim [including the experts' reports and statements] and attempt to define and narrow the issues [including those issues the subject of discussion by the experts].

22. Trial Bundle

The parties agree to file a trial bundle and exchange and file skeleton arguments and chronologies not more than 7 and not less than 3 days before the start of the trial.

23. Trial Timetable (only for use at final CMC or PTR)

(1) the parties agree a timetable for the trial, subject to the approval of the trial Judge, and file it with the trial bundle.

(2) subject to the approval of the trial Judge, the timetable for the trial will be:

- (a) opening speeches to last no more than   minutes,
- (b) the statements served stand as the evidence in chief of the Claimants' witnesses of fact who are to give evidence on the [first] morning/ afternoon/ day of the trial,
- (c) the statements served stand as the evidence in chief of the Defendants' witnesses of fact who are to give evidence on the   morning/afternoon/day of the trial,
- (d) the reports of the experts served stand as the evidence in chief and the expert(s) in the field(s) of   give oral evidence on the   morning/ afternoon/ day of the trial,
- (e) closing submissions be made on the   morning/ afternoon/ day of the trial.

24. Settlement

If the claim or part of the claim is settled the parties must immediately inform the Court, whether or not it is then possible to file a draft Consent Order to give effect to the settlement.

25. Other Directions

26. Costs

the costs of this application be;

- (a) in the case, or
- (b) summarily assessed at £   and paid by   , or
- (c) the   in any event to be the subject of a detailed assessment,
- (d) the   pay the   the sum of £   on account of such costs on or before

Dated

21 Form N252 – Notice of Commencement of Assessment of Bill of Costs

> *Handwritten annotation:* Receiving party serves on paying party after costs order is made along with the copy of the bill of costs.

Notice of commencement of assessment of bill of costs

In the	
Claim No.	
Claimant (include Ref.)	
Defendant (include Ref.)	

To the claimant(defendant)

Following an _____ (*insert name of document eg. order, judgment*) dated _____ (copy attached) I have prepared my Bill of Costs for assessment. The Bill totals *£ _____ If you choose to dispute this bill and your objections are not upheld at the assessment hearing, the full amount payable (including the assessment fee) will be £ _____ (together with interest (*see note below*)). I shall also seek the costs of the assessment hearing

Your points of dispute must include

- details of the items in the bill of costs which are disputed
- concise details of the nature and grounds of the dispute for each item and, if you seek a reduction in those items, suggest, where practicable, a reduced figure

You must serve your points of dispute by _____ (*insert date 21 days from the date of service of this notice*) on me at:- (*give full name and address for service including any DX number or reference*)

You must also serve copies of your points of dispute on all other parties to the assessment identified below (*you do not need to serve your points of dispute on the court*).

I certify that I have also served the following person(s) with a copy of this notice and my Bill of Costs:- (*give details of persons served*)

If I have not received your points of dispute by the above date, I will ask the court to issue a default costs certificate for the full amount of my bill (*see above**) plus fixed costs and court fee in the total amount of £ _____

Signed _____ Date _____
(Claimant)(Defendant)('s solicitor)

Note: Interest may be added to all High Court judgments and certain county court judgments of £5,000 or more under the Judgments Act 1838 and the County Courts Act 1984.

The court office at _____ is open between 10 am and 4 pm Monday to Friday. When corresponding with the court, please address forms or letters to the Court Manager and quote the claim number.

N252 Notice of commencement of assessment of bill of costs (12.99)   *The Court Service Publications Unit*

22 Precedent A – Bill of Costs

SCHEDULE OF COSTS PRECEDENTS
PRECEDENT A

IN THE HIGH COURT OF JUSTICE   2000 - B - 9999

QUEEN'S BENCH DIVISION

BRIGHTON DISTRICT REGISTRY

BETWEEN

AB   Claimant

- and -

CD   Defendant

**CLAIMANT'S BILL OF COSTS TO BE ASSESSED PURSUANT
TO THE ORDER DATED 26th JULY 2000**

V.A.T. No. 33 4404 90

In these proceedings the claimant sought compensation for personal injuries and other losses suffered in a road accident which occurred on Friday 1st January 1999 near the junction between Bolingbroke Lane and Regency Road, Brighton, East Sussex. The claimant had been travelling as a front seat passenger in a car driven by the defendant. The claimant suffered severe injuries when, because of the defendant's negligence, the car left the road and collided with a brick wall.

The defendant was later convicted of various offences arising out of the accident including careless driving and driving under the influence of drink or drugs.

In the civil action the defendant alleged that immediately before the car journey began the claimant had known that the defendant was under the influence of alcohol and therefore consented to the risk of injury or was contributorily negligent as to it. It was also alleged that, immediately before the accident occurred, the claimant wrongfully took control of the steering wheel so causing the accident to occur.

The claimant first instructed solicitors, E F & Co, in this matter in July 2000. The claim form was issued in October 2000 and in February 2001 the proceedings were listed for a two day trial commencing 25th July 2001. At the trial the defendant was found liable but the compensation was reduced by 25% to take account of contributory negligence by the claimant. The claimant was awarded a total of £78,256.83 plus £1,207.16 interest plus costs.

The claimant instructed E F & Co under a conditional fee agreement dated 8th July 2000 which specifies the following base fees and success fees.

    Partner - £180 per hour plus VAT
    Assistant Solicitor - £140 per hour plus VAT
    Other fee earners - £85 per hour plus VAT
    Success fees exclusive of disbursement funding costs: 40%
    Success fee in respect of disbursement funding costs: 7.5% (not claimed in this bill)

Except where the contrary is stated the proceedings were conducted on behalf of the claimant by an assistant solicitor, admitted November 1999.

E F & Co instructed Counsel (Miss GH, called 1992) under a conditional fee agreement dated 5th June 2001 which specifies a success fee of 75% and base fees, payable in various circumstances, of which the following are relevant

> Fees for interim hearing whose estimated duration is up to 2 hours: £600
> Brief for trial whose estimated duration is 2 days: £2,000
> Fee for second and subsequent days: £650 per day

264 Civil Litigation

Item No.	Description of work done	V.A.T.	Disburse-ments	Profit Costs
	8th July 2000 - F & Co instructed			
	22nd July 2000 - A I with Eastbird Legal Protection Ltd			
1	Premium for policy	-	£ 120.00	
	7th October 2000 - Claim issued			
2	Issue fee	-	£ 400.00	
	21st October 2000 - Particulars of claim served			
	25th November 2000 - Time for service of defence extended by agreement to 14th January 2001			
3	Fee on allocation	-	£ 80.00	
	20th January 2001 - case allocated to multi-track			
	9th February 2001 - Case management conference at which costs were awarded to the claimant and the base costs were summarily assessed at £400 (paid on 24th February 2001)			-
	23rd February 2001 - Claimant's list of documents			
	12th April 2001 - Payment into court of £25,126.33			
	13th April 2001 - Filing pre-trial checklist			
4	Fee on listing	-	£ 400.00	
5	28th June 2001 - Pre trial review: costs in case Engaged 1.5 hours £210.00 Travel and waiting 2.00 hours £280.00 Total solicitor's base fee for attending			£ 490.00
6	Counsel's base fee for pre trial review (Miss GH)		£ 600.00	
7	25th July 2001 - Attending first day of trial: adjourned part heard Engaged in Court 5.00 hours £700.00 Engaged in conference 0.75 hours £105.00 Travel and waiting 1.5 hours £210.00 Total solicitor's base fee for attending			£1,015.00
8	Counsel's base fee for trial (Miss GH)		£2,000.00	
9	Fee of expert witness (Dr. IJ)	-	£ 850.00	
10	Expenses of witnesses of fact	-	£ 84.00	
11	26th July 2001 - Attending second day of trial when judgment was given for the claimant in the sum of £78,256.53 plus £1207.16 interest plus costs Engaged in Court 3.00 hours £420.00 Engaged in conference 1.5 hours £210.00 Travel and waiting 1.5 hours £210.00 Total solicitor's base fee for attending			£ 840.00
12	Counsel's base fee for second day (Miss GH)		£ 650.00	
	To Summary	£ -	£5,184.00	£2,345.00

Item No.	Description of work done	V.A.T.	Disburse-ments	Profit Costs
	Claimant			
13	8th July 2000 - First instructions: 0.75 hours by Partner: base fee			£ 135.00
14	Other timed attendances in person and by telephone - See Schedule 1 Total base fee for Schedule 1 - 7.5 hours			£1,050.00
15	Routine letters out and telephone calls - 29 (17 + 12) total base fee			£ 406.00
	Witnesses of Fact			
16	Timed attendances in person, by letter out and by telephone - See Schedule 2 Total base fee for Schedule 2 - 5.2 hours			£ 728.00
17	Routine letters out, e mails and telephone calls - 8 (4 + 2 + 2)total base fee			£ 112.00
18	Paid travelling on 9th October 2000	£ 4.02	£ 22.96	
	Medical expert (Dr. IJ)			
19	11th September 2000 - long letter out 0.33 hours: base fee			£ 46.20
20	30th January 2001 - long letter out 0.25 hours base fee			£ 35.00
21	23rd May 2001 - telephone call 0.2 hours base fee			£ 28.00
22	Routine letters out and telephone calls - 10 (6 + 4) total base fee			£ 140.00
23	Dr. IJ's fee for report	-	£ 350.00	
	Defendant and his solicitor			
24	8th July 2000 - timed letter sent 0.5 hours: base fee			£ 70.00
25	19th February 2001 - telephone call 0.25 hours: base fee			£ 35.00
26	Routine letters out and telephone calls - 24 (18 + 6) total base fee			£ 336.00
	Communications with the court			
27	Routine letters out and telephone calls - 9 (8 + 1) total base fee			£ 126.00
	Communications with Counsel			
28	Routine letters out, e mails and telephone calls - 19 (4 + 7 + 8) total base fee			£ 266.00
29	**Work done on documents** Timed attendances - See Schedule 3 Total base fees for Schedule 3 - 0.75 hours at £180, 44.5 hours at £140, 12 hours at £85			£7,385.00
30	**Work done on negotiations** 23rd March 2001 - meeting at offices of Solicitors for the Defendant Engaged - 1.5 hours £210.00 Travel and waiting - 1.25 hours £175.00 Total base fee for meeting			£ 385.00
31	**Other work done** Preparing and checking bill Engaged: Solicitor - 1 hour £140.00 Engaged: Costs Draftsman - 4 hours £340.00 Total base fee on other work done			£ 480.00
	To Summary	£ 4.02	£ 372.96	£11,763.20

Item No.	Description of work done	V.A.T.	Disburse-ments	Profit Costs
32	Success fee on solicitor's base fee on interim orders which were summarily assessed (40% of £400) plus VAT at 17.5%	£ 28.00		£ 160.00
33	VAT on solicitor's other base fees (17.5% of £14,108.20)	£ 2,468.94		
34	Success fee on solicitor's other base fees (40% of £14,108.20) plus VAT at 17.5%	£ 987.58		£ 5,643.28
35	VAT on Counsel's base fees (17.5% of £3,250)'	£ 568.75		
36	Success fee on Counsel's base fee (75% of £3,250) plus VAT at 17.5%'	£ 426.57	£ 2,437.50	
	To Summary	£ 4,479.84	£ 2,437.50	£ 5,803.28
	SUMMARY			
	Page 3 £	-	£ 5,184.00	£ 2,345.00
	Page 4 £	4.02	£ 372.96	£ 11,763.20
	Page 5 £	4,479.84	£ 2,437.50	£ 5,803.28
	Totals:	£ 4,483.86	£ 7,994.46	£ 19,911.48
	Grand total:			£ 32,389.80

23 Precedent G – Points of Dispute

SCHEDULE OF COSTS PRECEDENTS
PRECEDENT G

IN THE HIGH COURT OF JUSTICE 2000 B 9999

QUEEN'S BENCH DIVISION

BRIGHTON DISTRICT REGISTRY

B E T W E E N

AB

Claimant

- and -

CD

Defendant

POINTS OF DISPUTE SERVED BY THE DEFENDANT

Item	Dispute	Claimant's Comments
General point	Base rates claimed for the assistant solicitor and other fee earners are excessive. Reduce to £100 and £70 respectively plus VAT. Each item in which these rates are claimed should be recalculated at the reduced rates.	
(1)	The premium claimed is excessive. Reduce to £95.	

CIVIL PROCEDURE RULES SEPTEMBER 2003 PRACTICE DIRECTION Parts 43–48/page 103

Item	Dispute	Claimant's Comments
(14)	The claim for timed attendances on claimant (schedule 1) is excessive. Reduce to 4 hours ie. £400 at reduced rates.	
(29)	The total claim for work done on documents by the assistant solicitor is excessive. A reasonable allowance in respect of documents concerning court and counsel is 8 hours, for documents concerning witnesses and the expert witness, 6.5 hours, for work done on arithmetic, 2.25 hours and for other documents, 5.5 hours. Reduce to 22.25 hours ie. £2,225 at reduced rates (£3,380 in total).	
(31)	The time claimed is excessive. Reduce solicitors time to 0.5 hours ie. to £50 at reduced rates and reduce the costs draftsman's time to three hours ie. £210 (£260 in total).	
(32)	The success fee claimed is excessive. Reduce to 25% ie. £100 plus VAT of £17.50.	
(33)	The total base fees when recalculated on the basis of the above points amount to £7,788, upon which VAT is £1,362.90.	
(34)	The success fee claimed is excessive. Reduce to 25% of £7,788 ie £1,947.50 plus VAT of £340.73.	
(36)	The success fee claimed is excessive. Reduce to 50% ie £1,625 plus VAT of £284.38.	

Served on .... [date] by .... [name] [solicitors for] the Defendant.

24 Practice Direction – Protocols

GENERAL

1.1 This Practice Direction applies to the pre-action protocols which have been approved by the Head of Civil Justice.

1.2 The pre-action protocols which have been approved are set out in para 5.1. Other pre-action protocols may subsequently be added.

1.3 Pre-action protocols outline the steps parties should take to seek information from and to provide information to each other about a prospective legal claim.

1.4 The objectives of pre-action protocols are:

    (1)   to encourage the exchange of early and full information about the prospective legal claim,

    (2)   to enable parties to avoid litigation by agreeing a settlement of the claim before the commencement of proceedings,

    (3)   to support the efficient management of proceedings where litigation cannot be avoided.

Compliance With Protocols

2.1 The Civil Procedure Rules enable the court to take into account compliance or non-compliance with an applicable protocol when giving directions for the management of proceedings (see CPR rules 3.1(4) and (5) and 3.9(e)) and when making orders for costs (see CPR rule 44.3(a)).

2.2 The court will expect all parties to have complied in substance with the terms of an approved protocol.

2.3 If, in the opinion of the court, non-compliance has led to the commencement of proceedings which might otherwise not have needed to be commenced, or has led to costs being incurred in the proceedings that might otherwise not have been incurred, the orders the court may make include:

    (1)   an order that the party at fault pay the costs of the proceedings, or part of those costs, of the other party or parties;

    (2)   an order that the party at fault pay those costs on an indemnity basis;

    (3)   if the party at fault is a claimant in whose favour an order for the payment of damages or some specified sum is subsequently made, an order depriving that party of interest on such sum and in respect of such period as may be specified, and/or awarding interest at a lower rate than that at which interest would otherwise have been awarded;

    (4)   if the party at fault is a defendant and an order for the payment of damages or some specified sum is subsequently made in favour of the claimant, an order awarding interest on such sum and in respect of such period as may be specified at a higher rate, not exceeding 10% above base rate (cf. CPR rule 36.21(2), than the rate at which interest would otherwise have been awarded.

2.4 The court will exercise its powers under paragraphs 2.1 and 2.3 with the object of placing the innocent party in no worse a position than he would have been in if the protocol had been complied with.

3.1 A claimant may be found to have failed to comply with a protocol by, for example:

    (a)   not having provided sufficient information to the defendant, or

    (b)   not having followed the procedure required by the protocol to be followed (eg not having followed the medical expert instruction procedure set out in the Personal Injury Protocol).

3.2 A defendant may be found to have failed to comply with a protocol by, for example:

    (a)   not making a preliminary response to the letter of claim within the time fixed for that purpose by the relevant protocol (21 days under the Personal Injury Protocol, 14 days under the Clinical Negligence Protocol),

(b) not making a full response within the time fixed for that purpose by the relevant protocol (3 months of the letter of claim under the Clinical Negligence Protocol, 3 months from the date of acknowledgement of the letter of claim under the Personal Injury Protocol),

(c) not disclosing documents required to be disclosed by the relevant protocol.

3.3 The court is likely to treat this practice direction as indicating the normal, reasonable way of dealing with disputes. If proceedings are issued and parties have not complied with this practice direction or a specific protocol, it will be for the court to decide whether sanctions should be applied.

3.4 The court is not likely to be concerned with minor infringements of the practice direction or protocols. The court is likely to look at the effect of non-compliance on the other party when deciding whether to impose sanctions.

3.5 This practice direction does not alter the statutory time limits for starting court proceedings. A claimant is required to start proceedings within those time limits and to adhere to subsequent time limits required by the rules or ordered by the court. If proceedings are for any reason started before the parties have followed the procedures in this practice direction, the parties are encouraged to agree to apply to the court for a stay of the proceedings while they follow the practice direction.

Pre-action behaviour in other cases

4.1 In cases not covered by any approved protocol, the court will expect the parties, in accordance with the overriding objective and the matters referred to in CPR 1.1(2)(a), (b) and (c), to act reasonably in exchanging information and documents relevant to the claim and generally in trying to avoid the necessity for the start of proceedings.

4.2 Parties to a potential dispute should follow a reasonable procedure, suitable to their particular circumstances, which is intended to avoid litigation. The procedure should not be regarded as a prelude to inevitable litigation. It should normally include-

(a) the claimant writing to give details of the claim;

(b) the defendant acknowledging the claim letter promptly;

(c) the defendant giving within a reasonable time a detailed written response; and

(d) the parties conducting genuine and reasonable negotiations with a view to settling the claim economically and without court proceedings.

4.3 The claimant's letter should-

(a) give sufficient concise details to enable the recipient to understand and investigate the claim without extensive further information;

(b) enclose copies of the essential documents which the claimant relies on;

(c) ask for a prompt acknowledgement of the letter, followed by a full written response within a reasonable stated period;

(For many claims, a normal reasonable period for a full response may be one month.)

(d) state whether court proceedings will be issued if the full response is not received within the stated period;

(e) identify and ask for copies of any essential documents, not in his possession, which the claimant wishes to see;

(f) state (if this is so) that the claimant wishes to enter into mediation or another alternative method of dispute resolution; and

(g) draw attention to the court's powers to impose sanctions for failure to comply with this practice direction and, if the recipient is likely to be unrepresented, enclose a copy of this practice direction.

4.4 The defendant should acknowledge the claimant's letter in writing within 21 days of receiving it. The acknowledgement should state when the defendant will give a full written response. If the time for this is longer than the period stated by the claimant, the defendant should give reasons why a longer period is needed.

4.5 The defendant's full written response should as appropriate-

(a) accept the claim in whole or in part and make proposals for settlement; or

(b) state that the claim is not accepted.

If the claim is accepted in part only, the response should make clear which part is accepted and which part is not accepted.

4.6 If the defendant does not accept the claim or part of it, the response should–

(a) give detailed reasons why the claim is not accepted, identifying which of the claimant's contentions are accepted and which are in dispute;

(b) enclose copies of the essential documents which the defendant relies on;

(c) enclose copies of documents asked for by the claimant, or explain why they are not enclosed;

(d) identify and ask for copies of any further essential documents, not in his possession, which the defendant wishes to see; and

(The claimant should provide these within a reasonably short time or explain in writing why he is not doing so.)

(e) state whether the defendant is prepared to enter into mediation or another alternative method of dispute resolution.

4.7 If the claim remains in dispute, the parties should promptly engage in appropriate negotiations with a view to settling the dispute and avoiding litigation.

4.8 Documents disclosed by either party in accordance with this practice direction may not be used for any purpose other than resolving the dispute, unless the other party agrees.

4.9 The resolution of some claims, but by no means all, may need help from an expert. If an expert is needed, the parties should wherever possible and to save expense engage an agreed expert.

4.10 Parties should be aware that, if the matter proceeds to litigation, the court may not allow the use of an expert's report, and that the cost of it is not always recoverable.

INFORMATION ABOUT FUNDING ARRANGEMENTS

4A.1 Where a person enters into a funding arrangement within the meaning of rule 43.2(1)(k) he should inform other potential parties to the claim that he has done so.

4A.2 Paragraph 4A.1 applies to all proceedings whether proceedings to which a pre-action protocol applies or otherwise.

(Rule 44.3B(1)(c) provides that a party may not recover any additional liability for any period in the proceedings during which he failed to provide information about a funding arrangement in accordance with a rule, practice direction or court order.)

COMMENCEMENT

5.1 The following table sets out the protocols currently in force, the date they came into force and their date of publication:

Protocol	Coming into force	Publication
Personal Injury	26 April 1999	January 1999
Clinical Negligence	26 April 1999	January 1999
Construction and Engineering Disputes	2 October 2000	September 2000
Defamation	2 October 2000	September 2000
Professional Negligence	16 July 2001	May 2001
Judicial Review	4 March 2002	3 December 2001

Disease and Illness	8 December 2003	September 2003
Housing Disrepair	8 December 2003	September 2003

5.2 The court will take compliance or non-compliance with a relevant protocol into account where the claim was started after the coming into force of that protocol but will not do so where the claim was started before that date.

5.3 Parties in a claim started after a relevant protocol came into force, who have, by work done before that date, achieved the objectives sought to be achieved by certain requirements of that protocol, need not take any further steps to comply with those requirements. They will not be considered to have not complied with the protocol for the purposes of paragraphs 2 and 3.

5.4 Parties in a claim started after a relevant protocol came into force, who have not been able to comply with any particular requirements of that protocol because the period of time between the publication date and the date of coming into force was too short, will not be considered to have not complied with the protocol for the purposes of paragraphs 2 and 3.

25 Professional Negligence Pre-action Protocol

THIS PROTOCOL MERGES THE TWO PROTOCOLS PREVIOUSLY PRODUCED BY THE SOLICITORS INDEMNITY FUND (SIF) AND CLAIMS AGAINST PROFESSIONALS (CAP)

A Introduction

A1. This protocol is designed to apply when a Claimant wishes to claim against a professional (other than construction professionals and healthcare providers) as a result of that professional's alleged negligence or equivalent breach of contract or breach of fiduciary duty. Although these claims will be the usual situation in which the protocol will be used, there may be other claims for which the protocol could be appropriate. For a more detailed explanation of the scope of the protocol see Guidance Note C2.

A2. The aim of this protocol is to establish a framework in which there is an early exchange of information so that the claim can be fully investigated and, if possible, resolved without the need for litigation. This includes:

(a) ensuring that the parties are on an equal footing

(b) saving expense

(c) dealing with the dispute in ways which are proportionate:

   (i) to the amount of money involved

   (ii) to the importance of the case

   (iii) to the complexity of the issues

   (iv) to the financial position of each party

(d) ensuring that it is dealt with expeditiously and fairly.

A3. This protocol is not intended to replace other forms of pre-action dispute resolution (such as internal complaints procedures, the Surveyors and Valuers Arbitration Scheme, etc). Where such procedures are available, parties are encouraged to consider whether they should be used. If, however, these other procedures are used and fail to resolve the dispute, the protocol should be used before litigation is started, adapting it where appropriate. See also Guidance Note C3.

A4. The Courts will be able to treat the standards set in this protocol as the normal reasonable approach. If litigation is started, it will be for the court to decide whether sanctions should be imposed as a result of substantial noncompliance with a protocol. Guidance on the courts' likely approach is given in the Protocols Practice Direction. The Court is likely to disregard minor departures from this protocol and so should the parties as between themselves.

A5. Both in operating the timetable and in requesting and providing information during the protocol period, the parties are expected to act reasonably, in line with the Court's expectations of them. See also Guidance Note C1.2.

B The Protocol

B1. Preliminary Notice (See also Guidance Note C3.1)

B1.1 As soon as the Claimant decides there is a reasonable chance that he will bring a claim against a professional, the Claimant is encouraged to notify the professional in writing.

B1.2 This letter should contain the following information:

(a) the identity of the Claimant and any other parties

(b) a brief outline of the Claimant's grievance against the professional

(c) if possible, a general indication of the financial value of the potential claim B1.3 This letter should be addressed to the professional and should ask the professional to inform his professional indemnity insurers, if any, immediately.

B1.4 The professional should acknowledge receipt of the Claimant's letter within 21 days of receiving it. Other than this acknowledgement, the protocol places no obligation upon either party to take any further action.

B2. Letter of Claim

B2.1 As soon as the Claimant decides there are grounds for a claim against the professional, the Claimant should write a detailed Letter of Claim to the professional.

B2.2 The Letter of Claim will normally be an open letter (as opposed to being 'without prejudice') and should include the following:

(a) The identity of any other parties involved in the dispute or a related dispute.

(b) A clear chronological summary (including key dates) of the facts on which the claim is based. Key documents should be identified, copied and enclosed.

(c) The allegations against the professional. What has he done wrong? What has he failed to do?

(d) An explanation of how the alleged error has caused the loss claimed.

(e) An estimate of the financial loss suffered by the Claimant and how it is calculated. Supporting documents should be identified, copied and enclosed. If details of the financial loss cannot be supplied, the Claimant should explain why and should state when he will be in a position to provide the details. This information should be sent to the professional as soon as reasonably possible.

If the Claimant is seeking some form of non-financial redress, this should be made clear.

(f) Confirmation whether or not an expert has been appointed. If so, providing the identity and discipline of the expert, together with the date upon which the expert was appointed.

(g) A request that a copy of the Letter of Claim be forwarded immediately to the professional's insurers, if any.

B2.3 The Letter of Claim is not intended to have the same formal status as a Statement of Case. If, however, the Letter of Claim differs materially from the Statement of Case in subsequent proceedings, the Court may decide, in its discretion, to impose sanctions.

B2.4 If the Claimant has sent other Letters of Claim (or equivalent) to any other party in relation to this dispute or related dispute, those letters should be copied to the professional. (If the Claimant is claiming against someone else to whom this protocol does not apply, please see Guidance Note C4.)

B3. The Letter of Acknowledgment

B3.1 The professional should acknowledge receipt of the Letter of Claim within 21 days of receiving it.

B4. Investigations

B4.1 The professional will have three months from the date of the Letter of Acknowledgment to investigate.

B4.2 If the professional is in difficulty in complying with the three month time period, the problem should be explained to the Claimant as soon as possible. The professional should explain what is being done to resolve the problem and when the professional expects to complete the investigations. The Claimant should agree to any reasonable request for an extension of the three month period.

B4.3 The parties should supply promptly, at this stage and throughout, whatever relevant information or documentation is reasonably requested. (Please see Guidance Note C5.)

(If the professional intends to claim against someone who is not currently a party to the dispute, please see Guidance Note C4.)

B5. Letter of Response and Letter of Settlement

B5.1 As soon as the professional has completed his investigations, the professional should send to the Claimant:

(a) a Letter of Response, or

(b) a Letter of Settlement; or

(c) both.

The Letters of Response and Settlement can be contained within a single letter.

The Letter of Response

B5.2 The Letter of Response will normally be an open letter (as opposed to being 'without prejudice') and should be a reasoned answer to the Claimant's allegations:

(a) if the claim is admitted the professional should say so in clear terms.

(b) if only part of the claim is admitted the professional should make clear which parts of the claim are admitted and which are denied.

(c) if the claim is denied in whole or in part, the Letter of Response should include specific comments on the allegations against the professional and, if the Claimant's version of events is disputed, the professional should provide his version of events.

(d) if the professional is unable to admit or deny the claim, the professional should identify any further information which is required.

(e) if the professional disputes the estimate of the Claimant's financial loss, the Letter of Response should set out the professional's estimate. If an estimate cannot be provided, the professional should explain why and should state when he will be in a position to provide an estimate. This information should be sent to the Claimant as soon as reasonably possible.

(f) where additional documents are relied upon, copies should be provided.

B5.3 The Letter of Response is not intended to have the same formal status as a Defence. If, however, the Letter of Response differs materially from the Defence in subsequent proceedings, the Court may decide, in its discretion, to impose sanctions.

The Letter of Settlement

B5.4 The Letter of Settlement will normally be a without prejudice letter and should be sent if the professional intends to make proposals for settlement. It should:

(a) set out the professional's views to date on the claim identifying those issues which the professional believes are likely to remain in dispute and those which are not. (The Letter of Settlement does not need to include this information if the professional has sent a Letter of Response).

(b) make a settlement proposal or identify any further information which is required before the professional can formulate its proposals.

(c) where additional documents are relied upon, copies should be provided.

Effect of Letter of Response and/or Letter of Settlement

B5.5 If the Letter of Response denies the claim in its entirety and there is no Letter of Settlement, it is open to the Claimant to commence proceedings.

B5.6 In any other circumstance, the professional and the Claimant should commence negotiations with the aim of concluding those negotiations within 6 months of the date of the Letter of Acknowledgment (NOT from the date of the Letter of Response).

B5.7 If the claim cannot be resolved within this period:

(a) the parties should agree within 14 days of the end of the period whether the period should be extended and, if so, by how long.

(b) the parties should seek to identify those issues which are still in dispute and those which can be agreed.

(c) if an extension of time is not agreed it will then be open to the Claimant to commence proceedings.

B6. Alternative Dispute Resolution

B6.1 The parties can agree at any stage to take the dispute (or any part of the dispute) to mediation or some other form of alternative dispute resolution (ADR).

B6.2 In addition, any party at any stage can refer the dispute (or any part of the dispute) to an ADR agency for mediation or some other form of ADR.

B6.3 When approached by a party or an ADR agency with a proposal that ADR be used, the other party or parties should respond within 14 days stating that:

(a) they agree to the proposal; or

(b) they agree that ADR will be or may be appropriate, but they believe it has been suggested prematurely. They should state when they anticipate it would or may become appropriate; or

(c) they agree that ADR is appropriate, but not the form of ADR proposed (if any). They should state the form of ADR which they believe to be appropriate; or

(d) they do not accept that any form of ADR is appropriate. They should state their reasons.

This letter should be copied to the other party or parties and can be disclosed to the court on the issue of costs.

B6.4 It is expressly recognised that no party can or should be forced to mediate or enter into any other form of ADR.

B7. Experts

(The following provisions apply where the claim raises an issue of professional expertise whose resolution requires expert evidence.)

B7.1 If the Claimant has obtained expert evidence prior to sending the Letter of Claim, the professional will have equal right to obtain expert evidence prior to sending the Letter of Response/Letter of Settlement.

B7.2 If the Claimant has not obtained expert evidence prior to sending the Letter of Claim, the parties are encouraged to appoint a joint expert. If they agree to do so, they should seek to agree the identity of the expert and the terms of the expert's appointment.

B7.3 If agreement about a joint expert cannot be reached, all parties are free to appoint their own experts.

(For further details on experts see Guidance Note C6.)

B8. Proceedings

B8.1 Unless it is necessary (for example, to obtain protection against the expiry of a relevant limitation period) the Claimant should not start Court proceedings until:

(a) the Letter of Response denies the claim in its entirety and there is no Letter of Settlement (see paragraph B5.5 above); or

(b) the end of the negotiation period (see paragraphs B5.6 and B5.7 above); or

(For further discussion of statutory time limits for the commencement of litigation, please see Guidance Note C7.)

B8.2 Where possible 14 days written notice should be given to the professional before proceedings are started, indicating the court within which the Claimant is intending to commence litigation.

B8.3 Proceedings should be served on the professional, unless the professional's solicitor has notified the Claimant in writing that he is authorised to accept service on behalf of the professional.

C Guidance Notes

C1. Introduction

C1.1 The protocol has been kept simple to promote ease of use and general acceptability. The guidance notes which follow relate particularly to issues on which further guidance may be required.

C1.2 The Woolf reforms envisage that parties will act reasonably in the pre-action period. Accordingly, in the event that the protocol and the guidelines do not specifically address a problem, the parties should comply with the spirit of the protocol by acting reasonably.

C2. Scope of Protocol

C2.1 The protocol is specifically designed for claims of negligence against professionals. This will include claims in which the allegation against a professional is that they have breached a contractual term to take reasonable skill and care. The protocol is also appropriate for claims of breach of fiduciary duty against professionals.

C2.2 The protocol is not intended to apply to claims:

  (a) against Architects, Engineers and Quantity Surveyors - parties should use the Construction and Engineering Disputes (CED) protocol.

  (b) against Healthcare providers - parties should use the pre-action protocol for the Resolution of Clinical Disputes.

  (c) concerning defamation - parties should use the pre-action protocol for defamation claims.

C2.3 'Professional' is deliberately left undefined in the protocol. If it becomes an issue as to whether a defendant is or is not a professional, parties are reminded of the overriding need to act reasonably (see paragraphs A4 and C1.2 above). Rather than argue about the definition of 'professional', therefore, the parties are invited to use this protocol, adapting it where appropriate.

C2.4 The protocol may not be suitable for disputes with professionals concerning intellectual property claims, etc. Until specific protocols are created for those claims, however, parties are invited to use this protocol, adapting it where necessary.

C2.5 Allegations of professional negligence are sometimes made in response to an attempt by the professional to recover outstanding fees. Where possible these allegations should be raised before litigation has commenced, in which case the parties should comply with the protocol before either party commences litigation. If litigation has already commenced it will be a matter for the Court whether sanctions should be imposed against either party. In any event, the parties are encouraged to consider applying to the Court for a stay to allow the protocol to be followed.

C3. Inter-action with other pre-action methods of dispute resolution

C3.1 There are a growing number of methods by which disputes can be resolved without the need for litigation, eg internal complaints procedures, the Surveyors and Valuers Arbitration Scheme, and so on. The Preliminary Notice procedure of the protocol (see paragraph B1) is designed to enable both parties to take stock at an early stage and to decide before work starts on preparing a Letter of Claim whether the grievance should be referred to one of these other dispute resolution procedures. (For the avoidance of doubt, however, there is no obligation on either party under the protocol to take any action at this stage other than giving the acknowledgment provided for in paragraph B1.4).

C3.2 Accordingly, parties are free to use (and are encouraged to use) any of the available pre-action procedures in an attempt to resolve their dispute. If appropriate, the parties can agree to suspend the protocol timetable whilst the other method of dispute resolution is used.

C3.3 If these methods fail to resolve the dispute, however, the protocol should be used before litigation is commenced. Because there has already been an attempt to resolve the dispute, it may be appropriate to adjust the protocol's requirements. In particular, unless the parties agree otherwise, there is unlikely to be any benefit in duplicating a stage which has in effect already been undertaken. However, if the protocol adds anything to the earlier method of dispute resolution, it should be used, adapting it where appropriate. Once again, the parties are expected to act reasonably.

C4. Multi-Party Disputes

C4.1 Paragraph B2.2(a) of the protocol requires a Claimant to identify any other parties involved in the dispute or a related dispute. This is intended to ensure that all relevant parties are identified as soon as possible.

C4.2 If the dispute involves more than two parties, there are a number of potential problems. It is possible that different protocols will apply to different defendants. It is possible that defendants will claim against each other. It is possible that other parties will be drawn into the dispute. It is possible that the protocol timetable against one party will not be synchronised with the protocol timetable against a different party. How will these problems be resolved?

C4.3 As stated in paragraph C1.2 above, the parties are expected to act reasonably. What is 'reasonable' will, of course, depend upon the specific facts of each case. Accordingly, it would be inappropriate for the protocol to set down generalised rules. Whenever a problem arises, the parties are encouraged to discuss how it can be overcome. In doing so, parties are reminded of the protocol's aims which include the aim to resolve the dispute without the need for litigation (paragraph A2 above).

C5. Investigations

C5.1 Paragraph B4.3 is intended to encourage the early exchange of relevant information, so that issues in the dispute can be clarified or resolved. It should not be used as a 'fishing expedition' by either party. No party is obliged under paragraph B4.3 to disclose any document which a Court could not order them to disclose in the pre-action period.

C5.2 This protocol does not alter the parties' duties to disclose documents under any professional regulation or under general law.

C6. Experts

C6.1 Expert evidence is not always needed, although the use and role of experts in professional negligence claims is often crucial. However, the way in which expert evidence is used in, say, an insurance brokers' negligence case, is not necessarily the same as in, say, an accountants' case. Similarly, the approach to be adopted in a £10,000 case does not necessarily compare with the approach in a £10 million case. The protocol therefore is designed to be flexible and does not dictate a standard approach. On the contrary it envisages that the parties will bear the responsibility for agreeing how best to use experts.

C6.2 If a joint expert is used, therefore, the parties are left to decide issues such as: the payment of the expert, whether joint or separate instructions are used, how and to whom the expert is to report, how questions may be addressed to the expert and how the expert should respond, whether an agreed statement of facts is required, and so on.

C6.3 If separate experts are used, the parties are left to decide issues such as: whether the expert's reports should be exchanged, whether there should be an expert's meeting, and so on.

C6.4 Even if a joint expert is appointed, it is possible that parties will still want to instruct their own experts. The protocol does not prohibit this.

C7. Proceedings

C7.1 This protocol does not alter the statutory time limits for starting Court proceedings. A Claimant is required to start proceedings within those time limits.

C7.2 If proceedings are for any reason started before the parties have followed the procedures in this protocol, the parties are encouraged to agree to apply to the court for a stay whilst the protocol is followed.

Appendix B
Miscellaneous Documents

1 *Tomlin* order

2 Guideline figures for summary assessment of costs

1 Tomlin Order

[handwritten: Why? 1) keep terms of settlement secret 2) to include terms that go beyond the boundaries of the litigation or which are beyond the powers of the court.]

IN THE HIGH COURT OF JUSTICE   2002 L 164

QUEEN'S BENCH DIVISION

WEYFORD DISTRICT REGISTRY

BETWEEN

              LA BOULE S.A.   Claimant

              and

              CHRISTALINE LTD   Defendant

ORDER BY CONSENT

UPON the parties having agreed terms of settlement

BY CONSENT IT IS ORDERED THAT:

1. All further proceedings in this action shall be stayed upon the terms set out in the attached schedule, except for the purpose of carrying such terms into effect.
2. Each party shall have liberty to apply to the court if the other party does not give effect to the terms set out in the schedule. *[handwritten: either party can revive original claim if settlement is not performed through]*
3. The Defendant do pay the Claimant on or before 13 August 2004 the sum of £10,000 in respect of the Claimant's costs.

*[handwritten: * If one party is to pay the other's costs, this must be set out here (rather than in the schedule) if the court are to assess the amount for these costs]*

Dated: ....

We consent to the making of an order in the above terms.

....

Swallows & Co., Solicitors for the Claimant

....

Singleton Trumper & Co., Solicitors for the Defendant

SCHEDULE

1. The Defendant shall pay or cause to be paid to the Claimant the sum of £50,000 on or before 13 August 2004 in full and final satisfaction of all claims and counterclaims arising in this action.

2. In the event of late payment, the Defendant will pay interest on the sum of £50,000 or any part remaining due at a daily rate equal to 3% above the base lending rate of Barcloyds Bank plc as at 13 August 2004.

3. The Claimant and the Defendant have entered into a distribution agreement dated 2 August 2004 as part of the compromise of this action.

2 Guideline figures for summary assessment of costs

Solicitors' hourly rates

The guideline rates for solicitors are broad approximations only. In any particular area the Designated Civil Judge may, after consultation between District Judges and local Law Societies, supply more exact guidelines for rates in that area. Also the costs estimate provided by the paying party may give further guidance if the solicitors for both parties are based in the same locality. The grades of fee earner have been agreed between representatives of the Supreme Court Costs Office, the Association of District Judges and the Law Society. The categories are as follows:

- A. Solicitors with over eight years post qualification experience including at least eight years litigation experience.
- B. Solicitors and legal executives with over four years post qualification experience including at least four years litigation experience.
- C. Other solicitors and legal executives and fee earners of equivalent experience.
- D. Trainee solicitors, para legals and other fee earners.

'Legal Executive' means a Fellow of the Institute of Legal Executives. Those who are not Fellows of the Institute are not entitled to call themselves legal executives and in principle are therefore not entitled to the same hourly rate as a legal executive.

Unqualified clerks who are fee earners of equivalent experience may be entitled to similar rates and in this regard it should be borne in mind that Fellows of the Institute of Legal Executives generally spend two years in a solicitor's office before passing their Part 1 general examinations, spend a further two years before passing the Part 2 specialist examinations and then complete a further two years in practice before being able to become Fellows. Fellows therefore possess considerable practical experience and academic achievement. Clerks without the equivalent experience of legal executives will be treated as being in the bottom grade of fee earner ie trainee solicitors and fee earners of equivalent experience. Whether or not a fee earner has equivalent experience is ultimately a matter for the discretion of the court.

Many High Court cases justify fee earners at a senior level. However the same may not be true of attendance at pre-trial hearings with counsel. The task of sitting behind counsel should be delegated to a more junior fee earner in all but the most important pre-trial hearings. As with hourly rates the costs estimate supplied by the paying party may be of assistance. What grade of fee earner did they use?

In the table which follows the date given alongside the locality is the date when the figures were notified to the SCCO.

In those cases marked 'SCCO' no figures have been received and figures have been inserted based on comparable areas.

'Prov' indicates that the consultation for that particular area is not yet complete.

Guideline Rates for Summary Assessment

January 2003

Band One	Grade*			
Guideline Rates	A	B	C	D
	175	155	130	95
Aldershot, Farnham, Bournemouth				
Birmingham Inner				
Cambridge City Centre				
Canterbury, Maidstone, Medway & Tunbridge Wells				
Cardiff (Inner)				
Kingston/Guildford/Reigate/Epsom				
Leeds Inner (within 1 kilometer radius of the City Art Gallery)				
Lewes				
Liverpool, Birkenhead				
Manchester Central				
Newcastle – City Centre (within a 2 mile radius of St Nicholas Cathedral)				
Norwich				
Nottingham City				
Southampton, Portsmouth				
Swindon, Basingstoke				

Band Two	Grade*			
Guideline Rates	A	B	C	D
	165	145	120	90
Bath, Cheltenham and Gloucester				
Bristol				
Bury				
Chelmsford North, Cambridge County, Peterborough, Bury St E, Norfolk, Lowestoft				
Chelmsford South				
Hampshire, Dorset, Wiltshire, Isle of Wight				
Hull (City)				
Leeds Outer, Wakefield & Pontefract				
Leigh				
Luton, Bedford, St Albans, Hitchin, Hertford				
Manchester Outer/ Oldham/ Bolton/ Tameside				
Oxford (Inner/Outer), Reading, Slough				

Band Two	Grade*
Milton Keynes, Aylesbury	
Sheffield and South Yorkshire	
Southport	
St Helens	
Stockport/Altrincham/Salford	
Swansea, Newport, Cardiff (Outer)	
Watford	
Wigan	
York, Harrogate	

Band Three	Grade*			
Guideline Rates	A	B	C	D
	150	135	115	85
Birmingham Outer				
Bradford (Dewsbury, Halifax, Huddersfield, Keighley & Skipton)				
Chester & North Wales				
Coventry, Rugby, Nuneaton, Stratford and Warwick				
Cumbria				
Devon, Cornwall, Exeter, Taunton & Yeovil				
Grimsby				
Hull Outer				
Kidderminster				
Lincoln				
Newcastle (other than City Centre)				
Northampton & Leicester				
Nottingham & Derbyshire				
Plymouth				
Preston, Lancaster, Blackpool, Chorley				
Accrington, Burnley, Blackburn, Rawenstall & Nelson				
Scarborough & Ripon				
Stafford, Stoke, Tamworth				
Teesside				
Trowbridge				
Weston				
Wolverhampton, Walsall, Dudley & Stourbridge				
Worcester, Hereford, Evesham and Redditch				
Shrewsbury, Telford, Ludlow, Oswestry				
South & West Wales				

London Bands	Grade*			
Guideline Rates	A	B	C	D
City of London**	342	247	189	116
Central London	263	200	163	105
Outer London (including Bromley, Croydon, Dartford, Gravesend and Uxbridge)	189–221	142–189	137	100

*   There are four grades of fee earner:
A.   Solicitors with over 8 years post qualification experience including at least 8 years litigation experience.
B.   Solicitors and legal executives with over 4 years post qualification experience including at least 4 years litigation experience.
C.   Other solicitors and legal executives and fee earners of equivalent experience.
D.   Trainee Solicitors, para legals and fee earners of equivalent experience.

Note: 'legal executive' means a Fellow of the Institute of Legal Executives.

**   Although a guideline figure is given for the top grade of fee earner in the City of London, it is recognised that in certain complex, major litigation the appropriate rate may exceed the guideline by a significant margin.

Counsel's Fees

The following table sets out figures based on Supreme Court Costs Office statistics dealing with run of the mill proceedings in the Queens Bench and Chancery Division and in the Administrative Court. The table gives figures for cases lasting up to an hour and up to half a day, in respect of counsel up to five years call, up to ten years call and over ten years call. It is emphasised that these figures are not recommended rates but it is hoped that they may provide a helpful starting point for judges when assessing counsel's fees. The appropriate fee in any particular case may be more or less than the figures appearing in the table, depending up the circumstances

The table does not include any figures in respect of leading counsel's fees since such cases would self evidently be exceptional. Similarly, no figures are included for the Commercial Court or the Technology & Construction Court.

Table of Counsel's Fees

Queens Bench	1 hour hearing	Half day hearing
Junior up to 5 years call	£220	£385
Junior 5–10 years call	£330	£655
Junior 10+ years call	£500	£1,000

Chancery Division	1 hour hearing	Half day hearing
Junior up to 5 years call	£250	£475
Junior 5–10 years call	£425	£800
Junior 10+ years call	£650	£1,200

Administrative Court	1 hour hearing	Half day hearing
Junior up to 5 years call	£325	£500
Junior 5–10 years call	£600	£1,000
Junior 10+ years call	£850	£1,500

If the paying parties were represented by counsel, the fee paid to their counsel is an important factor but not a conclusive one on the question of fees payable to the receiving party's counsel.

In deciding upon the appropriate fee for counsel the question is not simply one of counsel's experience and seniority but also of the level of counsel which the particular case merits.

Counsel's fees should not be allowed in cases in which it was not reasonable to have instructed counsel, but it must be borne in mind that, especially in substantial hearings, it may be more economical if the advocacy is conducted by counsel rather than a solicitor. In all cases the court should consider whether or not the decision to instruct counsel has led to an increase in costs and whether that increase is justifiable.

Appendix C
Flow Diagrams

1. Overview of the Five Stages of Llitigation
2. Determining Jurisdiction where the Defendant is Domiciled in an EU State
3. Consequences of Part 36 Payment
4. Consequences of Offer Made by Claimant under Part 36 – Defendant Accepts Offer
5. Consequences of Offer Made by Claimant under Part 36 – Claimant Beats Own Offer at Trial
6. Consequences of Offer Made by Claimant under Part 36 – Claimant Fails to Beat Own Offer
7. Consequences of Offer Made by Claimant under Part 36 – Claimant Loses at Trial
8. Possible Responses by Defendant to a Claim
9. Table 1 – Admission of Claim in Whole but Request Time to Pay
10. Table 2 – Admission of Part of Claim – Specified Amount
11. Table 3 – File Acknowledgment of Service
12. Table 4 – Default Judgment

1 Overview of the Five Stages of Litigation

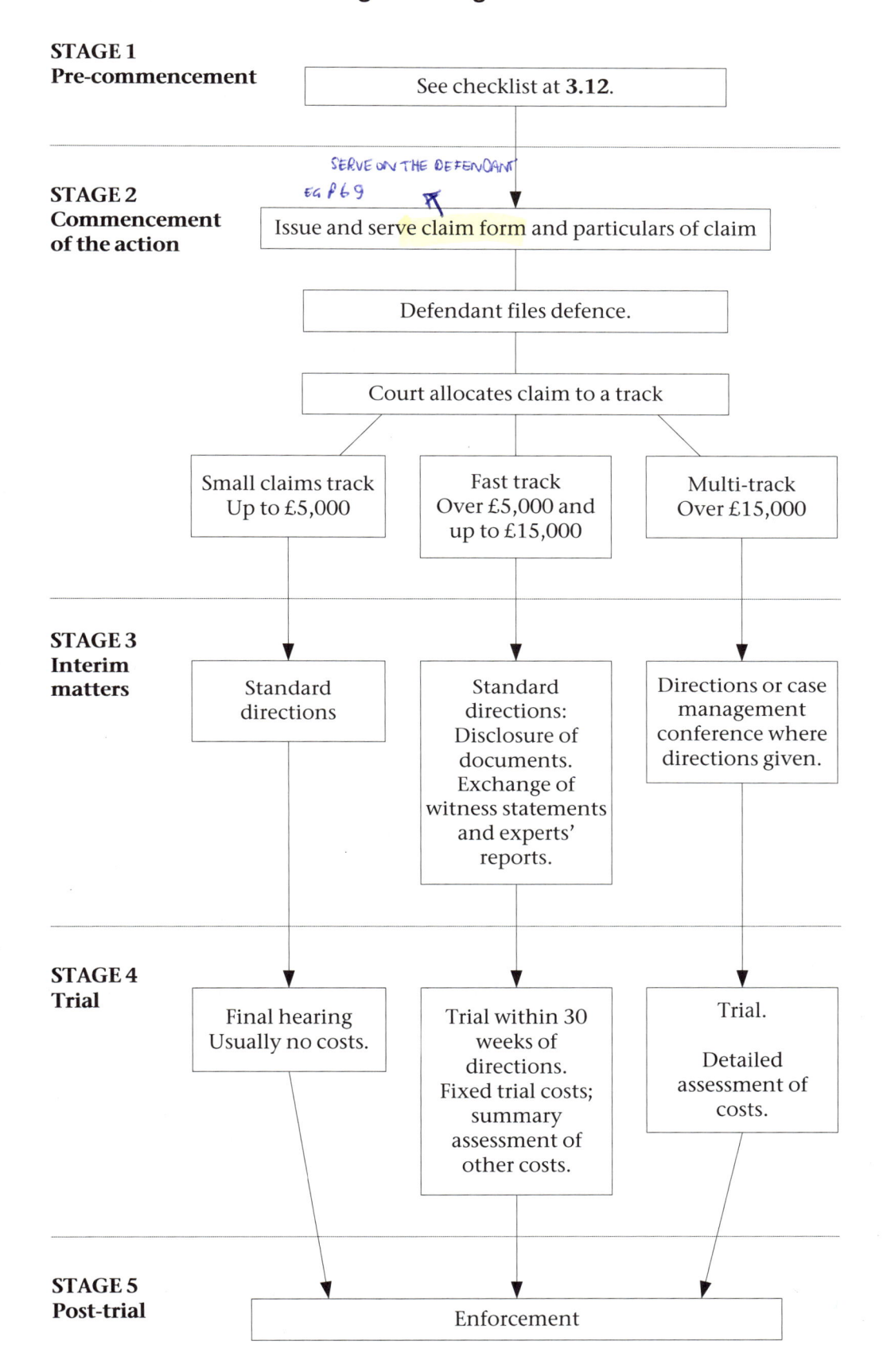

STAGE 1
Pre-commencement

See checklist at **3.12**.

STAGE 2
Commencement of the action

[handwritten: SERVE ON THE DEFENDANT EG P 69]

Issue and serve claim form and particulars of claim

Defendant files defence.

Court allocates claim to a track

| Small claims track Up to £5,000 | Fast track Over £5,000 and up to £15,000 | Multi-track Over £15,000 |

STAGE 3
Interim matters

| Standard directions | Standard directions: Disclosure of documents. Exchange of witness statements and experts' reports. | Directions or case management conference where directions given. |

STAGE 4
Trial

| Final hearing Usually no costs. | Trial within 30 weeks of directions. Fixed trial costs; summary assessment of other costs. | Trial. Detailed assessment of costs. |

STAGE 5
Post-trial

Enforcement

Flow Diagrams 291

2 Determining Jurisdiction where the Defendant is Domiciled in an EU State

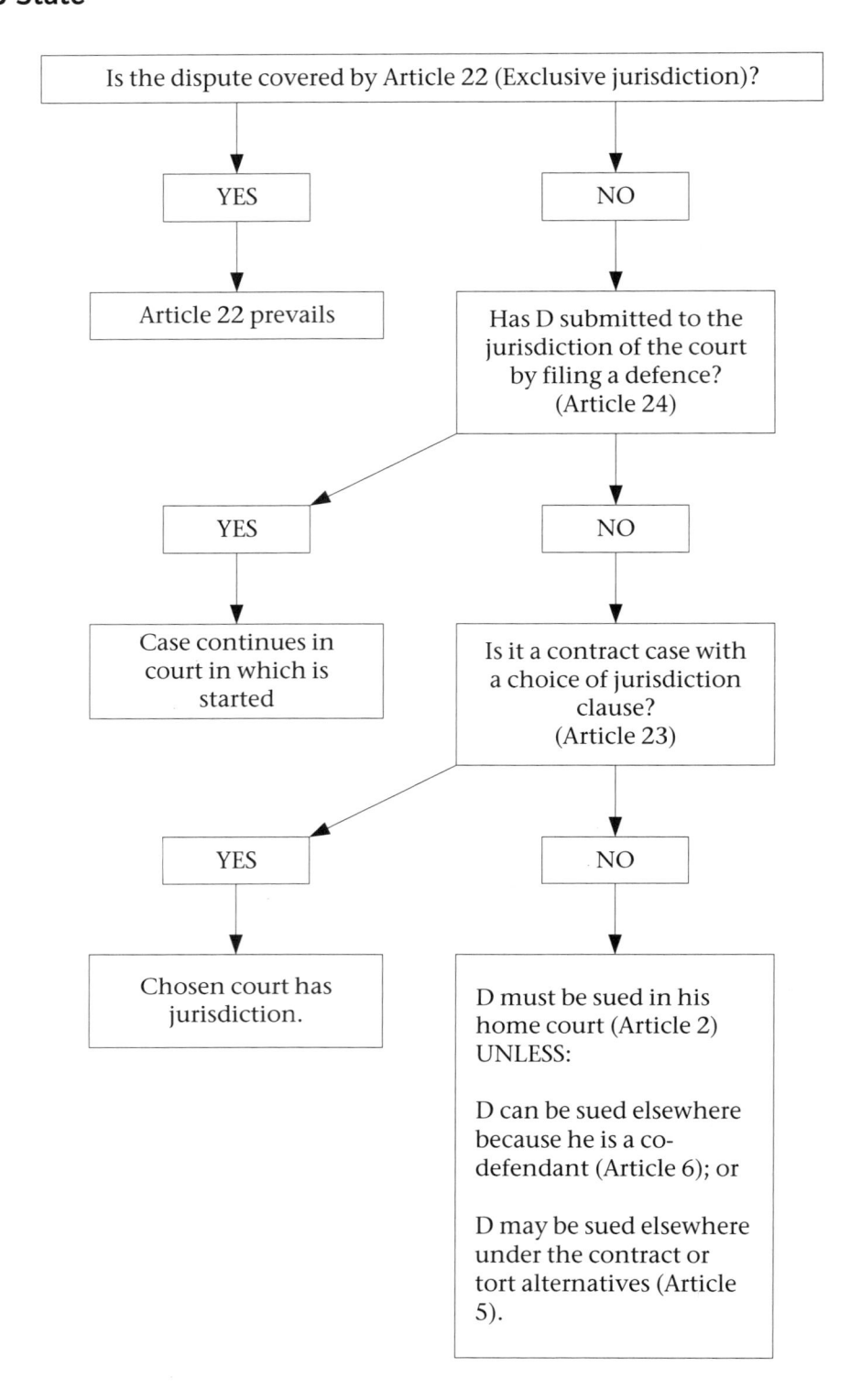

```
┌─────────────────────────────────────────────────────────┐
│ Is the dispute covered by Article 22 (Exclusive jurisdiction)? │
└─────────────────────────────────────────────────────────┘
         │                                    │
         ▼                                    ▼
      ┌─────┐                              ┌─────┐
      │ YES │                              │ NO  │
      └─────┘                              └─────┘
         │                                    │
         ▼                                    ▼
 ┌──────────────────┐              ┌──────────────────────┐
 │ Article 22       │              │ Has D submitted to the│
 │ prevails         │              │ jurisdiction of the court│
 └──────────────────┘              │ by filing a defence?  │
                                   │ (Article 24)          │
                                   └──────────────────────┘
                                      │              │
                                      ▼              ▼
                                   ┌─────┐        ┌─────┐
                                   │ YES │        │ NO  │
                                   └─────┘        └─────┘
                                      │              │
                                      ▼              ▼
                           ┌──────────────────┐  ┌──────────────────────┐
                           │ Case continues in │  │ Is it a contract case with│
                           │ court in which is │  │ a choice of jurisdiction│
                           │ started          │  │ clause?              │
                           └──────────────────┘  │ (Article 23)         │
                                                 └──────────────────────┘
                                                    │              │
                                                    ▼              ▼
                                                 ┌─────┐        ┌─────┐
                                                 │ YES │        │ NO  │
                                                 └─────┘        └─────┘
                                                    │              │
                                                    ▼              ▼
                                         ┌──────────────────┐  ┌──────────────────────┐
                                         │ Chosen court has │  │ D must be sued in his │
                                         │ jurisdiction.    │  │ home court (Article 2)│
                                         └──────────────────┘  │ UNLESS:              │
                                                               │                      │
                                                               │ D can be sued elsewhere│
                                                               │ because he is a co-  │
                                                               │ defendant (Article 6); or│
                                                               │                      │
                                                               │ D may be sued elsewhere│
                                                               │ under the contract or│
                                                               │ tort alternatives (Article│
                                                               │ 5).                  │
                                                               └──────────────────────┘
```

Note: as to Denmark and the EFTA States, see **Chapter 2**.

What if C fails to beat D's Part 36 payment at trial?

Flow Diagrams 293

3 Consequences of Part 36 Payment

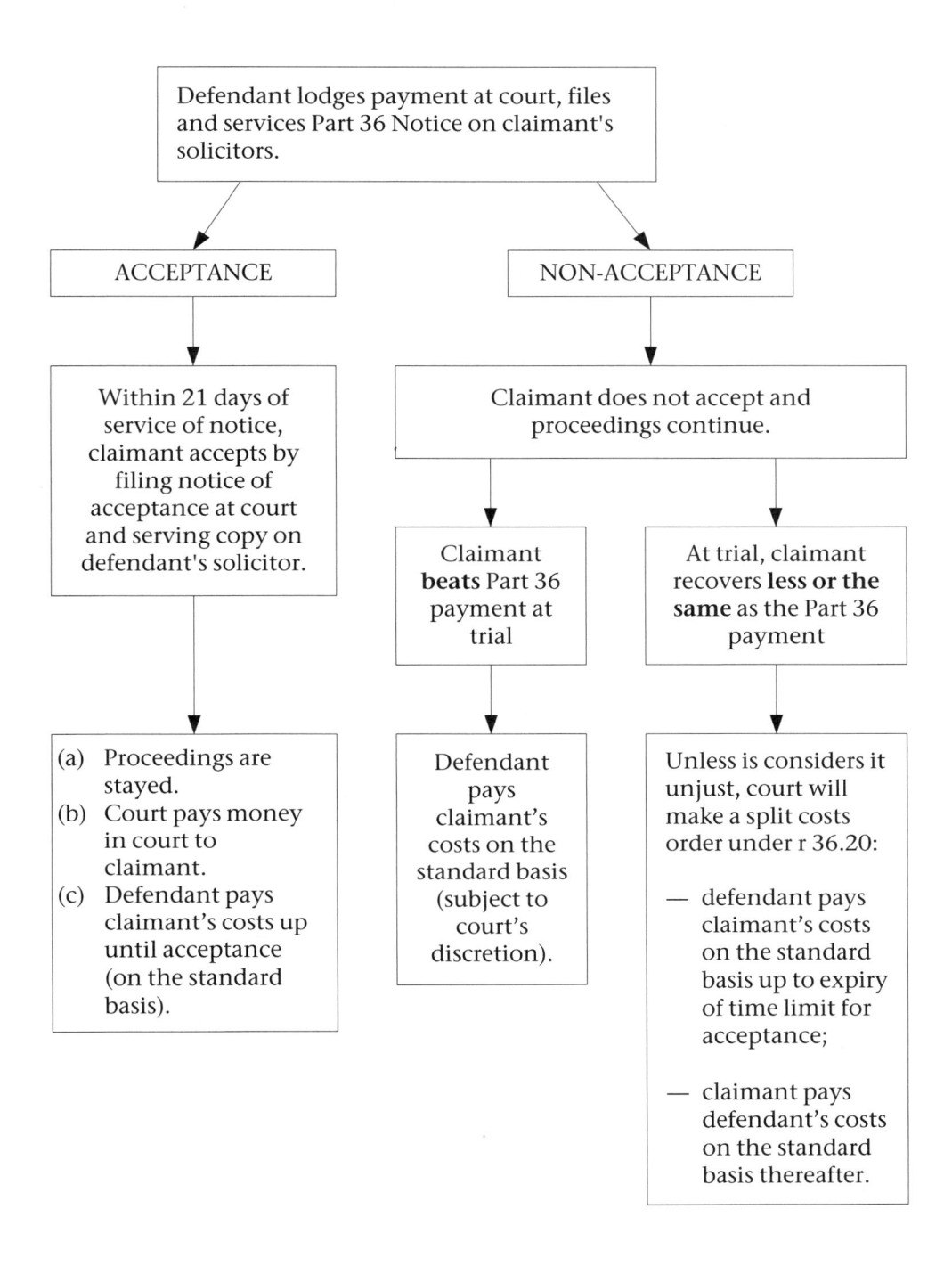

```
        Defendant lodges payment at court, files
        and services Part 36 Notice on claimant's
                      solicitors.
                  /              \
         ACCEPTANCE            NON-ACCEPTANCE
              |                        |
   Within 21 days of         Claimant does not accept and
   service of notice,          proceedings continue.
   claimant accepts by              /          \
   filing notice of
   acceptance at court    Claimant          At trial, claimant
   and serving copy on    beats Part 36     recovers less or the
   defendant's solicitor. payment at        same as the Part 36
                          trial             payment
              |                 |                  |
   (a) Proceedings are    Defendant          Unless is considers it
       stayed.            pays               unjust, court will
   (b) Court pays money   claimant's         make a split costs
       in court to        costs on the       order under r 36.20:
       claimant.          standard basis
   (c) Defendant pays     (subject to        — defendant pays
       claimant's costs up court's              claimant's costs
       until acceptance   discretion).          on the standard
       (on the standard                         basis up to expiry
       basis).                                  of time limit for
                                                acceptance;

                                             — claimant pays
                                                defendant's costs
                                                on the standard
                                                basis thereafter.
```

4 Consequences of Offer Made by Claimant under Part 36 – Defendant Accepts Offer

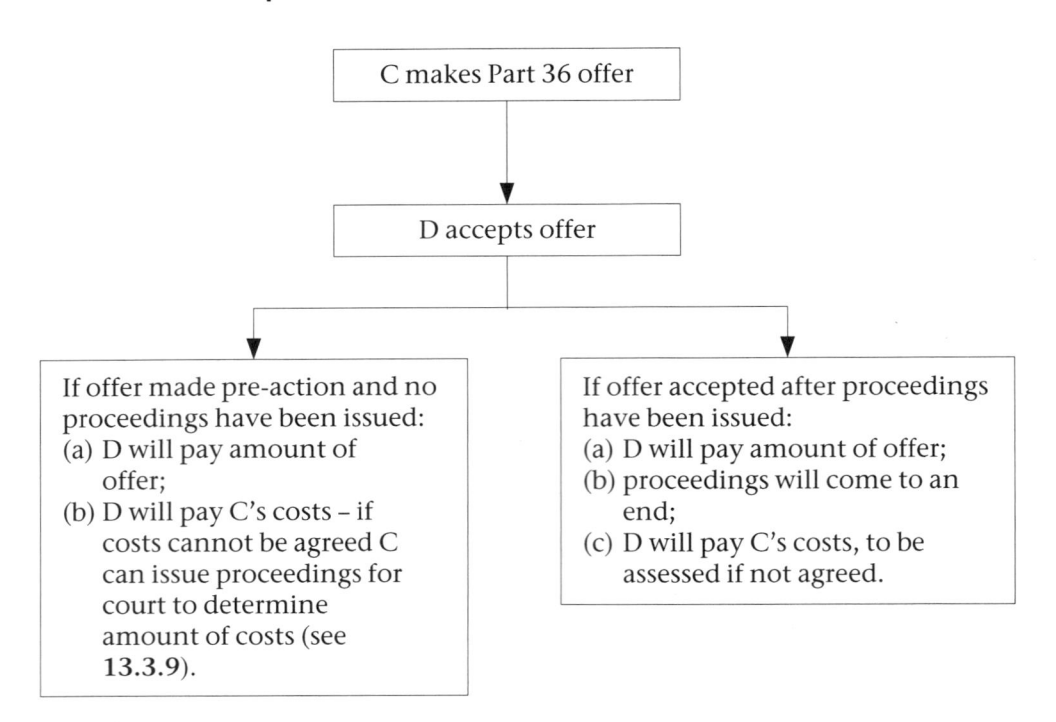

```
            ┌─────────────────────────┐
            │  C makes Part 36 offer  │
            └───────────┬─────────────┘
                        │
                        ▼
            ┌─────────────────────────┐
            │      D accepts offer    │
            └───────────┬─────────────┘
                        │
           ┌────────────┴────────────┐
           ▼                         ▼
```

| If offer made pre-action and no proceedings have been issued:
(a) D will pay amount of offer;
(b) D will pay C's costs – if costs cannot be agreed C can issue proceedings for court to determine amount of costs (see 13.3.9). | If offer accepted after proceedings have been issued:
(a) D will pay amount of offer;
(b) proceedings will come to an end;
(c) D will pay C's costs, to be assessed if not agreed. |

what if C beats his own Part 36 offer at trial?

5 Consequences of Offer Made by Claimant Under Part 36 – Claimant Beats Own Offer at Trial

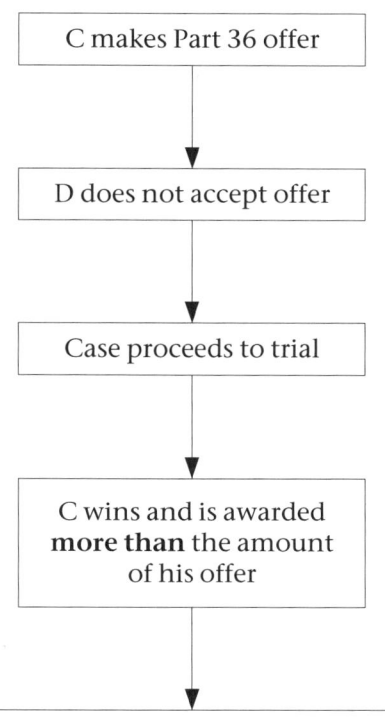

```
C makes Part 36 offer
        ↓
D does not accept offer
        ↓
Case proceeds to trial
        ↓
C wins and is awarded
more than the amount
of his offer
        ↓
```

C will receive:
(a) the damages awarded by the court;
(b) interest at the court's discretion on the damages provided claimed in the particulars of claim (usually) from the date the cause of action arose up to judgment;
(c) enhanced interest on the damages under r 36.21 from the last date when D could have accepted the offer without needing the court's permission until judgment at a maximum rate of 10% over base rate **less** interest already awarded under (b) for the same period;
(d) costs on the standard basis from when first incurred up to the last date for acceptance of the offer without needing the court's permission;
(e) costs on the indemnity basis under r 36.21 from the day after the last date for acceptance of the offer without needing the court's permission up to judgment;
(f) interest on the indemnity basis costs under r 36.21 at a maximum rate of 10% over base rate.

6 Consequences of Offer Made by Claimant under Part 36 – Claimant Fails to Beat Offer

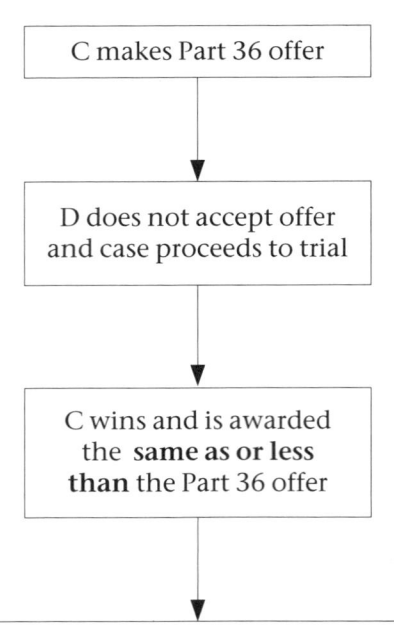

```
┌─────────────────────────┐
│  C makes Part 36 offer  │
└─────────────────────────┘
             │
             ▼
┌─────────────────────────┐
│  D does not accept offer│
│  and case proceeds to trial│
└─────────────────────────┘
             │
             ▼
┌─────────────────────────┐
│  C wins and is awarded  │
│  the **same as or less**│
│  **than** the Part 36 offer│
└─────────────────────────┘
             │
             ▼
```

C will receive:
(a) the damages awarded;
(b) interest at the court's discretion on the damages provided claimed in the particulars of claim (usually) from the date the cause of action arose up to judgment;
(c) subject to the court's discretion his costs on the standard basis.
Note: PD – Costs (Parts 43 to 48), para 8.4 provides that where a claimant has made a Part 36 offer and fails to obtain a judgment which is more advantageous than that offer, that circumstance alone will not lead to a reduction in the costs awarded to the claimant.

7 Consequences of Offer Made by Claimant Under Part 36 – Claimant Loses at Trial

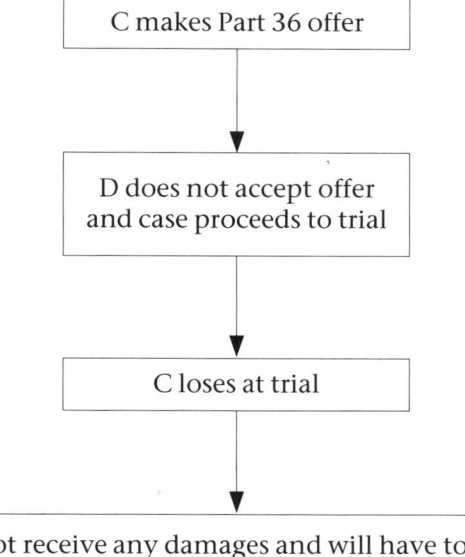

```
┌─────────────────────┐
│ C makes Part 36 offer │
└─────────┬───────────┘
          ▼
┌─────────────────────────┐
│ D does not accept offer │
│ and case proceeds to trial │
└─────────┬───────────────┘
          ▼
┌─────────────────────┐
│   C loses at trial  │
└─────────┬───────────┘
          ▼
```

C will not receive any damages and will have to pay:
(a) subject to the court's discretion, D's costs of the proceedings on the standard basis.
(b) his own costs (subject to any CFA, etc).

8 Possible Responses by Defendant to a Claim

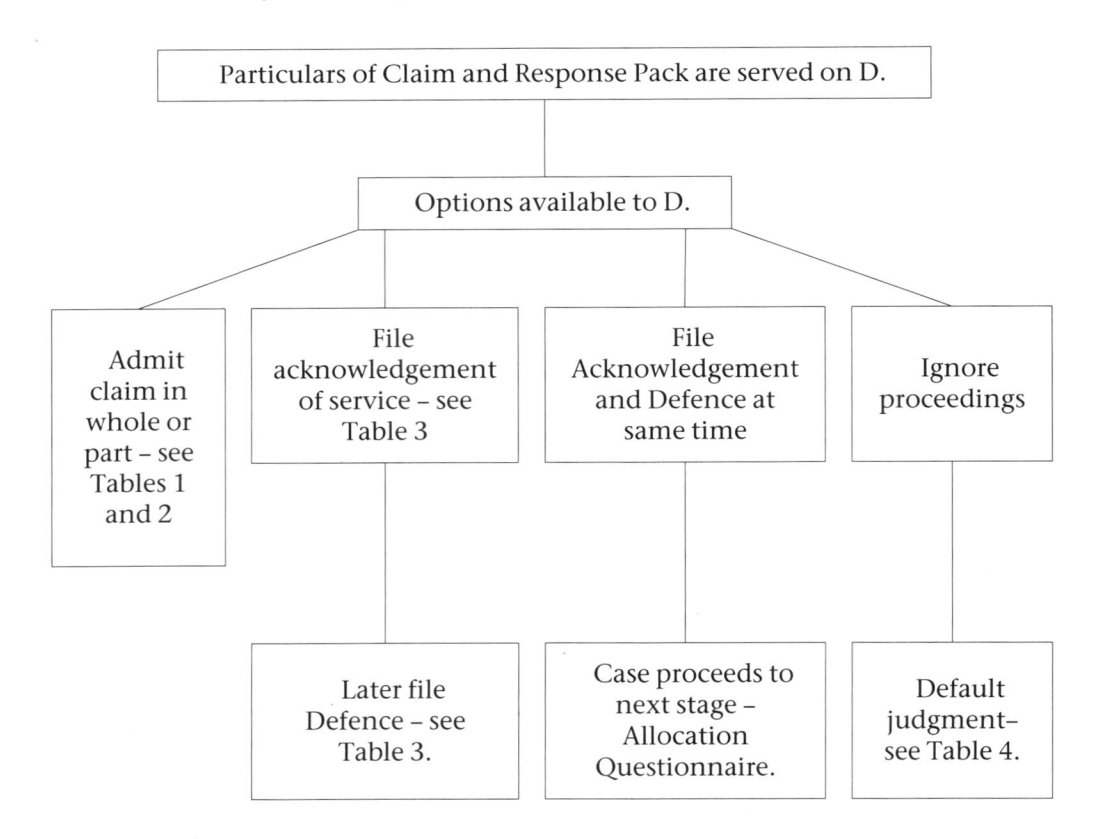

```
         Particulars of Claim and Response Pack are served on D.
                                    │
                          Options available to D.
         ┌──────────────┬───────────┴──────────┬──────────────┐
   Admit claim      File              File                Ignore
   in whole or      acknowledgement   Acknowledgement     proceedings
   part – see       of service – see  and Defence at
   Tables 1         Table 3           same time
   and 2
                         │                     │                  │
                    Later file         Case proceeds to      Default
                    Defence – see      next stage –          judgment–
                    Table 3.           Allocation            see Table 4.
                                       Questionnaire.
```

9 Table 1 – Admission of Claim in Whole but Request Time to Pay

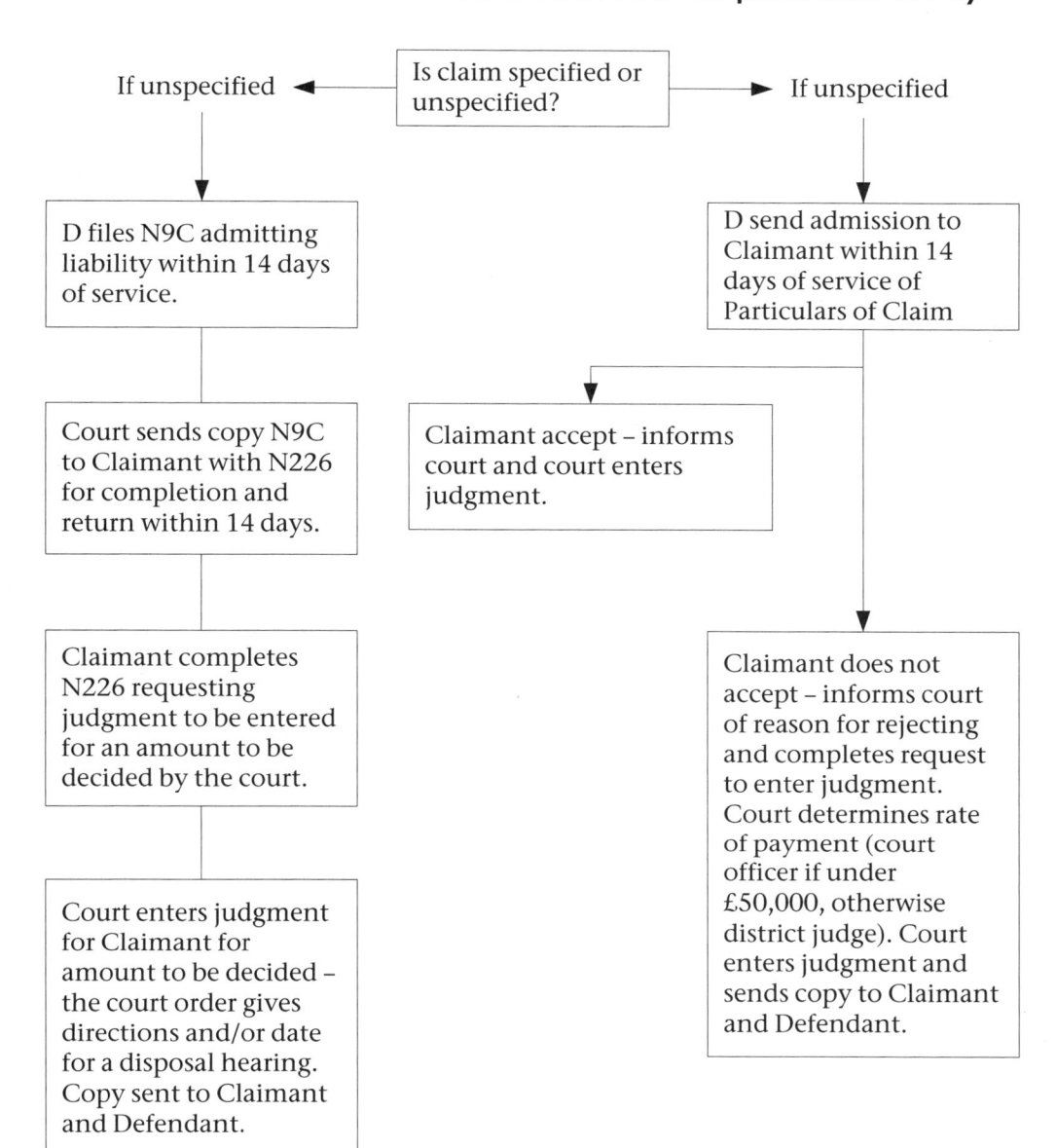

Is claim specified or unspecified?

If unspecified (left branch):

- D files N9C admitting liability within 14 days of service.
- Court sends copy N9C to Claimant with N226 for completion and return within 14 days.
- Claimant completes N226 requesting judgment to be entered for an amount to be decided by the court.
- Court enters judgment for Claimant for amount to be decided – the court order gives directions and/or date for a disposal hearing. Copy sent to Claimant and Defendant.

If unspecified (right branch):

- D send admission to Claimant within 14 days of service of Particulars of Claim
- Claimant accept – informs court and court enters judgment.
- Claimant does not accept – informs court of reason for rejecting and completes request to enter judgment. Court determines rate of payment (court officer if under £50,000, otherwise district judge). Court enters judgment and sends copy to Claimant and Defendant.

10 Table 2 – Admission of Part of Claim – Specified Amount

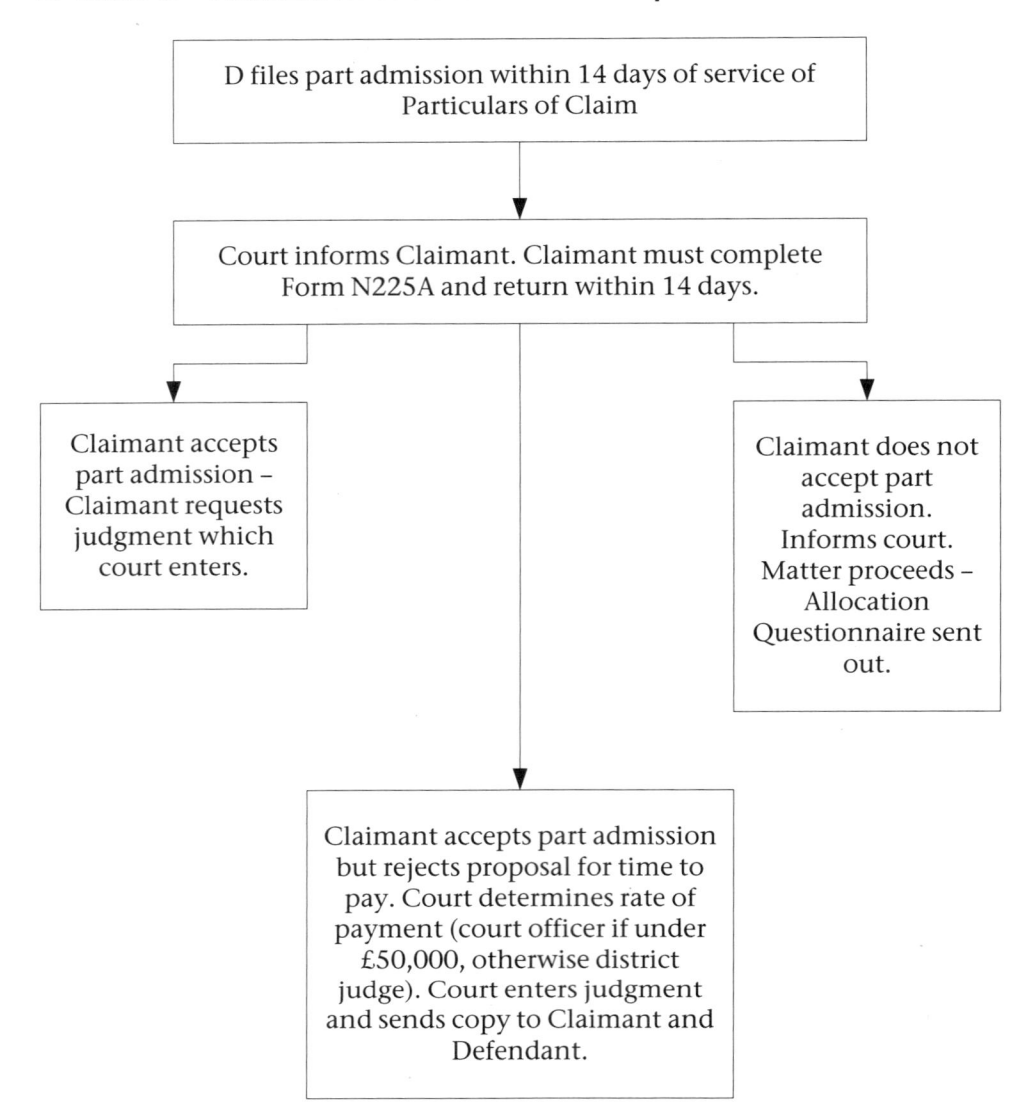

```
┌─────────────────────────────────────────────────┐
│ D files part admission within 14 days of service│
│              of Particulars of Claim             │
└─────────────────────────────────────────────────┘
                         │
                         ▼
┌─────────────────────────────────────────────────┐
│   Court informs Claimant. Claimant must complete│
│       Form N225A and return within 14 days.      │
└─────────────────────────────────────────────────┘
         │               │                │
         ▼               ▼                ▼
┌─────────────────┐             ┌─────────────────┐
│ Claimant accepts│             │ Claimant does not│
│ part admission –│             │   accept part   │
│Claimant requests│             │    admission.   │
│ judgment which  │             │  Informs court. │
│  court enters.  │             │ Matter proceeds –│
└─────────────────┘             │    Allocation   │
                                │Questionnaire sent│
                                │       out.      │
                                └─────────────────┘
                 ▼
        ┌──────────────────────────────────┐
        │ Claimant accepts part admission  │
        │ but rejects proposal for time to │
        │ pay. Court determines rate of    │
        │ payment (court officer if under  │
        │  £50,000, otherwise district     │
        │ judge). Court enters judgment    │
        │ and sends copy to Claimant and   │
        │            Defendant.            │
        └──────────────────────────────────┘
```

11 Table 3 – File Acknowledgement of Service

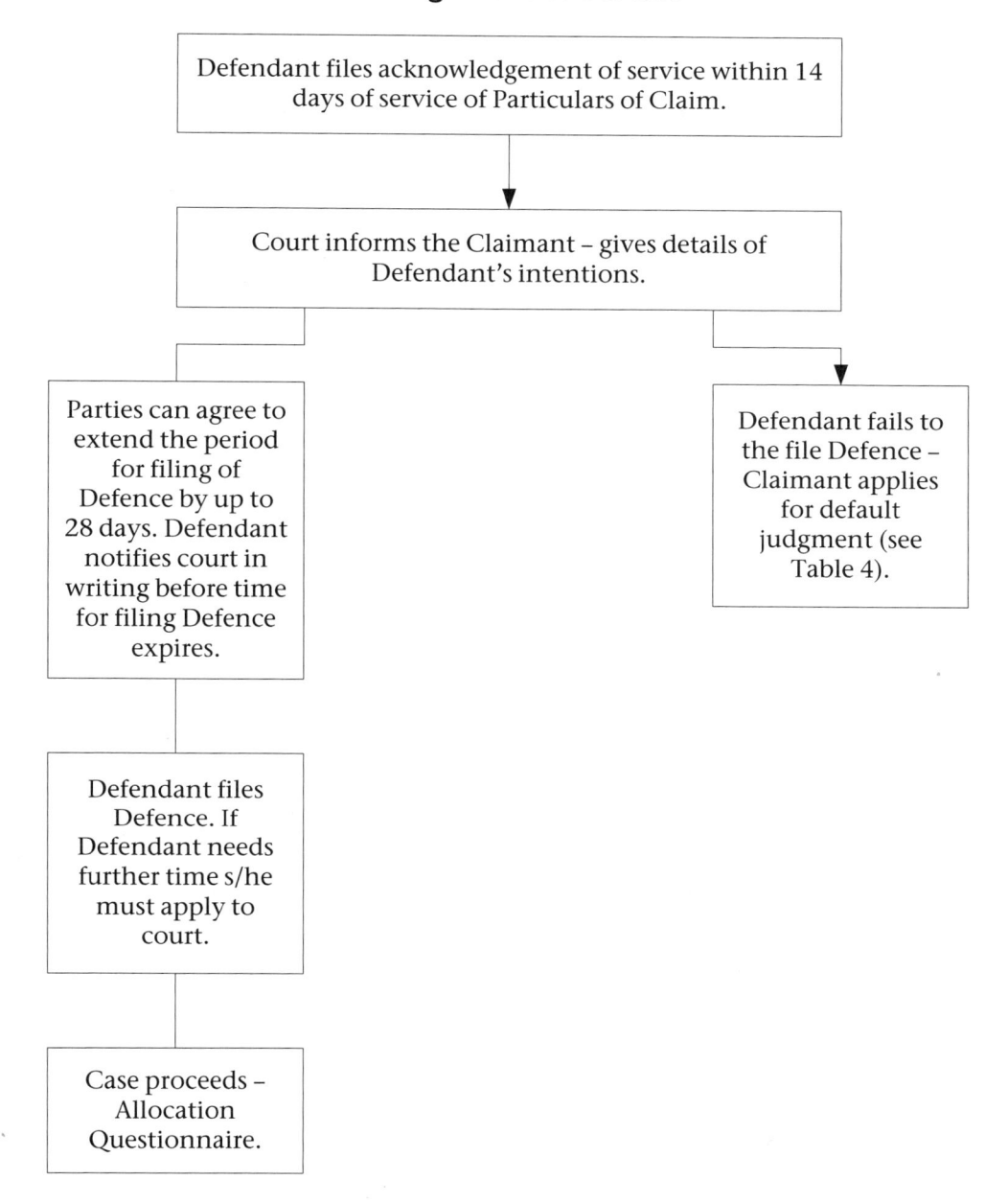

```
┌─────────────────────────────────────────────┐
│ Defendant files acknowledgement of service  │
│ within 14 days of service of Particulars of │
│ Claim.                                      │
└─────────────────────────────────────────────┘
                       │
                       ▼
┌─────────────────────────────────────────────┐
│ Court informs the Claimant – gives details  │
│ of Defendant's intentions.                  │
└─────────────────────────────────────────────┘
            │                           │
            ▼                           ▼
┌───────────────────────┐   ┌───────────────────────┐
│ Parties can agree to  │   │ Defendant fails to    │
│ extend the period     │   │ the file Defence –    │
│ for filing of         │   │ Claimant applies      │
│ Defence by up to      │   │ for default           │
│ 28 days. Defendant    │   │ judgment (see         │
│ notifies court in     │   │ Table 4).             │
│ writing before time   │   └───────────────────────┘
│ for filing Defence    │
│ expires.              │
└───────────────────────┘
            │
            ▼
┌───────────────────────┐
│ Defendant files       │
│ Defence. If           │
│ Defendant needs       │
│ further time s/he     │
│ must apply to         │
│ court.                │
└───────────────────────┘
            │
            ▼
┌───────────────────────┐
│ Case proceeds –       │
│ Allocation            │
│ Questionnaire.        │
└───────────────────────┘
```

12 Table 4 – Default Judgment

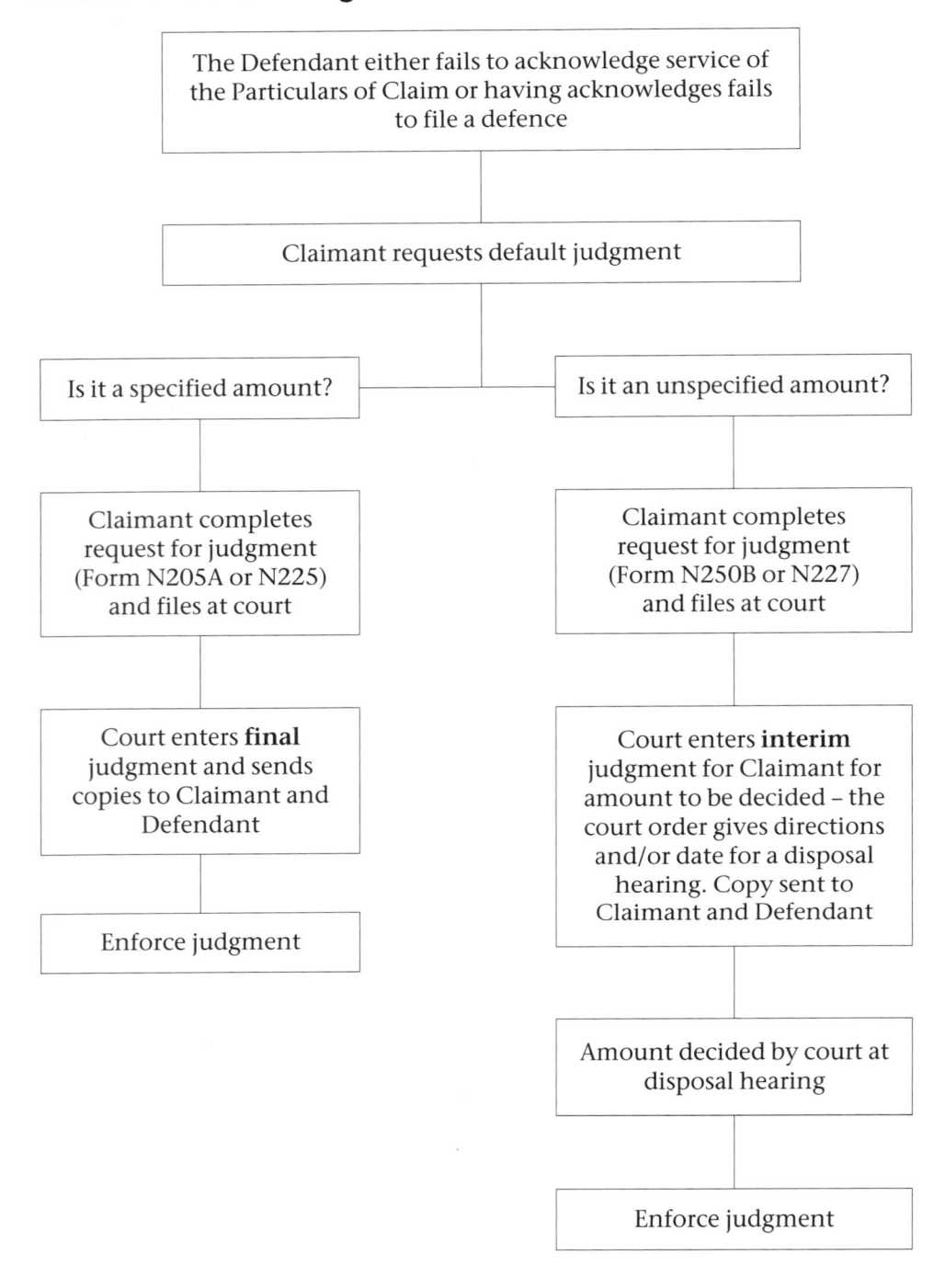

```
┌─────────────────────────────────────────────────────┐
│ The Defendant either fails to acknowledge service of│
│ the Particulars of Claim or having acknowledges     │
│ fails to file a defence                             │
└─────────────────────────────────────────────────────┘
                           │
                           ▼
┌─────────────────────────────────────────────────────┐
│           Claimant requests default judgment        │
└─────────────────────────────────────────────────────┘
              │                           │
              ▼                           ▼
   ┌──────────────────────┐    ┌──────────────────────┐
   │ Is it a specified    │    │ Is it an unspecified │
   │ amount?              │    │ amount?              │
   └──────────────────────┘    └──────────────────────┘
              │                           │
              ▼                           ▼
   ┌──────────────────────┐    ┌──────────────────────┐
   │ Claimant completes   │    │ Claimant completes   │
   │ request for judgment │    │ request for judgment │
   │ (Form N205A or N225) │    │ (Form N250B or N227) │
   │ and files at court   │    │ and files at court   │
   └──────────────────────┘    └──────────────────────┘
              │                           │
              ▼                           ▼
   ┌──────────────────────┐    ┌──────────────────────┐
   │ Court enters final   │    │ Court enters interim │
   │ judgment and sends   │    │ judgment for Claimant│
   │ copies to Claimant   │    │ for amount to be     │
   │ and Defendant        │    │ decided – the court  │
   └──────────────────────┘    │ order gives          │
              │                │ directions and/or    │
              ▼                │ date for a disposal  │
   ┌──────────────────────┐    │ hearing. Copy sent   │
   │ Enforce judgment     │    │ to Claimant and      │
   └──────────────────────┘    │ Defendant            │
                               └──────────────────────┘
                                          │
                                          ▼
                               ┌──────────────────────┐
                               │ Amount decided by    │
                               │ court at disposal    │
                               │ hearing              │
                               └──────────────────────┘
                                          │
                                          ▼
                               ┌──────────────────────┐
                               │ Enforce judgment     │
                               └──────────────────────┘
```

Appendix D
Case Study Documents

1 Letter of Claim

2 Particulars of Claim

3 Defence and Part 20 Counterclaim

4 Reply and Defence to Part 20 Counterclaim

5 Case Summary for Use at Case Management Conference

6 Order for Directions

7 Experts' Without Prejudice Meeting Statement

8 (Defendant's) Brief to Counsel

9 Consent Order

1 Letter of Claim

SOLICITORS LLP
1 Avenue Road
Nowhere
Mythshire
MC1V 2AA

Our reference: 1234/PO

Mr G Templar
1 The Cottage
Grassy Knowle
Nowhere
Mythshire MY76 9T

27 August 2004

Dear Sir,

Incident at Bliss Lodge, Steep Lane, Nowhere on 1 August 2004
Letter of Claim

We are instructed by Mr W Simpson and Dr R Simpson in connection with a claim for damages following an incident which occurred at their home on 1 August 2004.

The facts

Our clients advise us that at approximately 11 pm on 1 August 2004 you drove your motor car, a Land Cruiser 4x4, 4.5 litre turbo model, registration GIT 1 ('the Car'), on their drive. We understand you were about to take up a short-term let in part of the premises. The Car crashed into the recently completed extension of our clients' property causing serious damage to the garden, building, furnishings and fittings.

Legal basis of claim

By entering our clients' premises it became your responsibility to ensure that you drove with the degree of care and skill that would be expected from a competent driver.

Factual basis of claim

We are instructed that you drove up the drive at excessive speed and without properly controlling the Car. As a result you drove into our client's extension at their property. Our preliminary investigations have revealed that the entire extension will have to be demolished, rebuilt and refitted.

Responsibility

We have advised our clients that your actions on 1 August 2004 were negligent and that they are entitled to be compensated by you.

Calculation of damage to the extension at 'Bliss Lodge'

	£
Putting right damage to garden & drive	8,000
Demolishing and rebuilding extension	96,000
Kitchen refit	57,000
Bedroom refit	10,000
TOTAL	**171,000**

The above figures are based on current available estimates copies of which are enclosed.

In addition to the above losses our clients have been put to considerable expense in making safe the extension.

Calculation of loss in making safe the extension at 'Bliss Lodge'

	£
Weather-proofing the extension	8,000
Installing a temporary alarm system for the parts of 'Bliss Lodge' accessible from the extension	5,000
Making safe the electrical supply to and in the extension	1,000
Sealing off the plumbing supply to the extension	500
TOTAL	**14,500**

We enclose copies of receipted invoices for these matters.

Response

Please acknowledge safe receipt of this letter promptly, and by no later than 17 September 2004. Please also note that unless a full written response is received by 24 September 2004 we are instructed to start proceedings for damages, interest and costs without further notice to you.

We advise you to take independent legal advice. Should you choose not to instruct solicitors, we enclose a copy of a Practice Direction issued by the courts and we draw your attention to the power of the courts to impose sanctions under paragraph 4.3(g). We understand that you are insured with Raven Lunar Insurance Plc. We enclose a copy of a letter we have sent to that company giving formal notification of the possible commencement of the proceedings.

Yours faithfully,

2 Particulars of Claim

IN THE HIGH COURT OF JUSTICE WF-04-1234
QUEEN'S BENCH DIVISION
WEYFORD DISTRICT REGISTRY

BETWEEN MR WILLIAM ULYSSES SIMPSON (1) Claimants
DR RUPINDER SIMPSON (2)

and

MR GEOFFREY IAN TEMPLAR Defendant

PARTICULARS OF CLAIM

1. At all material times the Claimants owned the property known as 'Bliss Lodge', Steep Lane, Nowhere, Mythshire, GU15 6AB ('the Property').

2. On 1 August 2004 at about 11.00 pm, the Defendant drove a Land Cruiser 4x4, 4.5 litre turbo model registration number GIT 13 ('the Car') down the driveway leading to the Property.

3. Owing to the negligent driving of the Defendant, the Car left the driveway and collided with the Property, partially destroying a recently-constructed two-storey extension.

PARTICULARS OF NEGLIGENCE

The Defendant drove negligently in that he:

(a) drove at excessive speed;
(b) lost control of the Car;
(c) swerved repeatedly on and off the driveway;
(d) failed to apply the Car's brakes sufficiently or at all;
(e) failed to steer, manage, control or stop the Car so as to avoid the collision.

4. Owing to the Defendant's negligence, the Claimants have suffered loss and damage.

PARTICULARS OF LOSS AND DAMAGE

	£
Costs incurred rendering the extension safe following the collision:	
– Weather-proofing the extension	8,000.00
– Installation of temporary alarm system for parts of Bliss Lodge accessible from the extension	5,000.00
– Making safe electrical supply to and in the extension	1,000.00
– Sealing off plumbing supply to the extension	500.00
	14,500.00

Particulars of the estimated costs that follow are given in the attached Schedule.

Estimated costs to be incurred repairing damage to the extension:–

– demolishing and rebuilding the extension	96,000.00
– refitting custom-made kitchen	57,000.00
– refitting bedroom	10,000.00
– remedial and reinstatement works to garden and driveway	8,000.00
	171,000.00
TOTAL	185,500.00

5. In respect of damages awarded to them the Claimants claim interest under s.35A of the Supreme Court Act 1981 at such rate and for such period as the court thinks fit.

AND THE CLAIMANTS CLAIM:

(1) Damages as stated in paragraph 4 above;
(2) Interest as stated in paragraph 5 above.

Dated 19 January 2005   Signed: *Solicitors LLP*

<u>STATEMENT OF TRUTH</u>

We believe that the facts stated in these Particulars of Claim are true.

Signed: *William Ulysses Simpson*   *Rupinder Simpson*
              WILLIAM ULYSSES SIMPSON   RUPINDER SIMPSON
              FIRST CLAIMANT   SECOND CLAIMANT

The Claimants' solicitors are Solicitors LLP, 1 Avenue Road, Nowhere, Mythshire, MC1V 2AA where they will accept service of proceedings on behalf of the Claimants.

To: the Defendant
To: the Court Manager

3 Defence and Part 20 Counterclaim

IN THE HIGH COURT OF JUSTICE WF-04-1234
QUEEN'S BENCH DIVISION
WEYFORD DISTRICT REGISTRY

BETWEEN   MR WILLIAM ULYSSES SIMPSON (1)
               DR RUPINDER SIMPSON (2)

Claimants/Part 20 Defendants

and

MR GEOFFREY IAN TEMPLAR

Defendant/Part 20 Claimant

DEFENCE AND PART 20 COUNTERCLAIM — *title to proceedings change once there is a Part 20 counterclaim*

DEFENCE

1. The Defendant admits paragraph 1 of the Particulars of Claim. The Claimants were the occupiers of the Property and the Defendant was a visitor within the meaning of the Occupiers' Liability Act 1957 ('the Act'). The Defendant visited the Property at the Claimants' invitation on 1 August 2004 to use accommodation in a converted stable block there.

2. The Defendant admits paragraph 2.

3. Save that the Defendant admits that he lost control of the Car and that it collided with the Property, the Defendant denies for the reasons that follow that he drove negligently as alleged in paragraph 3 or at all or that the matters complained of were caused as alleged or at all.

4. Further or alternatively, the collision was caused or contributed to by the breach of statutory duty of the Claimants.

PARTICULARS OF BREACH OF STATUTORY DUTY

The Claimants acted in breach of statutory duty in that they:

(a) unknown to the Defendant caused or allowed shards of broken glass to be present on the driveway of the Property which caused the front and rear offside tyres of the Car to suddenly burst, thus resulting in him losing control of the Car;

(b) failed by means of notices or otherwise to warn the Defendant of the presence and position of the glass referred to in (a);

(c) required or allowed the Defendant to use the driveway when it was unsafe;

(d) exposed the Defendant to danger and a foreseeable risk of damage to his property;

(e) failed to take proper care for the Defendant's safety.

5. As to paragraph 4, the Defendant admits that the Property was damaged by the collision but denies for the reasons set out above that he caused any damage. The Defendant otherwise makes no admissions as to the loss or damage alleged by the Claimants in paragraph 4 of the Particulars of Claim as he has no knowledge of such.

6. In the circumstances, the Defendant denies that the Claimants are entitled to the relief claimed in paragraph 4 or any relief.

PART 20 COUNTERCLAIM

7. The Defendant repeats paragraphs 1 to 5 of the Defence.

8. Owing to the above matters, the Defendant has suffered loss and damage.

<u>PARTICULARS OF LOSS AND DAMAGE</u>

	£
Value of Defendant's Car irreparably damaged	58,995.00
Value of other items in the Car irreparably damaged: – Diasan PC notebook computer – Mercuriam satellite mobile phone	6,500.00 2,000.00
Towing charges paid to We-Haul in removing the Car	440.63
Cost of storing the Car at We-Haul's premises for nine weeks at £50.00 per week and continuing	450.00
Alternative car hire charges for nine weeks at £150.00 per week and continuing	1,350.00
Additional cost of alternative accommodation in Nowhere	450.00
TOTAL	70,185.63

9. The Defendant therefore counterclaims from the Claimants damages in respect of the above.

10. The Defendant claims interest under s.35A of the Supreme Court Act 1981 on damages awarded to him at such rate and for such period as the court thinks fit.

AND THE DEFENDANT COUNTERCLAIMS:

(1) Damages as stated in paragraph 9 above;

(2) Interest as stated in paragraph 10 above.

Dated 4 February 2005   Signed: Advocates & Co

STATEMENT OF TRUTH

I believe that the facts stated in this Defence and Part 20 Counterclaim are true.

Signed: *G I Templar*
....
GEOFFREY IAN TEMPLAR
DEFENDANT

The Defendant's solicitors are Advocates & Co, 30 Cheapway, Nowhere, Mythshire, MB2X 5PP where they accept service of proceedings in behalf of the Defendant.

To: the Claimants / Part 20 Defendants

To: the Court Manager

4 Reply and Defence to Part 20 Counterclaim

IN THE HIGH COURT OF JUSTICE WF-04-1234
QUEEN'S BENCH DIVISION
WEYFORD DISTRICT REGISTRY

BETWEEN   MR WILLIAM ULYSSES SIMPSON (1)
                 DR RUPINDER SIMPSON (2)

Claimants/Part 20 Defendants

and

MR GEOFFREY IAN TEMPLAR

Defendant/Part 20 Claimant

REPLY AND DEFENCE TO PART 20 COUNTERCLAIM

REPLY

1. The Claimants admit paragraph 1 of the Defence.

2. The Claimants deny that they were in breach of statutory duty as alleged in paragraph 4 of the Defence or at all. The Claimants also deny that the collision was caused or contributed to by their breach of statutory duty. The Claimants contend that:

    (a) There was no broken glass and/or debris on the driveway. Alternatively, if there was broken glass and/or debris on the driveway, it was placed there by the actions of the Defendant, referred to in paragraph (b) below, whereby the Defendant swerved onto broken glass and/or debris on the grass and thereby caused it to scatter;

    (b) There was a small amount of builders' debris on the grass bordering the right hand side of the driveway. The debris was well away from the normal passage of any vehicle and did not constitute a hazard. It was solely due to the Defendant's excessive speed that he lost control of the Car, veered off the driveway onto the grass and drove onto the debris;

    (c) If the Defendant had been driving at an appropriate speed, he should have been able to control the Car, after the front and rear offside tyres burst, so as to avoid colliding with the Property.

3. Except where the Defendant has made admissions and except as appears in this statement of case, the Claimants join issue with the Defendant upon his Defence.

DEFENCE TO PART 20 COUNTERCLAIM

4. The Claimants repeat paragraphs 1, 2 and 3 above.

5. As to paragraph 8 of the Part 20 Counterclaim, the Claimants admit that the Defendant's Car suffered damage but deny for the reasons given above that they caused such loss and damage. The Claimants otherwise do not admit the loss and damage alleged in paragraph 8 of the Part 20 Counterclaim as they have no knowledge of such.

6. In the circumstances the Claimants deny that the Defendant is entitled to any damages whatsoever.

Dated: 18 February 2005. Signed: *Solicitors LLP*

STATEMENT OF TRUTH

We believe that the facts stated in this Reply and Defence to Counterclaim are true.

Signed: *William Ulysses Simpson* *Rupinder Simpson*
....
WILLIAM ULYSSES SIMPSON RUPINDER SIMPSON
FIRST CLAIMANT SECOND CLAIMANT

The Claimants' solicitors are Solicitors LLP, 1 Avenue Road, Nowhere, Mythshire, MC1V 2AA where they will accept service of proceedings on behalf of the Claimants.

To: the Defendant / Part 20 Claimant
To: the Court Manager

5 Case Summary for Use at Case Management Conference

IN THE HIGH COURT OF JUSTICE WF-04-1234
QUEEN'S BENCH DIVISION
WEYFORD DISTRICT REGISTRY

BETWEEN   MR WILLIAM ULYSSES SIMPSON (1)
               DR RUPINDER SIMPSON (2)

Claimants/Part 20 Defendants

and

MR GEOFFREY IAN TEMPLAR

Defendant/Part 20 Claimant

Case Summary agreed by the parties for the purpose of the case management conference to be held on 21 April 2005

Chronology of Proceedings

Claim form	19 January 2005
Particulars of claim	19 January 2005
Acknowledgment of service	25 January 2005
Defence and Part 20 Counterclaim	4 February 2005
Reply and defence to Part 20 Counterclaim	18 February 2005
Allocation questionnaires	10 March 2005

Agreed Issues of Fact

1. On 19 July 2004 the Defendant agreed with the Claimants to rent the stable block of Bliss Lodge, Steep Lane, Nowhere, Mythshire, the Claimants' property and home known as 'Bliss Lodge' for the period of two weeks commencing on 1 August 2004.
2. The Defendant drove onto the driveway leading to 'Bliss Lodge' on 1 August 2004 at about 11.00 pm.
3. The Defendant's car crashed into Bliss Lodge.
4. The car was a Land Cruiser registration no. GIT 13. The car is a write-off.
5. There was substantial damage done to Bliss Lodge.
6. The quantum of the Defendant's Part 20 Counterclaim is agreed, subject to liability, as follows:

	£
Land Cruiser	58,995.00
Diasan Notebook	6,500.00
Mercuriam mobile telephone	2,000.00
We-Haul Ltd towage charges	440.63
We-Haul Ltd storage charges	800.00
Excess accommodation costs for 2 weeks	450.00
Car hire 16 weeks	2,400.00
	71,585.63

Issues in Dispute – Claim

1. Was the Defendant driving negligently by going too fast and/or without due care and attention down the Claimants' drive?
2. Was there glass on or near the drive?
3. If so, should the Defendant have been in a position to take appropriate avoiding action?
4. Did the Defendant's negligence cause the damage to the Claimants' property?
5. Were the Claimants contributorily negligent in leaving glass on or near the drive?
6. What are the Claimants' losses and can these be recovered in full from the Defendant?

Issues in Dispute – Part 20 Counterclaim

1. Were the Claimants in breach of their duties under the Occupiers' Liability Act 1957 in leaving or allowing their builders to leave glass on the drive?
2. Did the Claimants' breach of statutory duties cause the damage to the Defendant's car and possessions?
3. Was the Defendant contributorily negligent in any way?
4. Can the Defendant's losses be recovered in full from the Claimants?

The Evidence Required to Deal with the Disputed Issues

The Claimants

The First Claimant will give evidence as to the Defendant's driving, the accident and consequent damage.

The Second Claimant will give evidence about the location of the glass, the accident and consequent damage.

As to expert evidence, the Claimant wishes to rely on:

(a) Anthony Bacon: accident reconstruction expert: as to the cause of the accident
(b) Fiona McFadden: structural engineer: in respect of structural damage to the Claimant's property
(c) John Eaves: quantity surveyor: as to quantum of the Claimants' claim in respect of structural damage to their property.

The Defendant

The Defendant will give evidence as to his driving, the accident and consequent damage.

Colonel Trudge, the Claimants' neighbour, will give evidence as to the Defendant's driving and consequent damage.

Mrs Hilda Trudge will give evidence as to the location of the glass.

As to expert evidence, the Defendant wishes to rely on:

(a) Raymond Crow: an accident reconstruction expert: as to the cause of the accident
(b) Kieran O'Donnell: building surveyor: in respect of structural damage to the Claimant's property and its quantum.

The Defendant does not agree with the Claimants that evidence from a structural engineer is required.

Signed:

Solicitors LLP

Solicitors LLP

Dated 14 April 2005

Advocates & Co

Advocates & Co

Dated 14 April 2005

6 Order for Directions

IN THE HIGH COURT OF JUSTICE WF-04-1234
QUEEN'S BENCH DIVISION
WEYFORD DISTRICT REGISTRY
DISTRICT JUDGE HARDCASTLE

BETWEEN MR WILLIAM SIMPSON (1)
DR RUPINDER SIMPSON (2)

Claimants/Part 20 Defendants

and

MR GEOFFREY IAN TEMPLAR

Defendant/Part 20 Claimant

ORDER FOR DIRECTIONS

Upon hearing the solicitors for the parties and upon reading the agreed Case Summary dated 14 April 2005

IT IS ORDERED as follows:

DISCLOSURE OF DOCUMENTS

1. Disclosure will take place as follows:-
    (a) each party will give standard disclosure by list no later than 12 May 2005;
    (b) inspection will be completed and/or copies served no later than 26 May 2005.

WITNESSES OF FACT

2. Each party will serve on every other party the witness statements of all witnesses of fact on whom he wants to rely by simultaneous exchange no later than 30 June 2005.
3. Only the evidence of those witnesses whose evidence is exchanged may be called at trial.

EXPERT EVIDENCE

4. The parties have permission to use the following expert witnesses:
    (a) One expert on accident reconstruction each.
    (b) One building surveyor each.
5. The parties will simultaneously exchange expert reports setting out the substance of any expert evidence on which they intend to rely no later than 28 July 2005.
6. Questions to the expert witnesses must be served by 25 August 2005 and replies must be provided by 8 September 2005.
7. Reports must be agreed, if possible, no later than 22 September 2005.
8. If the reports are not agreed within that time there will be a without prejudice discussion between the relevant experts no later than 6 October 2005 to identify whether there are any issues that can be agreed between them and to agree those issues.
9. The experts will prepare for and file with the court a statement of the issues on which they agree and on which they disagree with a summary of their

reasons and that statement will be filed with the court with the pre-trial checklist, listing questionnaire.

10. The experts have permission to give oral evidence at the trial provided that the substance of the evidence to be given has been disclosed as above and has not been agreed.

REQUESTS FOR INFORMATION ETC.

11. Each party will serve any requests for information or clarification based on any document disclosed or statement served by another party no later than 14 days after disclosure or service.
12. Any such request will be dealt with within 21 days of service.

DOCUMENTS TO BE FILED WITH PRE-TRIAL CHECKLISTS, LISTING QUESTIONNAIRES

13. The parties must file with their pre-trial checklists, listing questionnaires copies of their experts' reports, witness statements and any replies to requests for further information.

DATES FOR FILING PRE-TRIAL CHECKLISTS, LISTING QUESTIONNAIRES AND THE TRIAL

14. Each party must file a completed pre-trial checklist, listing questionnaire no later than 20 October 2005.
15. The trial of this case will take place on a date to be fixed between 9 January and 30 January 2006.

COSTS

16. The costs of the case management conference be costs in the case.

Dated 21 April 2005.

7 Experts' Without Prejudice Meeting Statement

SIMPSON AND SIMPSON -v- TEMPLAR

CASE No. WF-03-1234

NOTE OF 'WITHOUT PREJUDICE' MEETING BETWEEN MR JOHN EAVES AND MR KIERAN O'DONNELL ON 30 SEPTEMBER 2005 IN ACCORDANCE WITH THE ORDER FOR DIRECTIONS DATED 21 APRIL 2005

[*must be addressed to the court, not the instructing party*]

To: the court

Date: 30 September 2005

The meeting took place at the offices of O'Donnell & Co, at 64 High Street, Nowhere at 9.30 am. It was followed by a short site visit to the Claimants' property at Bliss Lodge, Steep Lane, Nowhere.

Agreed Issues

We agreed that:

1. The sum of £8,000 claimed in respect of emergency weatherproofing work following the accident was reasonable in all the circumstances given the inclement weather in August 2004.
2. A sum of £2,275 is agreed in respect of the installation of a temporary security system at the property pending full repairs.
3. £1,500 is reasonable for the associated electrical and plumbing work.
4. There was no structural damage to the main fabric of Bliss Lodge arising from the accident. We agreed that the evidence of slight subsidence in the back of the playroom where the extension abuts the house pre-dates the accident and is in any event not a cause for concern.
5. There is structural damage to the extension's joists. These will need to be stripped out and re-fixed. As a result the extension's roof will need to be removed and rebuilt.
6. The extension's foundations are only marginally damaged and can be made good with minor repairs.
7. The cost of refitting the kitchen is agreed at £38,775. It is agreed that the majority of the units will need to be replaced because of water damage.

Disputed Issues

1. Mr Eaves for the Claimants maintains that the load-bearing walls of the extension are fundamentally damaged and need to be demolished and rebuilt. This effectively means that the whole extension has to be demolished.

   Mr O'Donnell for the Defendant maintains that only part of one load-bearing wall must be rebuilt. There is no requirement to demolish the whole extension and the extent of any rebuilding work can be limited to the removal and repair of the roof and joists referred to in paragraph 5 above and the repair *in situ* of the one damaged wall.

In terms of cost (all figures exclude VAT), the figures are as follows:

	Mr Eaves	Mr O'Donnell
Demolition work	£25,600	Nil
Clear site	£8,645	Nil
Rebuild walls	£36,600	£12,460
Make good interior plastering and tiling	£6,700	£5,000

2. The cost of removing the roof, repairing the joists and replacing the roof is disputed:-

   Mr Eaves   £18,550
   Mr O'Donnell   £14,750

3. The extent of repairs required to the bedroom and the associated costs are not agreed:-

Mr Eaves	Strip out, replaster and rewallpaper and make good windows and paintwork	£6,560
	Make good floor joists and boards and re-carpet	£4,200
Mr O'Donnell	Minor repairs to lower half of walls in bedroom including re-wallpaper where necessary	£1,300
	Make good floor joists, boards and re-carpet	£2,300

John Eaves
....
John Eaves
(for the Claimants)

Kieran O'Donnell
....
Kieran O'Donnell
(for the Defendant)

8 (Defendant's) Brief to Counsel

IN THE HIGH COURT OF JUSTICE   WF-04-1234
QUEEN'S BENCH DIVISION
WEYFORD DISTRICT REGISTRY

BETWEEN   MR WILLIAM ULYSSES SIMPSON (1)
                           DR RUPINDER SIMPSON (2)
                                                        Claimants/Part 20 Defendants

                                          and

                              MR GEOFFREY IAN TEMPLAR
                                                        Defendant/Part 20 Claimant

BRIEF TO COUNSEL TO APPEAR ON BEHALF OF THE DEFENDANT AT THE TRIAL OF THE ACTION ON 10 JANUARY 2006

Counsel has the following copy documents:

(1) Bundle of correspondence between the parties and solicitors;
(2) Statements of case;
(3) Allocation questionnaires and pre-trial checklists;
(4) Orders made during the action;
(5) Claimants' Part 36 offer letter;
(6) Case summary from case management conference;
(7) Documents obtained from the Claimant on inspection;
(8) The Defendant's documents in Part 1 of his list;
(9) Exchanged witness statements;
(10) Civil Evidence Act Hearsay Notice
(11) Exchanged expert reports;
(12) Replies from experts to parties' questions;
(13) Experts' 'without prejudice' statements filed at court;
(14) Case summary from pre-trial review hearing;
(15) Directions for trial;
(16) Proposed index for trial bundle;
(17) Proposed index for core bundle;
(18) Previous instructions to counsel and advice.

BACKGROUND

1. We act for the Defendant in this action. Counsel will be familiar with the main issues having advised on evidence after disclosure. The action is fixed for trial on 10 January 2006 at 10 am at Weyford District Registry.

FACTS

2. Counsel is referred to the case summaries prepared in advance of the case management conference and pre-trial review. The facts are briefly as follows.

3. On 1 August 2004 the Defendant drove his brand new car, a 4x4 Land Cruiser to the Claimants' property Bliss Lodge, where he was due to take up a

two week tenancy in that property's converted stable block. The Claimants had given him directions. He arrived at about 11 pm. This was observed by the Claimants' neighbour, Colonel Trudge. According to his wife, Mrs Hilda Trudge, the Claimants' builders had earlier that day dropped a pane of glass on the Claimants' driveway. It is the Defendant's case that some broken glass was left on the drive. The Defendant drove over the glass which caused his two offside tyres to burst. The car went out of his control. The drive was relatively steep and the Defendant's car careered into Bliss Lodge itself, severely damaging the Claimants' newly built extension.

Issues – liability

4. The issues in the action turn mainly on whether:
   (a) the Defendant can be shown to have driven negligently; and
   (b) the Claimants breached their duty, as occupiers, to the Defendant under the Occupiers' Liability Act 1957, in failing to clear away the broken glass and debris and/or warn the Defendant adequately of its presence. It is clear from Mrs Trudge's statement for the Defendant that the Claimants were aware of the glass on and around the drive and there are no issues arising about the liability of the builders.

5. There is a dispute on the facts about the precise location of the pile of glass and debris. The Claimants maintain that it was to the side of the drive and that the Defendant, in driving too fast down the drive, drove slightly off the drive and over the glass. Their position is that if he had not been driving negligently he would not have strayed off the drive and would not have hit the glass. This is supported by their expert, Mr Bacon.

6. Clearly if the Claimants succeed on these points, the counterclaim on the Occupiers' Liability Act is likely to fail at least in part. The Defendant will then face at least partial liability for the damage to Bliss Lodge. The evidence on these points is dealt with in more detail below.

Evidence on liability

7. Counsel is referred to the reports of the accident reconstruction experts, Mr Bacon for the Claimants and Mr Crow for the Defendant and to the witness statements of Mr Simpson, Colonel and Mrs Trudge. The witness statements are self-explanatory.

8. Neither expert's report is favourable to the Defendant in terms of the speed at which he was allegedly driving before the accident.

9. The experts' reports are inconclusive on the question of whether the broken glass was originally on or beside the drive. Therefore, this remains a disputed fact and will have to be resolved by non-expert evidence only (see above). Mr Bacon says that there is evidence of tyre tracks on the grass and he thinks it likely that they were made before the car hit the glass. This opinion is based on the car's subsequent erratic route. However, Mr Crow says he is unable to tell whether the car went over the grass or glass first. He may well be vulnerable in cross-examination. Both experts are of the view that the car hit the house at something approaching 35 to 40 mph. It appears from the reports that there was glass both on and next to the drive at the time of the inspections, possibly as a result of the accident.

10. Subject to the above comments we have advised the Defendant that there is a risk that the Judge may find in favour of the Claimants. We have discussed settlement and the possibility of a Part 36 payment into court in order to try to protect his position as to costs. Nevertheless, he is determined to defend

the action and pursue his counterclaim. Please would Counsel telephone upon receipt of these instructions to discus. A pre-trial conference can be arranged should counsel consider it necessary.

Claimant's Part 36 Offer

11. Counsel will note that the Claimants made a Part 36 offer that expired on 24 March 2005 to settle the claim for £175,000 inclusive of interest and taking the Defendant's Part 20 Counterclaim into account. We have advised the Defendant of the potential additional interest and costs payable under CPR Rule 36.21 should the Claimants better that offer at trial.

Issues – quantum

12. The quantum of the Part 20 counterclaim is agreed, subject to liability, at £71,585.63 (see the case summaries). The only two continuing items of loss ceased immediately before the case management conference as the Defendant had taken delivery of his replacement car and the car involved in the incident was then scrapped.

13. The Claimants' quantum is not agreed. Full details of the issues which are still disputed appear in the without prejudice meeting statement filed by the parties' respective experts on 30 September 2005.

14. There are no issues of remoteness of damage arising and the dispute on quantum relates almost wholly to the scope of demolition and repair work required to the Claimants' extension. The difference amounts to approximately £75,000.

Trial

15. Amanda Frost of Instructing Solicitors will be attending the trial. We will make the necessary arrangements to ensure that Colonel Trudge attends. Mrs Trudge will not be attending trial. Mrs Trudge is in Australia caring for her ailing sister. A Civil Evidence Act Hearsay Notice was served when her witness statement was exchanged and the Claimants' solicitors have not objected to her absence.

16. Counsel is asked to liaise with Amanda Frost as to the final content of the Trial and Core Bundles.

17. Please let us know if Counsel requires any further information.

Counsel is briefed to appear at the trial of the action on 10 January 2006 at Weyford District Registry at 10 am.

Advocates & Co
7 December 2005

9 Consent Order

IN THE HIGH COURT OF JUSTICE WF-04-1234
QUEEN'S BENCH DIVISION
WEYFORD DISTRICT REGISTRY

BETWEEN MR WILLIAM ULYSSES SIMPSON (1)
DR RUPINDER SIMPSON (2)

Claimants/Part 20 Defendants

and

MR GEOFFREY IAN TEMPLAR

Defendant/Part 20 Claimant

CONSENT ORDER

Upon the parties agreeing to settle this matter

AND BY CONSENT

IT IS ORDERED THAT

1. The Defendant pay the Claimants the sum of £170,000 by 2.30 p.m. on Monday 16 January 2006;
2. Upon payment, claim WF-04-1234 and its associated Part 20 counterclaim be stayed;
3. There be no order as to costs.

We consent to the terms of this order.	We consent to the terms of this order.
Solicitors LLP	Advocates & Co
Solicitors LLP	*Advocates & Co*
Dated 5 January 2006	Dated 5 January 2006

Index

Academy of Experts 200
Access to Justice (Woolf Report) 1-4
acknowledgement of service 57, 58-9
   flow diagram 301
addition of parties 49-50
admissibility
   hearsay evidence 143-4
admissions
   challenging court's decision 61
   form N9A 59-60, 212-13, 216-17
   interest 61-2
   notice to admit documents 146
   notice to admit facts 146, 231
   specified amount 59-60, 212-13
      part admission 60, 300
   time to pay request 299
   unspecified amount 60-1, 216-17
   variation of payment rate 62
ADR Group 200
affidavits 141
   oath 141
after-the-event insurance 20-1
allocation to track 6, 93-4
   allocation questionnaire
      completion 94-5
      failure to complete 96
      failure to pay fee 93
      Form N150 94, 234-8
   county court track 96-105
   dissatisfaction with allocation 97
   fast track 99-101
   financial value of claim 97
   multi-track 102-5
   small claims track 97-8
alternative dispute resolution (ADR) 5, 12, 27
   Academy of Experts 200
   ADR Group 200
   advantages 196
   agreement 200
   arbitration 26-7, 195
   cases where not appropriate 198
   Centre for Dispute Resolution 200
   Chartered Institute of Arbitrators 200
   choice of 201
   commercial reality 197
   conciliation 198
   confidentiality clause 201
   costs 196, 197
   criminal compensation order 28
   Criminal Injuries Compensation Authority 28
   disadvantages 197-8
   disclosure obligations 198, 200
   enforcement 197-8
   expert appraisal 27, 199
   expert determination 27, 199

alternative dispute resolution (ADR) – *continued*
   final offer arbitration 199
   flexibility 197
   independent third party 196
   insurance 27
   judicial appraisal 199
   'Med-arb' 198-9
   mediation 27, 198
   Mediation UK 200
   mini-trial 199
   Motor Insurers Bureau 28
   nature of 195
   negotiation 27, 195
   non-binding nature 197
   non-co-operation 201
   non-disclosure 198, 200
   organisations providing 200
   preserving business relationship 197
   privacy 197
   professional bodies 200
   Royal Institution of Chartered Surveyors 200
   speed 196, 198
   structured settlement procedure 199
   third parties 197
   trade schemes 27
   use 200-1
   voluntary nature 195
appeals
   assessment of costs 181
   interim order 112-13
applications to court
   appeals against interim order 112-13
   choice of court 107
   consent order 108
      sample 323
   content 107-8
   draft order 108
   evidence in support
      attached to notice 108
      preparation 109-10
   Form N244 107, 245-6
   freezing injunction 119
   further information 117-18
   human rights aspects 122
      public access 123
      security for costs 123
      summary judgment 122-3
      without notice 122
   interim costs 110-12
   interim order appeals 112-13
   interim payments 119-20
      consequences of order 121-2
      discretion of court 121
      grounds 120-1
      poverty and 120

applications to court – *continued*
　procedure 120
　interim remedies 118-19
　　evidence in support 119
　search order 118, 119
　security for costs 122
　　human rights 123
　service 108
　setting aside default judgment 113-14
　specific disclosure 132-3
　summary judgment
　　conditional orders 116-17
　　costs 117
　　directions 117
　　grounds 114-15
　　human rights 122-3
　　orders 116-17
　　procedure 115-16
　telephone hearings 109
　video conferencing 109
　without notice 122
　without notice orders 108-9
appraisal
　expert 27, 199
　judicial 199
arbitration 26-7, 195
　enforcement of award 197-8
　final offer arbitration 199
　see also **alternative dispute resolution (ADR)**
assessment of costs
　agreeing costs 181
　bill of costs 179, 180, 262-6
　counsel's fees 286-7
　detailed 7
　　appeals 181
　　challenging the bill 181
　　conditional fee agreements 182-3
　　interim orders 182
　　late commencement of assessment 180
　　offer to settle 182
　factors taken into account 177-8
　fast track 178-9
　guideline figures 178, 283-7
　indemnity basis 174, 176-7
　multi-track 179-82
　notice of commencement (Form N252) 179, 181, 261
　points of dispute service 181, 267-8
　procedure 178
　standard basis 176-7
　statement of costs 178, 247-8
　summary 7, 178, 283-7
　　conditional fee agreements 112, 182-3
　　statement of costs 111-12, 178, 247-8
assessors 151
attachment of earnings 192-3

balance of probabilities 12
bankruptcy 193-4
bill of costs
　challenging 181

bill of costs – *continued*
　notice of commencement of assessment 179, 181, 261
　points of dispute service 181, 267-8
　precedent 179, 180, 262-6
briefing counsel 35-6, 167
　sample brief 320-2
burden of proof
　balance of probabilities 12
　legal 12

case analysis 7
case management
　allocation to tracks *see* **track allocation**
　case summary for conference 313-15
　conditions 89-90
　conference
　　case summary for 313-15
　　multi-track 102-3
　　preparation 104
　　topics considered 103-4
　directions 6
　disclosure 6
　inadequate statements of case 90-1
　non-compliance sanctions 90
　　costs 92
　　interest 92
　　limiting issues 92
　　relief 92-3
　　striking out 90-2
　powers of court 89-90
　powers of judges 45
　striking out sanction 90-2
　timetables 3-4, 6
　track allocation *see* **track allocation**
　unless order 92
Centre for Dispute Resolution 200
certificate of service (N215) 51, 53, 54, 228-9
charging order
　on land
　　choice of court 190
　　notice 190
　　order for sale 190
　　procedure 190-1
　　restrictions on making 190
　on securities 191
Chartered Institute of Arbitrators 200
children
　limitation 10
　oath 172-3
　party to proceedings 46-50
　settlements 48-9, 165
　as witnesses 172-3
　see also **litigation friend**
choice of court
　applications to court 107
　charging order on land 190-1
　commencement of proceedings 43-4
　execution of judgment 188
　third party debt orders 191
Civil Procedure Rules 4
　overriding objective 1-2

Civil Procedure Rules – *continued*
  reserved rules 4
  Woolf reforms 1-4
claim form
  amount claimed 45
  claimant details 45
  completion 6, 45-7
  court fees 46
  defendant details 45
  details of claim 45
  Form N1 45, 205-6
  Form N1A notes for claimant 13
  Form N2 notes for claimant 45, 207-8
  Form N211 Part 20 claims 222-6
  High Court cases 46
  human rights issues 46
  particulars of claim 46
  service 54
    time for 55
  solicitor's costs 46
  statement of truth 46-7
claim, letter of *see* **letter of claim**
closing speeches 173
co-defendants
  default judgment 63
  foreign elements 25
commencement of proceedings
  choice of court 43-4
  claim form 45-7
  costs, assessment *see* **assessment of costs**
  issuing proceedings 45-7
  overview 6, 291
  particulars of claim *see* **particulars of claim**
  parties *see* **parties to proceedings**
  service *see* **service**
commercial debts, late payment 14, 15
  particulars of claim 67-8
Community Legal Service
  website 7
competence
  hearsay evidence 144
compromise 165
computation of time 57-8
conciliation 198
conditional fee agreements 16-21, 182-3
  disbursements 20-1
  drafting 19
  interim application costs assessment 112
  notification 21, 227
  opponent's costs 20-1
  paying party funded 112
  receiving party funded 112
  success fee 19-20, 182-3
confidentiality 23
  ADR agreement clause 201
  Part 36 offer or payment 164
conflict of interest 23
consent orders 108, 154
  sample 323
contingency fees 21

contract
  damages 13
  foreign elements 25
  interest claims 14-15
  limitation 9-10
contribution
  Part 20 claim 84
copies
  disclosure 126
costs
  alternative dispute resolution 196, 197
  amended statements of case 80
  in any event 110
  in the application 110
  applications to court 110-12
  assessment *see* **assessment of costs**
  between parties 15-16
  bill of costs 179, 262-7
    bill of costs 180
    challenging 181
  in the case 110
  of and caused by 111
  CFA agreements and 112
  claimant's 110
  conditional fee agreements 16-21, 182-3
  conduct of parties 175
  contingency fees 21
  defendant's 110
  discontinuance of claim 165
  discretion of court 174
  fast track
    summary assessment of other costs 179
    trial costs 178
    valuing claim 178-9
  here and below 111
  indemnity basis 176-7
  indemnity principle 174
  information at first interview 15-23
  interest 153-4
    after judgment 174
    up to date of judgment 173-4
  multi-track 179-82
    agreeing costs 181
    bill of costs, challenging 181
    interim orders 182
    late commencement of assessment 180
    notice of commencement (Form N252) 179, 261
    offer to settle 182
  no order as to 111
  non-acceptance of Part 36 payment 157-8
  non-compliance sanction 92
  notice of commencement of assessment (Form N252) 181
  offer to settle 182
  orders 175
  own costs 111
  payment 7
  points of dispute service 181, 267-8
  pre-action settlement 154
  reserved 110
  security for
    application 122, 123

costs – *continued*
    human rights issue 122
    solicitor and client costs 15-16
    'split costs' order 158
    standard basis 176-7
    statement of costs 111-12, 178, 247-8
    success fee 19-20, 182-3
    summary judgment applications 117
    third party debt orders 192
    thrown away 111
costs estimates 105-6, 239-41
    inaccurate 175
costs judge 7
costs only proceedings 183
counsel
    briefing 35-6, 167, 320-2
    conference 35
    fees 286-7
    method of instructing 35-6
    sample brief 320-2
    use 35
counterclaims
    Form N9B 59, 214-15, 218-19
    Part 20 84, 309-12
    procedure 84-6
    reply and defence to 311-12
county courts 43
    execution 188, 189
    interest on judgment debts 185-6
    particulars of claim 69-70
    track allocation 96-105
Court Service website 4, 7
courts
    choice
        applications to court 107
        charging order on land 191
        commencement of proceedings 43-4
        execution of judgment 188
        third party debt orders 191
    county courts *see* **county courts**
    High Court *see* **High Court**
    personnel 45
    transfers 44
credibility
    hearsay evidence 145
criminal compensation order 28
Criminal Injuries Compensation Authority 28
cross-examination 171

damages 12-13
    contract 13
    duty to mitigate loss 13
    tort 13
debt action 13
    interest claims 14-15
default judgment
    co-defendants 63
    failure of defendant to respond 62
    flow diagram 302
    human rights issues 64
    interest 63
    Part 20 claims 86

default judgment – *continued*
    procedure 62
    request Form N227 62, 221
    setting aside 63
        application 113-14
        claimant's duty 114
        discretionary grounds 113-14
        mandatory grounds 113
    specified amounts 62
    unspecified amounts 63
    where not available 62
defence 65
    comprehensive response 74-5
    example, High Court 75-6
    filing 59
    Form N9B 59, 218-19
    Form N9C 59
    reply to 76
    to each allegation 75
    see also **statements of case**
defence and counterclaim
    Form N9 59, 214-15, 218-19
    procedure 84
    sample 309
defendants
    acknowledgement of service 57, 58-9
    admissions
        challenging court's decision 61
        Form N9A 59-60, 212-13, 216-17
        part claim 300
        specified amount 59-60, 212-13, 300
        time to pay request 299
        unspecified amount 60-1, 216-17
        variation of payment rate 62
    capacity 11
    counterclaim 59, 214-15, 218-19
    default judgment 62-4
    defence 59, 214-15, 218-19
    details in claim form 45
    disputing jurisdiction 58-9
    identification 11
    notes for defendants (N1C) 57, 209-10
    response flow diagram 298
    response pack (N9) 57, 211-19
    solvency 11
    status 11
    whereabouts 12
Department of Constitutional Affairs
    website 7
directions 6
    fast track 99, 252-4
        exchange of expert reports 100-1
        exchange of witness statements 100-1
        failure to comply 100
        listing directions 101
        timetable 99
        variation 99-100
        variation by consent 100
    multi-track 102
        case management conference 102-4
        order for 102
        non-compliance 105
        order for 255-60

directions – *continued*
    variation 104-5
    order for 316-17
    Part 20 claims 86
    summary judgment applications 117

disclosure 6, 32
    continuing obligation 128
    copies 126
    definition 126
    documents defined 126
    duty to search 126-7
    failure to disclose 132
    Form N265 127, 131-2, 134, 232-3
    human rights 134
    inadvertent 131
    list of documents 131-2, 232-3
    non-party 133-4
    order 38-9
    pre-action 38-9, 133
    privilege *see* **privilege**
    purpose 125-6
    searches 126-7
    solicitors' duties 135
    specific 132-3
    standard 126
      procedure 127
    statement 128
    subsequent use of documents 132
    third parties 133-4
    'without prejudice' documents 131
    see also **inspection of documents**

discontinuance of claim
    costs 165
    general position 165
    procedure 165

district judges 45

documents
    definition 126
    disclosure *see* **disclosure**
    inspection *see* **inspection of documents**
    meaning 32
    notice to admit 146
    notice to prove 146
    preservation 32
    service *see* **service**
    'without prejudice' 39-40, 131

enforcement 7
    alternative dispute resolution awards 197-8
    attachment of earnings 192-3
    bankruptcy 193-4
    charging order on land
      choice of court 190
      notice 190
      order for sale 190
      procedure 190-1
      restrictions on making 190
    charging order on securities 191
    enquiry agents 186-7
    execution
      choice of court 188

enforcement – *continued*
      county courts 188, 189
      High Court 188
      items exempt from seizure 189
      walking possession 189
    interest on judgment debts
      county courts 185-6
      High Court 185
    investigation of means 186
    money judgments 185-94
    outside jurisdiction
      Brussels Convention 194
      countries outside EU and conventions 194
      EU Regulation 194
      Lugano Convention 194
      United States 194
    third party debt orders 191-2
      choice of court 191
      costs 192
      deposit taking institution 192
      procedure 191-2
    tracing 186
    walking possession 189
    winding up 194

enquiry agents 186-7

European Court of Justice
    website 7

evidence
    affidavits 141
    assessors 151
    at trial 171-3
    exchange before trial 6
    exhibits 139
    experts *see* **expert evidence**
    hearsay *see* **hearsay evidence**
    human rights 151
    models 145-6
    notice to admit documents 146
    notice to admit facts 146
    notice to prove documents 146
    opinion 141-2
    oral 137-8
    photographs 145-6
    plans 145-6
    previous inconsistent statement 145, 171
    Rules 137
    in support of application
      attached to notice 108
      interim remedies 119
      preparation 109-10
    trial bundle 168-9, 170
    witness evidence 137-8
    witness statements 138-40
    witness summaries 32, 139-40

execution of judgment
    county courts 188, 189
    High Court 188
    items exempt from seizure 189
    walking possession 189

expert appraisal 27, 199

expert determination 27, 199

expert evidence
  assessors 151
  attendance at trial 168
  court power to restrict 147
  directions 147
  discussion between experts 149
  duty of expert 146-7
  fees 147
  form of 148
  human rights 151
  instructions 33, 146, 147-8
  opinion 34
  oral 147
  privilege 147-8
  questions to expert 149
  report 33-4, 147
    content 148-9
    exchange 100-1
    statement of truth 149
  restrictions on use 34
  single joint expert 34, 149-50
  'without prejudice' meeting statement 318-19

fast track
  allocation to 99-101
  costs
    summary assessment of other costs 179
    trial costs 178
    valuing claim 178-9
  costs estimates 105-6, 239-41
  directions
    exchange of expert reports 100-1
    exchange of witness statements 100-1
    failure to comply 100
    listing 101
    standard 99, 252-4
    timetable 99
    variation 99-100
  listing directions 101
  listing questionnaire 101, 249-51
  pre-trial checklist 101, 249-51
  timetable 169-70
  trial 7
final offer arbitration 199
first interview 5
  alternative remedies 12
  burden of proof 12
  capacity of defendant 11
  confirmation of instructions 31
  costs information 15-16
    see also funding
  damages 12-13
  debt actions 13, 15
  identification of defendants 11
  interest 14-15
  limitation 5, 9-11
  merits of claim 12
  money claims 13-14
  public funding 22-3
  purpose 9
  remedy sought 12-15
  solvency of defendant 11

first interview – *continued*
  standard of proof 12
  viability of claim 11-12
  whereabouts of defendant 12
foreign elements
  co-defendants 25
  contract 25
  domicile 25
  EU Member States 24-6
  exclusive jurisdiction 25
  local courts 25
  Lugano Convention states 24-6
  rest of the world 26
  submission to jurisdiction 25-6
  third parties 25
  tort 25
  see also **jurisdiction**
forms
  N1 45, 205-6
  N1A notes for claimant 13, 45, 207-8
  N1C notes for defendants 57, 209-10
  N9 response pack 57, 211-19
  N9A admissions 59-60, 212-13, 216-17
  N9B defence and counterclaim 59, 214-15, 218-19
  N9C 59
  N150 allocation questionnaire 94, 234-8
  N205A 62
  N205B 62
  N208 Part 8 claim form 87
  N211 Part 20 claims 222-6
  N215 certificate of service 51, 53, 54, 228-9
  N218 service on partner 51, 230
  N225 request for judgment 62, 220
  N227 request for judgment in default 62, 221
  N242A notice of payment into court 156, 242-3
  N243A notice of acceptance of payment 156, 244
  N244 application notice 107, 245-6
  N252 notice of commencement of assessment 179, 181, 261
  N260 statement of costs 111, 247-8
  N265 standard disclosure documents 127, 131-2, 134, 232-3
freezing injunctions
  affidavit evidence 141
  applications 119
funding
  after-the-event insurance 20-1
  conditional fee agreements 16-21, 182-3
    interim application costs notice 21, 227
  contingency fees 21
  costs information 15-16
  human rights 28-9
  insurance 22
  public 22-3
  success fee 19-20, 182-3
  trade unions 22

further information
  applications to court 117-18
  requests for 80

hearsay evidence 142-5
  admissibility 143-4
  competence 144
  credibility 145
  cross-examination on 144
  definition 142-3
  first-hand 143
  human rights 151
  multiple 143
  notice 143-4
  previous inconsistent statements 145
  use 143-4
  weight attached 144
  witness statements as 139, 140, 144
High Court 43-4
  claim form 46
  example defence 75-6
  execution 188
  interest on judgment debts 185
  particulars of claim 71-2
hostile witness 172
human rights
  applications to court 122
  declaration of incompatibility 52
  default judgment 64
  disclosure 134
  evidence 151
  expert evidence 151
  funding 28-9
  hearsay evidence 151
  limitation 28
  public access 123
  security for costs 123
  summary judgment 122-3
  trial 183
  without notice applications 122

indemnity
  costs basis 176-7
  Part 20 claim 84
  principle 174
inspection of documents
  failure to allow 132
  purpose 125-6
  right 127
  withholding *see* **privilege**
  see also **disclosures**
instructions
  counsel 35-6, 167
  expert witness 33-4, 146, 147-8
  writing to confirm 31
insurance 22
  after-the-event 20-1
  alternative dispute resolution (ADR) 27
  notifying other side 21
interest
  admissions 61-2
  after judgment 174
  breach of contract 14-15

interest – *continued*
  debt action 15
  default judgment 63
  on judgment debts
    county courts 186
    High Court 185
  non-compliance sanction 92
  Part 36 offer 155, 156, 161
  particulars of claim 14
  pre-action settlement 153-4
  tort actions 15
  up to date of judgment 173-4
interim costs
  applications to court 110-12
interim matters
  overview 6-7, 291
interim payments
  applications to court 119-22
  consequences of order 121-2
  discretion of court 121
  grounds 120-1
  poverty and 120
  procedure 120
interim remedies
  applications to court 118-19
  evidence in support 119
interview with solicitor
  first *see* **first interview**
interviewing witnesses 31-2
investigation of means
  defendant 11
  judgment debtor 186-7

judgment
  in default *see* **enforcement**
  delivery of 173
  request for 62, 220-1
  summary *see* **summary judgment**
judgment debtor
  investigation of means 186-7
  obtaining information
    application 187
    hearing 187
judgment debts
  enforcement *see* **enforcement**
judicial appraisal 199
jurisdiction
  co-defendants 25
  contract claims 25
  defendant served in England and Wales 26
  determination for EU domicile 25, 292
  disputed 58-9
  domicile 25, 292
  EU Member States 24-6
  exclusive 25
  local courts 25
  Lugano Convention states 24-6
  rest of the world 26
  service
    in England and Wales 26
    outside jurisdiction 26, 54-5
  submission to 25-6

jurisdiction – *continued*
   third parties 25
   tort claims 25

latent damage
   limitation 10
legal burden 12
legal professional privilege
   advice privilege 129
   expert evidence 147-8
   litigation privilege 129-30
   third parties 129-30
   waiver 130
letter of claim 5-6
   content 37-8
   drafting 37
   response of defendant 6, 38
   sample 305-6
   sending out 37-8
letter of response 6, 38
limitation 5, 9-11
   contract actions 9-10
   human rights 28
   latent damage 10
   persons under disability 10
   solicitor's role 10
   tort actions 9-10
limited companies
   parties to action 49
   service on 52
list of documents
   standard disclosure 127, 232-3
listing questionnaire
   fast track 101, 249-51
   multi-track 105
litigation
   last resort 5
   overview flow diagram 291
litigation friend
   actions by 48
   cessation of appointment 48
   requirement for 47-8

masters 45
'Med-arb' 198-9
mediation 27, 198
Mediation UK 200
mini-trial 199
minors *see* **children**
mitigation of loss 13
models 145-6
money claims
   specified 13-14
   unspecified 13-14
money judgments
   enforcement *see* **enforcement**
Motor Insurers Bureau 28
multi-track
   case management conference 102-3
      preparation 104
      topics considered 103-4
   costs
      agreeing costs 181

multi-track – *continued*
      bill of costs 179, 180, 262-6
         challenging 181
      detailed assessment 179-82
      interim orders 182
      late commencement of assessment 180
      notice of commencement (N252) 179, 261
      offer to settle 182
   costs estimates 105-6, 239-41
   directions 102
      hearing 103
      non-compliance 105
      order for 102, 255-60
      variation 104-5
   listing questionnaire 105
   Part 8 claims 87
   pre-trial checklist 105
   timetable 169-70
   trial 7

negotiation 195
   authority of solicitor 153
   basis on which to conduct 153
notice of acceptance of payment (N243A) 156, 244
notice of commencement of assessment 179, 181, 261
notice of payment into court (N242A) 156, 242-3
notice of service on partner (N218) 51, 230
notice to admit facts 146, 231

oaths
   affidavits 141
   children 172-3
obtaining information
   application 187
   hearing 187
offer to settle
   detailed assessment of costs 182
   'without prejudice' 164
   see also **Part 36 offer**
ombudsmen schemes 199-200
opinion evidence 141-2
order for directions
   sample 316-17
overriding objective 1-2
overview
   commencement of action 6
   flowchart 291
   interim matters 6-7
   post-trial 7
   pre-commencement procedure 5-6
   trial 7

Part 8 claims
   claim Form N208 87
   multi-track 87
   procedure 87
   types of claim 87

Part 20 claims 83-4
   application for permission to make 85
   claim Form N211 222-6
   contribution or indemnity between co-defendants 84
   directions 86
   judgment in default 86
   procedure 87
   service 85-6
   third parties 85
   title of proceedings 86
Part 36 offer 154-5
   assessment of terms 164
   children 165
   claimant's 155-6
     acceptance 161
     failure to beat offer 161
     interest 161
     non-acceptance 161-3
     succeeding in beating offer 161-3
     tactical considerations 164
   defendant's 155-6
     acceptance 160
     made during proceedings 160-1
     mixed claims 160
     non-acceptance 160
   flow diagrams 294-7
   interest 155, 156
   patients 165
   secrecy 164
   'split costs' order 158
Part 36 payment
   assessment of terms 164
   children 165
   consequences flow diagram 293
   late acceptance 157
   mixed monetary on non-monetary claims 160
   non-acceptance 157-8
   notice of acceptance 156, 244
   notice of payment 156, 242-3
   part of proceedings only 157
   patients 165
   permission to withdraw or reduce 156
   secrecy 164
   'split costs' order 158
   tactical considerations 159-60
particulars of claim 46, 65
   breach and damage 73
   chronology of material facts 73
   contents 66-8
   example
     county court 69-70
     High Court 71-2
   sample 307-8
   service 55
   statement of truth 73
   summary for relief 73
   see also **statements of case**
parties to proceedings
   addition 49-50
   children 47-9
   limited companies 49

parties to proceedings – *continued*
   litigation friend 47-8
   partnerships 49
   persons under disability 47-9
     limitation 10
   sole traders 49
   substitution 49-50
partnerships
   notice of service on 51, 230
   party to proceedings 49
patients
   parties to proceedings 47-9
   settlements 165
personal injury actions
   pre-action disclosure 39
persons under disability
   limitation 10
   parties to proceedings 47-9
   settlements 165
photographs
   as evidence 145-6
   site visits 34
plans 145-6
   site visits 34
post-trial procedure
   overview 7, 291
Practice Direction protocols 5, 269-72
practitioner works 40
pre-action checklist 29
pre-action disclosure 38-9, 133
pre-action protocols 5
   aims 36
   cases not covered by 37
   non-compliance costs 36
   Practice Direction 5, 36, 269-72
   professional negligence 36, 273-8
pre-action settlement
   costs 153-4
   interest 153-4
   recording 154
pre-commencement procedure
   ADR 5, 6, 12
   costs 5
   costs information *see* **funding**
   first interview 5
     limitation 5, 9-11
     purpose 9
   jurisdiction 5
   letter of claim 5-6
   letter of response 6
   limitation 5, 9-11
   parties 5
   pre-action protocols 5
pre-trial checklist
   fast track 101, 249-51
   multi-track 105
preparations for trial
   attendance of witnesses
     experts 168
     general 167-8
   briefing counsel 35-6, 167, 320-2
   case summary 169
   skeleton arguments 169

preparations for trial – *continued*
   trial bundle 168-9, 170
preservation of documents 32
previous inconsistent statements 145, 171
privilege
   challenging claim for 130
   claim in list of documents 131-2
   inadvertent disclosure 131
   legal professional
      advice privilege 129
      expert evidence 147-8
      litigation privilege 129-30
      third parties 129-30
      waiver 130
   public policy 130, 134
   self-incrimination 130
   'without prejudice' documents 131
professional negligence pre-action protocol 36, 273-8
proof of evidence 32
public funding 22-3
   human rights 28-9
   statutory charge 23
public policy privilege 130, 134

re-examination 172
recognised practitioner works 40
remedies
   damages 12-13
   debt action 13
   interest 14-15
   interim *see* **interim payments; interim remedies**
   money claims 13-14
reply and defence to counterclaim 311-12
reply to defence 76
request for further information
   application for court order 81
   no response 81
   request 80
   response to request 81
request for judgment
   Form N225 62, 220
request for judgment in default
   Form N227 62, 221
reserved rules 4
response
   defendant's response pack 57, 211-19
   flow diagram 298
   to letter of claim 38
Royal Institution of Chartered Surveyors 200

search
   standard disclosure duty 126-7
search orders
   affidavit evidence 141
   application 118, 119
security for costs
   application to court 122, 123
   human rights 123

seizure
   exempt items 189
self-incrimination privilege 130
service 50-1
   acknowledgement of 57, 58-9, 301
   address for 53
   application notice 108
   by court 52-3
   by party 52-3
   certificate of service (N215) 51, 53, 54, 228-9
   claim form 54
      time for 55
   deemed date calculation 52
   document exchange 51
   electronic means 51-2
   email 51-2
   fax 51
   first-class post 51
   foreign elements 26
   leaving at address 51
   limited companies 52
   notice of service on partner 51, 230
   out of jurisdiction 26
      EU countries 54
      non-EU countries 54-5
   Part 20 claims 85-6
   particulars of claim 55
   partnerships 51
   personal 51
   postal 51
setting aside default judgment 63
   application 113-14
   claimant's duty 114
   discretionary grounds 113-14
   mandatory grounds 113
settlements
   after issue of proceedings 154
   children's claims 48-9, 165
   compromise 165
   consent orders 154
   discontinuance 165
   judgments 154
   negotiations 39-40
      authority of solicitor 153
      basis on which to conduct 153
   offer to settle
      'without prejudice' 164
      see also **Part 36 offer**
   Part 36 offers and payments *see* **Part 36 offers; Part 36 payment**
   patients 165
   persons under disability 165
   pre-action
      costs 153-4
      interest 153-4
      recording 154
   Tomlin orders 154, 281-2
   'without prejudice' correspondence 39-40
single joint expert 34
site visits 34
skeleton arguments 169

small claims track
   allocation to 97-8
   trial 7
sole traders 49
solicitors
   confidentiality duty 23
   confirmation of instructions 31
   conflict of interest 23
   disclosure duties 135
   duty as advocate 24
   duty to court 2, 24
   instructing counsel 35-6, 167
   instructing expert witnesses 33-4, 146, 147-8
   interviewing witnesses 31-2
   preservation of documents 32
   researching the law 40-1
   site visits 34
   warranty of authority 24
   writing to client after first interview 31
'split costs' order 158
standard of proof 12
statement of costs
   summary assessment 111-12, 247-8
statement of truth 46-7
   amended statements of case 79
   evidence in support of application 108
   expert report 149
   particulars of claim 73
   witness statements 139
statements of case
   amendments 79
     before service 79
     costs 80
     directions following 79
     outside limitation period 79
     with permission 79
     statement of truth 79
     without permission 80
   defence *see* **defence**
   defining issues 78
   formalities 65-6
   further information *see* **requests for further information**
   particulars of claim *see* **particulars of claim**
   reply to defence 76
   role 77-8
   statement of truth 46-7
   witnesses 77
statutory charge 23
striking out
   case management power 90-2
   inadequate statements of case 90-1
   non-compliance sanction 91-2
structured settlement procedure 199
substitution of parties 49-50
success fee 19-20, 182-3
summary judgment applications
   costs 117
   directions 117
   grounds 114-15
   human rights 122-3

summary judgment applications – *continued*
   orders 116-17
   procedure 115-16
telephone hearings 109
third parties
   disclosure 133-4
   foreign elements 25
   Part 20 claims 85
third party debt orders 191-2
   choice of court 191
   costs 192
   deposit taking institutions 192
   procedure 191-2
timetables
   case management 3-4, 6, 99
   for trial 169-70
***Tomlin* orders 154, 281-2**
tort
   damages 13
   foreign elements 25
   interest claims 15
   limitation 9-10
tracing 186
track allocation 6, 93-4
   allocation questionnaire
     completion 94-5
     failure to complete 96
     failure to pay fee 93
     Form N150 94, 234-8
   county court track 96-105
   dissatisfaction with allocation 97
   failure to pay fee 93
   fast track 99-101
   financial value of claim 97
   multi-track 102-5
   small claims track 97-8
trade unions
   funding litigation 22
trial
   briefing counsel 35-6, 167, 320-2
   bundles 168-9, 170
   child witnesses 172-3
   claimant's case
     cross-examination 171
     evidence 170-2
     examination in chief 171
     re-examination 172
   closing speeches 173
   costs *see* **costs**
   cross-examination 171
   defendant's case 172
   examination in chief 171
   final preparations 167-9
   hostile witness 172
   human rights 183
   judgment 173
   order of proceedings 170-2
   overview 7, 291
   previous inconsistent statement 171
   re-examination 172
   small claims track 7

trial – *continued*
    timetable 169-70
    venue 169
    witnesses
        attendance 167-8
        experts 168

unless order 92

video conferencing 109

walking possession 189
winding up
    enforcement by 194
'without prejudice' documents 131
    settlement negotiations 39-40
'without prejudice' meeting of experts
    sample statement 318-19
witness statements 32, 77
    as evidence in chief 140, 145
    exchange 137-8
        fast track 100-1
    exhibits in connection with 139

witness statements – *continued*
    form 138-9
    hearsay evidence 139, 140, 144
    late service 140-1
    new evidence 139
    non-service sanctions 140-1
    opinion evidence 142
    statement of truth 139
    in support of application 119
    sworn *see* **affidavits**
    use at trial 139
witness summary 32, 139-40
witnesses
    attendance at trial 167-8
    children 172-3
    compulsory attendance 32
    experts *see* **expert evidence**
    hostile 172
    interview by solicitor 31-2
    oral evidence 137-8
    statements *see* **witness statements**
    in statements of case 77
    summaries 140
Woolf reforms 1-4